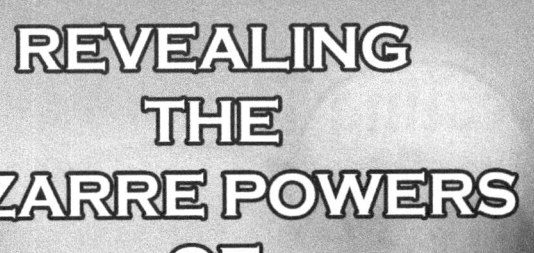

REVEALING THE BIZARRE POWERS OF HARRY HOUDINI
UPDATED

**PSYCHIC?
MEDIUM?
PROPHET?
CLAIRVOYANT?**

AN EXPOSE BY SIR ARTHUR CONAN DOYLE
WITH HARRY HOUDINI
EDITED BY TIMOTHY GREEN BECKLEY

GLOBAL COMMUNICATIONS

Revealing The Bizarre Powers of Harry Houdini

UPDATED

By Sir Arthur Conan Doyle
Harry Houdini
Timothy Green Beckley

Copyright © 2010/2014 – Timothy Green Beckley
DBA Global Communications, All Rights Reserved

Nonfiction

No part of this book may be reproduced, stored in retrieval system or transmitted in any form or by any means, electronic, mechanical, photocopying, recording, without express permission of the publisher.

Timothy Green Beckley: Editorial Director
Carol Rodriguez: Publishers Assistant
Sean Casteel: Associate Editor
Tim R. Swartz: Associate Editor

Printed in the United States of America

For free catalog write:
Global Communications
P.O. Box 753
New Brunswick, NJ
08903

Free Subscription to Conspiracy Journal E-Mail Newsletter www.ConspiracyJournal.com

Contents

The Untold Story: Doyle Vs. Houdini - Were They Spirit Worlds Apart?
    By Timothy Green Beckley .... - 9 -

The Riddle of Houdini by Sir Arthur Conan Doyle .... - 11 -

A Magician Among The Spirits by Houdini .... - 53 -
    Introduction .... - 55 -
    Preface .... - 59 -
    Chapter 1 The Founders of Modern Spiritualism .... - 61 -
    Chapter 2 The Davenport Brothers .... - 69 -
    Chapter 3 Daniel Dunglas Home .... - 79 -
    Chapter 4 Palladino .... - 85 -
    Chapter 5 Ann O'delia Diss Debar .... - 93 -
    Chapter 6 Dr. Slade and His Spirit Slates .... - 99 -
    Chapter 7 Slate Writing And Other Methods .... - 109 -
    Chapter 8 Spirit Photography .... - 117 -
    Chapter 9 Sir Arthur Conan Doyle .... - 125 -
    Chapter 10 Why Ectoplasm? .... - 137 -
    Chapter 11 By-Products of Spiritualism .... - 143 -
    Chapter 12 Investigations -- Wise and Otherwise .... - 149 -
    Chapter 13 How Mediums Obtain Information .... - 159 -
    Chapter 14 What You Must Believe To Be A Spiritualist .... - 165 -
    Chapter 15 Magicians As Detectors of Fraud .... - 171 -
    Chapter 16 Conclusion .... - 181 -
    Appendix .... - 183 -
        A Statement of Margaret Fox .... - 183 -
        B Irving's Speech .... - 183 -
        C Lord Adare's Story. .... - 184 -
        D Luther R. Marsh and the Huylers .... - 185 -
        E Police Record of Ann O'Delia Diss Debar. .... - 185 -
        F Judge Edmonds .... - 186 -
        G Doyle and the "Denver Express." .... - 186 -
        H Exposure of Mrs. Stewart .... - 187 -

Appendix – Sir Arthur Conan Doyle: Research and Rebuttal to
    Houdini's Debunking of Famous Mediums .... - 199 -
The Fox Sisters by Sir Arthur Conan Doyle .... - 201 -
    The Hydesville Episode .... - 201 -
    Statement By John D. Fox .... - 204 -
The Davenport Brothers by Sir Arthur Conan Doyle .... - 209 -
The Career of Eusapia Palladino by Arthur Conan Doyle .... - 213 -
Daniel D. Home By Arthur Conan Doyle .... - 220 -
Henry Slade by Arthur Conan Doyle .... - 229 -

THE AMAZING HARRY HOUDINI

THE years have passed and their feud should have long since been forgotten.

But both Harry Houdini, famed escape artist and magician, and Sir Arthur Conan Doyle, creator of master detective Sherlock Holmes, still linger in our memories. To many, it is as if they are still alive today.

As this is being written, we have heard that the SyFy Network is developing a series based on the rivalry between these two famous gentlemen.

Says a report from "Deadline Hollywood" . . .

"The cable network has secured the rights to *Among the Spirits*, a mystery show centered around legendary magician and escape artist Harry Houdini and British novelist Sir Arthur Conan Doyle. The show is based on the self-published graphic novel of the same name. Writers Steve Valentine and Paul Chart will transition to the TV project, producing along with Daniel J. Frey. Frey is a newcomer, whose only IMDb credits are art department roles on 2009's underwhelming *Gamer*, indie movie *Parasomnia* and Discovery's short-lived *Bone Detectives*.

"*Among the Spirits* will play out in 1920s America, as the duo solves suspicious murders with the aid of a female police detective. According to Syfy original programming president Mark Stern, the show will draw heavily upon the 'Steampunk' artistic aesthetic that's become popular in the last few years."

While only getting it "half right" the "Deadline Hollywood" report continues by talking about Houdini and Doyle's "friendship":

"In the real world, Houdini and Doyle were fast friends, and the showmanship of the former complemented the practicality of the latter. In an interesting twist, Houdini was a fierce opponent of anyone who claimed to be a medium or fortune-teller and would go to great lengths to disprove them. Arthur Conan Doyle was, in his later years, a great believer in the supernatural and an outspoken member of the Spiritualist movement. Houdini's expose-style book, *A Magician Among The Spirits,* (from which the Syfy project gets its name) was at direct odds with Doyle's beliefs and caused the two to have a falling out. Presumably, the historical figures' personal beliefs will be played as a counterpoint for the series . . ."

Although the last we heard was that the project was only in its development stage, we hope those involved in the venture press on with it so that the entire nation can enjoy what would seem to be a fascinating concept.

Late word also has it that the famous Steven Spielberg studio Dreamworks will produce its own Doyle/Houdini big screen epic, having acquired *"Voices From the Dead,"* an original script by J. Michael Straczynski. Little has been said about this proposed project, so we will all just have to stay tuned.

I truly believe this is the most complete book ever written on the feud between these important figures in history over spiritualism and psychic phenomena – with the added twist that Doyle sincerely believed that Houdini was really a clairvoyant and a "magician" in the true sense of the word.

It's all here, Watson, in the pages of this book. It's up to us to unravel the mysteries.

Timothy Beckley
New York
2013
mrufo8@hotmail.com

The Untold Story: Doyle Vs. Houdini - Were They Spirit Worlds Apart?
By Timothy Green Beckley

What twelve-year-old boy wouldn't be fascinated by the likes of Harry Houdini, the greatest escape artist who ever lived and an unprecedented talent among magicians? He came along at the height of an international media frenzy where attention was being given for the first time to celebrities on both sides of the great Atlantic Ocean. He also was a master showman who knew the meaning of "hype" well over half a century before the word became part of our lexicon. Above all else, he was a master manipulator on and off the stage. To use a well-worn phrase . . . the spin stops here!

I probably read about Houdini for the first time when I was in the third or fourth grade. Scholastic Books was offering a paperback for some loose change (that would be fifty cents in those days . . . yep, that's what they went for. How inflation and the years have grown and flown). The authors were Beryl Williams and Samuel Epstein (I know because I just used Google to track it down for old time's sake) and what they said about Houdini was more than flattering; for the most part, they made him sound like a superhero. Well, they got only part of the story correct as far as I am concerned, but this soft cover pulp got me interested enough in Houdini to want to research his life and publish this book even after many decades have passed.

What wasn't brought out in this paperback was Houdini's animosity toward the world of parapsychology and spiritualism in particular. Not that it's that much different these days with the Amazing Randi attempting to expose the likes of Uri Geller (a friend from way back) and anyone else who claims second sight. It seems that most magicians have an inbred hatred caused by paranoia of the paranormal because they sincerely feel that a belief in the world of phantoms takes away a bit of their thunder. After all, who needs to sit in an audience and have their mind read through trickery when you can get a more accurate "cold reading" from someone like John Edwards, who might actually bring grandma back to say hello from the spirit world. Now believe you me, I am not talking off the cuff. I know Randi. I was on his all night radio show back in the mid-sixties on New York City radio station WOR several times when he took over from Long John Nebel, who had switched to NBC and a bigger paycheck. In fact, Randi and I shared a small office at 303 Fifth Ave in Manhattan that was also occupied by Jim Moseley of UFO fame. I traveled with Randi to several of his gigs. I remember one in particular at a high school gym where he levitated a young lady and the curtain shook behind him (no room to "hide" the equipment, or a real ghost perhaps?).

Now me, I tend toward the other side of the invisibility spectrum. I have had enough personal experience to know that something strange is afoot. I have seen UFOs, done a bit of astral projection and witnessed ghostly phenomenon in the house that I grew up in. So I know where Sir Arthur Conan Doyle is coming from. I understand his passion for the unexplained. It's something that grows on you, that grabs you by the scruff of your neck and drags you screaming into the night in search for answers. I can't say I have known any physical mediums really well, but I have seen Uri Geller do some absolutely incredible things. Like bending my key, which wasn't even in his hand, but across the room lying on a desk in my friend's apartment. Or there was the time we took Uri to meet Mohammad Ali at the champ's training camp in Pennsylvania and he put a rather impressive impression in the Saint Christopher medal worn by Ali's sparing partner. A bit later we were off to the side with Ali's wife Belinda, when Uri took her hand and asked her to tell us all if she felt something happening. He placed his hand over her hand and about thirty seconds later she said she felt a tingling sensation. When he let go momentarily, something damn odd had happened to the ring she was wearing. The stone was missing – vanished! – and the setting was slightly twisted. I suppose Uri could have had a jeweler's tool tucked away on his person to commit fraud in both cases. Randi might say so. But I didn't see any signs of subterfuge. Maybe I am blind!

Sir Arthur Conan Doyle and Houdini started out close friends, but their relationship grew more strained as the real life Sherlock Holmes professes to have actually caught Houdini deceiving an investigating committee from the prestigious "Scientific American" into believing one of the most famous mediums of the era was fraudulent. He tried to humiliate and disgrace the highly regarded spiritualist "Margery" by rigging a specially built box that the medium was enclosed in and which should have prevented her from moving about when the lights were turned down and ringing an electric bell nearby that Margery claimed her brother in spirit was triggering as proof of an afterlife. Houdini had hidden a ruler inside the body restrainer so that later he could assert upon examination of the device that Margery had held the ruler in her mouth – her head protruding from the enclosure so she could breath, how nice of the committee – and triggered the bell by poking at it this way. No easy task even so, I would say!

In fact, if it wasn't for the medium's brother on the other side of the pale, Houdini might have gotten away with his stunt to convince the millions around the world who were waiting for evidence of eternal life that the medium Margery was a complete and utter charlatan. Suddenly, just before the séance was to begin, a phantom voice from out of the darkness screamed: "Houdini, you – blackguard! You have put a ruler into the cabinet. You! Remember, Houdini, you won't live forever. Someday you've got to die!" Those in the room who had sat at one of Margery's séances previously immediately recognized the voice as that of her departed brother. Her brother Walter's voice was certainly very masculine, not the soft and tender voice of the medium at all!

Says Sir Arthur about Houdini's disposition at this juncture of Houdini's career:

"His anti-Spiritualist agitation became more and more unreasoning until it bordered upon a mania which could only be explained in some quarters by supposing that he was in the pay of certain clerical fanatics, an accusation which I do not believe. It is true that, in order to preserve some show of reason, he proclaimed that he wished only to attack dishonest mediums, but as in the same breath he would assert that there were no honest ones. His moderation was more apparent than real."

The claims and counterclaims of both Doyle and Houdini went on for decades becoming, at times, rather outlandish and childish. Doyle ended up believing that Houdini was a sort of "Psychic Charlatan," that he really was psychic himself and a gifted medium and was using his debunking skills as sort of a smoke screen to cover up the true nature of his blockbuster performances that he had convinced his audiences were nothing more than fabulous feats of non-supernatural magic.

Doyle was convinced – from what he personally witnessed and what others confided in him – that Houdini could read minds, dematerialize, possessed supernatural strength, and was guided by angelic forces which shielded him from harm even during the most dangerous of escape performances which likely would have caused death to others.

Doyle stated that Houdini had once remarked, "There are some of my feats which my own wife does not know the secret of." And a famous Chinese conjurer who had seen Houdini perform added, "This is not a trick, it is a gift." Sadly, many of Houdini's feats died with him, even though they would have been an invaluable asset. "What can cover all these facts," states Doyle, "save that there was some element in his power which was peculiar to himself, that could only point to a psychic element – in a word, that he was a medium."

Being as unfair and unbalanced as my bones will allow, I hereby offer the stage to Doyle followed by the greatest skeptic of them all, Houdini. I doubt if anything will be resolved or finalized, but the debate is as relevant today as it was when Doyle and his provocateur lectured on spiritualism and psychic phenomenon in concert halls throughout the States and in Europe. Here then is both sides of the story - in the actual words of the famed Sherlock Holmes' originator and Houdini himself, who went out of his way to create the impression that fakes and phonies were afoot everywhere in the "shady world" of table tapping, levitating trumpets, spirit photography, slate writing, as well as the materialization of ectoplasmic forms in the darkening shadows of the séance room everywhere!

The Riddle of Houdini
by Sir Arthur Conan Doyle

WHO WAS the greatest medium-baiter of modern times? Undoubtedly Houdini. Who was the greatest physical medium of modern times? There are some who would be inclined to give the same answer. I do not see how it can ever now be finally and definitely proved, but circumstantial evidence may be very strong, as Thoreau said when he found a trout in the milk jug. I foresee that the subject will be debated for many years to come, so perhaps my opinion, since I knew him well, and always entertained this possibility in my mind, may be of interest. If others add their experience in order to support or disprove my own surmises, then some result may eventually be obtained.

I will first give some of my own personal impressions of Houdini. I will then dwell on some phases of his career which show his singular character, and I will then endeavour to give the argument as to the source of his unique powers.

Let me say, in the first instance, that in a long life which has touched every side of humanity, Houdini is far and away the most curious and intriguing character whom I have ever encountered. I have met better men, and I have certainly met very many worse ones, but I have never met a man who had such strange contrasts in his nature, and whose actions and motives it was more difficult to foresee or to reconcile.

I will first, as is only proper, dwell upon the great good which lay in his nature. He had the essential masculine quality of courage to a supreme degree. Nobody has ever done, and nobody in all human probability will ever do, such reckless feats of daring. His whole life was one long succession of them, and when I say that amongst them was the leaping from one aeroplane to another, with handcuffed hands at the height of three thousand feet, one can form an idea of the extraordinary lengths that he would go. In this, however, as in much more that concerned him, there was a certain psychic element which he was ready to admit freely. He told me that a voice which was independent of his own reason or judgment told him what to do and how to do it. So long as he obeyed the voice he was assured of safety. "It all comes as easy as stepping off a log," said he to me, "but I have to wait for the voice. You stand there before a jump, swallowing the yellow stuff that every man has in him. Then at last you hear the voice and you jump. Once I jumped on my own and I nearly broke my neck." This was the nearest admission that I ever had from him that I was right in thinking that there was a psychic element which was essential to every one of his feats.

Apart from his amazing courage, he was remarkable for his cheery urbanity in every-day life. One could not wish a better companion so long as one was with him, though he might do and say the most unexpected things when one was absent. He was, like most Jews, estimable in his family relationships. His love for his dead mother seemed to be the ruling passion of his life, which he expressed on all sorts of public occasions in a way which was, I am sure, sincere, but is strange to our colder Western blood. There were many things in Houdini which were as Oriental as there were in our own Disraeli. He was devoted also to his wife, and with good reason, for she was as devoted to him, but again his intimacy showed itself in unconventional ways. When in his examination before the Senatorial Committee he was hard-pressed by some defender of Spiritualism who impugned his motives in his violent and vindictive campaign against mediums, his answer was to turn to his wife and to say, "I have always been a good boy, have I not?"

Another favourable side of his character was his charity. I have heard, and am quite prepared to believe, that he was the last refuge of the down-and-outer, especially if he belonged to his own profession of showman. This charity extended even beyond the grave, and if he heard of any old magician whose tombstone needed repair he took it upon himself at once to set the matter right. Willie Davenport in Australia, Bosco in Germany, and many others of his profession were the objects of these pious offices. Whatever he did was done upon a large scale. He had many pensioners whom he did not know by sight. One man embraced him in the street, and upon Houdini angrily demanding who the devil he was, he answered, "Why, I am the man whose rent you have paid for the last ten years." He was devoted to children, though he had none of his own. He was never too busy to give a special free performance for the youngsters. At Edinburgh he was so shocked at the bare feet of the kiddies that he had them all into the theatre, and fitted them then and there with five hundred pairs of boots. He was the greatest publicity agent that ever lived, so that it is not ill-natured to surmise that the local papers had been advised beforehand, and that the advertisement was well worth it. There were other occasions, however, when his charity was less ostentatious. Animals too were loved by him, and he had a peculiar talent for taming them and teaching them tricks. All these ingredients in one impulsive personality surely make up a very lovable man. It is true that his generosity was curiously mixed with frugality, so that even while he was giving away his earnings at a rate which alarmed his wife, he would put an indignant comment in his diary because he had been charged two shillings for the pressing of his clothes.

So much for his virtues—and most of us would be very glad to have as goodly a list. But all he did was extreme, and there was something to be placed in the other scale.

A prevailing feature of his character was a vanity which was so obvious and childish that it became more amusing than offensive. I can remember, for example, that when he introduced his brother to me, he did it by saying, "This is the brother of the great Houdini." This without any twinkle of humour and in a perfectly natural manner.

This enormous vanity was combined with a passion for publicity which knew no bounds, and which must at all costs be gratified. There was no consideration of any sort which would restrain him if he saw his way to an advertisement. Even when he laid flowers upon the graves of the dead it was in the prearranged presence of the local photographers.

It was this desire to play a constant public part which had a great deal to do with his furious campaign against Spiritualism. He knew that the public took a keen interest in the matter, and that there was unlimited publicity to be had from it. He perpetually offered large sums to any medium who would do this or that, knowing well that even in the unlikely event of the thing being done he could always raise some objection and get out of it. Sometimes his tactics were too obvious to be artistic. In Boston he arrived by prearrangement before a great crowd at the City Hall and walked solemnly up the steps with ten thousand dollars' worth of stock in his hand, which represented one of his perennial stakes against phenomena. This was in connection with his engagement on a tour of the music-halls. His favourite argument, and that of many of his fellow-conjurers, was this flourishing of dollar-wads. It is obviously absurd, since the money will only be paid if you satisfy the challenger, and since the challenger has to pay the money he naturally never will be satisfied. The classical instance is that of the *Scientific American* magazine, which offered a large sum for any well-attested psychic phenomenon, but on being confronted with the Crandon phenomena, which are perhaps the best attested in the whole annals of psychical research, found reasons for withholding the money. I remember that when I arrived in New York, Houdini offered some huge sum that he could do anything which I had ever seen a medium do. I at once accepted his challenge, and proposed as a test that he should materialize the face of my mother in such a way that others besides myself who had known her in life could recognize it. I heard no more of the matter after that, and yet in England a medium had actually done this. I would have brought my witnesses across the Atlantic had the test been accepted.

I am quite prepared to think that Houdini's campaign against mediums did temporary good so far as false mediums goes, but it was so indiscriminate and accompanied by so much which was intolerant and offensive that it turned away the sympathy and help which Spiritualists, who are anxious for the cleanliness of their own movement, would gladly have given him. The unmasking of false mediums is our urgent duty, but when we are told that, in spite of our own evidence and that of three generations of mankind, there are no real ones we lose interest, for we know that we are speaking to an ignorant man. At the same time, the States, and in a lesser degree our own people, do need stern supervision. I admit that I underrated the corruption in the States. What first brought it home to me was that my friend Mrs. Crandon told me that she had received price lists from some firm which manufactures fraudulent instruments for performing tricks. If such a firm can make a living, there must be some villainy about, and a more judicious Houdini might well find a useful field of activity. It is these hyenas who retard our progress. I have myself had a hand in exposing more than one of them.

There was a particular Hall in Boston which Houdini used for his tirades against the spirits. Some weeks after his campaign a curious and disagreeable phenomenon broke out there. Showers of gravel or of small pebbles fell continually among the audience, and several people suffered minor injuries. A police watch was kept up for some time, and eventually it was shown that a staid employee, whose record was an excellent one, was in the habit, without rhyme or reason, of stealing up to the gallery and throwing these missiles down into the stalls. When tried for the offense he could only say that a senseless but overpowering impulse caused him to do it. Many psychic students would be prepared to consider that the incident would bear the interpretation of a poltergeist on the one side and an obsession on the other.

There was another incident at Boston of a very much more serious kind, and one which bears out my assertion that where there was an advertisement to be gained Houdini was a dangerous man. The remarkable psychic powers of Mrs. Crandon, the famous "Margery," were at that time under examination by the committee of the *Scientific American*. Various members of this committee had sat many times with the Crandons, and some of them had been completely converted to the psychic explanation, while others, though unable to give any rational explanation of the phenomena, were in different stages of dissent. It would obviously be an enormous feather in Houdini's cap if he could appear on the scene and at once solve the mystery. What a glorious position to be in! Houdini laid his plans and was so sure of success that before going to Boston he wrote a letter, which I saw, to a mutual friend in London, announcing that he was about to expose her. He would have done it, too, had it not been for an interposition which was miraculous. I think well enough of Houdini to hope that he would have held his hand if he could have realized the ruin and disgrace which his success would have brought upon his victims. As it was, the thought of the tremendous advertisement swallowed up his scruples. All America was watching, and he could not resist the temptation.

He had become familiar in advance with the procedure of the Crandon circle, and with the types of phenomena. It was easy for him to lay his plans. What he failed to take into account was that the presiding spirit, Walter, the dead brother of Mrs. Crandon, was a very real and live entity, who was by no means inclined to allow his innocent sister to be made the laughing-stock of the continent. It was the unseen Walter who checkmated the carefully-laid plans of the magician.

The account of what occurred I take from the notes which were taken by the circle at the time. The first phenomenon to be tested was the ringing of an electric bell which could only be done by pressing down a flap of wood, well out of the reach of the medium. The room was darkened, but the bell did not ring. Suddenly the angry voice of Walter was heard.

"You have put something to stop the bell ringing, Houdini, you—" he cried.

Walter has a wealth of strong language and makes no pretence at all to be a very elevated being. They all have their use over there. On this occasion, at least, the use was evident, for when the light was turned up, there was the rubber from the end of a pencil stuck into the angle of the flap in such a way as to make it impossible that it could descend and press the bell. Of course, Houdini professed complete ignorance as to how it got there, but who else had the deft touch to do such a thing in the dark, and why was it only in his presence that such a thing occurred? It is clear that if he could say afterwards, when he had quietly removed the rubber, that his arrival had made all further trickery impossible, he would have scored the first trick in the game.

He should have taken warning and realized that he was up against powers which were too strong for him, and which might prove dangerous if provoked too far. But the letters he had written and boasts he had made cut off his retreat. The second night landed him in a very much worse mess than the first one. He had brought with him an absurd box which was secured in front by no fewer than eight padlocks. One would have thought that it was a gorilla rather than a particularly gentle lady who was about to be confined within. The forces behind Margery showed what they thought of this contraption by bursting the whole front open the moment Margery was fastened into it. This very unexpected development Houdini endeavoured to explain away, but he found it difficult to give a reason why, if the box was so vulnerable, it was worth while to bring it with so much pomp and ceremony, with eight padlocks and many other gadgets, all the way from New York to Boston.

However, much worse was to come. The lady was put into the reconstituted box, her arms protruding through holes on each side. Houdini was observed without any apparent reason to pass his hand along the lady's arm, and so into the box. Presently, after some experiments, the lady's arms were placed inside and the attempt was to be made to ring the bell-box while only her head projected. Suddenly the terrible Walter intervened.

"Houdini, you——blackguard!" he thundered. "You have put a rule into the cabinet. You——! Remember, Houdini, you won't live for ever. Some day you've got to die."

The lights were turned on, and, shocking to relate, a two-foot folding rule was found lying in the box. It was a most deadly trick, for, of course, if the bell had rung Houdini would have demanded a search of the cabinet, the rule would have been found, it would, if held between the teeth, have enabled the medium to have reached and pressed down the flap of the bell-box, and all America would have resounded next day with the astuteness of Houdini and the proven villainy of the Crandons. I do not think that even the friends of the latter could have got over the patent facts. It was the most dangerous moment of their career, and only Walter saved them from ruin.

For the moment Houdini was completely overcome, and cowered, as well he might, before the wrath of the unseen. His offence was so obvious that no better excuse occurred to him, when he had rallied his senses, than that the rule had been left there by accident by some subordinate. When one considers, however, that no other tool upon earth, neither a hammer, a chisel, nor a wrench, but only a folding two-foot rule, could have sustained the charge, one realizes how hopeless was his position. But one of Houdini's characteristics was that nothing in this world or the next could permanently abash him. He could not suggest that they were guilty considering that the Crandons had actually asked to have the cabinet examined after she had entered, and Houdini had refused. Yet, incredible as it may seem, he had his advertisement after all, for he flooded America with a pamphlet to say that he had shown that the Crandons were frauds, and that he had in some unspecified way exposed them. Since the cabinet had become a delicate subject his chief accusation was that Mrs. Crandon had in some way rung the bell-box by stretching out her foot. He must have known, though his complaisant audiences did not, that the bell-box was continually rung while some sitter was permitted to hold it in his hands, and even to rise and walk away with it.

Speaking with a full knowledge, I say that this Boston incident was never an exposure of Margery, but it was a very real exposure of Houdini, and is a most serious blot upon his career.

To account for the phenomena he was prepared to assert that not only the doctor, but that even members of the committee were in senseless collaboration with the medium. The amazing part of the business was that other members of the committee seemed to have been overawed by the masterful conjurer, and even changed their very capable secretary, Mr. Malcolm Bird, at his behest. Mr. Bird, it may be remarked, with a far better brain than Houdini, and with a record of some fifty séances, had by this time been entirely convinced of the truth of the phenomena.

It may seem unkind that I should dwell upon these matters now that Houdini has gone to his account, but what I am writing now I also published during his lifetime. I deal gently with the matter, but I have to remember that its importance far transcends any worldly consideration, and that the honour of the Crandons is still impugned in many minds by the false charges which were not only circulated in print, but were shouted by Houdini from the platforms of a score of music-halls with a violence which browbeat and overbore every protest from the friends of truth. Houdini did not yet realize the gravity of his own actions, or the consequences which they entailed. The Crandons are themselves the most patient and forgiving people in the world, treating the most irritating opposition with a good-humoured and amused tolerance. But there are other forces which are beyond human control, and from that day the shadow lay heavy upon Houdini. His anti-Spiritualist agitation became more and more unreasoning until it bordered upon a mania which could only be explained in some quarters by supposing that he was in the pay of certain clerical fanatics, an accusation which I do not believe. It is true that in order to preserve some show of reason he proclaimed that he wished only to attack dishonest mediums, but as in the same breath he would assert that there were no honest ones, his moderation was more apparent than real. If he had consulted the reports of the National Association of American Spiritualists he would have found that this representative body was far more efficient in exposing those swindlers than he had ever been, for they had the necessary experience by which the true can be separated from the false.

I suppose that at that time Houdini was, from an insurance point of view, so far as bodily health goes, the best life of his age in America. He was in constant training, and he used neither alcohol nor tobacco. Yet all over the land warnings of danger arose. He alluded in public to the matter again and again. In my own home circle I had the message some months before his death, "Houdini is doomed, doomed, doomed!" So seriously did I take this warning that I would have written to him had I the least hope that my words could have any effect. I knew, however, by previous experience, that he always published my letters, even the most private of them, and that it would only give him a fresh pretext for ridiculing that which I regard as a sacred cause.

But as the months passed and fresh warnings came from independent sources, both I and, as I believe, the Crandons became seriously alarmed for his safety. He was, on one side of his character, so fine a fellow that even those who were attacked in this monstrous way were unwilling that real harm should befall him.

But he continued to rave, and the shadow continued to thicken. I have an American friend who writes in the press under the name of Samri Frikell. He is really Fulton Oursler, the distinguished novelist, whose *Step-child of the Moon* is, in my judgment, one of the best of recent romances. Oursler was an intimate friend of Houdini, and he has allowed me to quote some of his experiences.

"You know him as well as I do," writes Oursler. "You knew the immense vanity of the man. You know that he loved to be important. My experience with him for the last three months of his life was most peculiar. He would call me on the telephone at seven o'clock in the morning and he would be in a quarrelsome mood. He would talk for an hour telling me how important he was and what a great career he was making. In his voice was a hysterical, almost feminine, note of rebellion, as if his hands were beating against an immutable destiny.

"In all these cases Houdini portrayed to me a clear sense of impending doom. This is not an impression which I have received subsequent to his death. But I commented upon it at the time. I believe that Houdini sensed the coming of his death, but did not know that it meant death. He didn't know what it meant, but he hated it and his soul screamed out in indignation."

Some time later he telephoned to the same friend in a way which showed that his surmise had become more definite. "I am marked for death," said he. "I mean that they are predicting my death in spirit circles all over the country." At that time he was starting in perfect health upon that tour of the Vaudevilles which was destined to be the last of his career. Within a few weeks he was dead.

The details of that death were in many ways most singular. On October 11th he had a painful but, as everyone thought, an unimportant accident, when during his performance his ankle sustained an injury. The incident was treated quite lightly by the Press, but was regarded more seriously by those who had other sources of information. On October 13th, two days after the accident, the gentleman already quoted had a letter from a medium, Mrs. Wood.

"Three years ago," said this ill-omened epistle, "the spirit of Dr. Hyslop said, 'The waters are black for Houdini,' and he foretold that disaster would befall him while performing before an audience in a theatre. Dr. Hyslop now says that the injury is more serious than has been reported, and that Houdini's days as a magician are over."

The sad prophecy proved to be only too true, though the injured leg was only the prelude of worse disaster. It seemed indeed to be a sign that the protective mantle which had been around him had for some reason been withdrawn. The ankle continued to pain him, though he managed for some weeks to give his accustomed show. At Montreal a member of the audience rose to protest against the violence with which he raved against Spiritualism, and very particularly against me. Such personal attacks were not to be taken too seriously, for it was part of his perfervid nature that anyone who had experiences which differed from his own was either a dupe or a scoundrel. He bore up with great bravery against the pain from which he must have continually suffered, but in less than a fortnight, while on the stage at Detroit, he completely collapsed, and was carried to that hospital from which he never emerged alive.

There were some remarkable points about his death. It seems that upon Friday, October 22nd, he was lying in his dressing-room, reading his letters. It was about five in the afternoon. He had lectured at McGill University a few days before, and with his usual affability he allowed some of the students to come in and see him. What followed may be taken verbatim from the report of one of these young men.

" 'Houdini,' he says, 'was facing us and lying down on a couch at the time reading some mail, his right side nearest us.' This first-year student engaged Houdini more or less continually in a conversation whilst my friend Mr. Smilovitch continued to sketch Houdini. This student was the first to raise the question of Houdini's strength. My friend and I were not so much interested in his strength as we were in his mental acuteness, his skill, his beliefs and his personal experiences. Houdini stated that he had extraordinary muscles in his forearms, in his shoulders and in his back, and he asked all of us present to feel them, which we did.

"The first-year McGill student asked Houdini whether it was true that punches in the stomach did not hurt him. Houdini remarked rather unenthusiastically that his stomach could resist much, although he did not speak of it in superlative terms. Thereupon he gave Houdini some very hammer-like blows below the belt, first securing Houdini's permission to strike him. Houdini was reclining at the time with his right side nearest Whitehead, and the said student was more or less bending over him. These blows fell on that part of the stomach to the right of the navel, and were struck on the side nearest us, which was in fact Houdini's right side; I do not remember exactly how many blows were struck. I am certain, however, of at least four very hard and severe body blows, because at the end of the second or third blow I verbally protested against this sudden onslaught on the part of this first-year student, using the words, 'Hey there. You must be crazy, what are you doing?' or words to that effect, but Whitehead continued striking Houdini with all his strength.

"Houdini stopped him suddenly in the midst of a punch, with a gesture that he had had enough. At the time Whitehead was striking Houdini, the latter looked as though he was in extreme pain and winced as each blow was struck.

"Houdini immediately after stated that he had had no opportunity to prepare himself against the blows, as he did not think that Whitehead would strike him as suddenly as he did and with such force, and that he would have been in a better position to prepare for the blows if he had arisen from his couch for this purpose, but the injury to his foot prevented him from getting about rapidly."

There is no doubt that the immediate cause of the death was ruptured appendix, and it was certified as traumatic appendicitis by all three doctors who attended him. It is, however, a very rare complaint, one of the doctors asserting that he had never seen a case before. When one considers how often boxers are struck violent blows in this region, one can understand that it is not usually so vulnerable. From the time that he reached hospital he seems to have known that he was doomed.

Even after death strange things continued to happen which seem to be beyond the range of chance or coincidence. Some little time before Houdini had ordered a very ornate coffin, which he proposed to use in some sensational act. He paid no less than two thousand five hundred dollars for it. The idea was, I believe, to have a glass face to it and to exhibit the magician within it after it was hermetically sealed up, for he had shown in a previous experiment an inexplicable capacity for living without air. He carried this coffin about with him in one of the very numerous crates in which all his apparatus was packed. After his death all his goods were, I am told, sent on to New York. It was found, however, that by some blunder one box had been left behind. On examination this was found to contain the show coffin, which was accordingly used for his burial. At that burial some curious and suggestive words were used by the presiding rabbi, Barnard Drachman. He said: "Houdini possessed a wondrous power that he never understood, and which he never revealed to anyone in life." Such an expression coming at so solemn a moment from one who may have been in a special position to know must show that my speculations are not extravagant or fantastic when I deal with the real source of those powers. The rabbi's speech is to be taken with Houdini's own remark, when he said to my wife: "There are some of my feats which my own wife does not know the secret of." A famous Chinese conjurer who saw him perform said, "This is not a trick, it is a gift." He frequently said that his work would die with him, and he has left no legacy of it so far as can be seen, though it would clearly be a very valuable asset. What can cover all these facts, save that there was some element in his power which was peculiar to himself, and that could only point to a psychic element—in a word, that he was a medium?

In the remarkable ceremony performed beside his coffin by his brother-magicians, the spokesman broke a symbolic wand and said:

"The wand is broken. God touched him with a wondrous gift, and our brother used it. Now the wand is broken." It may indeed have been not mere trickery but a God-given gift which raised Houdini to such a height. And why should he not use it, if it were indeed the gift of God? I see no reason why the medium, like other God-endowed men—the painter, the poet, or the romancer—should not earn money and renown by his gift. Let him hesitate, however, before he makes rash attacks upon those who are using the same gift, and for higher ends.

Other curious points, which may possibly come within the range of coincidence, are connected with the death of Houdini. For example, there was a Mr. Gysel, who had shared in Houdini's views as to Spiritualism. He wrote thus to my friend:

"MR. FRIKELL,—
"Something happened to me in my room on Sunday night, October 24th, 1926, 10:58: Houdini had given me a picture of himself which I had framed and hung on the wall. At the above time and date the picture fell to the ground, breaking the glass. I now know that Houdini will die. Maybe there is something in these psychic phenomena after all."

To this Mr. "Frikell" adds:

"As I think back on my own experience I am inclined to agree maybe there is indeed something to the psychic phenomena after all."

His admission is the more noteworthy as I remember the day when he was a strong and intelligent opponent.

I will now turn to a consideration of the nature of Houdini's powers, and in order to appreciate the argument one has to consider the nature of some of the feats which he did actually perform. A list of these would make a considerable pamphlet, but a few typical ones may be selected. A general outline of his life, too, may not be out of place.

Houdini's real name was Eric Weiss, and he was born in 1874, in the State of Wisconsin, in one of those small towns which seem to be the real centres of American originality. He was the seventh son of a Jewish rabbi, and he has left it on record that his mother did not even know the English language. He has also left it on record that in his early youth he had some connection with mediumship, though of a most doubtful variety. He has not scrupled to confess that he eked out any powers he may have had by the expedient of reading the names upon the graves in the local cemeteries. It was a good deal later than this that he first met a true medium in the shape of Ira Davenport, the only survivor of the famous brothers whose powers amazed all England in the 'sixties, and who, in spite of all the interested claims of Maskelyne and other conjurers, were never exposed, nor even adequately imitated. I have before me as I write a letter from Houdini himself, in which he tells me:

"I was an intimate friend of Ira Erastus Davenport. I can make the positive assertion that the Davenport Brothers never were exposed. I know more about the Davenports than anyone living."

He then adds the very curious and notable sentence:

"I know for a fact that it was not necessary for them to remove their bonds in order to obtain manifestations."

When one considers that these bonds were often handcuffs or twisted copper wire, and that the manifestations occurred in many cases within a few seconds of the closing of the cabinet, this admission by one, who claims that he knows, is of very great importance. We will return to this later, after we have enumerated a few of his results.

He could, and continually did, walk straight out of any prison cell in which he might be confined. They placed him at Washington in the cell in which Guiteau, the murderer of Garfield, had been locked, but he readily emerged. In the letter from which I have already quoted, he says to me:

"I pledge my word of honour that I was never given any assistance, nor was in collusion with anyone."

This was clearly the case, for he performed the feat many times in different places, and was always searched to prove that he had no tools in his possession. Sometimes the grinning warders had hardly got out of the passage before their prisoner was at their heels. It takes some credulity, I think, to say that this was, in the ordinary sense of the word, a trick.

Handcuffs might have been made of jelly, so easily did his limbs pass through them. He was heavily manacled at Scotland Yard, and placed behind a screen from over which a shower of manacles began to fall until he stepped out a free man. These things he could do in an instant. When I was lecturing at the Carnegie Hall in New York, my wife and Houdini walked down some side corridor after the lecture in order to rejoin me. They came to a padlocked door, and my wife was about to turn back. To her amazement, her companion put out his hand and picked off the locked padlock as one picks a plum from a tree. Was that a trick, or are all these talks about sleight of hand what Houdini himself would call "bunk" or "hokum"?

When Houdini was in Holland, he got the local basketmakers to weave a basket round him. Out of this he emerged. He was shut up later in a sealed paper bag and came out, leaving it intact. A block of ice was frozen round his body and he burst his way out. One who has attempted to bring his feats within the range of normal explanations tells us that he did this by "depressing his periphery as a prelude to dynamic expansion"—whatever that may mean. He was also buried six feet deep in California and emerged unhurt, though we are not told by what dynamic expansion the feat was achieved.

In Leeds he was coopered up in a cask by the brewers, but he was soon out. At Krupps' he defied the whole management, who constructed a special set of fetters for his behoof. They had no better luck than the others. He was put into the Siberian convict van at Moscow, but walked straight out of it. On December 2nd, 1906, he leaped from the Old Belle Isle Bridge at Detroit heavily handcuffed, and released himself under icy water, which would paralyse any man's limbs. On August 26th, 1907, he was thrown into San Francisco Bay with his hands tied behind his back and seventy-five pounds of ball and chain attached to his body. He was none the worse. He escaped from a padlocked United States mailbag, as many a parcel has done before him. Finally, he was manacled, tied up in a box, and dropped into the East River at New York, but lived to tell the tale.

Whatever may have been the true source of Houdini's powers—and I am not prepared to be dogmatic upon the point—I am very sure that the explanations of his fellow-conjurers do not always meet the case.

Thus we have Mr. Harry Kellock, to whose book I am indebted for much supplementary information, talking persuasively about the magician's skill with a pick-lock. He had told reporters that his method was to have a small instrument which was concealed by surgeon's plaster upon the sole of his foot. This would certainly seem to be very useful when he was lowered in a coffin to the bottom of the sea!

Of course, I am aware that Houdini really was a very skilful conjurer. All that could be known in that direction he knew. Thus he confused the public mind by mixing up things which were dimly within their comprehension with things which were beyond anyone's comprehension. I am aware also that there is a box trick, and that there is a normal handcuff and bag trick. But these are not in the same class with Houdini's work. I will believe they are when I see one of these other gentlemen thrown in a box off London Bridge. One poor man in America actually believed these explanations, and on the strength of them jumped in a weighted packing-case into a river in the Middle West; and one did so in Germany. They are there yet!

To show the difference between Houdini's methods and those by which the box trick is done by other conjurers, I will give a description of the latter by one who has all normal tricks at his finger-ends. He says:

"While the air-holes are there for ventilation they are there for another purpose, and that is that the man inside may get a catch or grip of that particular board. The first thing that is done by the man inside is to put his back up against the side next the audience and with his feet force off the board with the air-holes in it. After freeing this board, with a bit of string he lowers this board to the floor. If any obstruction comes in the way in the shape of a nail which he cannot force with his concealed lever and hammer, he cuts the nail with a fine saw. Thus his escape. The ropes are only a blind, as quite sufficient room can be got to get out between ropes. The procedure to close up again is simple. The iron nails are placed back upon the holes from which they were forced and squeezed in and knocked with a leather-covered hammer."

Such is the usual technique as described by an expert. Does anyone believe that all this could be done as I have seen Houdini do it in a little over a minute, or could one imagine it being carried out at the bottom of a river? I contend that Houdini's performance was on an utterly different plane, and that it is an outrage against common sense to think otherwise.

I will now take a single case of Houdini's powers, and of the sort of thing that he would say, in order to show the reader what he is up against if he means to maintain that these tricks had no abnormal element. The description is by my friend, Captain Bartlett, himself a man of many accomplishments, psychic and otherwise. In the course of their conversation he said to his guest:

" 'How about your box trick?'
"Instantly his expression changed. The sparkle left his eyes and his face looked drawn and haggard. 'I cannot tell you,' he said, in a low, tense voice. 'I don't know myself, and, what is more, I have always a dread lest I should fail, and then I would not live. I have promised Mrs. Houdini to give up the box trick at the end of the season, for she makes herself ill with anxiety, and for myself I shall be relieved too.'

"He stooped to stroke our cats, and to our amazement they fled from the room with their tails in the air, and for some minutes they dashed wildly up and down stairs, scattering the mats in all directions.

"After this we had an earnest talk on psychic phenomena, and he told me of strange happenings to himself, especially at the grave of his mother, to whom he was deeply attached.

"The trunk-makers of Bristol had made a challenge box from which he was billed to escape that evening. He begged me to be with him, explaining that he liked the support of a sensitive, more especially as he was feeling anxious.

"I willingly agreed, the more especially as he allowed me to bring a very observant friend, a civil engineer of repute.

"The box was made of inch planking, tongued and grooved, with double thickness at the ends. It was nailed herring-bone fashion, three-inch nails, three inches apart. Several auger holes were made at one end to admit air, and the whole thing was carefully and solidly finished. It was, as I have said, a challenge box, yet we thoroughly overhauled it and were satisfied that it contained no tricks.

"Houdini lay down in it, while the challengers climbed to the platform and nailed down the heavy top again, using three-inch nails as before. The box was then tightly roped, three men pulling on the cords. Meanwhile, Houdini inside the box called out that it was very hot, and, putting a finger through an air-hole, waggled it furiously.

"The box was then enclosed by a tent consisting of brass rods covered by a silken canopy.

"In ninety-five seconds Houdini was standing before his audience, breathless, and with his shirt in tatters. The boxmakers, after careful examination, in which we joined, declared that both box and roping were intact.

"Now, was Houdini's statement that he never knew how he got out of the box a mere blind, or did he employ supernormal forces and dematerialize? If I put a beetle in a bottle, hermetically sealed, and that beetle makes its escape, I, being only an ordinary human, and not a magician, can only conclude that either the beetle has broken the laws of matter, or that it possesses secrets that I should call supernormal."

I would also ask the reader to consider the following account by the late Mr. Hewat Mackenzie, one of the most experienced psychical researchers in the world. In his book, *Spirit Intercourse* (p. 86), he says:

"A small iron tank filled with water was deposited on the stage, and in it Houdini was placed, the water completely covering his body. Over this was placed an iron lid with three hasps and staples, and these were securely locked. The body was then completely dematerialized within the tank in one and a half minutes, while the author stood immediately over it. Without disturbing any of the locks Houdini was transferred from the tank direct to the back of the stage front, dripping with water and attired in the blue jersey-suit in which he entered the tank. From the time that he entered it to the time that he came to the front only one and a half minutes had elapsed.

"While the author stood near the tank during the dematerialization process a great loss of physical energy was felt by him, such as is usually felt by sitters in materializing séances who have a good stock of vital energy, as in such phenomena a large amount of energy is required. . . . This startling manifestation of one of Nature's profoundest miracles was probably regarded by most of the audience as a very clever trick."

In other words, in Mr. Mackenzie's opinion the audience was successfully bluffed by the commercialization of psychic power. It is remarkable and most suggestive that in this case, as in the Bristol one already given, Houdini was anxious that some psychic from whom he could draw strength should stand near him.

Can any reasonable man read such an account as this and then dismiss the possibility which I suggest as fantastic? It seems to me that the fantasy lies in refusing its serious consideration.

A point which is worth considering is, that even if we grant that enormous practice and natural advantages might conceivably give a man a facility in one direction which might appear preternatural, these feats of Houdini cover a larger range than could be accounted for by any one aptitude. This consideration becomes stronger still when one sees that his powers really covered the whole field of what we usually associate with physical mediumship in its strongest form, and can be covered so far as I can see by no other explanation whatever.

His friend Mr. Bernard Ernst, a well-known and very level-headed lawyer of New York, told me that on one occasion upon the veranda of his own country house at Long Island, Houdini proposed a séance. When hands were laid upon the table it began to rise up in the air. As Mrs. Houdini was present, Ernst took it for granted at first that the hands or feet were used to produce the effect. On examination, however, in good light he found that this was not so, and that there were no steel rods up the sleeve, which is a fraudulent method occasionally used. The feat appeared to him—and he is himself an experienced conjurer—to be clearly preternatural. Houdini himself rebuked a tendency towards levity upon the part of the company, and treated the matter with great gravity.

Now let us take the case of the séance which he gave to President Roosevelt—a bogus séance according to Houdini. It was on board the *Imperator* in June 1910. It followed the lines of the usual slate phenomenon as practised by many mediums, honest and otherwise. The written question, folded and sealed, is placed between the folding slates, and the answer is found upon one side of the slate when they are opened. Roosevelt wrote the question, "Where was I last Christmas?" folded, sealed in an envelope, and placed it between the slates with his own hand. When the slates were opened a map of the South American journey of Roosevelt was found to be drawn, with the legend "Near the Andes." The President was naturally greatly amazed and Houdini refused to give any explanation, though had it been a mere trick and there was no reason for secrecy, it would have been most natural that he should have explained it to so important a person, in order to show how easily fraudulent mediums can operate.

Long afterwards he did give an explanation, which is so incredible that I would take it as an extreme example of that contempt which Houdini had for the public intelligence, taking it for granted that they would swallow without question anything which he might put before them. To condense a long story which the curious may find on pages 244-6 of Kellock's very readable book, the "explanation" ran thus:

He knew that the President would be aboard and he received advance information about the South American travels from friends on the *Daily Telegraph*, which he made note of in case there should be a séance on board. So far we are on understandable ground. He suggested that such a séance should be held, and had the slates prepared. This also we may pass. He then asked for written questions from the passengers, and himself wrote several, "Where did I spend last Christmas?" which he placed upon the top of the pile. We are still on more or less solid ground, presuming that the passengers were so dense as not to see the change of slates from the one which they examined to the prepared one. But now comes the fatal link in the chain. He claims that, "no telepathy or thought-transference being involved," the President *by pure chance* asked the very question for which these elaborate preparations had been made. People will believe this, and yet accuse Spiritualists of credulity. Can anyone who has the least conception of what is probable or possible accept such an explanation? It is only in psychic and preternatural (not supernatural) regions that such things really do become commonplace.

Again, a friend reports:

"One day a sceptic called upon him. Houdini read the man's hand, prognosticated his future, and pronounced his past from a mere reading of his face, having only been told the day of his birth. This was done with an accuracy and vividness which astonished the subject."

This sounds like possible clairvoyance, but is hardly in the repertoire of the conjurer.

There were many indications that Houdini possessed that psychic sensibility which is the groundwork of mediumship, though it really indicates, in my opinion, an unusual degree of soul power in the subject itself, without necessarily implying any outside assistance. All thought-reading seems to come under this category. On one occasion Pulitzer, the famous proprietor of the *New York World*, had been interested in the telepathic results obtained by Professor Gilbert Murray in England. Houdini dashed in, in his usual impetuous fashion, and claimed that he could duplicate them. A committee assembled in his own house, and put him to the test, they sitting on the ground floor, and he being locked up in a room at the top of the house, with the door guarded. Out of four tests he got three more or less correctly. When asked for an explanation he refused to answer, save to say that it was "scientific trickery." As usual he took it for granted that the Press and public would readily accept his explanation, and experience showed that he was right.

If once the mind is adjusted to the false assumption that psychic powers do not exist, then all reasoning power seems to become atrophied, as is the case in all bigoted religions. As an example it was said, and is said, again and again, "How absurd for Doyle to attribute possible psychic powers to a man who himself denies them!" Is it not perfectly evident that if he did not deny them his occupation would have been gone for ever? What would his brother-magicians have to say to a man who admitted that half his tricks were done by what they would regard as illicit powers? It would be "exit Houdini."

Now, having considered some of Houdini's inexplicable powers, let us turn to his direct relations with Spiritualism.

PART II

In public, as is notorious, he posed as the uncompromising foe of Spiritualism. It is useless to pretend that it was only the fake medium that he was after. We are all out after that scoundrel, and ready to accept any honest help in our search for him. Houdini wrote in the *Christian Register* of July, 1925:

"Tell the people that all I am trying to do is to save them from being tricked in their grief and sorrows, and to persuade them to leave Spiritualism alone and take up some genuine religion."

Thus his attack was a general one upon the whole cult.

But this was not in the least his attitude in private. I suppose that there are few leaders of the movement, and few known mediums, who have not letters of his taking the tone that he was a sympathetic inquirer who needed but a little more to be convinced. His curious mentality caused him to ignore absolutely the experiences of anyone else, but he seemed to be enormously impressed if anything from an outside source came in his own direction. On one occasion he showed me a photograph which he had taken in California. "I believe it to be the only genuine spirit photograph ever taken!" he cried. To my mind, it was a very doubtful one, and one which no sane Spiritualist would have passed for a moment. But, in any case, if his was, as he claimed, genuine, why should he put down all others to fraud? He had another which he showed me with some disgust, but which seemed to me to be capable of a real psychic explanation, however unlikely. The sensitive film had been torn lengthways right down the plate, just as a sharp nail would have done. He assured me that he had put it into the carrier quite intact. It might, of course, have been some singular accident, or it might conceivably have been a sign of the same sort of disapproval, which was a possible explanation of the gravel-throwing in the music-hall of Boston.

His experience with decent mediums was exceedingly limited. He sat several times with Eva during the abortive investigation by the London Psychical Research Society. He wrote to me at the time, saying: "I found it highly interesting." There was no question of any exposure, and he admitted that he saw ectoplasm both come and go without being able to explain it. I believe that he once—and only once—sat with that great voice medium, Mrs. Wriedt, on which occasion nothing at all occurred, as will happen with all honest mediums, but does not happen with conjurers. There was certainly no talk of any exposure. He never sat with Miss Besinnet, nor with Mrs. Pruden, nor with Jonson of Pasadena, nor with Hope, nor with Mrs. Deane, nor with Evan Powell, nor Phoenix, nor Sloane. He claimed to have exposed P. L. O. Keeler, a medium whom I have heard quoted, but of whom I have no personal experience. Speaking generally, it may be said that his practical experience, save with a class of people whom a decent Spiritualist would neither use nor recommend, was very limited. His theoretical knowledge of the subject was also limited, for though he possessed an excellent library, it was, when I inspected it, neither catalogued nor arranged. I am told that his library was eventually put upon a more satisfactory basis, but I speak of it as I saw it. His book, *A Magician among the Spirits*, is full of errors of fact, and never for a moment did he show any appreciation of the higher religious claims of the movement.

In spite of this very limited basis, he gave the public the impression that his knowledge was profound. To one reporter he said that he had attended ten thousand séances. I pointed out at the time that this would mean one a day for thirty years. His accusations against Spiritualists were equally wild. A man, named Frank Macdowell, committed a peculiarly atrocious murder at Clearwater in Florida. Houdini broadcast the fact that it was due to spirit teaching. Fortunately, a resolute Spiritualist, Mr. Elliot Hammond, went into the matter, and showed clearly that the murderer gave his complete disbelief in life after death to have been at the root of his actions. Spiritualism would have saved him.

I repeat that Houdini's attitude in private was quite different to what it was in public. At one time we had him really converted without the slightest intention of causing such a result. It was at Atlantic City, in 1922. He had spoken in a touching manner of his mother, so my wife, who has the great gift of inspired writing—that is, of writing which appears to be quite disconnected from her own mentality—tried to see if she could get any message for him. It was done at my suggestion, and I well remember that my wife needed much persuasion. We had no sooner assembled in our quiet sitting-room than the power came, and the medium began to write with breathless and extraordinary speed, covering sheet after sheet, which I tore off and threw across to Houdini at the other side of the table. We gathered that it was a moving and impassioned message to her son from the dead mother. He asked a mental question of his mother without speech, and the medium's hand instantly wrote what he admitted to be an answer. Houdini was deeply moved, and there is no question that at the time he entirely accepted it.

When we met him two days later in New York, he said to us: "I have been walking on air ever since." I published the incident in my *American Adventure*, so that he had to explain it away to fit it into his anti-Spiritualistic campaign. The line of criticism which he took was that it could not have been from his mother, since a cross was put upon the top of the paper, and she was a Jewess. If he had cared to inquire we could have shown him that the medium *always* puts a cross on the top of her paper, as being a holy symbol. We consider that such exercises are, in the highest degree, religious. That is a complete answer to the objection.

His second criticism was that the letter was in English. This was plausible, but shows an ignorance of psychic methods. If a medium were in complete trance, it might well be possible to get an unknown tongue through her. Such cases are not very rare; but when the medium is not in trance, but writing by inspiration, it is the flood of thought and of emotion which strikes her, and has to be translated by her in her own vocabulary as best she can. As an illustration, I have notes of a case where two mediums in the same room both got an inspired message at the same moment. They each wrote down the same sense, but the wording was quite different. Thus the second criticism falls to the ground. In any case, one would imagine that he would have nothing but respect and gratitude for one who tried to help him, with no conceivable advantage to herself. No sign of this appears. It is the same queer mental twist which caused him first to take the name of the great Frenchman, and then to write a whole book, *The Unmasking of Houdin*, to prove that he was a fraud.

But there was another very curious and suggestive incident in connection with that sitting at Atlantic City. As Houdini, much moved, rose from the table, he took up the pencil, and, bending to the papers, he said: "I wonder if I could do anything at this!" The pencil moved and he wrote one word. Then he looked up at me and I was amazed, for I saw in his eyes that look, impossible to imitate, which comes to the medium who is under influence. The eyes look at you, and yet you feel that they are not focused upon you. Then I took up the paper. He had written upon it one word, "Powell." My friend, Ellis Powell, had just died in England, so the name had a meaning. "Why, Houdini," I cried, "Saul is among the prophets! You are a medium." Houdini had a poker-face and gave nothing away as a rule, but he seemed to me to be disconcerted by my remark. He muttered something about knowing a man called "Powell" down in Texas, though he failed to invent any reason why that particular man should come back at that particular moment. Then, gathering up the papers, he hurried from the room. It is probable that at that moment I had surprised the master secret of his life—a secret which even those who were nearest to him had never quite understood. Each fact alone may be capable of explanation, but when a dozen facts all point in the same direction, then surely there is a case to answer.

I have said that the Houdini mentality was the most obscure that I have ever known. Consider this manifestation of it. My wife and I were, as I have shown, endeavouring to help him, with no possible motive save to give him such consolation as we could, since he was always saying that he wished to get in touch with his mother. Such consolation has often been given to others. Even if we suppose, for argument's sake, that we were mistaken in our views, we were, as he often admits, in dead earnest. Then, as we rose, he wrote down the name Powell, which meant much to me. If it was not written under psychic influence, why should he write anything at all, since no one asked him to do so? He saw the difficulty when he had to explain it away, so in his book he says that it was a "deliberate mystification" upon his part, and that he wrote it entirely of his own volition. Thus by his own showing, while we were honest with him, he was playing what I will charitably describe as a practical joke upon us. Is it any wonder that we look back at the incident with some bitterness? He does not attempt to explain how it was that out of all his friends the name that he wrote was the very one which might well have wished to come through to me. There is a limit to coincidence.

It is a curious fact that neither my wife nor I knew what was in the mother's letter until I read it in his book. It was written so swiftly that the medium, in her half-unconscious state, could at best only have a very vague idea of its purport, while I never even glanced at it. Now that I read it, it seems to me to be a very beautiful letter, full of love and of longing. As I have explained, the thoughts are given and are largely translated by the medium. Therefore, there are some sentences in which I can recognize my wife's style of expression, but the greater part of it is far more fervid—one might almost say more Oriental—than anything I have known my wife do. Here is a short extract:

"Oh, my darling, my darling, thank God at last I am through. I've tried, oh, so often. Now I am happy. Of course, I want to talk to my boy, my own beloved boy. . . . My only shadow has been that my beloved one has not known how often I have been with him all the while. . . . I want him only to know that—that—I have bridged the gulf—that is what I wanted—oh, so much. Now I can rest in peace."

It was a long and very moving message and bore every internal sign of being genuine. There is no question at all in my mind that Houdini was greatly shaken at the time and for some days afterwards. His objections were all afterthoughts in order to save the situation.

In the account of the matter which Houdini gave, he lays stress upon the fact that Mrs. Houdini had spoken to my wife the night before as to Houdini's affairs, with many details as to his habits when with his mother. Now if the message had really come from my wife's subconscious self I think it is certain that some of this information would have come through. I have known this to happen in the case of perfectly honest mediums and for this reason it is better never to tell a medium anything at all before a séance. A blank slate is the best to write upon. In the long message, however, which my wife gave there was no trace at all of the knowledge which she had normally gained, and which could have been used so effectively if anyone had been so wicked as to play a trick. This is, I think, a very clear sign that the message was not subconscious but did really come from the source it claimed. Houdini's objection that the mother made no mention of the fact that it was her own birthday has no relevancy. What are birthdays on the other side? It is the death day which is the real birthday. In her rush of joy and emotion why should she pause to mention such a fact? The method in which Houdini tried to explain away, minimize and contort our attempt at consolation, which was given entirely at his own urgent request and against my wife's desire, has left a deplorable shadow in my mind which made some alteration in my feelings for him. Conscious as I was of his many excellent and wonderful qualities, such incidents took the edge off my sympathies, and put a strain upon our friendship.

When my friend, the late Miss Scatcherd, was in New York, some years ago, she saw a good deal of Houdini, and got, I fancy, as nearly into his complete confidence as anyone could do. To her, as to me, he showed no animosity to psychic things, but, on the contrary, he was eager to show her the one and only true medium whom he had discovered in America. Miss Scatcherd was not, I gather, much impressed by his find, having known many better ones. She did not fail, however, to point out to him that in admitting the one medium he had really given away his whole case, and agreed that the Spiritualists had a solid foundation for their cult. She then accused him of being a powerful medium himself, for she was a strong sensitive, and all her psychic powers told her that he was the same. She also scolded him in her charming, good-natured way for having behaved shamefully in the "Margery" case, which he did not deny. The climax came, however, when, far out on the Atlantic, she received the following wireless message:

"From a sensitive to a sensitive. Wishing you a pleasant voyage.—Houdini."

A sensitive is a medium, and what is the logic of denouncing all mediums as frauds from the public platforms, and at the same time declaring in a telegram that you are one yourself?

Let us now follow a fresh line of thought. There can be no question at all, to anyone who has really weighed the facts, that Ira Davenport was a true medium. Apart from the evidence of thousands of witnesses, it is self-evident that he could at any time, by announcing himself and his brother as conjurers, and doing his unique performances as tricks, have won fame and fortune. This would seem a dreadful thing to do from the point of view of a good Spiritualist, and the Davenports went to the last possible limit by leaving the source of their powers to the audience to determine. Houdini has endeavoured to take advantage of this and to make out that Ira admitted in his old age that his feats were tricks. To clear away such an idea, I append the following letter, written by Ira in 1868 to *The Banner of Light*:

"It is singular that any individual, sceptic or Spiritualist, could believe such statements after fourteen years of the most bitter persecution, culminating in the riots of Liverpool, Hudderfield, and Leeds, where our lives were placed in imminent peril by the fury of brutal mobs, our property destroyed, all because we would not renounce Spiritualism and declare ourselves jugglers when threatened by the mob and urged to do so. In conclusion, we denounce all such statements as base falsehoods."

We happen to be particularly well informed about the Davenports, for, apart from long statements from many well-known people who examined them, there are three books by people who knew them well, and who could not possibly have been deceived had they been swindlers.

The smaller book, by Orrin Abbott, covers the early days, and the author tells how he was intimate with the brothers when they were little boys, and how at that time he had every opportunity of observing and testing their wonderful powers. These seem, as is often the case with mediums, to have been stronger in childhood than in later life, the power of levitation being one which Abbott witnessed, but which is not recorded of them elsewhere. The second and fullest is Dr. Nicol's biography, while the third and most valuable is found in the *Supramundane Facts* of the Rev. J. B. Ferguson. Ferguson was a man of very high character, with a notable record behind him, and he travelled with the Davenports during their tour in England. He was with them at all hours of the day and night, and he has left it on record that their experiences when in private were quite as wonderful as anything that the public ever saw. It is notable that these well-attested feats included not only the instant freedom from ropes, however carefully fastened and sealed by the spectators, but also, on occasion, the freedom from handcuffs or twisted wire, and the power of opening locked doors. In a word, the Davenport powers were the Houdini powers, save that the latter had physical strength and agility which may have helped him to extend them.

My argument now begins to emerge. If it be true that the Davenports were real mediums (and let the inquirer really read their record before he denies it),[1] and if Houdini produced exactly similar results, which have in each case been inexplicable to their contemporaries, then is it conceivable that they were produced in entirely different ways? If Ira Davenport was a medium, then there is a strong primâ facie case that Houdini was a medium too. Now we come upon some explanation of the cryptic saying of the rabbi by the graveside: "He possessed a wondrous power that he never understood, and which he never revealed to anyone in life." What could that power be, save what we have called the power of the medium?

A singular incident is narrated by Mrs. Houdini and is incorporated in Mr. Kellock's biography. Shortly after his marriage, Houdini took his girl wife and his brother to a lonely place, where he halted them upon a bridge at midnight. When the hour came he made them both raise their hands in the air and said to them, "Beatrice, Dash, raise your

[1] It will be found epitomized in my *History of Spiritualism* (Cassell).

hands to heaven and swear that both of you will be true to me. Never betray me in any way, so help you God!" I would not put too much stress upon this incident. It may have been the considered act of one who already had some strange and secret knowledge which he foresaw might be used in the future and might be surprised by those around him.

I would not, in probing this difficult problem, pass too lightly over the considered words of the rabbi, that he had a wondrous power and did not himself understand it. This phrase fits very exactly into what has been stated to me by those who were nearest to him in life. "If it was so, he did not know it," they have answered when I hinted at my conclusions. It seems hard to comprehend, and yet there may be something in this view. He was not a clear thinker, and he had no logical process in his mind. That surely is evident when in the same breath he denies all mediumship and claims to have discovered the greatest medium in America; or when he scoffs at spirit pictures but brings me a very indifferent one which he had taken himself. Imagine that such a man finds himself one minute inside a box; there is an interval of semi-trance during which his mind is filled with a vague feeling of confused effort, and then he finds himself outside the box. There is no obvious intervention of spirits, or of any outside force, but it just happens so. He has the same power in emerging from fetters, but he has no sort of philosophy by which he can explain such things. If we could imagine such a very strange and unlikely state of things as that, it would, at least, have the merit that it would give some sort of honest and rational explanation of a good deal which at present is dark. It is no unusual thing for a medium to fail to understand his own results, but it would certainly seem almost incredible that anyone could have such results for many years and never correlate them with the experience of others. I, as his former friend, would welcome such an explanation if it could be sustained.

But how does the good rabbi know that he did not understand it? Only one man could say with authority, but he has passed away with closed lips, leaving, however, many signs behind for those who have the wit to follow them. There is one thing certain, and that is that the fate of the Davenports must have been a perpetual warning to Houdini. They had been ruined and hunted off the stage because it was thought that their claim was psychic. If his powers were to be drawn from that source, and if he were to avoid a similar fate, then his first and fundamental law must be that it be camouflaged in every possible way, and that no one at all should know his secret. If this be granted, a great many disconnected points become at once a connected whole. We see what he meant when he said that his own wife did not know how he produced his effects. We understand the voice of which he spoke. We comprehend dimly the unknown power of the rabbi. We can even imagine that a campaign against mediums, fortified by the knowledge that false mediums do exist, would be an excellent smoke-screen, though probably he had never thought out what view the unseen powers might take of such a transaction, any more than he calculated upon the interposition of Walter in the case of the conspiracy against the Crandons. I cannot say that all this is certain. I can only say that it covers the facts as I know them.

Of course, I know that he had a trick-box. I know also who constructed it, and the large amount that he paid for it. When I know also that he could do his escapes equally well in any local box, I am not inclined to attach much importance to the matter. He was a very astute man, and what he did he would do thoroughly, but he became too careless in his methods as he found he could do them with impunity.

Houdini is curiously contradictory in his account of the methods of Davenport. In his book *A Magician among the Spirits*, he says:

"Their method of releasing themselves was simple. When one extended his feet the other drew his in, thus securing slack enough in the wrist rope to permit working their hands out of the loops. The second brother was released by reversing the action."

But, as I have shown, in a letter to me he said:

"I know for a positive fact that it was not essential for them to release the bonds in order to obtain manifestations."

So the previous explanation would seem to have been a fake in order to conceal the real one.

In another letter he says:

"I am afraid I cannot say that all of their work was accomplished by spirits."

The "all" is suggestive. I would be the last to suggest that all of Davenport's or indeed that all of Houdini's work could be due to spirits. For that matter, we have to remember that we are ourselves spirits here and now, and that a man may very well be producing psychic effects without going beyond his own organism. It is in this sense that I suspect the Houdini results as being psychic, and I do not at all insist upon the interposition of outside forces. The two things are not far apart, however, and very easily slide into each other. There is, I hold, the medium's use of his own power, there is a vague borderland, and there is a wide world beyond where his power is used by forces outside himself. I am convinced, for example, that raps may be produced voluntarily by a medium by a psychic effort, and I am equally convinced that at another stage these same raps may be used for purposes quite beyond his knowledge or control.

It is possible for a man to be a very powerful medium all his life, to use that power continually, and yet never to realize that the gifts he is using are those which the world calls mediumship? If that be indeed possible, then we have a solution of the Houdini enigma. One who knew him well and worked with him often wrote to me as follows:

"Often he would get a difficult lock. I would stand by the cabinet and hear him say: 'This is beyond me.' After many minutes, when the audience became restless, I would say, 'If there is anything in this belief in Spiritism why don't you call on them to assist you?' And before many minutes had passed Houdini had mastered the lock. He never attributed this to psychic help. He just knew that that particular instrument was the one to open that lock, and so he did all his tricks."

It is only fair to state, however, that this correspondent, who was in a good position to know, would not admit the mediumship. And yet if "that particular instrument" was, as stated, an appeal to spirits, it seems difficult to claim that the result was natural.

I would not limit my hypothesis to the idea that it was only when he met the Davenports that he first developed these strange powers. He seems only to have met Ira in 1909, and he had certainly done many marvellous feats himself before then. But the history and object-lesson of the Davenports must have been well known to him, and have shown him what to avoid.

In putting forward such a view as I have here expressed it is natural that a critic should demand that I should show that similar results to those of Houdini have actually been produced by psychic power. Of this there can be no possible doubt upon the part of anyone who has studied the subject. I have already mentioned the case of the Davenports who were so badly treated by the English mob, and so maligned by Maskelyne and other English conjurers who produced a feeble imitation of their results and called it an exposure. They freed themselves with the greatest ease from metal bands as well as from the tightest ligatures. Such results can only be obtained by the passage of matter through matter—of the wrist for example through the metal—and though such a thing may seem inconceivable to the prosaic scientist of to-day, he would have pronounced wireless or flying to be equally impossible a generation or so in the past. We seem to need no spirit intervention here, but to be within the region of the latent powers of the human organism in peculiarly constituted individuals. There is, I believe, a constructive and a destructive power in thought alone which is akin to that "faith which moves mountains." What sort of vibration it can be which is shot out from the human brain and separates for a moment the molecules of that solid object towards which it is directed I do not know, but the results are clear and perhaps in the near future the cause may become equally so. From personal observation I have assured myself that mediums in sealed bonds can cast those bonds, walk about the room, and be found later with the sealed bonds as before. If they could get out by a trick I see no way in which they could get back. I am forced, therefore, to predicate the existence of such a dematerializing and reconstructing force, which would amply cover most of the phenomena both of the Davenports and of Houdini. Such a force was demonstrated also in the experiments which were made with Slade by Zöllner and three other German professors, and described by him in his *Transcendental Physics*. In this book many instances, closely observed, of the passage of matter through matter were recorded, accompanied by the interesting observation that the phenomenon was accompanied often by heat and a strong smell of burning.[2] Bellachini, the Court conjurer, deposed that the results he saw were out of the region of conjuring altogether.[3] But suppose that Slade had

[2] *Transcendental Physics*, by Prof. Zöllner (English translation), p. 113.
[3] *Vide* appendix of the above book.

gone round the world doing such things and allowing people to believe that they were tricks, while confusing the public by mixing them up with real tricks, would not his position have been very close to that of Houdini?

We come, however, upon a more advanced class of phenomenon when we consider the case of the passage of a human body through a solid obstacle and its reassembly on the other side. If I can show that such cases have upon most unquestionable evidence occurred then I shall have got a possible line upon Houdini's performance. In the April number of *Psychic Science* there is the report by an American lady, Mrs. Hack, of the phenomena at a circle sitting in the Castle Millesimo, which is near Genoa. Mrs. Hack was herself present, as were the well-known Professor Bozzano, and other first-class witnesses. The Marquis Centurione Scotto, the owner of the castle, was one of the company. Suddenly in the midst of the proceedings he vanished from his chair. His friends were horrified. They searched the room and the castle, but he was gone. Finally, after hours of agitation he was found in a deep trance in an outhouse, which was separated by several locked doors from the main building. He was led back; and had no recollection how he had got there. Such in a few words is the gist of a case which was closely observed and fully reported. In it a human body is passed through several solid obstacles and reassembled on the other side. How does this differ from the passage of Houdini's body through wooden planks, brick walls, paper bags, glass tanks, or whatever else was used to confine him?[4]

In Mr. Campbell Holms' book, *The Facts of Psychic Science*, which is, and will be always, a most exact and valuable book of reference, there are a number of cases given where people have been transported through solid objects. Inexperienced and foolish people may jeer, but they will find it easier to do so than to refute the evidence. For example, upon June 3rd, 1871, Mrs. Guppy was floated from her own house in Highbury, and appeared upon the table of a room at 61 Lambs Conduit Street, where a séance was being held behind locked doors. A document was signed by the eleven sitters to testify to the fact and they had no possible object in perjuring themselves about the matter. Mrs.

[4] These remarkable experiences are more fully described in Mrs. Hack's *Modern Psychic Mysteries* (Rider).

Guppy said that the last thing she could remember was sitting with her friend Miss Neyland. That lady deposed that Mrs. Guppy had suddenly vanished from her sight. Four of the sitters accompanied Mrs. Guppy home and heard what her friend had to say. It is difficult to find any flaw in such evidence and it would certainly have been conclusive in a court of law had it been a criminal case. But surely such a transposition is more remarkable than any of Houdini's, and had she done similar things in public her reputation would have been similar to his own.

In another case, that of Mr. Henderson, a photographer, quoted by Mr. Campbell Holms and described in the *Spiritual Magazine* of 1874 (p. 22), no less than ten persons saw him vanish from a room, while nine others deposed to his arrival almost instantaneously at a point more than a mile distant. The idea that these nineteen witnesses can be disregarded is surely an impossible one, and yet here again we have evidence of the possibility by psychic means of passing a human body through solid obstacles by a process of dematerialization and reassembly. I could quote a number of other cases, but the sum of it all is that Houdini's exploits, which are inexplicable in any other way, come into line at once if we compare them with other well-attested examples of psychic power. When one adds this evidence to the various other indications of similar powers which I have assembled here, the case seems to me to be greatly strengthened.

That Houdini's performances were on a different level from those of other magicians is shown by the fact that men who took a pride in fathoming such problems, and who were usually successful, were utterly foiled in their attempts to explain them in any reasonable way. Thus Mr. H. L. Adam, an English journalist who is an expert in such matters, writes to me that he could understand much that was done by Maskelyne and others, but

"I have never been able to discover anything about Houdini's tricks. Why? I have stood quite near him on the stage during the performances of many of his tricks, but it was like looking at a brick wall, so impenetrable were they. I remember on one occasion, while Houdini was waiting at the side of the stage ready for his 'turn,' he sat in a chair, threw his head back, closed his eyes, and appeared plunged in the profoundest meditations. A few moments before he had been talking confidentially to me. After the lapse of perhaps ten minutes, he 'came to' and continued his conversation with me as though nothing had intervened."

"Houdini once suggested to me that he should, by way of advertisement, profess to 'give away' his handcuff trick, which I was to publish. But it struck me that the volunteered so-called explanation, which included a hidden key, was too feeble to be convincing, and it was never developed. This was the nearest approach he ever came to discussing any of his secrets with me."

Here again in that trance-like condition before a performance we seem to get a glimpse of some psychic influence.

Houdini continually admitted that there were psychic things which he could not understand. I would say in parenthesis that one may be a strong medium oneself and yet have very small understanding of other people's phenomena. That was conspicuous in the case of D. D. Home. Here is a Houdini story told by Don Ryan[5]:

"Houdini had gone in a spiritualist church in Los Angeles, taking a camera-man, who carried a camera concealed. They made themselves inconspicuous till the witching hour at which the ghost was accustomed to walk. The hour came and with it the spirit. The leader of the group was holding conversation with the invisible spirit when the camera was trained on the spot without the knowledge of anybody save Houdini and his photographer.

"The developed plate which Houdini showed me revealed a well-defined transparent human figure draped in white.

" 'I can't explain it and I don't know what to think of it,' said Houdini that day, and I could see that the thing had made a decided impression on him.

" 'It's no more astonishing than your staying under water for an hour and a half in a lead-lined coffin,' I told him.

" 'Ah,' replied Houdini, 'but I know how that is done.' "

The attempts upon the part of his brother-magicians to give some sort of explanation of Houdini's feats only serve to deepen the mystery. Mr. Howard Thurston, for whose opinion I have respect, for he seemed to me to be the only American conjurer who had some real accurate knowledge of psychic matters, says that his feats all come within the power of advanced conjuring. I know that feats with the same name do so, but I venture to express the opinion that such feats as Houdini did have never been explained and are in an altogether different class. So too,

[5] *New York American,* February 11th, 1928.

Mr. Will Goldston, who is well known and respected as an authority on conjuring, has actually described in a book how they are done. Here again he seems to me to be describing the accepted methods, which by no means covers Houdini's results. To show the inadequacy of Mr. Goldston's "explanations"[6] he says in talking of the escape under water, "Without giving away his secrets I may say that he was always practically out of the box before it reached the water." Considering that the screwed and corded box was in full sight of hundreds of spectators as it sank beneath the waves, it is difficult to accept such a solution as this. I admit that I am at a disadvantage when opposed to the technical knowledge of such men as Goldston and Thurston, but on the other hand I have my own technical and expert knowledge of psychic possibilities, and I put up a case for consideration and discussion.

He had, as already stated, a sitting with the medium Eva, and under the stringent and very deterrent conditions imposed by the London Psychical Research Society, which will be found described in their unsatisfactory and self-contradictory report, he did seem to have made acquaintance with ectoplasm in its very humblest form. He says in a letter to me written the next morning (June 22nd, 1920):

"They made Eva drink a cup of coffee and eat some cake (I presume to fill her up with some food-stuff), and after she had been sewn into the tights, and a net over her face, she manifested.

1. "Some froth-like substance, inside of net, 'twas long, about five inches, she said it was elevated, but none of us four watchers saw it 'elevate.'
2. "A white plaster-looking affair over her right eye.
3. "Something that looked like a small face, say four inches in circumference. Was terra-cotta coloured, and Dingwall, who held her hand, had the best look at the 'object.'
4. "Some substance, froth-like, exuding from her nose, and Baggeley and Fielding say it protrudes from her nose, but Dingwall and I are positive that it was inside of net and was not extending from her nose, as I had the best view from two different places I deliberately took advantage to see just what it was.
5. "Medium asked permission to remove something in her mouth, show her hands empty, and took out what appeared to be a rubberish substance, which she disengaged, showed us plainly, we held the electric torch, all saw it

[6] *Sunday Express*, November 7th, 1926.

plainly, when presto! it vanished. It was a surprise effect indeed! The séance started at 7:30 and lasted past midnight.

"We went over the notes, and no doubt you will get a full report. I found it highly interesting."

It will be found from these extracts that when faced with facts his attitude was very different from what his public utterances would lead one to expect.

Be his mystery what it may, Houdini was one of the most remarkable men of whom we have any record, and he will live in history with such personalities as Cagliostro, the Chevalier D'Eon, and other strange characters. He had many outstanding qualities, and the world is the poorer for his loss. As matters stand, no one can say positively and finally that his powers were abnormal, but the reader will, I hope, agree with me that there is a case to be answered.

Arthur Conan Doyle

Creator of Sherlock Holmes

An Expose By Sir Arthur Conan Doyle

2D BIG WEEK!
GREATEST SENSATION IN YEARS
THE ACTUAL EXPOSE OF A WORLD PROBLEM
METHODS OF FAKE MEDIUMS BROUGHT BEFORE YOUR EYES BY

HOUDINI

AFTER SEEING HIS EXHIBITION THIS WEEK YOU CAN HAVE A THOUSAND THRILLS AT HOME. BE YOUR OWN MEDIUM. IT IS POSITIVELY EASY AND SIMPLE.

OPEN FORUM OF FIVE MINUTES AFTER ACT.
MR. HOUDINI CANNOT GIVE A PRIVATE AUDIENCE WITHOUT APPOINTMENT

PSYCHIC CHALLENGED BY MAGICIAN

MRS. L. R. G. CRANDON ("MARGERY")
Boston psychic whom Houdini declares he will denounce on his arrival here today. He will deposit $5,000 with Boston's mayor as a guarantee of his project.

TO DEPOSIT $5,000 AT CITY HALL

Will Forfeit the Cash if He Cannot Expose Hub Psychic's "Tricks"

Harry Houdini, famous man of magic, arrived in Boston today prepared, in his own words, to denounce and expose the psychic "Margery" and her husband, Dr. Le Roi G. Crandon.

Houdini will deposit $5,000 with Mayor Curley. This $5,000 the famous magician will forfeit if he cannot duplicate by trick or explain away manifestations produced by "Margery."

Upon his arrival here Houdini repeated his challenge to Dr. William McDougall, Harvard professor of psychology.

If the Harvard professor, who has taken exception to Houdini's statements regarding manifestations by "Margery," will allow himself to be nailed inside a weighted packing case and thrown into the Charles River Houdini will pay him a sum equal to a year's salary at Harvard.

The arrival of Houdini in Boston today is the culmination of controversy which have arisen over the proposed award of the Scientific American committee to the Crandons for genuine display of psychic powers.

Charges and counter charges came to a head a week ago when Houdini claimed that the powers of magic and darkness were being called upon to bring about his death.

HOUDINI

Exposes the tricks used by the
Boston Medium "Margery"
to win the $2100 prize offered by the Scientific American

Also a complete exposure of
ARGAMASILLA
The famous Spaniard who baffled noted Scientists of Europe and America, with his claim to
X-RAY VISION

HILL STREET THEATRE
"The Pride of Los Angeles"
Junior Orpheum Circuit Phone Pico 6640 Eighth & Hill

SPECIAL PERFORMANCE
Friday Morning Only
April 27, 1923 — 11 a.m.

The Famous Psychic Investigator

"THE GENIUS OF ESCAPE"
HOUDINI (IN PERSON)
WHO WILL STARTLE AND AMAZE

With a Lecture on
"FRAUD MEDIUMS and MIRACLE MONGERS"

A SENSATIONAL AND STARTLING EXPOSE
Read Further Particulars Inside

MARGERY GENUINE, SAYS CONAN DOYLE; HE SCORES HOUDINI

MEDIUM AND HER NEW CHAMPION

MRS. MINA CRANDON
Who, as Margery, is Storm Centre in Psychic Controversy

SIR ARTHUR CONAN DOYLE
Who Comes to Defense of Mrs. Crandon
(Daily News Service)

CRITICIZES THE EXPERT BODY IN SEVERE TERMS

All but Bird and Carrington Derelict in Silence Under Attack

HE ANALYZES ALL EVIDENCE ADDUCED

Surprised American Gentlemen Should Tolerate Wizard's Conduct

Using the methods of deduction made famous in his Sherlock Holmes stories, Sir Arthur Conan Doyle analyzes the phenomena shown by Mrs. Le Roi G. Crandon, the famous medium, "Margery," and vigorously defends their authenticity in a statement which he sent to The Herald yesterday.

He finds after a minute examination of the proceedings of the Scientific American investigating committee, which held more than 90 séances with the wife of the Boston surgeon, that the charges of fraud made by Houdini, the magician, were entirely groundless, that the other experts, with the exception of E. Malcolm Bird and Hereward Carrington, were derelict in remaining silent after the handcuff king's attack. He also declares that Dr. Crandon was entirely too forbearing in permitting the tests to continue after his wife's honesty was impugned.

MAKES COUNTER-CHARGES

Counter-charges against the members of the committee who opposed Bird's and Carrington's proposal of a favorable report and a sense of amazement at their stubborn incredulity characterizes Sir Arthur's message. He states that a cabal, headed by Houdini, was undoubtedly organized against Bird and Bird, resulted in his removal as secretary of the body.

Sir is particularly bitter in his criticism of Houdini and states that "he left Boston a very discredited man so far as psychic research is concerned." In conclusion he expresses his "amazement" that the committee, consisting of "honorable gentlemen" should permit the attack on the reputation of a lady and permitted a man "with entirely different standards to make this outrageous attack," and adds that by doing so they practically made themselves responsible for it.

By SIR ARTHUR CONAN DOYLE

It is Christmas morning and I sit at a table which is heaped with documents and photographs. They are the dossier of the Crandon case. Perhaps one should not work upon Christmas day, and yet surely there is no day so holy that one may not use it for the fight for truth, the exposure of evil and the defense of the honor of a most estimable lady.

The Margery case will live in history and perhaps it is fitting that I should have some hand in the record, since the matter was in a double sense of my begetting. In the first place 12 members of the Scientific American newspaper was instituted in consequence of my psychic lectures in 1922. In the second it was I who, with her consent, introduced Margery to their notice.

CHARMING, CULTIVATED

Margery is a most charming and cultivated lady. A year or two back she found that she possessed certain psychic powers which ran in the direction of physical phenomena. Her husband, as a man of science, was naturally interested in this development. Hearing that the committee of the "Scientific American" found it hard to get the services of professional mediums, Margery took the brave resolution of revealing her powers for examination.

HOUDINI STIRRED BY ARTICLE, MAY SUE SIR ARTHUR

Noted Magician Is Angry at Creator of Sherlock Holmes for Published Attack.

NEW YORK, Jan. 27—Houdini, the magician, "contemplates legal action" against Sir Arthur Conan Doyle as a result of remarks about him contained in a copyrighted article by Dr. Doyle, published yesterday in the Boston Herald. Sir Arthur's article was an answer to Houdini's attack on the genuineness of Margery, the Boston medium, whom the committee of the Scientific American has been investigating.

Margery is Mrs. Le Roi G. Crandon, wife of a Boston physician, and Dr. Doyle introduced her to the public as a medium when he was here three years ago. He believes her alleged communications with her dead brother, Walter, are valid.

Houdini said yesterday he does not propose to let Sir Arthur get away with certain harsh remarks contained in the article. He will have a retraction, or "communicate with his lawyer." Also, Sir Arthur is a bit senile, says Houdini, and therefore easily bamboozled. Houdini has been investigating mediums for 35 years and he says he has never had a valid manifestation of communication with the other world. Furthermore, he thinks that a bit of the sharpness contained in Sir Arthur's remarks may have been occasioned by the fact that he, Houdini, once expressed the belief that Lady Doyle was not a valid medium either.

Doyle Defends Margery.

In his article, Sir Arthur declares he is "rushing to the defense of a most estimable lady."

He describes two sittings which Houdini attended. He says Margery's dead brother, "Walter," warned beforehand that Houdini would attempt a trick. When the séance started "Walter," in a very loud and angry voice, asked Houdini, "How much are they paying you to stop these phenomena?" Then "Walter" demanded that a certain box, on which was a bell the spirits were supposed to ring, be taken into the light and examined. Doyle says somebody had placed a rubber under the bell to keep it from ringing and thus discredit Margery.

Sir Arthur accuses Houdini of "self-advertising." He says Houdini left Boston "a very discredited man so far as psychic research is concerned." He hopes Houdini will "confine himself in future to that art in which he is famous and leave a field for which his strong prejudices and unbalanced judgment entirely unfit him."

Houdini Denies Charge.

"There is not a word of truth in his charges against me," said Houdini. "Sir Arthur has been sadly misinformed. Anyhow, I fail to see how he, being 3500 miles away, qualifies as a judge.

"I have posted $10,000 with Mayor Curley of Boston to be given to charity if she makes good before a committee chosen by Mayor Curley.

"The truth of the whole matter is that Margery, in my belief, is a social climber."

An Expose By Sir Arthur Conan Doyle

"Can the Dead Speak to the Living?"
An Expose of Fraudulent Spiritual Communication with Sensational Demonstrations

HIPPODROME

One of the best shows of the season at the Hippodrome, with business heavy Monday night, due, unquestionably, to the "draw" of the headliner, Houdini (New Acts) in his spiritualistic expose of the medium "Margery," and all fake psychics. The Houdini act, next to closing, ran 41 minutes and could have composed the entire half of the bill, such was the intense interest of the packed house in the handcuff king's showup of the gypping table knockers, bell ringers and astral body producers.

Houdini is the greatest showman in vaudeville today and a tremendous draw. His latest act surpasses anything he has ever attempted before on account of the world-wide interest in spiritualism. The humanitarian qualities of the turn can never be imagined by a layman unfamiliar with the hoaxes perpetrated by fake mediums on believers. Last wills and testaments have been changed through the trickery of mediums, where messages from the dead were used as the motivating power to induce some rich convert his or her fortune should be left to the scheming individuals who employed the fake mediums.

CONAN DOYLE "SPIRIT" PHOTOGRAPH

Vicar's Claim to Have Received First.

AT SEANCE.

TO-DAY the *Daily Dispatch* is able to reproduce remarkable "spirit" photographs of Sir Arthur Conan Doyle, who died on July 7, taken by the Rev. Charles L. Tweedale, Vicar of Weston, near Otley, an earnest investigator into spirit phenomena, whose book, "Man's Survival After Death," is an accepted standard work.

Mr. Tweedale states that he was certain that Sir Arthur, whom he knew very well, would manifest himself soon after his death, and that on July 8 and 9 messages were received at their séance, the first of which was read by Mrs. M. L. Tweedale and Dorothy M. Tweedale, the second by Mrs. Tweedale and himself, and the third by Mr. Tweedale, Mrs. Tweedale and Mr. Tweedale.

An original photograph of Sir Arthur Conan Doyle.

By the Rev. CHARLES L. TWEEDALE,
VICAR OF WESTON, NEAR OTLEY.

Friday, July 11, 4.40 a.m.—I awoke, woke my wife, and we exchanged a few words and composed ourselves for sleep again. My mind reverted to the Doyle message, and there and then I prayed earnestly that God would bless the manifestations and the evidence to the furtherance of the truth.

The moment my prayer ended, the door of the room where we sit for spirit communication, and which is a few feet to the left of our bedroom and on the other side of the passage, to which it forms a "cul-de-sac," began to be fiercely shaken. Owing to the door frame being twisted it needs a strong pull to be made to make a grating noise. Then it suddenly gestures into the frame with a loud bang.

The door closed in this manner with a loud bang twice in a way heard by both of us, the moment my prayer was ended, and as though in immediate answer.

It was daylight, our room door was open and no one passed it. The room where we sit for the messages has no door on the window, was closed, and no one outside could do this.

WRITTEN MESSAGE

At the first sitting a spirit control declared "A said 'Doyle is sitting in the outer dark,' and required to try to get him to send a message through Alice."

At a sitting at 12.45 p.m. on July 8, Aunt Mary Tweedale, "A" came and said that my mother and Sir Arthur might now show themselves photographically together next week."

At a later sitting the same day "A" gave a written message from Sir Arthur, through communicator "B" because "B's" writing was smaller to which Sir Arthur said:

"Mr. Tweedale, I have arrived here in Paradise. That is how I express my joy, but wait till about ... a charming time to see a crowd here to welcome you. Paradise is far too heavy for a poet. Prose wins. I am still testing. I begin from time to time just you. I ascribe holy connection."

"B" concluding, said, "Sir Arthur has just been heard. He is off in rapture; he has had ignite an earthly taste for the evening, and is used to it."

Mr. Tweedale takes up the narrative in this point.

TAKING THE PHOTOGRAPHS

Monday, July 14.—Set with the comforted psychic, Mr. William Hope, who came under good test conditions. Took a new, unopened packet of plates, tested the foil, and signed the plates myself, carefully inspected and cleaned the slide, which had such touch marked. After backing the slide, I put it in my pocket and proceeded to the house, took the back to the dark room after the exposure, where I developed the plates myself, and Hope was not allowed to touch them or place his hands over them.

I took three more exposures and two more plates, recognisable persons of Sir Arthur.

On the first plate are four faces in their forms of a lighted, around my head upon which the face is partly superimposed. Here are all pictures of the same person, and two of them are clearly recognisable pictures of Sir Arthur, the drooping moustache and head, and the sweep of the hair on the right being clearly apparent; also, as far as we can discern, building the forehead of Doyle.

A picture showing the manifestation of Sir William Crookes.

The photograph enlarged for the purpose of newspaper reproduction showing two faces of Sir Arthur Conan Doyle as they appeared with that of the Rev. C. L. Tweedale.

FACE THAT MOVED.

After the exposure and development of the first pair of plates a remarkable thing happened. Seeing that the faces were in a cloudy band of ectoplasm and that one was superimposed on my own head, before the second pair of plates were exposed I called down the superintendence the exposures were made. Will the manifesting personality please take care not to show up on my face?

On developing these exposures, I found that the face had left the ring of ectoplasm above me, as requested, and thrown itself as a smaller but more distinct face close to, but not touching, my head.

This picture shows Sir Arthur as a much younger man, but comparison with the photograph facing pages 64 and 72, and also with the frontispiece in his book, "Wanderings of a Spiritualist," show the identity of features beyond question.

LEARNING WAY ABOUT.

Representing, as they do, Sir Arthur's first attempts to show himself photographically, these pictures are remarkable, seeing that he only passed over a few days ago.

The pictures are rather faint, though clearly recognisable. I hope they will be strong enough to reproduce for Press illustration.

These first psychic pictures are wonderful as representing Sir Arthur's first attempt to show himself in this way, he having only been a few days in the spirit world, and, in the words of a message received from him last night: "Only just beginning to know his way about."

What can be done by a spirit who has been passed over some time will be seen by examining the accompanying picture of Sir William Crookes, the great scientist, who manifested with me on March 25, 1929, and whose features are more clearly shown than my own.

HONOR POE IN LONDON.

Conan Doyle Acknowledges His Inspiration at Authors Club Dinner.

LONDON, March 1.—A brilliant company gathered to-night at the invitation of the Authors Club at a banquet to celebrate the centenary of the birth of Edgar Allan Poe. Sir Arthur Conan Doyle presided, and was supported by Ambassador Reid and Mrs. Humphry Ward, many leading British authors and a large number of American residents of London. Among the guests was Capt. Poe, the oldest surviving member of the Poe family. The speeches, which were delivered by Ambassador Reid and Sir Conan Doyle, Capt. Poe, Charles Garvice, the novelist, and Francis Henry Gribble, the critic, were interspersed with recitations of Poe's poems.

Sir Conan Doyle, after referring to the tragedy of Poe's life, paid a glowing tribute to Poe's work, saying: "It is the irony of Fate that he, as he said, should have died in poverty, for if every man who wrote a story which was indirectly inspired by Poe were to pay a tithe toward a monument it would be such as would dwarf the pyramids."

The speaker credited the inspiration for his own detective stories to Poe.

Ambassador Reid said the lateness of the celebration was quite in keeping with Poe's career.

"Everything came to him too late, in life, as in death, especially in his own country," said the Ambassador. "Even when good fortune seemed ready to press itself upon him more than once during his life his temperamental waywardness, heedlessness, and irresponsibility kept him from appreciating the opportunity until it was too late.

"Now, long after his unhappy death and long after the English and French literary tribunals have accepted him as one of the immortals, his countrymen still wait even beyond the century to place him with their other literary figures, some surely far smaller, in their hall of fame. Yet with all the abatements Poe's place surely is in the front rank, if not at the very head, of the world's tellers of short stories."

Among the patrons of the celebration besides those already named were J. Ridgeley Carter, Secretary of the American Embassy; Rear Admiral Stockton, U. S. N.; Prof. George Grafton Wilson of Brown University, who was a Delegate to the recent International Naval Conference; the Duchess of Marlborough, the Marchioness of Dufferin; Cora, the Countess of Strafford; Mrs. Cornwallis-West, Lord Fairfax, Robert Newton Crane, and Justin McCarthy.

An Expose By Sir Arthur Conan Doyle

KERNAN'S THEATRICAL BULLETIN

THE ONLY PAPER PUBLISHED EXCLUSIVELY FOR THE THEATRE GOER.

Vol. 2.   Baltimore, Md., Week of February 25, 1907   No. 22

THE TALK OF THE TOWN!
Novel Challenge Week of
HOUDINI
With New Surprises and Sensations

Maryland Theater

Week of

Feb. 25th

Matinee Daily

POPULAR PRICES

Daring Escapes

ASTOUNDING FEATS

Marvelous Tricks

Houdini, the Handcuff King.
The Greatest Mystery of the Age
New Miracles at Every Performance

HOUDINI'S CHALLENGE WEEK.

Houdini has accepted many novel challenges and arranged a highly interesting program of sensational feats and surprises for this week, which will include a number of feats he has never before attempted in public, and which are startling surprises.

The program is as follows: Monday Matinee, Hindoo needle trick, which is over 20 years old. Houdini swallows fifty or more needles and then a dozen yards of thread, after which he pulls up the thread with every needle threaded on it. Monday evening he will escape from an extra heavy packing box built on the stage by the Adam's Hardware Company, in which he will be nailed, roped and sealed. Tuesday afternoon he will escape from a State asylum straight jacket, such as are used for confining the violently insane, and in the evening will perform the seemingly impossible feat of escaping from a "Crazy Crib" such as are used to confine maniacs. Wednesday matinee, he will be tied in several hundreds of yards of rope, from which he will escape, and in the evening he will be locked and sealed in an extra heavy and strong mail pouch, made of leather by the Douglass Shoe Co. Thursday afternoon he will repeat the needle trick and make an escape from a pillory. He will get out of a locked iron hamper at the evening performance. Friday matinee he will be handcuffed, chained and tied to a wooden door, from which he will escape, and in the evening he will be bound in a genuine Blackwell's Island straight jacket, from which he will attempt escape. Saturday matinee, his feat will be an escape from an iron bound wicker hamper, which is locked, lashed with ropes and sealed. Saturday evening he will attempt to break all his previous time records in getting out of a full length straight jacket, in which the most dangerous maniacs of the State asylums have been successfully confined.

Harry Houdini
— THE —
Handcuff King.

THE WORLD FAMOUS SELF-LIBERATOR
HOUDINI,
Presenting the Greatest Performance of his Strenuous Career, liberating himself after being Locked in a
WATER TORTURE CELL
(Houdini's own Invention) whilst Standing on his Head, his Ankles Clamped and Locked above in the centre of the Massive Cover.

A FEAT WHICH BORDERS ON THE SUPERNATURAL
$1,000
HOUDINI offers this sum to any one proving that it is possible to obtain air in the upside-down position in which he releases himself from this
Water Filled Torture Cell.

LOAN STACK

GIFT

HOUDINI CHALLENGED

The genius of escape, Houdini, has received at the Orpheum the following challenge from Roos Bros.' expert shipping man:

Roos Bros.
Clothiers to Men, Women & Children
Washington Street
at Thirteenth
Oakland.

Challenge to Houdini

Having witnessed the Monday night's performance at which you escaped from a packing case, we, the undersigned, hereby challenge you to permit us to bring to the Orpheum Theatre, timber, nails and ropes, and in full view of the audience we will construct a strong packing case, you to enter at once, to prevent preparation, and we defy you to escape without demolishing the same after we have secured you in the box according to our ideas.

Yours very truly,
ROOS BROS.
E. McDonough

Houdini has accepted the above challenge from the Roos Bros. and will meet the challenger and attempt to escape from the Roos Bros.' box on the stage of the Orpheum Wednesday night, the day before Thanksgiving.

A Magician Among The Spirits
by Houdini

SIR ARTHUR CONAN DOYLE AND HOUDINI PHOTOGRAPHED
AT THE AUTO CLUB, LONDON, ENGLAND

Houdini, pictured here in 1924 in one of his many disguises, led the crusade against fraudulent Spiritualists.

Sir Arthur Conan Doyle

Introduction

FROM my early career as a mystical entertainer I have been interested in Spiritualism as belonging to the category of mysticism, and as a side line to my own phase of mystery shows I have associated myself with mediums, joining the rank and file and held séances as an independent medium to fathom the truth of it all. At the time I appreciated the fact that I surprised my clients, but while aware of the fact that I was *deceiving* them I did not see or understand the seriousness of trifling with such sacred sentimentality and the baneful result which inevitably followed. To me it was a lark. I was a mystifier and as such my ambition was being gratified and my love for a mild sensation satisfied. After delving deep I realized the seriousness of it all. As I advanced to riper years of experience I was brought to a realization of the seriousness of trifling with the hallowed reverence which the average human being bestows on the departed, and when I personally became afflicted with similar grief I was chagrined that I should ever have been guilty of such frivolity and for the first time realized that it bordered on crime.

As a consequence my own mental attitude became considerably more plastic. I too would have parted gladly with a large share of my earthly possessions for the solace of one word from my loved departed--just one word that I was sure had been genuinely bestowed by them--and so I was brought to a full consciousness of the sacredness of the thought, and became deeply interested to discover if there was a possible reality to the return, by Spirit, of one who had passed over the border and ever since have devoted to this effort my heart and soul and what brain power I possess. In this frame of mind I began a new line of psychical research in all seriousness and from that time to the present I have never entered a séance room except with an open mind devoutly anxious to learn if intercommunication is within the range of possibilities and with a willingness to accept any demonstration which proves a revelation of truth.

It is this question as to the truth or falsity of intercommunication between the dead and the living, more than anything else, that has claimed my attention and to which I have devoted years of research and conscientious study. Sir Arthur Conan Doyle says in one of his lectures:

"When one has a knock at the door, one does not pause, but goes further to see what causes it and investigates, and sooner or later one discovers that a message is being delivered, . . ."

So I have gone to investigate the knocks, but as a result of my efforts I must confess that I am farther than ever from belief in the genuineness of Spirit manifestations and after twenty-five years of ardent research and endeavor I declare that nothing has been revealed to convince me that intercommunication has been established between the Spirits of the departed and those still in the flesh.

I have made compacts with fourteen different persons that whichever of us died first would communicate with the other if it were possible, but I have never received a word. The first of these compacts was made more than twenty-five years ago and I am certain that if any one of the persons could have reached me he would have done so. One compact was made with my private secretary, the late John W. Sargent, a man of mature years. We were very much attached to each other. The day before he underwent an operation he said to me:

"Houdini, this may be the end. If it is, I am coming back to you no matter what happens on the other side provided there is any way I can reach you. And if I can come, you will know it is I because I am going to will it so strong that you cannot be mistaken."

He died the next day. That was more than three years ago and there has been no sign. I have waited and watched believing that if any man ever could have sent back word he would have been the man. And I know that our minds were so close to each other that I would have received the signal that my friend wanted to call me. No one could accuse me of being unwilling to receive such a sign because it would have been the greatest enlightenment I could possibly have had in this world.

An Expose By Sir Arthur Conan Doyle

Sir Arthur Conan Doyle, a sincere and confirmed believer in Spirit phenomena whose acquaintance I esteem, advises me that I do not secure convincing results because I am a skeptic and I therefore want to make it clear that I am not a scoffer. I firmly believe in a Supreme Being and that there is a Hereafter. Therefore since their departure from this earth it has been my practice, as a final duty, to visit the sacred resting places of my dearly beloved parents, and ask their protection and silent blessings through the Omnipotent Almighty. The very first place I visit when I return from a trip is this same hallowed spot. Both promised me faithfully innumerable times in this life that if they could aid and protect me from their graves or from the Great Beyond, they would do so. My mind has always been open and receptive and ready to believe. In attending séances I have always made a pledge of honor with myself to banish all profane thoughts from my mind to the utmost of my ability. I further pledge myself to concentrate. I have persuaded my whole soul, brain and thought to a point where the medium has my attention to such an extent that at the finish I feel as much exhausted as the medium who shows to those present the effects of great strain irrespective of its cause. Thus it must be seen that I am not a skeptic. However, it has been my life work to invent and publicly present problems, the secrets of which not even the members of the magical profession have been able to discover, and the effects of which have proved as inexplicable to the scientists as any marvel of the mediums, and I claim that in so far as the revelation of trickery is concerned my years of investigation have been more productive than the same period of similar work by any scientist; that my record as a "mystifier of mystifiers" qualifies me to look below the surface of any mystery problem presented to me and that with my eyes trained by thirty years' experience in the realms of mystery and occultism it is not strange that I view these so-called phenomena from a different angle than the ordinary layman or even the expert investigator.

A memorable incident in my life and one that shows how little the world at large understands the methods by which my mysteries are produced and also shows how easy it is for even a great intellect, faced with a mystery it cannot fathom, to conclude that there is something supernatural involved, has to do with Madame Sarah Bernhardt.

During one of my various engagements in Paris she had witnessed my performances and was anxious to see one of my outdoor exploits, so, when we were both playing at the same time in Boston, out of good camaraderie I gave a special performance at my hotel adding a few extra experiments for her benefit. As we were seated in the motor car on the way to my demonstration she placed her arm gently around my shoulder, and in that wonderful speaking voice with which she was gifted and which has thrilled thousands of auditors, but now stilled forever, she said to me:

"Houdini, you do such marvellous things. Couldn't you--could you bring back my leg for me?"

I looked at her, startled, and failing to see any mischievous sparkle in her eye replied:

"Good heavens, Madame, certainly not; you cannot be serious. You know my powers are limited and you are actually asking me to do the impossible."

"Yes," she said as she leaned closer to me, "but you do the impossible."

We looked at each other; she, the travel-worn, experienced woman of the world; I, the humble mystifier, nonplussed and thunderstruck at the extraordinary, unintentional compliment she was paying me. Then I asked:

"Are you jesting?"

"Mais non, Houdini, j'ai jamais ete plus serieux dans ma vie,"[1] she answered as she slowly shook her head.

"Madame, you exaggerate my ability," I told her.

Each of the marvels of modern scientific achievement such as the telephone, radio, flying machine, radium, etc., were at one time classed as impossible and would have been looked upon as supernatural, if not Spiritual manifestations. Similar mysteries, but more frail in principle and constructive detail, were the instruments used by the priestcraft of ancient religious cults for the purpose of holding the mass of unintelligent beings in servitude.

---

[1] "Oh, no, Houdini, I never was more serious in my life."

It is not unusual for the eye or ear to play tricks with one but when such illusions and delusions are taken for the Spirit forms of the departed and voices of the dead instead of being recognized as some subjective phenomena brought about by a physical cause the situation takes on a grave aspect. It is this transfer of an inner reaction to an external object which constitutes practically all that is necessary to be placed in the category of "psychics," who represent the priests and ministers of Spiritualism.

Distressed relatives catch at the least word which may remotely indicate that the Spirit which they seek is in communication with them. One little sign even, which appeals to their waiting imagination, shatters all ordinary caution and they are converted. Then they begin to accept all kinds of natural events as results of Spirit intervention. This state of mind is productive of many misfortunes, including suicides by those who think they are going to happiness with loved ones beyond the pale. When in Europe in 1919 finishing an engagement interrupted by the World War I was impressed by the eagerness of grief-stricken parents for the solace of a word from the boy who had passed on and my desire for the truth was renewed with fresh vigor. I am informed that so great has the "medium" craze become in Berlin that the grief-stricken residents have spent great sums of money in the hope of discovering mediums who will "guarantee them a glimpse behind the veil." It is with the deepest interest and concern that I have watched this great wave of Spiritualism sweep the world in recent months and realized that it has taken such a hold on persons of a neurotic temperament, especially those suffering from bereavement, that it has become a menace to health and sanity.

Professor George M. Robertson, eminent psychopathologist, and Physician-Superintendent of the Royal Edinburgh Mental Hospital, made the danger of insanity resulting from strong belief in Spiritualism by neurotics the subject of a part of his annual report in 1920. He says:

"Those who had sustained bereavements during the war and bore them with equanimity in the days of crowded incidents and amidst the pressure of war activities, such as Red Cross and other work, find it much harder to bear up now, although time has elapsed. Some have broken down since the war came to an end. Many, as a solace to their feelings, have taken an interest in Spiritualism. Since Dr. Charles Mercier quoted in the preface of his book 'Spiritualism and Sir Oliver Lodge' my warning on the danger of neurotic persons engaging in practical inquiries of a Spiritualistic nature, I have received many requests to say more on the subject. I have little to add save to reaffirm the statement then made.

"I do not consider either Sir Arthur Conan Doyle or Sir Oliver Lodge to be safe judges, whose opinion should be accepted on this difficult and important subject, in view of their bereavement and unconscious desires. If the wish be father to the thought, it is mother to the hallucination of the senses.

"The tricks the brain can play without calling in Spiritualistic aids are simply astounding, and only those who have made a study of morbid as well as normal psychology, realize the full truth of this."

I have read with keen curiosity the articles by leading scientists on the subject of psychic phenomena, particularly those by Sir Arthur Conan Doyle and Sir Oliver Lodge, in which they have discussed their respective conversions to a belief in communication with the dead. There is no doubt in my mind that some of these scientists are sincere in their belief but unfortunately it is through this very *sincerity* that thousands become converts. The fact that they are *scientists* does not endow them with an especial gift for detecting the particular sort of fraud used by mediums, nor does it bar them from being deceived, especially when they are fortified in their belief by grief, for the various books and records of the subject are replete with deceptions practised on noted scientists who have essayed to investigate prominent mediums. It is perfectly rational to suppose that I may be deceived once or twice by a new illusion, but if my mind, which has been so keenly trained for years to invent mysterious effects, can be deceived, how much more susceptible must the ordinary observer be.

During my last trip abroad, in 1919, I attended over one hundred séances with the sole purpose of honest investigation; these séances were presided over by well-known mediums in France and England. In addition to attending these séances I spent a great deal of time conferring with persons prominently identified with Spiritualism. In the course of my intense investigations I have met most of the famous mediums of our time. I have submitted to conditions imposed by them and religiously awaited results, but I still question any so-called proof of the existence of Spirits who are interested in any way, physically or mentally, in the welfare of mortal men. It is not within the province of this book, which is the result of my years of investigation, to give all the historical detail concerning every medium mentioned, though enough are furnished in each instance to establish my claims, each of which is based on a thorough study of the records as are also my statements many of which are supported by documentary evidence in my possession.

I have spent a goodly part of my life in study and research. During the last thirty years I have read every single piece of literature on the subject of Spiritualism that I could. I have accumulated one of the largest libraries in the world on psychic phenomena, Spiritualism, magic, witchcraft, demonology, evil spirits, etc., some of the material going back as far as 1489, and I doubt if any one in the world has so complete a library on modern Spiritualism, but nothing I ever read concerning the so-called Spiritualistic phenomena has impressed me as being genuine. It is true that some of the things I read seemed mystifying but I question if they would be were they to be reproduced under different circumstances, under *test conditions,* and before expert mystifiers and open minded committees. Mine has not been an investigation of a few days or weeks or months but one that has extended over thirty years and in that thirty years I have not found one incident that savoured of the genuine. If there had been any real unalloyed demonstration to work on, one that did not reek of fraud, one that could not be reproduced by earthly powers, then there would be something for a foundation, but up to the present time everything that I have investigated has been the result of deluded brains or those which were too actively and intensely willing to believe.

HOUDINI.

Houdini Historical Center, Boldt Collection

This photo of Rabbi Mayer Samuel Weiss, Harry Houdini's father, was taken in Appleton around 1880.

Houdini and his Mother

Preface

GLADLY would I embrace Spiritualism if it could prove its claims, but I am not willing to be deluded by the fraudulent impositions of so-called psychics, or accept as sacred reality any of the evidence that has been placed before me thus far.

The ancients' childish belief in demonology and witchcraft; the superstitions of the civilized and uncivilized, and those marvellous mysteries of past ages are all laughed at by the full grown sense of the present generation; yet we are asked, in all seriousness, by a few scientists and scholars, to accept as absolute truth such testimony as is built up by their pet mediums, which, so far, has been proven to be nothing beyond a more or less elaborate construction of fiction resting on the slenderest of foundations, or rather, absolutely no foundation.

Not only educated men and women with emotional longings for some assurance of the continued existence of departed loved ones, but people of all phases and conditions of life, have completely surrendered themselves to belief in the most monstrous fiction, vouched for by only a single witness of the so-called phenomenon, and that too when the medium, through whom the phenomenon was supposed to have presented itself, had been caught cheating time and again.

I believe in a Hereafter and no greater blessing could be bestowed upon me than the opportunity, once again, to speak to my sainted Mother who awaits me with open arms to press me to her heart in welcome, Just as she did when I entered this mundane sphere.

Spring, 1924. H.

Houdini with his wife and mother

Harry Houdini   Sir Arthur Conan Doyle

Houdini Historical Center, Hyman Collection, 1995.83.1

Houdini posing in January 1907 with the two women in his life: his wife, Bess, and his mother, Cecilia Weiss. Houdini continued to visit Appleton until his mother's death in 1913.

Houdini and Teddy Roosevelt on board the Imperator, *June 23, 1914.*

Houdini Historical Center, R1988.1623

Houdini Giving Testimony in Congressional Hearing

Houdini Demonstrating Spiritualist Fraud Before Members of Congress

A Young Houdini

Chapter 1
The Founders of Modern Spiritualism

THE story of modern spirit manifestations, so called, dates from 1848 and the "solitary farmhouse" of John D. Fox and his wife in the village of Hydesville, in New York State, and centres around their two little girls, Margaret, eight, and Kate, younger by a year and a half. Successfully exploited while still children; credited with occult power; becoming world-famous as "The Fox Sisters,"--their record is, without exception, one of the most interesting in the history of spiritualism.

John Fox and his wife appear to have been of the "good, honest," but not mentally keen type of farmer folk. Of the two, the wife was the more "simple minded," and when the "nervous, superstitious woman" began to hear unusual noises which she could not account for, and which seemed in some peculiar manner connected with her children, she concluded at once that the sounds were "unnatural" and began to brood over the matter. Her fears increased with the persistent recurrence of the mysterious sounds, and before long she took some of the neighbors into her confidence. They were as puzzled as the mother, the Fox home became an object of suspicion and the neighborhood set itself the task of solving the mystery.

With the increase of interest came a proportionate increase in the noises, which commenced to be known as "rappings," and which, in spite of the positive denials by the children of any knowledge of how they were produced, regularly answered by an uncanny code questions asked the two girls. The possibility of duplicity in such children never occurred to any one in Hydesville, with the result that the timid hint of a "disembodied spirit" soon became a theory. Some one asked the girls if a murder had ever been committed in the house. The ominous sounds of the code answered in the affirmative and at once to the eager investigators, the theory became a proven fact and there flashed up in their minds the vision of a personality in the Spirit World endeavoring by crude means, which somewhat resembled telegraphy, to give to human beings the benefit of its vaster knowledge, the whole affair in some obscure manner being connected with two little girls.

At this critical moment a married daughter of John D. Fox and his wife came home to Hydesville for a visit. Twenty-three years older than little Margaret, of a very different type than either father or mother, she seems to have grasped instantly the possibilities in the "occult" powers of her little sisters and to have taken complete command of the Fox family's affairs at once. Her first move was to organize a "Society of Spiritualists" and encourage crowds to come to the house to see the children. Hydesville became famous almost overnight. News of the peculiar "rappings" spread with lightning-like rapidity and soon became an absorbing topic of conversation, not only in the United States, but in England, France, Italy, and Germany as well. Women like Harriet Martineau and Elizabeth Barrett Browning were said to have given their whole thought to it, and men of the strongest intellect and will to be "caught in the meshes it had woven in contemporaneous thought."

Hydesville became too small a field for the operations of Mrs. Fish, the older sister, very quickly, and soon she appears in Rochester with the girls, publicly exhibiting their feats to great crowds for money, realizing from one hundred to a hundred and fifty dollars a night in profits, which she pocketed. From Rochester she took them to New York City, and later the girls made a tour of the cities of the United States, attracting the "most prominent theologians, physicians, and professional men of all kinds, as well as great crowds everywhere." There is no record that the girls were ever under the management of Mrs. Fish after they left New York City although she menaced them continually and Margaret feared her as long as she lived.

The grand tour over, Kate, sponsored by Horace Greeley, went to school and Margaret, just developing into an attractive young woman, and destined to become the more famous of the two mediums, began a series of séances in rooms occupied by herself and mother at the Union Hotel in Philadelphia. There romance entered her life on a day in 1853 in the person of Dr. Elisha Kent Kane, the noted Arctic explorer.

His had been a remarkable career. Belonging to one of the most aristocratic families in Philadelphia; the son of a judge; handsome; still under thirty-four; graduated more than ten years previously from the University of Pennsylvania, he had gone out to China with Commodore Parker as "surgeon of the embassy," later obtained a leave of absence and travelled through Greece on foot, went up the Nile, toured India, Ceylon, and the South Sea Islands, and even "dared the Himalayas." The Mexican War had furnished him an opportunity to "win spurs for gallantry," and, this over, he had joined a relief expedition which went in search of Sir John Franklin in 1850.[2]

This much travelled, much experienced man of the world was instantly and irresistibly attracted to the young medium. An acquaintance was formed and it was not long before Doctor Kane determined that, regardless of all obstacles, she should be his wife. In spite of the efforts of his family, he soon made arrangements to educate Margaret, and she was placed with a tutor in a quiet suburb of Philadelphia, where an aunt of the doctor's could have an oversight of her and where in addition to her other studies she was to be made proficient in French, German, and Italian, as well as vocal and instrumental music. Her vacations were spent with a sister of Senator Cockrell. For some three or four years she was thus sheltered from the world, while the doctor did all in his power to eradicate from her mind everything connected with spiritualism and "rappings." Then came the turn of the tide.

The doctor became broken in health as a result of exposure in the Arctic and decided to go abroad. There had been neither civil or religious ceremony to mark his marriage to Margaret, but just before he sailed, in the presence of her mother and other witnesses, he declared that they were husband and wife. His health grew worse in London and he left there for the West Indies, where Margaret and her mother were to join him, but their preparations for the journey were cut short by the announcement in the papers of his death in Havana on the 16th of February, 1857. Margaret was prostrated by the blow. A long sickness followed and when she finally recovered it was to face the world, not only friendless and alone, but penniless as well, for, owing to a compromise, she did not share in the doctor's estate. Disappointed, disheartened, and bitter she went back to her Spiritualism and "rappings." For thirty years she wandered from place to place holding séances. For thirty years she suffered the tortures of remorse and ill health. She believed she was being driven "into hell." She loathed the thing she was, and tried at times to drown her troubles in wine. For thirty years she lived in constant fear of her older sister. Then Margaret Kane found a temporary solace in the Catholic Church. But there were still more months of struggle before she finally found courage to tell the story of the world-famous "rappings" in a signed confession given to the press in October, 1888.[3]

"I do this," she said, "because I consider it my duty, a sacred thing, a holy mission, to expose it (Spiritualism). I want to see the day when it is entirely done away with. After I expose it I hope Spiritualism will be given a death blow. I was the first in the field and I have a right to expose it.[4]

"My sister Katie and I were very young children when this horrible deception began. I was only eight, just a year and a half older than she. We were very mischievous children and sought merely to terrify our dear mother, who was a very good woman and very easily frightened.

"When we went to bed at night we used to tie an apple to a string and move the string up and down, causing the apple to bump on the floor, or we would drop the apple on the floor, making a strange noise every time it would rebound. Mother listened to this for a time. She would not understand it and did not suspect us as being capable of a trick because we were so young.

"At last she could stand it no longer and she called the neighbors in and told them about it. It was this that set us to discover a means of making the raps more effectually. I think, when I reflect about it, that it was a most wonderful discovery, a very wonderful thing that children should make such a discovery, and all through a desire to do mischief only.[5]

---

[2] Sir John Franklin was a celebrated Arctic explorer. In 1845 he was appointed to the command of an expedition sent out by the British Admiralty in search of the northwest passage. The expedition sailed from Greenhithe, May 18, 1845, and was last spoken off the entrance of Lancaster Sound, July 26, 1845. Thirty-nine relief expeditions, public and private, were sent out from England and America in search of the missing explorer between 1847 and 1857. McClintock found traces of the missing expedition in 1859, which confirmed previous rumors of its total destruction.

[3] *New York World*, October 21, 1888.

[4] See Appendix A.

[5] Could this possibly have been "in answer to prayer" as now claimed?

"Our oldest sister was twenty-three years of age when I was born. She was in Rochester when these tricks first began but came to Hydesville, the little village in central New York where we were born and lived.

"All the neighbors around, as I have said, were called in to witness these manifestations. There were so many people coming to the house that we were not able to make use of the apple trick except when we were in bed and the room was dark. Even then we could hardly do it, so the only way was to rap on the bedstead.

"And that is the way we began. First, as a mere trick to frighten mother, and then, when so many people came to see us children, we were ourselves frightened, and for self-preservation forced to keep it up. No one suspected us of any trick because we were such young children. We were led on by my sister purposely and by mother unintentionally. We often heard her say:

" 'Is this a disembodied spirit that has taken possession of my dear children?'

"That encouraged our fun and we went on. All the neighbors thought there was something and they wanted to find out what it was. They were convinced that some one had been murdered in the house. They asked the spirits through us about it and we would rap one for the spirit answer 'yes,' not three as we did afterwards. The murder they concluded must have been committed in the house. They went over the whole surrounding country trying to get the names of people who had formerly lived in the house. Finally they found a man by the name of Bell, and they said that this poor innocent man had committed a murder in the house and that the noises came from the spirit of the murdered person. Poor Bell was shunned and looked upon by the whole community as a murderer.[6]

"Mrs. Underhill, my eldest sister, took Katie and me to Rochester. There it was that we discovered a new way to make the raps. My sister Katie was the first to observe that by swishing her fingers she could produce certain noises with her knuckles and joints, and that the same effect could be made with the toes. Finding that we could make raps with our feet--first with one foot and then with both--we practiced until we could do this easily when the room was dark.

"Like most perplexing things when made clear, it is astonishing how easily it is done. The rappings are simply the result of a perfect control of the muscles of the leg below the knee, which govern the tendons of the foot and allow action of the toe and ankle bones that is not commonly known. Such perfect control is only possible when a child is taken at an early age and carefully and continually taught to practice the muscles, which grow stiff in later years. A child at twelve is almost too old. With control of the muscles of the foot, the toes may be brought down to the floor without any movement that is perceptible to the eye. The whole foot, in fact, can be made to give rappings by the use only of the muscles below the knee. This, then, is the simple explanation of the whole method of the knocks and raps.

"In Rochester Mrs. Underhill gave exhibitions. We had crowds coming to see us and she made as much as a hundred to a hundred and fifty dollars a night. She pocketed this. Parties came in from all parts to see us. Many as soon as they heard a little rap were convinced. To all questions we answered by raps. We knew when to rap 'yes' or 'no' according to certain signs which Mrs. Underhill gave us during the séance.

"A great many people when they hear the rapping imagine at once that the spirits are touching them. It is a very common delusion. Some very wealthy people came to see me some years ago when I lived in Forty-second Street and I did some rappings for them. I made the spirit rap on the chair and one of the ladies cried out:

" 'I feel the spirit tapping me on the shoulder.'

Of course that was pure imagination.

---

[6] Sir Arthur Conan Doyle in his book, "Our American Adventures," states: "The original house was removed by pious hands and reconstructed, as I understand it, at Lily Dale. It is not generally known that when it was pulled down or it may have been before, the bones of the murdered peddler and his tin box were discovered buried in the cellar, as was stated in the original rappings. The rappings were in 1848, the discovery in 1903. What have our opponents to say to this?" According to Margaret Fox's confession, Doyle's statements are misleading and contrary to the facts.

"Katie and I were led around like lambs. We went to New York from Rochester and then all over the United States. We drew immense crowds. I remember particularly Cincinnati. We stopped at the Burnett House. The rooms were jammed from morning till night and we were called upon by those old wretches to show our rappings when we should have been out at play in the fresh air.

"Nobody has ever suspected anything from the start in 1848 until the present day as to any trickery in our methods. There has never been a detection.[7] But as the world grew wise and science began to investigate we began to adapt our experiments to our audiences. Our séances were held in a room. There was a centre-table in the middle and we all stood around it.

"As far as *Spirits* were concerned neither my sister nor I thought about it. I know that there is no such thing as the departed returning to this life. Many people have said to me that such a thing was possible and seemed to believe so firmly in it that I tried to see, and I have tried in every form and know that it cannot be done.

"After I married, Dr. Kane would not let me refer to my old life--he wanted me to forget it. But when I was poor, after his death, I was driven to it again, and I wish to say clearly that I owe all my misfortune to that woman, my sister. I have asked her time and again:

" 'Now that you are rich why don't you save your soul?'

"But at my words she would fly into a passion. She wanted to establish a new religion and she told me that she received messages from spirits. She knew that we were tricking people but she tried to make us believe spirits existed. She told us that before we were born spirits came into her room and told her that we were destined for great things.

"Yes, I am going to expose Spiritualism from its very foundation. I have had the idea in my head for many a year but I have never come to a determination before. I have thought of it day and night. I loathe the thing I have been. I used to say to those who wanted me to give a séance:

" 'You are driving me into Hell.'

"Then the next day I would drown my remorse in wine. I was too honest to remain a 'medium.' That's why I gave up my exhibitions. I have seen so much miserable deception! Every morning of my life I have it before me. When I wake up I brood over it. That is why I am willing to state that Spiritualism is a fraud of the worst description. I have had a life of sorrow, I have been poor and ill, but I consider it my duty, a sacred thing, a holy mission to expose it. I want to see the day when it is entirely done away with. After my sister Katie and I expose it I hope Spiritualism will be given a death blow.

"I do not want it understood that the Catholic Church has advised me to make these public exposures and confession. It is my own idea. My own mission. I would have done it long ago if I could have had the necessary money and courage to do it. I could not find anyone to help me--I was too timid to ask.

"I am now very poor. I intend, however, to expose Spiritualism because I think it is my sacred duty. If I cannot do it who can? I who have been the beginning of it? At least I hope to reduce the ranks of the eight million Spiritualists in the country. I go into it as into a holy war. I am waiting anxiously and fearlessly for the moment when I can show the world, by personal demonstration, that all Spiritualism is a fraud and a deception. It is a branch of legerdemain, but it has to be closely studied to gain perfection. None but a child at an early age, would have ever attained the proficiency and wrought such widespread evil as I have.

"I trust that this statement, coming solemnly from me, the first and the most successful in this deception, will break the rapid growth of Spiritualism and prove that it is all a fraud, hypocrisy and delusion.

---

[7] There were three investigations by competent investigators. One in Buffalo by medical doctors, one in Philadelphia by the Seybert Commission of the University of Pennsylvania, and one in Boston by a committee of professors from Harvard University. Any one of the three would have resulted disastrously for the medium had the conditions and requirements demanded by the investigators been complied with. A suspicion was well founded in the minds of the investigators as to the actual solution of the problem, but they were not permitted to proceed to a finish, the mediums hedging each time when a crucial test was proposed.

(Signed) "Margaret Fox Kane."[8]

Mrs. Kane's "confession" was published in the Sunday edition of the New York *World* on October 21, 1888. Arrangements had been made for her to give a public demonstration and exposition of the so-called "marvellous" Spiritualistic "phenomena" that same evening at the Academy of Music in New York. Meanwhile, in order to foil the "attempts" of certain mediums to "kidnap her" she was being closely guarded at her hotel where during the day she was interviewed by newspaper men. Expecting when she left her room to answer questions only she nevertheless readily consented to give some evidence of "how the trick was done" in order to do all in her power to "complete the exposure and demonstrate the utter absurdity of the claim made by mediums that she was possessed of spiritual power in spite of her denials." The *World* reporter told of this private demonstration as follows:

" 'Now,' said Mrs. Kane, 'I will stand up before these folding-doors and you may stand as near as you please and I will call up any "spirit" that you wish and answer any questions. One rap means "no" and three raps mean "yes." Are you ready?'

" 'Is Napoleon Bonaparte present?' the reporter asked, watching Mrs. Kane closely. Three raps (yes).

" 'Does he know me? I mean did he ever meet and converse with me?' Three raps.

" 'That is strange, isn't it,' remarked Mrs. Kane, smiling, 'in view of the fact that he must have died before you were born? Try again.'

" 'Is Abraham Lincoln present?' Three raps. " 'Well you see the "spirits" are very obliging.' " 'Will Harrison be elected?' One loud rap (no). " 'Will President Cleveland get another term?' Three raps."

That night some two thousand or more persons crowded the Academy of Music to witness the sensational expose. Most of them were sober, sensible people who "hailed with delight" the announcement that one of the famous Fox Sisters was to make a "clean breast of her share in Spiritualistic humbuggery." But certain portions of the house were packed with pronounced Spiritualists, men and women who regarded all efforts to disillusion the public as so many personal insults, and when, previous to Mrs. Kane's appearance, Dr. C. M. Richmond, a prominent New York dentist who had spent twenty years and thousands of dollars investigating mediumistic tricks and wiles explained and demonstrated in full light the full methods of producing them, this Spiritualistic contingent became decidedly hostile and when Mrs. Kane finally stepped before the big audience to "confess orally what she had already confessed in print" she was laboring under too great a nervous strain to make any "intelligent utterance." Those in charge of the affair realizing that an address was out of the question at once suggested that she immediately give a demonstration of the "rap-pings." One of the New York papers the next morning published the following description of what happened.[9]

"But if her tongue had lost its power her preternatural toe joint had not. A plain wooden stool, or table, resting upon four short legs and having the properties of a sounding board was placed in front of her. Removing her shoe, she placed her right foot upon this little table.

---

[8] I have been warned while writing this book to be careful regarding my statement of the confession of Margaret Fox. I am also fully aware of the fact that Dr. Funk writes in his book, "The Widow's Mite":

"Margaret Fox, not long before her death, confessed that she and her sister had duped the public. This unfortunate woman had sunk so low that for five dollars she would have denied her own mother and sworn to anything. At that time her affidavit for or against anything should not be given the slightest weight."

Mr. W. S. Davis, himself a practicing medium, who knew Margaret Fox Kane personally, wrote me:

"One would think that Margaret Fox got drunk, and in that condition, was induced to confess that she was a fraud, but When she became sober she renounced her confession. That is what we would think to hear some Spiritualists talk. *She was sober when she made her confession; she was sober when she appeared* in *the theatre and gave her expose. In fact she was usually sober,* She drank considerably during the later years of her life, and often drank too much, *but usually she was sober.* One of her reasons for drinking was that her hypocrisy had become more and more distasteful to her. Living a constant lie got on her nerves, and, when the later years came, she didn't have the same degree of vital force that she had in her younger days to battle off the dictates of her conscience."

[9] *New York World,* October 22, 1888.

"The entire house became breathlessly still and was rewarded by a number of little short, sharp raps--those mysterious sounds which have for forty years frightened and bewildered hundreds of thousands of people in this country and in Europe.

"A committee consisting of three physicians taken from the audience then ascended the stage, and having made an examination of her foot during the progress of the rappings, unhesitatingly agreed that the sounds were made by the action of the first joint of her large toe.

"The demonstration was perfect and complete and only the most hopelessly prejudiced and bigoted fanatics of Spiritualism could withstand the irresistible force of this commonplace explanation and exhibition of how spirit rappings are produced."

The exposure attracted widespread attention. Letters poured in from far and wide begging for confirmation, explanation or denial. The rest of the tribe of mediums naively hinted that if there had been fraud it was well to have it exposed but of course *they* were genuine.

Many who had believed in Spiritualism wrote most pathetically. One of these writing from San Francisco says:

"I have been a believer in the phenomena from its first inception through you and your sister, believing it to be true since that time.

"I am now eighty-one years old and have but a short time of course, to remain in this world, and I feel a great anxiety to know through you if I have been deceived all this time in a matter of vital interest to us all."[10]

But perhaps of them all none better expresses what a blow the exposure was to thousands who had accepted as genuine the messages of the mysterious raps or describes more vividly the effect of Spiritualism on many who are attracted to it than the following from a woman in Boston.[11]

"Hundreds of thousands have believed through you and you alone. Hundreds of thousands eagerly ask you whether all the glorious light that they fancied you had given them, was but the false flicker of a common dip-candle of fraud.

"If, as you say, you were forced to pursue this imposture from childhood, I can forgive you, and I am sure God will; for he turns not back the truly repentant. I will not upbraid you. I am sure you have suffered as much as any penalty, human or divine, could cause you to suffer. The disclosures that you make take from me all that I have cherished most. There is nothing left for me now but to hope for the reality of that repose which death promises us.

"It is perhaps better that the delusion should be at last swept away by one single word, and that word 'fraud.'

"I know that the pursuit of this shadowy belief has wrought upon my brain and that I am no longer my old self. Money I have spent in thousands and thousands of dollars within a few short years to propitiate the 'mediumistic' intelligence. It is true that never once have I received a message or the token of a word that did not leave a still unsatisfied longing in my heart, a feeling that it was not really my loved one after all who was speaking to me, or if it was my loved one that he was changed, that I hardly knew him and he hardly knew me. But that must have been the true intuition. It is better that the delusion is past, after all, for had I kept on in that way, I am sure I should have gone mad. The constant seeking, the frequent pretended response, its unsatisfying meaning, the sense of distance and change between me and my loved one--oh! it has been horrible, horrible!

"He who is dying of thirst and has the sweet cup ever snatched from his lips, just as the first drop touches them --he alone can know what in actual things is the similitude of this Spiritualistic torture.

"God bless you, for I think that you now speak the truth. You have my forgiveness at least, and I believe that thousands of others will forgive you, for the atonement made in season wipes out much of the stain of the early sin."

Margaret Kane's "confession" did not bring her the relief or friends she had hoped for, nor did it end her connection with Spiritualism for, glad as she would have been to give it up for good, her

---

[10] From Ruben Briggs Davenport's "The Death Blow to Spiritualism."
[11] Ibid.

theatrical exposure was a financial failure and before long she was down and out again and once more she resorted to Spiritualism as a means of livelihood, giving séances and mediumistic meetings in a number of cities throughout the United States; but her power of fooling the public was gone.

Having confessed to deceit once, no amount of persuasion on her part could convince the public that she was genuine, and in place of the thousands who had flocked to her in her younger days she never had more than a handful at her meetings. Her only friends were Spiritualists for strangely enough some of them still had faith in her, even when she was exposing Spiritualism, believing that she had fallen into the hands of evil spirits when she confessed that she was a fraud.

Some time after the confession a "recantation" was circulated as coming from Mrs. Kane. I was never able to find any proof of its authenticity but my friend, Mr. W. S. Davis, who knew her well, informed me that she did make it--that she had to, or starve. It was not wholly voluntary though as Mr. Newton (then President of the First Society of Spiritualists) convinced her that it would be for her interest, and the interest of Spiritualism as well to do it. It made little difference, however, for the career of the unfortunate woman was nearly over. Frequently overcome by drink, forced on by privation and misery, death came to her, on March 8, 1895, less than seven years after she had stood in a crowded theatre and deliberately shown the method of making the raps which had brought her fame for four decades.

The Fox Sisters used Spiritualism only as a means to "get while the getting was good." Fortunately for the general public Spiritualism received a severe jolt in the confession of Margaret Fox Kane; there was an end to the Fox "swindle" and an untold amount of blood-money and grief saved to poor misguided souls so easily fooled by a simple physical trick.

An Expose By Sir Arthur Conan Doyle

Houdini at Seance with Walter Gibson

Houdini and Fake Ectoplasm

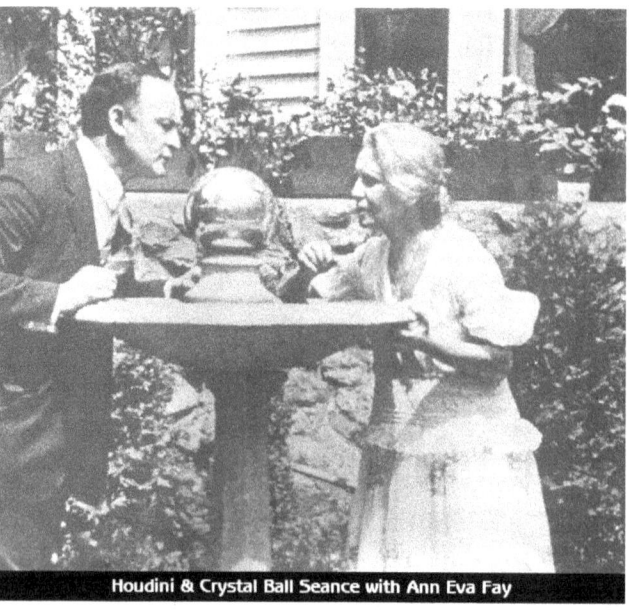

Houdini & Crystal Ball Seance with Ann Eva Fay

Chapter 2
The Davenport Brothers

SUCH evidence of spirits as the simple "rappings" of the Fox Sisters soon gave place to more elaborate "manifestations" and with the appearance of Ira Erastus Davenport and his brother William Henry Harrison Davenport, working together, and known as the "Davenport Brothers," these manifestations became complicated exhibitions involving the use of a cabinet, rope tricks, bells, and various horns and musical instruments. These brothers have always been, and are still, pointed to as being indisputable proof of the reality and genuineness of mediumistic phenomena and public interest in Spiritualism was greatly stimulated by the tremendous sensation and discussion caused by their demonstrations, yet an interesting train of circumstances put me in possession of facts more than sufficient to disprove their having, or even claiming, spiritualistic power.

During many of the years in which I have been making a study of Spiritualism I supposed both of the Davenports dead and when my friend, Harry Kellar, in recounting some of his early experiences and hardships told me that he had been associated with them at one time and that Ira Davenport was still living I was surprised indeed. I at once communicated with him and there followed a pleasant acquaintance which lasted until his death and furnished me with much of historic value concerning the brothers which has never appeared in print.

Heretofore all published accounts of the Davenport Brothers' doings have been vague, speculative, lacking in actual knowledge, and misleading because the authors have been victims of delusion, but the information here given is based on a long correspondence with Ira Davenport as well as an open hearted confession which he made to me shortly before his death, answering all my questions unreservedly and offering to assist me in every way he could as he wanted my statements[12] to be accurate in the book on Spiritualism which he knew I was writing.

The Davenport Brothers were devotedly attached to each other and when in 1877 William died while they were in Australia, Ira the surviving brother was completely upset. He made one feeble attempt to reinstate himself, but the "Spirit" was lacking and he returned, a discouraged man, to spend the remainder of his days in peace and quiet at home. While playing Australia early in 1910 for Harry Rickards I hunted up the grave of William Davenport and finding it sadly neglected I had it put in order, fresh flowers planted on it and the stone work repaired.[13] It was also on this trip that I met William M. Fay of "Davenport Brothers and Fay," who told me many interesting things about the brothers and on my return to America one of the first things which I did was to go to Maysville, Chautauqua County, New York, to make Ira Davenport a visit. He met me at the station and took me to his home, an exceptionally happy and restful one presided over by the second Mrs. Davenport, the first having died in childbirth.

This second marriage was most romantic. During a séance which the Brothers were giving in Paris[14] Ira noticed a strikingly beautiful Belgian girl intently watching him. After the performance he managed to meet her only to find that she could not speak a word of English. His French being limited to the usual two or three word table d'hote vocabulary of the average American tourist he called his interpreter and through him asked the girl to become his wife. Bewildered by such an audacious proposal she blushed deeply, and cast down her eyes, then slowly raising them looked straight into Ira's. There was a quick exchange of admiration and her woman's intuition must have read deeply and correctly for she then and there consented to wed this American who had so

---

[12] These statements are fully corroborated by letters on file in my library and I consider it not only a privilege, but a duty as well to truthfully present them here.

[13] Ira, the surviving brother, was so touched by this little act that he taught me the famous Davenport rope-tie, the secret of which had been so well kept that not even his sons knew it

[14] They were married in London during March, 1866.

unconventionally asked her to be his wife, a decision which she never had occasion to regret for they were a remarkably happy couple.[15]

In the tranquil atmosphere of his porch we turned back the pages of time, Mr. Davenport re-living in retrospect the trials, battles, praise and applause of long ago. Among other things we talked over the magical mystery performers of other days which led him to say very generously:

"Houdini, you know more about the old timers and my arguments, than I who lived through those troublesome times."

He said that he recognized in me a past master of the craft and therefore spoke openly and did not hesitate to tell me the secrets of his feats. We discussed and analyzed the statements made in his letters to me and he frankly admitted that the work of the Davenport Brothers was accomplished by perfectly natural means and belonged to that class of feats commonly credited to "physical dexterity." Not once was there even a hint that Spiritualism was of any concern to him, instead, discussing his work as straightforward showmanship.

For me it was a memorable day and did not end with the setting of the sun, for we talked far into the night,[16] I with notebook in hand, he with a long piece of rope initiating me into the mysteries of the real "Davenport tie," which converted thousands to a belief in Spiritualism and was the genesis[17] of the rope-tying stunts which gave such a stimulus to Spiritualistic discussion in connection with the brothers. Though many attempts were made to imitate it, to the best of my knowledge and belief, no one, not even the magical fraternity, was ever able to detect the method used in these famous rope tricks, the secret being guarded so carefully that Ira Davenport's children did not know it. I have tested it and for uses such as they made of it I consider it one of the best rope ties in existence to-day, and it is only because I want it on record when I eventually pass to the Beyond that I am explaining to the public the *modus operandi* which was as follows.

Built into either side of the cabinet used by the Davenports[18] was a bench through which two holes had been bored a little distance apart. The Brothers seated themselves on these benches, and opposite one another, with their feet squarely on the floor in front of them. The end of a rope was

---

[15] It was in Paris too that the other brother, William Henry Harrison Davenport, met the great Adah Isaacs Menken, called the "Bengal Tiger," and though not generally known she later became his wife. She was considered one of the "Ten Super-Women of the World." She was born within a few miles of New Orleans, La., in 1835. Upon the death of her father she embarked on her stage career and instantaneously won success. . . . She made her first appearance in New York City at the National Theatre in 1860. She was married a number of times. Her first marriage was to John C. Heenan, the prize fighter, better known as "Benicia Boy." She was the first woman to do the Mazeppa in tights, playing the role both in America and Europe. While in London she became the literary and professional star of the hour and her hotel was the meeting place for such men as Charles Dickens, Swinburne, Alexander Dumas, Charles Reade, Watts Phillips, John Oxenford, The Duke of Hamilton and many others. She wrote a book of poems named "Infelicity," which she dedicated to Charles Dickens. She had a penchant for being photographed with many of her admirers and there Is a rare photograph of her and Swinburne which he tried hard to suppress. Another famous one Is of Dumas and the fair lady.

[16] Long after Ira died his only daughter, Zellie, a well known actress, told me that while her father and I were so absorbed in discussing and experimenting with the rope trick she and her mother cautiously slipped behind the curtains and watched us through the bed-room window.

[17] Ira told me that at first they used to work unbound in a corner of the room with a curtain to conceal their methods. At one of their seances they were asked if the Spirits would work if the Brothers allowed themselves to be tied. This led them to try out different rope methods, gradually developing the one used all over the world which Ira taught me, saying smilingly after he had done so: "Houdini, we started it, you finish it."

[18] I had the honor of being Instrumental in launching and directing Dean Kellar's farewell at the Hippodrome in New York City and he selected me to be his last assistant. As a part of the performance he presented with *some* table tipping what he called the "Davenport Cabinet and Rope Mystery." After the performance he walked to the footlights and said:

"Ladies and gentlemen, I am finished giving performances to-night. As I will have no further use for the cabinet and table I publicly present them to my dear friend Houdini."

In this cabinet, made in imitation of the one used by the Davenport Brothers, the benches are fitted into a groove making it possible for them to be slipped out in case of an extra severe tie-up, giving enough freedom to ring bells and do a number of other things without releasing the hands in the usual way. This is something of an improvement in mystery cabinets.

passed around the legs of one of the brothers, close up by the knees, and tied. The rope was then wound around the legs several times, fastened at the ankles, the remaining portion carried straight across the cabinet to the other brother's ankles, fastened, wound about his legs and tied at the knees. A shorter piece of rope was then tied to each of their wrists with the knots lying next to the pulse. These ropes were threaded through the holes and the wrists drawn down to the benches, and the ends of the ropes fastened to the ankles.

Their method of releasing themselves was comparatively simple. While one extended his feet the other drew his in thus securing slack enough in the wrist ropes to permit working their hands out of the loops.[19] The second brother was released by reversing the action.

After the demonstrations were completed the brothers slipped their hands back into the loops from which they had drawn them, placed their feet in the original positions and were ready to be examined. When the cabinet was opened the ropes appeared as taut as when put on by the committee.

In order to disprove the frequently made claim that the Davenports left their benches to produce certain manifestations they asked investigating committees to place sheets of paper under their feet and mark around them with pencil or crayon thus making it seemingly impossible to move a foot without detection. But this in no way interfered or hindered in their performance for Ira told me they used to slide their feet, paper and all, and still keep the feet inside the marks, a method I can vouch for as being practical for I have tried it successfully.[20]

With the advantage of working together it was simply impossible to secure both of the brothers in such a manner as to prevent their producing the expected results. If one was in trouble the other was always ready to come to the rescue for no matter how securely the committee tied them one was sure to be more loosely tied than the other and could get a hand free to reach over and help.

"There was one chance in twenty million to hold us both at the same time," Ira told me.[21]

The Davenports' strictest test was known as "The Tie Around the Neck." This was also explained to me by Ira. A committee of three was called upon one of whom was a woman and for that reason the least suspected although in reality a confederate.[22] She and the Davenports were each in turn tied around the neck. The woman released herself by cutting the rope.[23] Hiding the pieces in her bloomers she performed her share of the manifestations and retied herself with a duplicate piece of rope. No one was the wiser for so curiously allied are our five senses that the committee, bereft of its sight while such dark deeds were being done, seemed to have lost the use of its reasoning power as well.

The first of the Davenports' public performances were given in a large hall with rows of seats for the audience and a small raised platform which served as a stage. Someone, thinking to prevent the possibility of assistance by visitors, or confederates in the audience, asked if it were possible to have the manifestations occur in a closet. Receiving an affirmative answer one was built with openings large enough to "insert the spirit hands." This closet was a decided advantage to the Brothers as it gave them an opportunity to work in total darkness which was an essential element of their performance. The closet was improved upon by placing a big box in the center of the stage and there gradually developed the cabinet[24] as we know it to-day.

---

[19] They rubbed vaseline into their hands and wrists to facilitate their movements. The rope generally used was similar to the Silver Lake sash cord.

[20] It was sometimes claimed that after their demonstrations were over the Davenports turned the papers and remarked them. This Ira said was a deliberate lie as they never left their places throughout the entire performance.

[21] At one of their seances a man tied the brothers so tightly that it was necessary for them to make a desperate struggle to effect a release. The next night the man tried a more difficult test, simply laying the ropes all over their bodies, but the Davenports worked so slowly, deftly, and with such inexhaustible patience that they saved their reputation.

[22] Nor did he hesitate to tell me that he sometimes used as many as ten confederates at a seance for protection.

[23] William Fay, in order to be prepared for an emergency, always carried a piece of rope in his mandolin, and boasted to his partners: "I'll not chaw the ropes like you fellows, I'll cut."

[24] The original cabinet of the Davenports, made of bird's-eye maple, was pawned for thirty pounds in Cuba many years ago and is still there.

During that eventful visit Ira emphatically denied many of the absurd tales and popular beliefs concerning the Brothers, among them being the "flour test," the "snuff test"[25] and such stories as the claim that when a boy at home he gave a séance for his parents and during levitation[26] was raised up until his head touched the ceiling breaking both lath and plaster; that he was once levitated across the Niagara River, a distance of three thousand yards, and the one telling of his having effected an escape by Spiritual means from a prison in Oswego, N. Y., in 1859.

The Davenports were constantly on their guard against surprise and exposure and Ira explained to me that when they were suspicious of a committeeman who wanted to go into the cabinet with them they would insist that he be tied too in order to prevent the audience from thinking he was a confederate. Fastened to a bench as well as to each of the Davenports he was absolutely helpless for while one was getting loose the other would strain the ropes on the committeeman's feet holding him tight.

He also told me that they were in the habit of reserving seats in the front row for their friends as a protection against anyone breaking through. At private circles they ran a cord through button holes on all present, ostensibly to "prevent collusion with the medium," but in reality as a protection against a surprise seizure. They once heard that the Pinkerton Detective agency had been hired to catch them and in order to effectually forestall any meddler, they had a confederate smuggle in a bear-trap and after the séance room was darkened set the trap in the aisle.

I called Ira's attention to a clipping concerning the "Dark Séances" from the London *Post,* a conservative paper, which read:

"The musical instruments, bells, etc., were placed on the table; the Brothers Davenport were then manacled, hands and feet, and securely bound to the chairs by ropes. A chain of communication (though not a circular one) was formed, and the instant the lights were extinguished *the musical instruments appeared to be carried all about the room. The current of air, which they occasioned in their rapid transit was felt upon the faces of all present.*

"The bells were loudly rung; the trumpets made knocks upon the floor, *and the tambourine appeared running around the room, jingling with all its might. At the same time sparks were observed as if passing from South to West. Several persons exclaimed that they were touched by the instruments, which on one occasion became so demonstrative that one gentleman received a knock on the nasal organ which broke the skin and caused a few drops of blood to flow.*"

After I finished reading it Ira exclaimed:

"Strange how people imagine things in the dark! Why, the musical instruments never left our hands yet many spectators would have taken an oath that they heard them flying over their heads."[27]

Ira Davenport positively disclaimed Spiritualistic power in his talk with me, saying repeatedly that he and his brother never claimed to be mediums or pretended their work to be Spiritualistic. He admitted, however, that his parents died believing that the boys had superhuman power. In this

---

[25] In order to prove to the public that they did not make use of their hands test conditions were imposed by filling both the brothers' hands with flour and then tying them behind their backs. Almost every publication that has written an expose of the Davenport Brothers claims with glee that the trick was performed by putting flour into their pockets from which they took a fresh handful after the manifestations were finished and pretending that their hands were clenched all the time. It is claimed that once a committeeman instead of placing flour in their hands filled them with snuff and after the manifestations had been performed they had their hands fulls of flour. Ira told me that this was a deliberate lie as they did not need to get rid of the flour in their hands as they could do all the tricks with their hands clenched using the free thumb.

[26] The levitation act which has helped to swell the ranks of the Spiritualists and which mystified scientist and laymen alike, was one of the simplest deceptions ever practiced on the guileless masses by cunning mediums. A reformed medium in Bristol, England, told me that he would endeavor to free himself from his restraints, and by deft manipulations managed to pick up a person who sat in a chair nearby. Although the sitter had only been lifted a few inches from the floor he believed in all good faith that his head had actually brushed the ceiling, this impression being created by the medium gently passing his hand over the top of the sitter's head.

[27] As to the delusion of sound. Sound waves are deflected just as light waves are reflected by the intervention of a proper medium and under certain conditions it is a difficult thing to locate their source. Stuart Cumberland told me an interesting test to prove the inability of a blindfolded person to trace sound to its source. It is exceedingly simple; merely clicking two coins over the head of the blindfolded person.

connection he told me of a family by the name of Kidder in which the boys faked Spiritualistic mediumship. The mother, a simple woman easily misled, became a confirmed believer. After a time the boys got tired of the game they were playing and confessed to her that it was all a fake. The shock of the disillusion almost drove her insane and Ira said it was the fear of a similar result which kept him from confessing to his father the true nature of their work. So when the father asked the boys to do tests for him they declared that the spirits said "no" and explained that they could only do what the *spirits* asked.

But if the Davenport Brothers did not claim spiritual powers themselves they nevertheless allowed others to claim them in their behalf. One of the first to do this was J. B. Ferguson, variously known as "Mr.," "Rev.," and "Dr.," but I have no way of knowing how his titles came to him or just what they represented. If I am not mistaken he had been a minister in the Unitarian Church. He travelled with the Davenports as their lecturer, a position filled later by Thomas L. Nichols. Ferguson positively believed that everything accomplished by the Davenports was done with the aid of spirits. That both Ferguson and Nichols believed in Spiritualism is shown by their writings. Neither of them were disillusioned regarding the spiritual powers of the Brothers, the secret of the manifestations being religiously kept from them. Their remarks were left to their own discretion, the Davenports thinking it better showmanship to leave the whole matter for the audience to draw its own conclusion after seeing the exhibition. Then too with a minister as a lecturer who sincerely believed the phenomena many were led to believe, which helped to fill the coffers, meet the expenses, and increase the publicity which was a necessary part of the game.

In one of the letters which Ira wrote me he says:

"We never in public affirmed our belief in Spiritualism, that we regarded as no business of the public; nor did we offer our entertainment as the result of sleight-of-hand, or on the other hand as Spiritualism. We let our friends and foes settle that as best they could between themselves, but unfortunately, we were often the victims of their disagreements."

In a letter which Ira wrote from Maysville, dated January 19, 1909, which I received while in Europe, he says:

"You must not fail to do me the honor of a visit when you return to America, although two years is quite a long time, and in the mean time, please let me hear from you whenever the *'Spirit'* moves.

"Regarding the future, I think the possibilities within your grasp are almost boundless, splendid new territory, all South of Central America, Mexico, Australia, New Zealand, India, Spain, Portugal and Africa."[28]

"My old-time travelling companion, William M. Fay, told me four years ago while on a visit here from Australia, that he and Harry Kellar cleared over $40,000 in about eight months in South America, and Mexico, and that was thirty-four years ago, and that the opportunities are now vastly improved, such as *railroads, instead of mules,* increase of population, advance in civilization in those backward countries. He says it would be a pleasure trip now to what it was when he and Kellar had to travel on muleback. He was very enthusiastic on the subject of making another tour and we would have done so but for the fact that his physicians strongly advised against it on account of poor health and weakened physical condition. He is living at present in Melbourne, Australia, having settled there with his family in 1877, shortly after the death of my brother, which occurred July 1, 1877. He is not at all contented, notwithstanding his pleasant surroundings and ample fortune; after a man has become a regular *'Globe Trotter,'* I don't think it possible for him to settle down and lead a quiet monotonous life. . . . I wish here to say that our first tour through Europe consumed four years, leaving this country, August 26, 1864, returning September 29, 1868. Our second trip took us over three years, leaving here March 22, 1874, and returning October 20, 1877, four months after the death of my brother."

---

[28] This refers to our contemplated tour of the world. When I first became acquainted with Ira Davenport in 1909 I found that he was very anxious to re-enter the entertainment field and we set about planning a tour of the world together. By combining his reputation and my knowledge and experience we would have been able to set the world agog. Under no circumstances, however, would we have claimed our performance Spiritualistic, but just a mystery entertainment.

When exhibiting in Liverpool the Davenports were the cause of quite a riot[29] which not only militated against them but stirred up some political strife as well. I will quote Ira's account of it from a letter to me dated January 19, 1909.

"Well, yes, regarding Liverpool, I have very vivid recollections, and after forty-four years they are far from being 'scenes of mystified events,' they were results of peculiar combinations, of unfortunate circumstances, *professional jealousy, religious prejudice, anti-American feeling,* with a few other disturbing elements thrown in, including 'fenianism,'[30] which was engaging the public attention at that time, all worked up to a *white heat* culminating in one of the most spectacular displays of 'English Fair Play' that was ever presented to an appreciative English public.... While in Liverpool and some other towns in England, we could not appear in the streets without being greeted by, threatening crowds, with such exclamations as 'Yankee Doodle,' 'John Brown's Body,' 'Barnum's Humbug,' 'Yankee Swindle,' 'Fegi Mermaid,' and many other nice things too numerous to mention....

"I think my experience in Liverpool stands out as the most prominent example of 'Fair Play' ever dealt out to any American citizens and a nauseating example to all foreigners of ' 'ow' the average Englishman does things at ' 'ome.' ... It was well known that we were Northern men, and the world knows how the English sympathized with the slave holders' rebellion, and they did not miss any opportunity of showing how they felt at the time on the subject. While pretending that their brutal displays of hostility were caused by our refusal to be tied by a particular kind of knot, in fact our only offence was, objecting to be tortured at the risk of being permanently maimed or crippled for life.... Our appeal to the British public at the time is a plain truthful statement of the facts, regarding the riots in Liverpool, Huddersfield, and Leeds which several of the English papers had the fairness to publish. All England seemed to have gone mad on the subject of cabinet smashing and speculative sharpers reaped a rich harvest selling bogus pieces of smashed Davenport cabinet. Wood enough was sold in small pieces to make ten times as many cabinets as the Davenport Brothers ever used during their public career.... Although I am now in my 70th year, I would not for one moment hesitate to face the public of Liverpool, Huddersfield, and Leeds, and try conclusions with them again, drawing no line or limitations except those of torturing or maiming one for life. ... I shall always feel a great deal of pleasure in your success, especially in meeting and overcoming anything in the nature of hostility and opposition. I remember seeing a notice of the death of Dr. Slade quite a while ago. I became acquainted with him in 1860. He then resided in the State of Michigan."

The above excerpt shows the pluck and courage of a genuine showman at the age of seventy, still ready for a tussle with an entertainment based on natural laws.

The Davenport Brothers while exhibiting in Manchester, England, had the distinction of being publicly imitated and ridiculed by two celebrated actors, Sir Henry Irving and Edward A. Sothern, who were appearing at the Theatre Royal. With some friends they had witnessed a performance by the Davenport Brothers and determined to expose what Irving termed a "shameful imposture." With the assistance of these men he gave a private performance in imitation of the Davenport séance at a popular club and was so successful that he was requested to repeat it in a large hall. So on Saturday, February 25, 1865, the Library Hall of the Man-Chester Athenaeum was filled with an audience invited to witness "a display of 'preternatural philosophy' in a private séance a la Davenport provided by some well-known members of the theatrical profession playing in the city.

A wig, a beard, a neckerchief, a tightly buttoned frock coat, and artistic makeup so completely transformed Irving that he looked the exact double of Dr. Ferguson. With his inimitable charm of manner Irving assumed the dignified air and characteristic gestures of the doctor and impersonating his reverend tones he gave an interesting and semi-jocose address with just enough seriousness to

---

[29] The start of the Liverpool riot can be laid Indirectly to Ferguson. He protested the way the boys had been secured and without waiting for instructions or a word from the Brothers, whipped out a knife and cut the ropes. Ira told me that it was too bad that Ferguson did that for they never could have secured them so they could not have produced some manifestations.

[30] Ira told me that during the disturbance in Liverpool, John Hughes, Fenian head, offered him five hundred Irishmen to clean up any mob of Englishmen.

keenly satirize the old doctor and at its close received thunderous applause from the delighted audience.[31]

Irving and his friends then proceeded to imitate the manifestations with a remarkable degree of accuracy. "The 'brothers' were tied hand and foot, placed in a cabinet, and immediately began their manifestations. Weird noises were heard, hands became visible through the opening in the cabinet, musical instruments were seen floating in the air, and the trumpet was several times thrown out. When the doors were opened, the brothers were shown to be securely tied. They reproduced every effect of the performances accompanied by appropriate remarks and delightful witticisms from Irving."

At the close of the séance, the performers received a vote of thanks, the audience cheering Irving repeatedly. The Manchester papers were filled for several days with accounts and letters concerning the Irving séance, and in response to many urgent requests it was repeated a week later in the Free Trade Hall, but the net result of the exposure to Irving was the loss of his engagement at the Theatre Royal as he refused to capitalize its success by giving nightly performances at the theatre.

The extent to which people allowed themselves to be deluded by the Davenport exhibitions is evident from the following passage taken from D. C. Donovan's "Evidences of Spiritualism." As a voluntary investigation committee of one he had been allowed to sit in the cabinet with the Brothers while the manifestations were in progress. In his account of his experiences he says:

"Whilst I was inside, several arms were thrust out at the openings and distinctly seen by persons outside. Now it is certain that these were not the arms of the Brothers, because they could not have reached the openings without rising from their seats, and had they done this, I should have detected it in an instant; moreover, if their hands had been free, they could not have played six instruments at once and still have hands left with which to touch my face and hands and pull my hair. Some of my friends endeavor to persuade me that the Davenports did move, but that being in the dark I did not notice it. Darkness, however, although highly unfavorable to seeing, is not at all so to feeling, and I had my hands on their shoulders, where the slightest muscular moving would have been detected."

In view of what Ira Davenport told me about their manipulations I cannot read the above account without feeling sorry for Mr. Donovan, who, if his belief was genuine, had reached the highest point of delusion.

Because of the particular qualifications and aptitude of magicians to detect fraud it is not surprising that Spiritualistic publications seize eagerly any word coming from them favorable to the cause of Spiritualism. With the comment, "it is well worth preserving and placing beside that of Belachini, the German conjuror, as an answer to those of our opponents, who, ignorant of legerdermain, declare our phenomena to be of that character," "The Spiritualist" of September 9, 1881, quoted from the Paris *"Revue Spirits"* the following statement of E. Jacobs, a French prestidigitator:

"Relating to phenomena which occurred in Paris in 1865, through the Brothers Davenport, spite of the assertions, more or less trustworthy, of the French and English journalists, and spite of the foolish jealousies of ignorant conjurors, I feel it my duty to show up the bad faith of one party, and chicanery of the other. . . . All that has been said or done adverse to these American mediums is absolutely untrustworthy. If we should judge rightly of a thing we must understand it, and neither the journalists nor the conjurors possess the most elementary knowledge of the science that governs these phenomena. As a Prestidigitator of repute and a sincere Spiritualist, I affirm that the mediumistic facts demonstrated by the two Brothers were absolutely true, and belong to the Spiritualistic order of things in every respect. . . . Messrs. Henri Robin and Robert Houdin, when attempting to imitate these said feats, never presented to the public anything beyond an infantine and almost grotesque parody of the said phenomena, and it would be an ignorant and obstinate person who could regard the question seriously as set forth by these gentlemen. If, as I have reason to hope, the psychical studies to which I am applying myself at this time, succeed, I shall be able to establish clearly (and that by

---

[31] Ira told me that he believed that their success so diminished the popularity of the theatre where Irving was playing that the stars were forced to resort to various schemes to counteract the dwindling receipts at the box office. See Appendix B for Irving's speech.

public demonstration) the immense line of demarcation which separates mediumistic phenomena from conjuring proper, and then equivocation will be no longer possible, and persons will yield to evidence, or deny through predetermination.

(Signed) "E. Jacobs.[32]
"Experimenter and President of Conference to the
Psychological Studies at Paris."

Dion Boucicault, an Irish Dramatist and actor of prominence in America and equally so in Europe, entertained the Davenports at his home in London (1865) where he felt assured that the room could not contribute to fraudulent results. Twenty-three friends, men of rank and some prominence, among them clergymen and medical doctors, were in attendance. He did not report if any were believers, but it is inferred from his writing that none were. As in other cases, the utmost precaution was taken to render conditions most acceptable to the investigators, nevertheless, the usual manifestations took place and Mr. Boucicault wrote lengthy reports as to details, and as a conclusion to his report he wrote:

"At the termination of the séance a general conversation took place on the subject of what we had heard and witnessed. Lord Bury suggested that the general opinion seemed to be that we should assure the Brothers Davenport and Mr. W. Fay, that after a very stringent trial and strict scrutiny of their proceedings, the gentlemen present could arrive at no other conclusion than that there was no trace of trickery in any form, and certainly there were neither confederates nor machinery and that all those who had witnessed the results would freely state in society in which they moved, that, so far as their investigations enabled them to form an opinion, the phenomena which had taken place in their presence were not the product of legerdemain. This suggestion was promptly acceded to by all present.

"Some persons think that the requirement of darkness seems to infer trickery. Is not a dark chamber essential in the process of photography? And what would we reply to him who would say, 'I believe photography to be a humbug--do it all in the light, and we will believe otherwise'? It is true that we know why darkness is necessary to the production of the sun-pictures; and if scientific men will subject these phenomena to analysis, we shall find out why darkness is essential to such manifestations. It is a subject which scientific men are not justified in treating with the neglect of contempt.--I am, etc.,

"Dion Boucicault."

Richard Francis Burton, eminent English traveller, writer, and translator of *The Arabian Nights*, wrote to Dr. Ferguson, Davenport Brothers' lecturer and manager:

"I have spent a great part of my life in oriental lands, and have seen there many magicians. ... I have read and listened to every explanation of the Davenport 'tricks' hitherto placed before the English public, and, believe me, if anything would make me take that tremendous jump 'from matter to spirit,' it is the utter and complete unreason of the reasons by which the 'manifestations' are explained."

Nor was it in England alone that able men were completely fooled by the Davenports' performance. Frenchmen as well, after seeing the exhibition, hastened to put their favorable opinions in writing. Hamilton, a well-known expert in the art of legerdemain, and son-in-law of Robert Houdin, the famous conjuror, wrote:

"Messrs. Davenport,--Yesterday I had the pleasure of being present at the séance you gave, and I came away from it convinced that jealousy alone was the cause of the outcry against you. The phenomena produced surpassed my expectations, and your experiments were full of interest for me. I consider it my duty to add that those phenomena are inexplicable, and the more so by such persons as have thought themselves able to guess your supposed secret, and who are, in fact, far indeed from discovering the truth.

"Hamilton."

---

[32] The reader should not confuse this man Jacobs with *Jacoby*, the German escape-artist, a rope specialist who invented a number of rope tricks that are still well worth presenting.

M. Rhys, a manufacturer of conjuring implements and himself an inventor of tricks, wrote the Davenports:

". . . I have returned from one of your séances quite astonished. As a person who has devoted many years to the manufacture of instruments for legerdemain performances, my statement made with due regard to fidelity, and guided by the knowledge long experience has given me, will, I trust, be of some value to you. . . . I was admitted to examine your cabinet and instruments . . . with the greatest care but failed to find anything that could justify legitimate suspicions. From that moment I felt that the insinuations cast about you were false and malevolent."

These are but a few of innumerable instances where men of culture, knowledge and experience, were deluded by the performance of the Davenport Brothers, just as men are to-day with my presentations, and when the reader takes into consideration the confession of Ira Erastus Davenport[33] to me in 1909, and the fact that he taught me his full method of manipulating séances, he can then form some conception of the extent to which the most intelligent minds can be led astray by what seem to them phenomena, but to me, mere problems susceptible of lucid explanation.

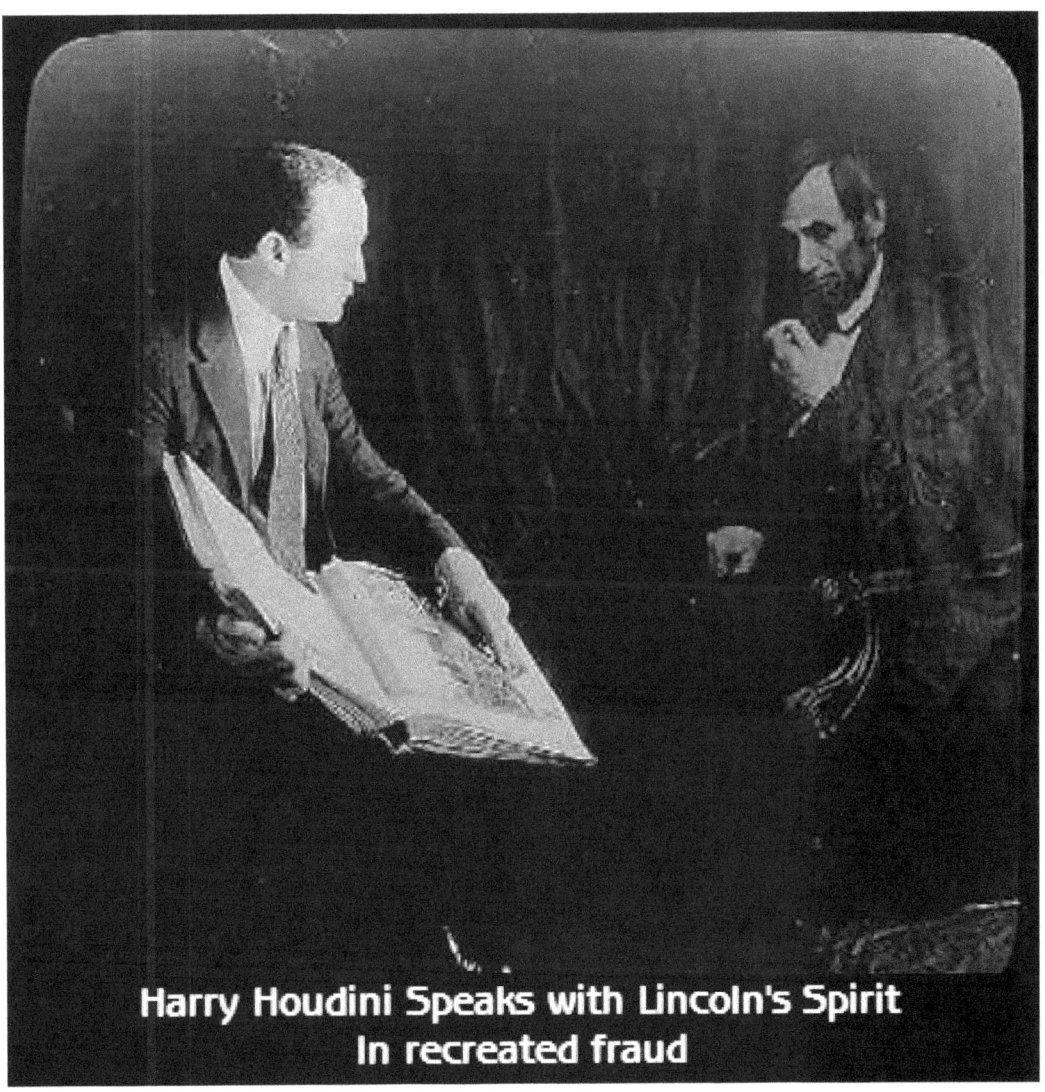

Harry Houdini Speaks with Lincoln's Spirit
In recreated fraud

---

[33] He wrote me a letter on July 5th, 1911, and was waiting to see me at the time of his death on the 8th. I was to leave New York on receipt of his letter but bis daughter Zelie wired me of his passing away.

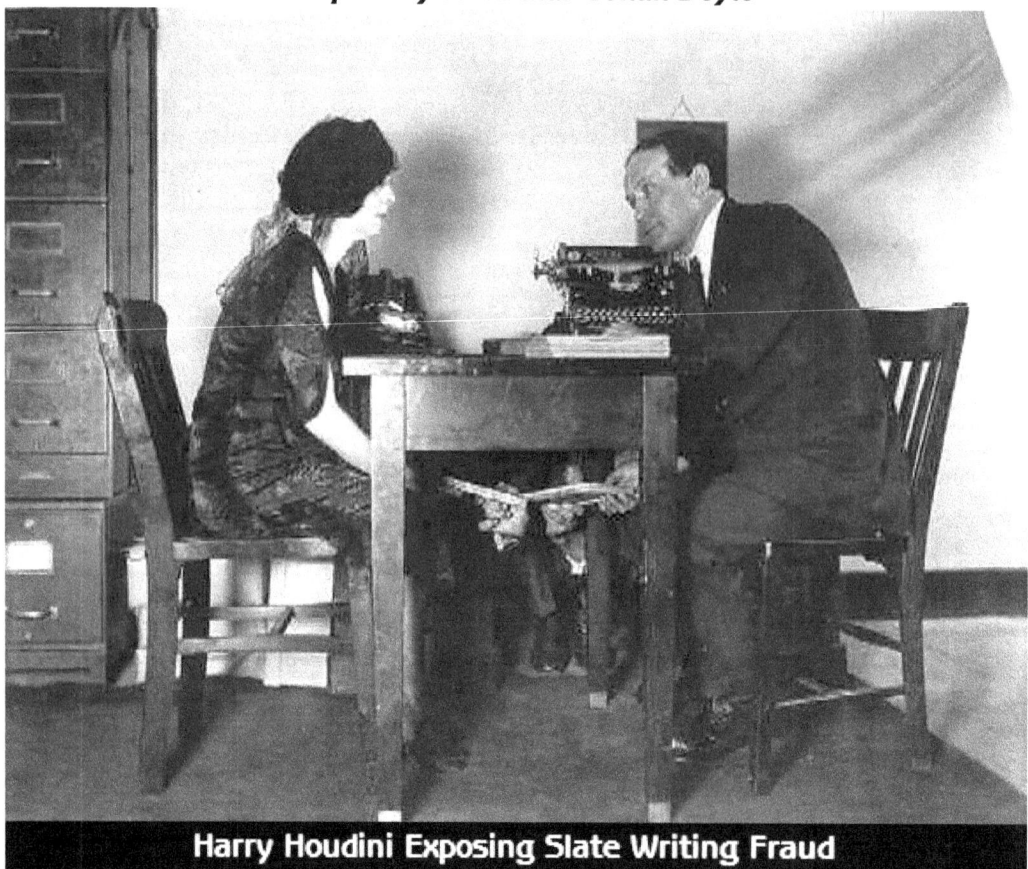
Harry Houdini Exposing Slate Writing Fraud

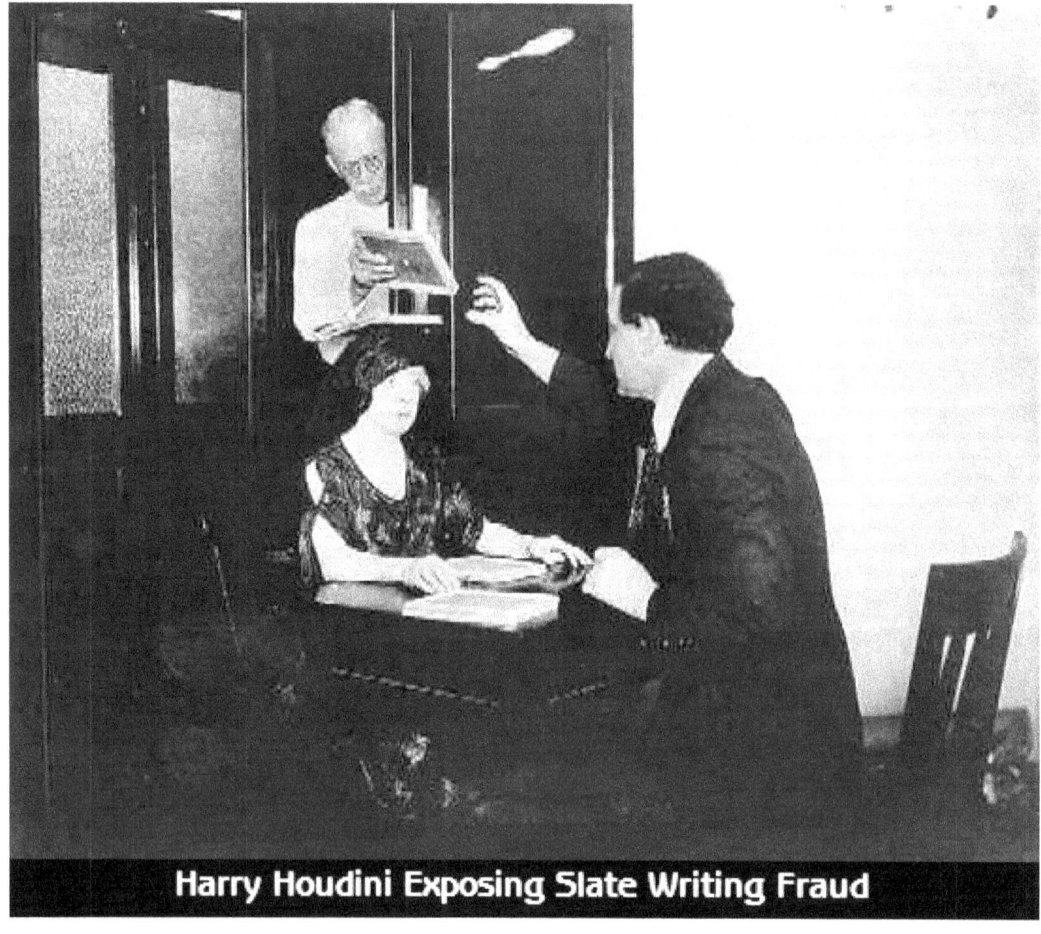
Harry Houdini Exposing Slate Writing Fraud

Chapter 3
Daniel Dunglas Home

FOLLOWING the first séances of the "Fox Sisters," in 1848, mediums sprang up all over the country like mushrooms but of this multitude there have not been more than a dozen whose work, in spite of repeated exposure, is still pointed to as proof of Spiritualism, and whose names have found a permanent place in connection with its development and history. Of these, one of the most conspicuous and lauded of his type and generation was Daniel Dunglas Home. He was the forerunner of the mediums whose forte is fleecing by presuming upon the credulity of the subject. A new and fertile field was opened and from that time to the present day there have been numerous cases of mediums falling into the clutches of the law as a direct result of using his methods, but Home had characteristics which went far in many cases to keep him out of trouble. Outwardly a lovable character with a magnetic personality and a great fondness for children; suave, captivating to the last degree, a good dresser fond of displaying jewelry; an appearance of ill-health which aroused sympathy and with an assumption of piety and devotion to established forms of religious worship, he made his way easily and found favor with many who would have spurned him under other conditions and this too, strange as it may seem, in spite of persistent *rumors* of immorality in his private life.

Home helped to build up his reputation by not charging for his mediumistic services. The claim that he did not accept fees for his sittings may, or may not, be quite true, but the fact remains that the spirits were good to him and provided for his temporal needs abundantly and sumptuously, and he subsisted on the bounty of his Spiritualistic friends who seemed to rival one another in entertaining him in their homes for long periods and showering him with gifts, a practice which began in America and was continued in England and on the Continent to an extent which made a life of positive luxury possible.

It is strongly intimated that the gifts which Home received were in many cases *suggested* by the *Spirits* he invoked and his spirit guide seems to have always kept a sharp eye on his need for earthly sustenance even to the point of satisfactorily bedecking his person with jewelry. This was always *materialized* for him when required, and since he, personally, could not be held responsible for what wicked spirits might do, and as they used good judgment in picking victims, nothing was said about it and he escaped the prison fate of Ann O'Delia Diss Debar.

His early life was spent in Connecticut but whether at the home of his aunt in Waterford or with his mother in Norwich, twelve miles away, is a question, but certain it is that at the death of his mother he went to the aunt's. This was when he was seventeen, two years after the "Fox Sisters" had begun their career in New York State. How much he had heard of them is uncertain, something no doubt, and it is not strange that a youth of his characteristics might want to emulate them. Then too his mother had the reputation of being possessed of so-called "second-sight" and he may have inherited traits which helped to make the life of a medium look attractive to him. At any rate, claiming the assistance of his mother's spirit, he tried out his mediumistic powers at the homes of the neighbors with such success that before long he announced to his aunt that he was going to set up as a *professional Spiritualist.* The lady, a devout Trinitarian, was so shocked and disturbed, he tells us, that "in her uncontrollable anger she seized a chair and threw it at me." But much as she disliked the idea of the young man becoming a medium his performances soon attracted so much attention that she was reconciled to his leaving her home in Norwich to go to Willimantic, Connecticut, where he began his life-long custom of living on the bounty of friends and dupes. His first feats were of the simplest kind such as are in the repertoire of every itinerant sideshow proprietor, but his success seems to have been instantaneous. One reason for this was that while mediums as a class were a lazy lot Home was an untiring worker as well as an unflinching egotist and his personal qualities went far to disarm suspicion and inspire confidence in the minds of his dupes.

Where he obtained his early education does not appear but the records are full of indications of considerable intellectuality. He claimed to have studied medicine and obtained a degree in New York but he never practiced. In his later years he set up a studio in Italy[34] and gave his attention to sculpture between séances and "sold busts at prices quite out of proportion to their artistic merits." He studied elocution too and is said to have given many successful readings.[35] He also had the credit of being quite a musician and playing several instruments, which partially explains his accordion trick. With it all he was considerable of a linguist, toward the last being able to speak most of the modern tongues. He was the author of two pretentious books[36] whose chief purpose seems to have been to establish the impression that while all other mediums cheated at times *Home was strictly honest* on all occasions, and in proof it was said that he was never exposed and never received a fee for his sittings. Nevertheless one charge of fraud was proven against him in court.[37] It may or may not be true that he was never completely exposed but many of his manifestations were discovered to be fraudulent and every one of them can be duplicated by modern conjurors under the same conditions. The principal reason why he was never *completely* exposed was that he gave no public sittings, always appearing as the guest of the family where he was living and as one writer expressed it, "one would no more think of criticising his host's guest than he would his host's wine."

On one occasion Robert Browning, the poet, attended one of Home's séances. He had become somewhat alarmed by his wife's interest in Spiritualism, and when a face was materialized and said to be that of a son who had died in infancy, Browning seized the supposed materialized head and discovered it to be *the bare foot of Mr. Home.* Incidentally, Browning had never lost an infant son. The living son, R. Barrett Browning, in a letter to the London *Times,* December 5, 1902, referring to this occurrence said, "Home was detected in a vulgar fraud." In the same letter he tells of the modification of His mother's belief after having been deceived by a *"trusted friend"* and his closing words were: "The pain of the disillusion was great, but her eyes were opened and she saw clearly."

What might be called Home's American apprenticeship began in 1850 and in spite of his youth and inexperience he succeeded in convincing many prominent persons of the genuineness of his phenomena, among them being such men as Judge Edmonds,[38] William Cullen Bryant, and Bishop Clarke of Rhode Island. In the spring of 1855 a committee of admirers collected a sum of money sufficient to send him to England and establish himself comfortably. He carried with him a letter of introduction to a man of scientific tastes by the name of Cox who was proprietor of Cox's Hotel, in Jermyn Street, and through whose influence he was able to arrange sittings with Lord Brougham, Sir David Brewster, Robert Owen, T. A. Trollope, Sir E. Bulwer Lytton, and others equally prominent.

After only a few months' stay in England Home went to Italy, ostensibly for his health, and for the next four years he lived on the Continent, travelling from place to place, living in luxury, being almost continually entertained in the homes of "friends," which in almost every case were people of rank and wealth. He seems to have had little difficulty in meeting royalty and nobility on terms of

---

[34] When Sir Arthur Conan Doyle was appearing in Australia in 1920 he met Bendigo Rymer, the grandson of J. S. Rymer, who had entertained Home lavishly. Bendigo showed Sir Arthur a number of letters from his grandfather which proved conclusively that Home had been guilty of taking advantage of the man's friendship. Rymer had entertained Home in England and sent him to Rome with his son to study art. From Rome young Rymer wrote his father that as soon as Home had been able to elbow his way into society he totally ignored him though as host he was paying Home's expenses. Finally Home ran away and lived with a titled English woman, shunning Rymer altogether.

Sir Arthur in his book, "The Wanderings of a Spiritualist," says in reference to Home: "For weeks he lived at her villa, although the state of his health would suggest that it was rather as a patient than a lover." In his introduction to Madame Home's book Sir Arthur entirely forgives this rude action of Home and strongly defends his base ingratitude.

[35] Home, the Spiritualist, is giving readings in Boston. Has he given up his Spiritualism in disgust at finding that people who strained at his manifestations have swallowed the Davenports? We are glad to think he has adopted an honest profession at last, and we hope before long to see his rivals rising to sweeping a crossing or something as respectable.—*London Fun,* 1864.

[36] "Incidents in My Life," London, 1863—"Lights and Shadows of Spiritualism," 1877.

[37] It is quite unnecessary for me to repeat the many proofs of fraud perpetrated by Home, but if the reader is interested he will find many such cases reported by Mr. Frank Podmore in "Modern Spiritualism," London, 1902, and "Newer Spiritualism," London, 1910. Mr. Podmore was a Spiritualist himself and a member of the Society of Psychical Research and would naturally make out as good a case for Home as he could honestly.

[38] See Appendix F.

intimacy even numbering among his patrons the Emperor and Empress of France as well as the Czar of Russia. From this clientele he received many and valuable gifts. At the Russian Court, with its leaning toward the occult, he was especially welcomed and lived for weeks at a time in the palace of the Czar, like the similar careers of Washington Irving Bishop, Mons. Phillipi, and Rasputin. During his stay in Russia he met a beautiful young lady of rank and with the approval of the Czar married her.[39]

Home at this time had already begun to show that fondness for precious stones which finally became so pronounced that a few years later an English writer in describing him said:

"But the salient feature of the man after all was his jewels. On the third finger of the left hand he wore an immense solitaire, which flashed imperial splendors with every movement; above that a sapphire of enormous size; on the other hand was a large yellow diamond and a superb ruby set in brilliants."

But these were not all for the writer adds a list of others in Home's possession which would easily arouse the envy of any multi-millionaire's wife. In view of this fondness for jewels an incident which occurred just prior to Home's leaving the Russian Court is interesting. The story was told me by Stuart Cumberland. I have heard him repeat it to others and he also tells it in his book, "That Other World," from which I quote.

"Whilst in Petrograd--so at least, a famous diplomat assured me when I was there--Home did a feat of de-materialization before the Court which, had it not been for the favor in which he was held in high places, might have curtailed his liberty for a period.

"He had dematerialized a splendid row of emeralds lent the "dear spirits" for the purpose of the test; but up to the time of his departure from the séance, the emeralds, for some occult reason, had declined to materialize and be given back to the confiding owner. They were, of course, in the spirit land engaging the attention of the spooks, who seemed to have a pretty taste for valuable jewels. But the chief of police had not that faith in spiritual probity generally accepted at the Court, and before leaving the palace, Home was searched, and--so the story came to me--the dematerialized emeralds were found materializing in his coat-tail pocket. They had been placed there by an evil spirit, of course, but the chief of police impressed upon the medium that the climate of the Russian Capital might not be good for his health-- that an early departure would probably benefit it. Home took the hint and his early departure. To his dying day, I think he regretted the interference of the evil spirit (or the police). It would have been so much more satisfactory for the jewels to have remained dematerialized in the spirit land, to be materialized at will with no interfering police around, for they, the jewels, were of great earthly value."

The year 1859 found Home back in England and marked the commencement of what proved to be the period of his greatest success. It was but a few years later that he attempted his most noted financial venture. He had become established in Sloane Street, London, as Secretary of what was called "The Spiritual Athenaeum." One day, late in 1866, there came to him a widow by the name of Jane Lyon who was anxious to join his society. She was seventy-five years old and besides being wealthy in her own right had been left ample means by her husband. Previous to calling on Home she had read his book, believed it, and in addition been having a series of unusual dreams. The medium had little difficulty in finding a way to make it possible for her to join the Athenaeum, and she told how later at this first meeting her husband's spirit "had communicated with her through Home, and knotted her handkerchief." Just all that the spirit of her husband said to her at this interview does not appear but it was enough to persuade her to give him twenty-four thousand pounds. The spirits became very much interested in Mrs. Lyon's affairs and in November, at their direction, Home burned her will and before long she gave him another six thousand pounds.

The attachment between the widow of seventy-five and the medium of thirty-three grew apace and soon the spirit of her husband suggested that she adopt Home as her son "for he would be such a comfort to her." The suggestion was immediately acted upon and the medium began to call himself Daniel Home Lyon. Nor was the spirit forgetful of the needs of a son, suggesting that an allowance of seven hundred pounds a year would be about right. In January (1867) Mrs. Lyon assigned a mortgage

---

[39] She only lived about four years

of thirty thousand pounds-to Home, only reserving the interest as an annuity for herself. Not until a month later did she become worried and consult a lawyer, who assured her that she had been imposed upon, but she was not convinced until she had questioned the spirits through a girl of twelve, the daughter of a flower medium by the name of Murray. As reported by this girl even the spirits seemed to think that Mrs. Lyon had been fleeced out of sixty thousand pounds and she accordingly demanded its return by Home. He ignored the demand but offered to return the mortgage if she would give him undisputed possession of the first thirty thousand pounds and allow him to drop the name of Lyon. She would not agree to this. Home was arrested and a suit for recovery begun. The litigation was long, the case finally ending in May, 1868, with a judgment in favor of Mrs. Lyon; the Court holding that as the transfer of money and deed had been accomplished by *fraud* it was therefore void. In his closing remarks the Vice Chancellor referred to Mrs. Lyon as an old lady with a mind *"saturated with delusion"* and characterized Spiritualism as being, according to the evidence, a "system of mischievous nonsense well calculated to delude the vain, the weak, the foolish, and the superstitious."[40]

DIAGRAM SHOWING ARRANGEMENT OF ROOMS, WINDOWS, ETC., WHERE HOME'S REPUTED FEAT OF FLOATING TOOK PLACE.

Home continued his mediumship, notwithstanding, and between 1870 and 1872 he held several séances with Sir William Crookes,[41] who was so impressed that he credited him with being "one of the most lovable of men--whose perfect genuineness was above suspicion," an opinion strikingly in contrast with the verdict in the case of Mrs. Lyon, but which shows how thoroughly and easily the followers of Spiritualism are beguiled and misled. *No* medium is *ever* open to suspicion by the faithful

---

[40] In his introduction to the 1921 edition of "D. D. Home's Life and Work," by Madame Home, Doyle declares that he commends the book to the student, saying:

"Very especially the second series is commended to the student of Home, because in it will be found all the papers dealing with the Home-Lyon lawsuit showing conclusively how honorable was the action of Home."

Does he wish us to infer that it was Home who brought the suit against Mrs. Lyon, rather than the opposite?

Does he wish it understood that he is *sincere* in his commendation of a charlatan?

Throughout the introduction he defends Home and seems to deliberately twist the history of the man.

[41] It is interesting to note that Sir William Crookes, the eminent scientist, who must have known of the history and character of Home as unveiled at the Lyon trial, should have permitted himself to fall within the mesh of D. D. Home.

and Sir William Crookes' statement encourages the belief that even scientists are not always immune from the influence of *personal magnetism.* He is also quoted as saying:

"As to the theory of fraud, it is obvious that this theory can account for a very small portion of the facts observed. I am willing to admit that some so-called mediums of whom the public have heard much, are arrant impostors, who have taken advantage of the public demand for Spiritualistic excitement, to fill their purses with easily earned guineas; *while others who have no pecuniary motive for imposture are tempted to cheat, it would seem, solely by a desire for notoriety.*"

So it will be seen that even Professor Crookes, while defending the so-called genuine medium, in the same breath admits that there are fraudulent practitioners.

Home gained wide notoriety for unusual phenomena by his reputed levitation acts, wherein he would slide from the chair on which he was sitting to a horizontal position, then ask to have the chair removed as it was not supporting him, and would "float" under a table and back, but his masterpiece, the incident oftenest referred to, was sailing out of a window feet first, and sailing into another, seven feet and four inches distant, landing feet first in an adjacent room, where he "sat down." Lord Adare, an observer, expressed surprise that he could have been carried through an aperture so narrow as eighteen inches whereupon "Home, still entranced said, 'I will show you,' *and then with his back to the window he leaned over and was shot out of the aperture, head first, with the body rigid, and then returned quite quietly.*"[42] [43]

This is the way the story has been recounted again and again by Spiritualist writers and speakers and to this day is told by Sir Arthur Conan Doyle with as much seriousness as if he had been an eyewitness of the occurrence in the full glare of a noon-day sun.

"When D. D. made that 'home-run' " around the outside of his house he seems to have been seeking an altitude rather than a speed record, as the three reliable (?) witnesses agree that the windows through which he floated were in the third story and either sixty or eighty feet from the ground. This would make the height of each story from twenty to twenty-seven feet, but *tall stories* appear to have been a specialty with these remarkably observant gentlemen.

In 1920 I made plans for reproducing this window feat under the same conditions as Home and the late Stuart Cumberland openly challenged Spiritualists that I was ready to submit to such a test but no response was received before I left Europe. Consequently I desire to go on record as being able to perform the same phenomena (?) provided I am given the same conditions and scope which Home was. I believe that those who witnessed the feat were sincere in giving credence to it but that it was an illusion and they were deceived by Home, for the mind of the average person accepts what it sees and is not willing to apply the laws of physics, no matter how much or how glaringly the act defies the fundamental principles upon which our very existence depends.

The years between 1859 and 1872 were those of Home's greatest success. Toward the end of this period, however, his popularity waned and having for a second time married a lady belonging to the Russian nobility, he gave up the practice of his profession, broke with nearly all his former friends and returned to the Continent where he devoted much of his time to writing. He died in 1886 and is buried at St. Germain-en-Laye.

His active career, his various escapades, and the direct cause of his death[44] all indicate that he lived the life of a hypocrite of the deepest dye. How strange that these inspired agents of

---

[42] Taking for granted that the committee in the room was not able to see or permitted to leave the table the method Home could have used with the greatest ease was: first actually get out of the window, or pretend to; then, go back and noiselessly crawl on all fours through the door into the next room and shake the window; and lastly, boldly return to the first room, closing the door with a bang.

There is a possibility that a man of Home's audacity with levitation feats might have resorted to swinging from one window to another, which means nothing to any acrobat with a wire properly placed in readiness.

The idea of Home losing his physical weight and floating out of the window head first is merely a suggestion of his, a ruse which is still being used by mediums.

[43] See Appendix C for Lord Adare's story.

[44] There are numerous versions of the cause of his death. Mme. Blavatsky, who made a special investigation of the deaths of prominent mediums, wrote; "This Calvin of Spiritualism suffered for years from a terrible spinal disease, brought on through his intercourse with the 'Spirits,' and died a perfect wreck." —"Key to Theosophy," 1890.

"Summerland," these human deliverers of messages, these stepping stones to the Beyond, are, for the greater part, moral perverts whose favorite defence is the claim that they are forced to do such deeds by the evil spirits which take possession of them.

Daniel Dunglas Home

Rare Photo of Houdini in Strait-Jacket Locked Inside Crate

Houdini & Fake Spirits

Young Houdini and Escape Box

Houdini the Aviator

Chapter 4
Palladino

EUSAPIA PALLADINO, an Italian, has to her credit the successful deception of more philosophic and scientific men than any other known medium, being regarded by some as the most famous of them all, notwithstanding the fact that she seems to have made no pretence of producing the class of miracles claimed by D. D. Home and many others. Materialization was rarely resorted to by her and there is very little variety in her program from 1892 up to the time of her death in 1918, evidently being content to astonish investigating scientists with the levitation and gyrating of inanimate things.[45]

Palladino was born in the Neapolitan district of poor peasants who died when she was a mere child. Naturally bright, even shrewd, her perceptive instinct seems to have developed early in life and continued throughout her career though she had no education and to the end was scarcely able to read or write.

Her first contact with the mysterious arts appears to have been when she was a mere child of thirteen (1867) in the service of an acrobat or *conjuror*[46] from whom she must have acquired some degree of skill and knowledge of the uncanny which she may have coupled up with the marvellous success achieved by Home, and her quick wit may have opened visions of a change from poverty to that affluence which she saw was the reward of the professional phenomena producer, for she began her Spiritualistic work just following his successful operations in Italy which served to spread Spiritualism in spite of Papal opposition. Her part must have been learned well and her plans carefully laid before she made her debut as a full fledged medium because she succeeded from the start in baffling brainy men of science, and while as the wife of a small shop-keeper she was very poor, she became wealthy within twenty years after taking up mediumistic work.

She did not attract the attention of the public until about 1880 when Professor Chiaia, who had been giving her a lot of attention without detecting her methods, challenged Professor Lombroso, at that time the most distinguished scientific man in Italy, to investigate her. Professor Lombroso did, but failed to detect any fraudulent work though his decision was delayed for so long a time that when it was finally given it was claimed that his mentality had weakened considerably.[47]

In 1892 Palladino had begun to attract the attention of scientific men in different Italian cities and had also been brought to the notice of some of the English Spiritualists but it was not until 1894 that she went to France. This trip was brought about through the influence of Professor Richet, and Sir Oliver Lodge, Professor Sidgwick, and Mr. Myers took part in the proceedings. On the return of Lodge and Myers to England they aroused interest in Palladino by reporting her phenomena to be genuine.

The first exposure of Palladino was made by Dr. Richard Hodgson in 1895. A committee from the English Society for Psychical Research, consisting of Hereward Carrington, Hon. Everard Feilding, and Wortly W. Baggally, which had held a series of test séances with Palladino in Italy, brought her to

---

[45] Table lifting was a strong card with her.

[46] "She was taken in a menial position into a family given to Spiritualistic practices. Being called one day to make up the circle at a seance, certain new and surprising manifestations took place, and she was pronounced to be a medium. So it appears that the Spiritualists actually pushed her into the matter, and she immediately took advantage of the opportunity."—Proceedings, Society for Psychical Research, November, 1909, pp. 311, 312.

[47] Robert Owen, Prof. Hare, Prof. Challis, Prof. Zollner, Prof. Weber, and Lombroso were all near the end of their lives when they embraced Spiritualism. —See "Spiritualism," by Joseph McCabe, page 207.

England for a fresh try-out and another series of sittings was held. Very early in the series suspicious movements on the part of the medium were observed. Later Dr. Hodgson joined the circle and was able to show conclusively that by clever manipulation--sheer trickery--she was getting one hand free and with it making the movements observed.

Her method[48] was to begin by allowing one hand to be firmly held by the sitter at her side (say on the left) and let the fingers of her other hand (right) rest on that of the sitter on her right. In the course of some rapid spasmodic movements she would bring the sitters' hands so close together that one of her own could do duty for two, being held by one sitter while its fingers rested on the hand of the other sitter,[49] leaving her (Palladino's) right hand free to produce the desired "phenomena" after which it was restored to its original position. Other devices equally dishonest were observed or inferred.

All of these men were experienced séance observers[50] but the report of their conclusions shows how easily such experts were deceived by the very tricks which were later proved fraudulent by the New York branch of The Society for Psychical Research. Mr. Feilding's reports were the least positive of the three and show that when the best phenomena were observed the control was not complete and that the stenographic notes were deficient, and when read over the day following the sitting they seemed weak in comparison with a recollection of the manifestations. That the final reports were based largely on these recollections is indicated by Mr. Feilding's statement that:

"We were forced from our proposed colorless attitude to one of almost proselyting affirmation."

When Palladino came to America in 1908 she was beginning to be world famous and her reputation was established; she was a shrewd woman with a large experience in the art of misdirection, and with a convenient subterfuge of unaccommodating Spirit guides whenever her own resources were exhausted because of some over-zealous observer. For twenty years or more she had avoided detection because she had fixed the conditions under which tests were made and consequently as scientific investigations they were simply farces. But in New York conditions were introduced which she did not approve for the simple reason that she did not know that they existed. Another difference was that in New York a number of rehearsals were held and each investigator was assigned to a special part of the work, thus guarding against the old trick of drawing the attention away from the place where a manifestation suddenly developed. The result was Palladino's downfall.

On her arrival in New York a group of Columbia professors became interested in Palladino and arranged for a series of ten test séances at one hundred and twenty-five dollars a sitting. Eight of the ten séances had been held and though a majority of the professors were satisfied that she was cheating they were unable to prove it. Although the séances were being conducted secretly by the scientists one of them, Professor Dickinson S. Miller, discussed Palladino's best trick, table levitation, with a friend of mine, Mr. W. S. Davis, himself an ex-medium whose séances were always given under test conditions. Davis not only explained to the Professor the probable method used by Palladino but demonstrated it as well with the result that the Professor declared that a full exposure of Palladino should be made even if it cost ten thousand dollars and invited Davis to aid at the next séance candidly admitting that he and his associates were incapable of proper investigation.

Davis replied that scientists were not the kind of men he could work with but if he would let him bring along a couple of "Flim-flam" men he would help. Professor Miller consented to this arrangement provided the men were palmed off as college professors as otherwise they would not be admitted. Davis then sent for John W. Sargent, a past-president of the Society of American Magicians, and for years my private secretary. He also sent for another magician, James L. Kellogg.

---

[48] Another adroit method of freeing one hand when the sitter thinks he has evidence that the two hands of the medium are being kept busy, is for the medium to keep up a continuous clapping of the hands, working the hands near the face or some other exposed part of the body and simply change the clapping of one hand against another to the clapping of one hand against the body. In the dark the effect is the same and the sitter believes that both the medium's hands are busily engaged in clapping.

[49] Not difficult to accomplish in the dark.

[50] Mr. Baggally had a reputation as a conjuror and I think he has done much in the way of exposing mediums. He is also a believer in telepathy and has recently published a book on that subject, "Telepathy, Genuine and Fraudulent," Chicago, 1918.

Both agreed with Davis that his theory of Palladino's method was correct. Professor Miller then suggested, that in order to make the discovery complete and to corroborate any and all observations, two other persons should be selected to watch the feet of the medium. Davis accordingly selected Joseph F. Rinn, another member of the magicians society, who had assisted in various exposures of pseudo-mediums and Professor Miller named Warner C. Pyne, a student at Columbia. It was agreed that these two should be clad in black even to a head covering and smuggled into the room under cover of darkness after the séance had convened and were to sprawl under the chairs and table in order that their heads might be near enough Palladino's feet to detect any movement. I am indebted to my friend Davis for the following inside story of the sitting just as he gave it to me.

"After the arrival of Eusapia and Mr. Livingston and when both had entered the séance room, Rinn and Pyne came downstairs and hid in the hall where they waited for their signal. When we were introduced and after the usual conversation, Eusapia said that she would begin. Before she had time to pick her controllers, Professor Miller ushered Kellogg and myself into the positions next to her. She took a seat at the narrow end of the table and with her back close to the cabinet curtains. (The cabinet was formed by placing curtains from the ceiling to the floor, extending out from one corner of the room). Kellogg sat at her right and I sat at her left. Eusapia sat close to the table and her black dress touched the table legs. She placed her right foot on the instep of Kellogg's left foot and her left foot on my right foot, which was her guarantee that her feet should play no part in the production of the phenomena. We did not reduce the light at the beginning of the séance.

"The rest of the party sitting around the table then placed their hands on its upper surface and formed the well known chain. Eusapia stamped Kellogg's foot and mine and asked us if the control was satisfactory which of course it was. Eusapia then drew her own hands away from ours and soon light raps were heard. *They were such as are easily and imperceptibly produced by sliding the finger tips upon the table top.*

"We were next favored with responsive raps,--doubling up her hands she beat the air with her fists in a jerky, spasmodic way when we heard the light noises on the wood. The exhibition above board did not occupy our entire attention. Every one in the party was interested in the theory of using a foot as a lever to raise the table. As she beat the air with her clenched fist, she correspondingly slid her feet away until we felt the pressure on the toe end of our feet only, whereas there had previously been pressure on the insteps. Kellogg and I both suspected that she had succeeded in removing one foot and was making the other do duty for two. From then on we commenced to get heavier raps, as though she struck the table leg with her foot.

"In striking the table leg with the side of her shoe, thus producing raps, Eusapia also got the exact position in which her foot should be placed for levitation. When she rocked the table from side to side it was only necessary to switch her toe an inch when the left leg of the table would come down on it, then all she had to do was to elevate her toe while the heel remained on the floor and either partial or complete levitation followed.

"We looked pleased and Eusapia began to feel at home. With a little rest, the rocking was resumed and she considered it safe to risk the entire levitation. Holding Kellogg's left hand up in the air with her right she put my right hand, palm down, on the top of the table, directly over the left table leg; then put her left hand over mine, the tips of the fingers extending rather over my hand and touching the table. No other hands were upon it. Then, after a few partial levitations, the table went up into the air with every leg off the floor. It was our first complete levitation. As beautiful as any on record and *given under bright lights."*

I asked Davis how he knew the levitation was fraudulent and he answered:

"(1) During the partial levitations I casually lifted my left foot, passed it over the right foot in the direction of Eusapia and was unable to touch her left leg in the place where it should have been. (2) Her black dress touched the table leg and as she took her toe suddenly out from under it, her dress moved accordingly. (3) By the thud which the table made when it was deprived of its very material perch. (4) By the fact that any juggler can perform the feat when the *'modus operandi'* is fully understood, though perhaps not with the same skill. (5) Every one present knew that the table was steadied at the top by Eusapia's hand, which rested upon mine, in turn bore down over the table leg, held up presumably by Eusapia's toe which formed a perfect human clamp.[51] (6) What Rinn and Pyne told us after the séance. They said that from their position under the chairs they saw Eusapia place her right foot upon Kellogg's left and her left foot upon my right, later they saw her tapping upon our feet with hers while she made some changes in the position of her feet. They also saw her slide her left foot away by a few hitches as her right was twisted around to cover my right foot which had previously been under her left foot. They distinctly saw Eusapia strike the table leg with the side of her foot to produce the raps and they also saw her slide her toe under the table leg and force the table up by toe leverage."[52]

During his narration I asked Davis to tell me if this astute Italian who had fooled the scientists of the world was not suspicious or did not sense that she was being checked up in her movements.

"No," he replied dryly, "once during the séance she asked every one to stand up. Two of the ladies in their inexperience proceeded to obey the command. We had two spies under our chairs and as we did not want her to see them something had to be done immediately, so I pretended to have severe cramps in my legs and while the interpreter told Eusapia of it Sargent and Kellogg nudged the ladies to sit down and the medium then resumed her seat."

I will not bore the reader with a detailed account of the cabinet phenomena at this séance under a subdued light but suffice to say that Davis and Kellogg tricked her as before and were able to explain every manifestation. The whole Miller séance was carried out as planned so carefully that Palladino on the way to her hotel afterwards told the Columbia student who had acted as interpreter[53] for her that she was well pleased with the evening and that the séance had been one of the most successful of the series.[54]

I quote by permission from a letter written me by Mr. Davis under date of June 22, 1923:

"Rupert Hughes, in an attack upon Spiritism some time ago, said that favorable reports on Palladino constituted a vast literature, and he was right. The public libraries both in this country and Europe contain many books in which it is claimed that it has been 'scientifically' demonstrated' that Eusapia possesses some occult power.

"Generations for centuries will probably be influenced by these books. They are only calculated to create superstition and ignorance and it is a shame that they are permitted to circulate. Eusapia was one of the world's greatest mountebanks. Her dupes were our foremost men of learning--they were not of the rabble. She was the greatest mountebank produced by modern Spiritism, and she duped more scientists than any other medium. In that respect D. D. Home does not compare with her. The *important lesson in the case is* that so-called 'scientific' testimony is just about worthless. That is an important educational fact and a valuable lesson to the general public."

Mr. Davis is quite right in his view of the seriousness of the possible danger and damage to the reading public from the effects of the grossly misapplied energy of the prominent scientists who have so unqualifiedly endorsed Eusapia Palladino as a genuine miracle worker, and the hosts of Spiritualistic enthusiasts who have repeated their published statements. Even Sir Arthur Conan Doyle unqualifiedly lauds Home and Palladino as patron saints of his psychic religion (?). He accepts as

---

[51] The "human-clamp" is one of the simplest and yet one of the most effective and mystifying means of table levitation. The medium and her subjects place the tips of their fingers on the top of the table lightly. The medium gently rocks the table back and forth until she gets it in a correct position to place her foot, or the hem of her dress, under one of the legs. When she perfects her position she presses down with the hand above the table leg that is resting on her foot. From then on it is only a matter of raising the foot to whatever height she wishes the table to rise. If she wants it levitated to a great height, she gives it an upward kick and then withdraws her foot, and the table rises and falls true to the laws of gravitation.

[52] At one time during the series of tests in New York City, a man from Philadelphia, Mr. Edgar Scott, who was standing in the background, took advantage of the darkness and crawled along the floor to the cabinet and attempted to grab Eusapia's foot while she was using it for trick purposes but just as his hand touched her foot Eusapia had a spasm of screeching. Professors Jastrow and Miller were witnesses of this fact.

[53] Palladino wanted her own interpreter, also a personal friend, but that obstacle was avoided. Neither was her business manager, Mr. Hereward Carrington, present on this particular occasion.

[54] The full details of this seance were published in the *Journal of the American Society for Psychical Research*, Section "B," August, 1910.

proof the fact that these learned scientists met their Waterloo in an attempt to fathom the simple tricks of impostors, and like all other Spiritualists refuses to accept the positive proof of the deception secured by men schooled in the science of magic which at times is as seemingly unexplainable as the more profound subjects of natural science.

The reader should bear in mind that Mr. Davis' *sincerity is* just as great as is Sir Arthur's. *Sincerity* is Sir Arthur's strong magnet and the reader should attach as much importance to *sincerity* on the part of an opponent. We must also take into consideration the fact that Mr. Davis was at one time a *medium* himself and he has had much opportunity for observing the qualifications of scientists as occult investigators. We must notice too the methods of conducting the séances in which such diverse results were obtained. Those held with only scientists as observers were under the full control of the medium and all her conditions were conformed to, but in New York it was practically a case of fighting fire with fire. It is proverbial that "it takes a rogue to catch a rogue"--just so a trickster is more capable of setting traps to detect trickery than the grave scientist in his endeavor to solve the problem by mathematics or logic. In the successful instance the plan of operation had been carefully worked out in every detail, each participant was assigned a specific work to do and did it. A number of rehearsals were held so that each person was familiar with their part. All the conditions so strenuously adhered to in previous séances, were safeguarded and the result was a successful exposure.

When Carrington brought Palladino to this country he announced that he did so in the interest of "science." Publicity was not to be ignored though and consequently the first séance was given before newspaper men. William A. Brady (the theatrical man) occupied the seat of honor which made it look as though Carrington hoped for some theatrical business as a side issue to the séances with scientists at a hundred and twenty-five dollars a sitting. It is also known that Carrington made a contract with a popular magazine which gave it an exclusive right to publish reports of the séances and naturally Carrington was to have received a liberal fee. But Mr. Davis in 1909 furnished the *New York Times* with two articles making a sensational attack on Palladino whereupon the magazine people cancelled their contract with Carrington on the ground that Davis had put a "frost" on their plans. As a result Carrington threatened the *Times* with a suit for a hundred thousand dollars damage. The threat was dropped after Palladino's complete exposure and her refusal to go to the Times Building and win the two thousand dollar prize offered by Rinn. In all the séances conducted by Carrington the program was the same and the phenomena of precisely the same character as in the one which resulted in Palladino's complete exposure. The value of Mr. Carrington's opinion as evidence may be judged from excerpts from an article in *McClure's Magazine* for October, 1909. In this article he answers his own question "Does Eusapia Deceive Her Investigators?" by saying:

"Well do I know the condition of mind induced by one or two séances with Eusapia. All one's previous experience is refuted, and the mind fails to grasp the facts or to accept them as real. It is incapable of absorbing them. It requires several séances before one is convinced of the reality of the phenomena, and of the fact that one's observation is not mistaken. Personally, I had to witness six séances before I was irrevocably and finally convinced of the reality of the fact. Before that, although I was quite unable to explain what I saw by any theory of fraud or trickery, and although I was quite certain the facts were not due to hallucination, still I could not believe them. I felt that there must be a loophole somewhere; and I know that my colleagues felt exactly as I did. But at the sixth séance when I was controlling the medium myself, in such a manner that I was quite sure as to the whereabouts of her whole body, and when it was, moreover, light enough to see the whole outline of her body clearly,--when, in spite of this, phenomena continued to take place all around us in the most bewildering manner and under the most perfect test conditions, I felt that there was no more to be said; certainty had been achieved; and from the sixth séance onward, and forever after, I shall remain as certain that these phenomena are facts, and form a part-- however sporadic--of nature, as I am that I write this article."

The foregoing shows how vacillating the mind of Mr. Carrington was at the time he was conducting the Palladino séances, and when after a personal contest with the medium he stated his conviction he should have known he was talking the impossible; that no one man could control Palladino beyond the possibility of fraud and at the same time detect her false moves. In the same article he writes:

"I may remark just here that this medium has been caught in trickery from time to time, and will almost invariably resort to it unless she is prevented from doing so by the rigidity of the control (that is, the degree of certainty obtained in holding her hands and feet). The reason for this is that Eusapia, knowing that the production of genuine phenomena will exhaust her nervous forces, resorts to this simpler method, if her sitters are sufficiently credulous to allow it, in order to save herself from the painful after effects of a genuine séance. Nearly every investigator has at one time or another discovered this fraud, which is petty, and more or less obvious to any careful investigator, and consists in the substitution of one hand for two, and in the production of phenomena with the remaining free hand. If, however, sufficient precautions are taken, it is a comparatively easy matter to frustrate her attempts at fraud; and when this is done so-called genuine phenomena are produced. Many of the phenomena are so incredible that by far the simplest explanation is that fraud has been operative in their production; but I can say positively (and I believe the records will show this) that fraud was quite impossible throughout our séances, not only because of the nature of our control of the medium, which was rigidly exacting, but because of the abundance of light. Any theory based upon the supposition that confederates were employed is absolutely discounted: first, because the séances were held in our own locked rooms in the hotel; and secondly, because throughout the séances it was light enough for us to see the whole room and its occupants. It is hardly necessary to add that we examined the cabinet, the table, instruments, and all articles of furniture, both before and after each séance."

This last seems just as a manager might be expected to talk of the merit of his own show. A salesman should not decry his wares.

There is no question but what Palladino was given to fraud.[55] In personal conversations with Hon. Everard Feilding, W. W. Baggally, E. J. Dingwall and Hereward Carrington, each stated positively that they had caught her cheating and that they knew her to be a fraud. They claimed that toward the end of her career she lost her occult power and at such times as the Spirits failed her she would resort to trickery rather than confess failure. They believed her a genuine medium because of the things which she did under test conditions which they could not explain, their knowledge of fraud being overpowered, apparently, by a willingness to believe in the impossible simply because they were not able to solve the problem.

If you go to a department store and ask for a well advertised bit of merchandise and when you get home you find the clerk has substituted "something just as good" you either report the clerk to the management or else you do not patronize the store again; if you go to a tailor and he sells you an "all-wool" suit and you find that most of the "wool" grew on cotton plants you pass that store by when you are ready to buy another suit; if you catch your best friend cheating at cards you refuse to play with him again ever and a life-time friendship is broken up. But Palladino cheated at Cambridge, she cheated in l'Aguelas, and she cheated in New York and yet each time that she was caught cheating the Spiritualists upheld her, excused her, and forgave her. Truly their logic sometimes borders on the humorous.

F. W. H. Myers wrote in "Borderland" in 1896:

"These frauds were practiced in and out of the real, or alleged, trance and were so skillfully executed that the poor woman must have practiced them long and carefully."

Palladino is summed up in these few lines. My opinion is that Palladino in her crafty prime may have possessed the agility and abundant skill in misdirection together with sufficient energy and nerve to bamboozle[56] her scientific and otherwise astute committeemen, but as time demanded its

---

[55] In an interview with Walter Littlefield, a noted journalist, Palladino revealed three methods by which she was able to employ substitution in regard to hands at the table, four in regard to foot substitution, half a dozen methods of table levitation, several ways of producing knocks, two ways in which she produced the illusion of a current of air coming from her forehead. She told him that she was not annoyed when caught practicing tricks, nor did she deny their use when caught. She said to him, *"All mediums indulge in tricks—all."* She also told him that she was a good Catholic, went to Mass, made her confession, and said she hated to hear people talk about "super-normal," or "supernatural" phenomena. The famous "current of air from the forehead" which Mr. Littlefield mentions was simply her breath blown with force and diverted by her under lip.

[56] I am informed on good authority that Eusapia threw her legs into the laps of her male sitters! That she placed her head upon their shoulders, and did various other things calculated to confuse and muddle men, all of which was

toll she probably lost her vim and nerve and became unable to present her "performances" with the success that attended her earlier demonstrations.

My old friend, John William Sargent, who died on September 24, 1920, was one of the committee which finally dethroned Palladino, and I believe it no more than just that the last word of this chapter should be said by him.

"Eusapia Palladino is dead and I have little doubt that she departed hence without forgiving me for the part I took in spoiling her business in America by assisting in the exposure of her little bag of tricks. It is an open question, however, whether the exposure of her trickery, or in fact of any of the class of sensation mongers to which she belonged, ever turned a soul from belief in Spiritism; some of the leading newspapers, in commenting on her death, show that in spite of the complete exposure of her methods, there still remains in the minds of many intelligent people the conviction that she was far from an impostor. I cannot understand how any reasonable person could see in this woman anything more than a fairly clever charlatan, whose success was due more to the credulity of her audiences than the skill of her performances. What did all her exposures amount to? Those who believed have continued to believe, and in spite of the old saw, 'Truth is mighty and must prevail,' the name of Eusapia Palladino will be on the lips of men long, long after her exposers are forgotten dust."

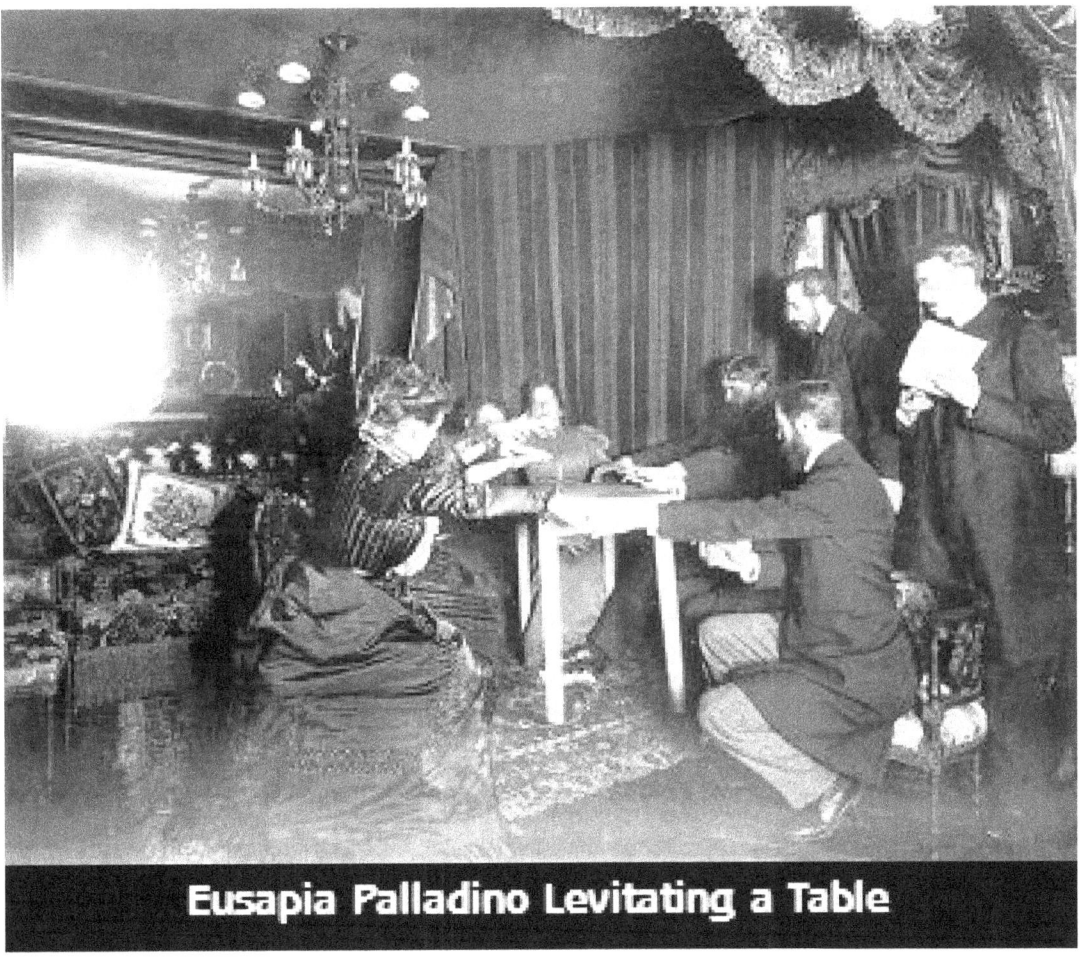

Eusapia Palladino Levitating a Table

---

explained on the theory of "hysteria." In her younger days Eusapia was a buxom woman and it is not strange that a lot of old scientists were badly flabbergasted by such conduct.

An Expose By Sir Arthur Conan Doyle

Eusapia Palladino

Eusapia Palladino Levitating a Mandoline

Houdini & His Ladder Escape

Eira Davenport and Harry Houdini

Houdini Escape Artist

Chapter 5
Ann O'delia Diss Debar

THE coming and going of Ann O'Delia Diss Debar are mysteries for there is no record of her birth and no trace of her death, but the "in between time" furnished material enough for an entire book rather than a single chapter, and gave her sufficient opportunity to have it said of her that she was "one of the most extraordinary fake mediums and mystery swindlers the world has ever known." Some even have classed her among the ten most prominent and dangerous female criminals of the world, and her repertoire is claimed to have run the full gamut from petty confidence games to elaborately contrived schemes aimed at the magnates of Wall Street. According to report she did not hesitate to victimize the innocent and the mentally unsound and left behind her a trail of sorrow, depleted pocket-books, and impaired morals that has seldom been equaled. Like many master criminals she escaped punishment for a time but in the end fell into the toils of the law and served time both here and in England. The marvellous tact with which she devoted her great powers to the purposes of self aggrandizement and profit is without parallel, and for cunning knavery, Cagliostro, by comparison, seems to have been an amateur. It is alleged that her crimes ranged from the smallest to the largest with morals as low as one can imagine in a human being while, worst of all, she flaunted this viciousness openly, making no effort whatever to cloak her degeneracy.

Nevertheless her name stands among the half score or more in the front ranks of the history of Spiritualism and with Daniel Dunglas Home shares the palm for the successful manipulation of big schemes. It was not unusual for her to make deals that ran into the hundreds of thousands of dollars and though the two were early in the mediumistic field, I believe that to this day they have had no peer in this respect. Possibly all other mediums combined could not have aggregated the amount of money obtained by these two.

Whether Home outbids Diss Debar for preeminence as to gain it is hard to say but it is certain that he "could not hold a candle" to her versatility. Both appear to have had the advantage of being scholastic, and well versed in historic lore and the classics, which gave them great prestige with cultured people, opening the doors to the social life of the "upper-ten," and bringing within their reach people of wealth as well as scholars and scientists, all of whom were apparently perfectly willing to be deceived, and to unwittingly aid in making the careers of these two adventurers "howling successes" up to the time of their undoing in the courts.

Unlike Home, who never in all the vicissitudes of his career denied his personality, Diss Debar as frequently as she changed her base of operations seems to have changed her name and her ancestry. Once in the heyday of her career she gave a series of interviews claiming to be the daughter of King Louis I of Bavaria and Lola Montez, a Spanish-Irish dancer who had a spectacular and adventurous career which covered Europe in its course, reached to the Russian Court and later America. It is supposed that Diss Debar was the daughter of a political refugee by the name of Salomen who settled in Kentucky and that she was born in 1849 although there is no documentary proof of it. According to the story she was named Editha and as she grew up became known as a wayward child bent on doing what she should not and perfectly callous to all restraining influence of parental affection. "At times her waywardness took such extraordinary turns that her parents thought she was not entirely sane and sought the advice of a doctor, who said she was really a sort of victim to an unholy passion, but that she would grow out of her failing as she grew older," a prophecy which never came true.

When Editha Salomen became of age she left home and for several years her father lost all track of her. Later, to his great astonishment, he discovered her settled in Baltimore, moving among the best of society, and posing as a member of European aristocracy. As the "Countess Landsfeldt and Baroness Rosenthal" of the peerage of Bavaria she availed herself of all the privileges which members of nobility enjoyed in the Republic, was courted by American youth and found American women "only too delighted to be led by a Countess."

Where the Kentucky girl with her peculiar temperament and characteristics could possibly have secured the education and knowledge which she displayed through all her exploits I am at a loss to understand. She must have inherited a liberal share of shrewdness, together with a fancy for reading ancient history, and at an early age realized that although not handsome she possessed some charm of personality which attracted attention and which enabled her to pose successfully as a member of the nobility.

It is said that in this role Editha had no difficulty in raising funds. It was easy to encourage a prosperous young man into a love trap and make him believe she would soon marry him. "Then one day she would find that she had to pay a large sum of money to meet a necessary obligation, that her careless bankers in Bavaria had failed to remit a few hundred thousand dollars, on account of which she most reluctantly accepted temporary relief from the rich suitor. She took as much as she dared and thereafter cut him." In this way she managed to cheat the youth of Baltimore out of about a quarter of a million dollars. She gave herself up to luxury and extravagance; took freely to smoking cigarettes impregnated with opium and was soon landed in Bellevue Hospital suffering from "acute nervous exhaustion."

One day, just as she was nearly cured, she sprang out of bed, stabbed an attendant and attempted to kill her doctor, and several persons were seriously wounded before she was secured. As a result she was sent to the asylum for the insane on Ward's Island, where she was detained for a year, during which time she showed no traces of insanity and it was concluded that her attempt at murder was premeditated; but as she had been committed as insane with no evidence to controvert it the law was powerless and she was released.

Her next venture was in the field of hypnotism, where she was an adept, but now known as Mrs. Messant and a widow, for though a young doctor, either through fear or fondness, had married her soon after her discharge from Ward's Island, he had survived the marriage less than a year. As "one can always find fools if one really looks for them" she had no difficulty in surrounding herself with dupes but as the widow of an obscure doctor was not *persona grata* in the circles of high society where the highest paying fools are to be found she set to work to find an entree. Her search was not for long. Soon she discovered a certain General Diss Debar; a man without money or "mind of his own" but he filled her need, easily yielded to her cajoleries and presently Editha Salomen, Countess Landsfeldt, Baroness Rosenthal, Messant became Ann O'Delia Diss Debar. As the wife of a general, society smiled on her again and she lived in comfort. The rich courted "hypnotism and general humbug and the wily woman was equal to the requirement." As time went on, however, she began to squander the money that flowed into her coffers. A couple of children were born to her. People began to tire of hypnotism, her income waned, and it became necessary for her to set her wits to work and cast her net for a fresh victim.

This proved to be Luther R. Marsh, a brilliant and wealthy lawyer of New York City. Mr. Marsh was an ideal subject for the hypnotizer's attention. Though a learned lawyer he was not free from superstition and his wife had died but a short time before he was discovered by Diss Debar. At an early opportunity she "received" messages from his spirit wife which the distinguished member of the bar accepted as genuine so gratefully and without question that the woman saw at once that she had opened up a new field with more and greater possibilities than she had ever worked before; she realized that she had gifts which fitted her to be a first class Spiritualistic medium. Nor was her judgment in error. The credulous lawyer proved an exceedingly easy mark. Very quickly she won his full confidence and it was not long before he invited her to share his hospitality at 166 Madison Avenue. There was no delay in her acceptance. With the owners' full consent the home was transformed into a Spiritualistic Temple in which Ann O'Delia Diss Debar was the high priestess. Soon it was evident that there were spirits in profusion and the new medium was able to produce any type of phenomena desired, even to spirit painting. The venture was a profound success and a flourishing business was developed with an upper-ten clientele in which Mr. Marsh became the chief and real victim.

Not only was Mr. Marsh mourning his wife but he had also lost a little daughter but a short time before and so when "Eva's" supposed spirit suggested to him that he make over his property at 166

Madison Avenue to Diss Debar the father was ready for the sacrifice.[57] The deeds were drawn and the transfer made but the medium was prevented from enjoying her booty by legal proceedings which vigilant relatives of Marsh instituted based on his mental condition.

Both Ann O'Delia Diss Debar and her husband, General Diss Debar, were arrested and held on bail for trial.[58] As not infrequently happens in such cases the litigation was long drawn out and much astonishing evidence produced.[59] When placed on the witness stand her first testimony demonstrated her character. A man by the name of Salomen had testified that he was her brother. She denied that he was and declared that he was a vile wretch who had come to her to borrow money. She admitted to an inspector afterwards that the man was her brother but that he would not dare go on the stand against her for she knew something about him that would blast him forever and would not hesitate for a second to tell it if she needed to.

Another indication of her character is furnished by the story that in choosing between two lawyers to represent her in court she not only inquired into their legal ability, but desired to know about their age and looks as well, finally deciding upon the younger and better looking.

She testified that all the trouble had been caused by Mr. Marsh giving her his house and in answer to a question as to why she did not get money from him instead of real estate she replied that she had tried to but that he was very mean with his cash. The last time she had gone to him for money he had refused it, offering her instead a deed of his property in Newport. This she had refused fearing it would get her into more trouble.

During the early part of the trial Diss Debar conceived the idea of consulting the spirit world in regard to her own course of action and soon after, on "the advice of Cicero and his colleagues in council of ten" she returned the deeds of the Madison Avenue property to Mr. Marsh.

One of the surprises of the trial was the calling by the prosecuting attorney of a professional illusionist, mesmerist, and conjuror, Carl Hertz, as a witness to prove by duplication that the tricks practiced on the unsuspecting Marsh by Diss Debar were simply applications of the ordinary laws of physics. This he succeeded in doing to the satisfaction of the court.

While Hertz was exhibiting "spirit message" reading on the stand Diss Debar did everything in her power to embarrass him but without success as he met every condition she suggested including some under which Diss Debar herself would have failed to "manifest." Mrs. Hertz had been her husband's assistant in reading the billets. Diss Debar proposed through her lawyer that she be allowed to take her place. Hertz readily consented. The Judge examined a fresh piece of paper and Hertz passed it to Diss Debar who deliberately tore it in two pieces and handing one of them back said to Hertz:

"I always mark mine; now let me see you do the trick with one of these pieces."

Hertz availed himself of the regular mediumistic subterfuge "unfavorable conditions" explaining that it was only a trick and being exhibited as such. To this Diss Debar retorted:

"I rest my honor upon its *all being done by Spiritual power* when I do it."

At this the court ordered her from the stand refusing to allow discussion along such lines. Later in the trial Hertz was recalled to the stand by Diss Debar's counsel and asked if he could produce the trick with Mr. Marsh as an assistant. He replied that he "could and would." From a newspaper

---

[57] See Appendix D.

[58] I have a full record of the proceedings in my reference file.

[59] In order to prove that fraud and trickery were the tools which had been used in fleecing the unwary, magicians were induced to appear in evidence, and on May 27, 1888, Alexander Hermann gave a public Demonstration at the Academy of Music in New York City for the purpose of duplicating the phenomena produced by Diss Debar and as an aid to the New York Press Club Fund.

The audience included many prominent people and notables including Col. Cockerell; Edward S. Stokes, of the Hoffman House; Joseph Howard; District Attorney Fellows; Ex-Judge Donohue; Lawyer Newcombe; Judge Hilton; *Luther R. Marsh;* and "Dr." Lawrence, one of the attaches of the Diss Debar Temple.

Professor Hermann read spirit messages, did table tipping, cabinet, light seance, and produced spook pictures, finishing with a dark seance of *ghostly* music and materializations.

account[60] we learn that excitement in the courtroom ran high while he proceeded with the trick. Diss Debar told Marsh to "mark the tablet."

The conditions were not favorable to the performance of a sleight-of-hand trick. Mr. Marsh and Mr. Hertz were less than two feet apart and people crowded around so close that the magician scarcely had room to move, and yet he succeeded completely in deceiving Mr. Marsh. When Hertz handed the tablet to Mr. Marsh he calmly said:

"If you wish to tear a corner off the tablet so as to identify it, I have no objections."

Mr. Marsh tore the corner off the tablet, nevertheless he was completely tricked, and he so admitted to the court.

Nothing could show more clearly the methods used by mediums than the following account, written by Hertz himself, of the means which he used in the demonstration described above. The letter was in response to one of mine in which I asked him to let me know the method he used as I thought it should be put in this record.

8 Hyde Park Mansions, London, N. W. July 16, 1923.

Dear Houdini:

I am in receipt of yours, with reference to the manner in which I manipulated the paper to fool Mme. Diss Debar. I worked it as follows: When she was in the witness box, I showed the jury and Mrs. Diss Debar a half sheet of plain white note paper with nothing on it. I then told her to examine it and fold it four times (I had a duplicate piece with a communication written on it palmed in my hand), when she handed it back to me, I quickly made the changes, and giving her the piece with the writing on it I told her to hold it against my forehead. She then stopped me and said: *"one moment please,* whenever I do this trick, *I let them mark the paper,"* and suiting the action to the word, she took the paper, and without opening it again, she tore a corner off the blank piece, but, as it was already changed it made no difference.

You will see, I took a big chance, but it came off. I had an idea she would do this, so I actually changed the papers before I should have done so in the ordinary way, and she was flabbergasted when she opened the paper and found a communication written upon it, and on the same piece of paper which she had marked.

The writing pad trick which I did in the witness box with Luther R. Marsh, I did as follows:--

The trick, if you remember, was to show a pad of about a hundred sheets of paper unwritten upon, and to wrap the pad up in a newspaper, and to allow Marsh to hold one end while she held the other. Then the sound of writing was heard as if some one was writing on the paper, and when the newspaper was opened every sheet in the pad was written upon.

I had two pads alike, one I had concealed under my waistcoat, and the other I gave to Marsh to examine; as I proceeded to wrap the pad up, under cover of the newspaper, I changed them, quickly drawing the pad from my waistcoat and leaving the other one in its place.

I then proceeded to wrap the pad up when Diss Debar shouted from her seat in the Court Room 'Don't let him fool you, mark it!' but as it was already changed, it did not matter so I let them tear a corner off.

I then let him hold one end, while I held the other, and amidst a great silence the sound of writing was heard, as if a pen was rapidly going over the paper, and I then told him to open the newspaper and look at the pad, when he found every sheet written upon.

I then showed the Court how I produced the sound of writing, by having the nail of my forefinger split, and simply scratching the newspaper underneath while I held it.

Kind regards to self and wife from both of us.

Yours sincerely,
(Signed) CARL HERTZ

---

[60] *New York Times,* April *21,* 1888,

Regardless of Carl Hertz's testimony and demonstration Mr. Marsh's belief in the genuineness of Spiritualistic phenomena was unshaken and remained so until the time of his death. Not only the extent of this belief and his mental condition, but his confidence in Diss Debar as well, are revealed in the following excerpt from the *New York Times's* account of the trial.

"A short communication from St. Paul was read by Mr. Howe (the Prosecuting Attorney) to the Court, and Mr. Marsh read a very long one from St. Peter. It required fifteen minutes and a half to read this communication, and Mr. Marsh said it had come in the tablet written in two minutes. Judge Cross and Luther Colby were in his study when it came. He knew that the tablet was blank before he and Mme. Diss Debar held it together in their hands.

"Mr. Howe asked Mr. Marsh if he really believed the communication was from St. Peter, the apostle, and Mr. Marsh replied that he knew it was.

" 'Then you still believe in it!' exclaimed Mr. Howe.

" 'I do,' was the firm reply, and the Spiritualistic element applauded vigorously. Mme. Diss Debar and Mr. Marsh both seemed pleased with this demonstration which the Court, however, stopped summarily."

Twelve ballots were taken by the jury before an agreement was reached due to the fact that one juror, evidently in sympathy with the accused, obstinately held out for acquittal. His reasons were as little logical as most Spiritualistic arguments and had no connection with the evidence. In fact the other jurors said that when they tried to talk evidence to him "he wouldn't have it, but hung to one line of thought, namely, that he believed Mrs. Diss Debar to be the daughter of Lola Montez and that a woman born out of wedlock was just as much entitled to consideration as one who was born in wedlock, and as Mrs. Ann O'Delia Diss Debar claimed all the honors of illegitimacy, he was on her side for keeps."

Finally after a long wrangle and with the prospect of being locked in a jury room over Sunday, an arrangement was reached whereby a verdict of guilty was to be brought in but with a recommendation for clemency. This was done and Diss Debar and her husband were sent to Blackwell's Island for six months.[61]

When she was released she disappeared from America only to reappear after a little in London, England, where under the names of Laura and Theodore Jackson she and her husband soon found themselves in trouble for starting an exceptionally immoral cult[62] which they called a "Theocratic Unity."[63] She was sentenced in December, 1901, to seven years of penal servitude in Aylesbury Prison. Even here her persuasive powers found a use for it is said that she gained favor because of the marvellous influence which she had over the refractory element which the officers in charge had difficulty in keeping in subjection. At any rate she was released after serving five years, "having obtained the maximum reduction of sentence for good behavior."[64]

Out in the world again she ventured into vaudeville and afterwards burlesque but in these roles she was a complete failure. Later she came back to America and was next heard of in Chicago as

---

[61] *New York World,* June 18, 1888.

[62] When the London press was full of sensational stories following the arrest of Laura and Theodore Jackson, Carl Hertz, on picking up his paper one morning, was astonished to recognize the woman who had lured young girls into joining her immoral cult as Ann O'Delia Diss Debar, with whom he had measured swords at the Marsh trial. He got in touch with Scotland Yard immediately and gave it all the information he had regarding Diss Debar's connection with fraud activities.

[63] "Miss Croisdale, who was one of the victims, testified that she had been initiated into the 'Theocratic Unity,' the sect which the Jacksons claimed to head, with a rope fastened about her; passes were made over her, she said, with a lamp, water and a saw: Jackson told her that he was Christ re-incarnated. Miss Croisdale then described the oath in which she swore she would allow no one else to hypnotize her and she would keep all the secrets under the penalty of 'submitting myself to a deadly and hostile current of will set in motion by the Chief of the order, with which I would be slain or paralyzed without visible weapons, as if blasted by lightning.' Mrs. Jackson (or Diss Debar) looked as if she wished to carry out the threat on the spot. Miss Croisdale further testified that Theodore had outraged her in his wife's presence. Jackson declared he was physically incapable and demanded a doctor's examination to prove his statement."—Dispatch from the *London Times* in the *New York Sun,* October 11, 1901.

[64] *Chicago Daily Tribune,* August 14, 1906.

Vera Ava. She succeeded in marrying a wealthy man there but before long was in more difficulties in connection with the pursuit of spookery and sentenced to the Joliet Penitentiary for two years.[65] Once more she appeared--in New Orleans as the Baroness Rosenthal--then in 1909 this creature, who for more than a quarter of a century had been swaying men of prominence and women of society, dropped out of sight and for the last fifteen years nothing has been known about her.[66]

In mothering this immoral woman, Spiritualism is guilty of the grossest misconduct and proves conclusively that she does not protect her own from the wiles and immorality of mediums even though they are found guilty of base criminality by the courts. Were I permitted to go into detail I could tell tales of Diss Debar that would shock even the worst roue of the Montmartre. Suffice to say that her crimes were not so much crimes of gain as they were insults to the decency and morality of the community.

Ann O'Delia Diss Debar's reputation [67] was such that she will go down in history as one of the great criminals. She was no credit to Spiritualism; she was no credit to any people, she was no credit to any country--she was one of these moral misfits which every once in awhile seem to find their way into the world. Better far had she died at birth than to have lived and spread the evil she did.

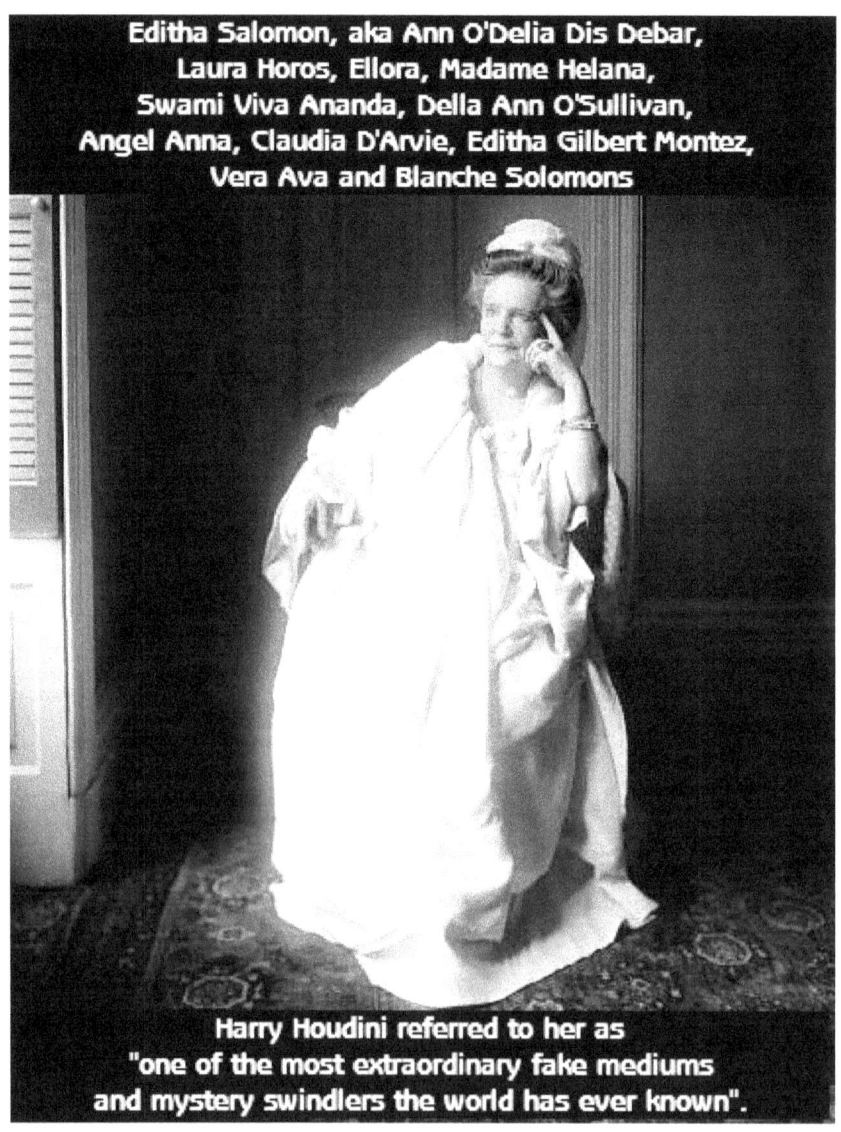

[65] New *York Sun,* October 11, 1901

[66] If alive she is now (1924) seventy-five years old.

[67] See Appendix E for Police Record.

Chapter 6
Dr. Slade and His Spirit Slates

SLATE writing was an especially fortunate "find" for mediums. Its results were obtained in full light and the whole thing seemed so simple and direct that apparently there was nothing to investigate and comparatively speaking there were no blank séances. Such success led to carelessness and exposures followed, so numerous and complete that it is quite unnecessary to list them all here.[68] Every once in a while though some medium still takes a chance when opportunity offers and gives a test to especially gullible sitters, but to-day no medium with any pretentions to "class" would think of anything so "common" as slate writing in its old form. Spirit slates are now listed in the catalogues of houses dealing in conjuring apparatus and the fraud mediums who formerly made use of them are employing the safer and easier swindles of automatic writing, trance or trumpet messages, and the "ouija board."

The infinite grafting possibilities of the Spirit slates seem to have been overlooked until adopted and put into usable form by Dr. Henry Slade,[69] a man who had acquired an unenviable reputation in New York City, but it is extremely doubtful if the present generation would have known anything about Dr. Slade had the perpetuation of his name been left to the quality of his mediumship, for he was only one of a large number of conjuring fakirs who bamboozled the credulous of his day. However, he was brought into the limelight on two notable occasions: first by being exposed and criminally prosecuted in London; and second when poor old Professor Zollner, a noted German astronomer and physicist, "fell" for his simple conjuring and fell so hard that he made Slade the hero of his great (?) work, "Transcendental Physics."

Like D. D. Home, and many others, after making a reputation in America, Slade jumped over to London, for England's arms seem ever open for the reception of mediums who have made good here and if a medium escapes the toils of American investigators he has little to fear from willing believers on the other side of the Atlantic, though as a matter of fact several were sent to jail there. Slade reached England in July, 1876, and began to hold sittings at once, and was soon "cleaning up" in fine shape. The late John Nevil Maskelyne, the great English magician, told me that:

"Crowds of people rushed to witness the phenomena (?) paying one guinea each for a sitting lasting but a few minutes. You would think they were giving gold guineas away. The 'Doctor' must have netted some hundreds of pounds weekly which in those days was rated a high sum of money for an individual 'performer.'"

Then, just as things were going so nicely for Slade there came a sudden crash, for which two men were responsible; Professor Ray Lankester (now Sir Ray Lankester) and Dr. Horatio Donkin (now Sir Horatio Donkin). These men applied certain effective methods of scrutiny to Slade's exhibitions which resulted in his arrest. The trial created a big sensation, not only in Spiritual circles, but throughout the civilized world, and the Bow Street Court was the most popular show in London for several days; the "top-liner" being J. N. Maskelyne, the magician, who performed all of Slade's tricks in the witness box.

Slade was convicted and sentenced to three months at hard labor. An appeal was taken and the decision quashed on account of a flaw in the indictment. While Sir Lankester was procuring new

---

[68] If the reader cares to look the matter up I would refer him to Podmore's "Modern Spiritualism," Vol. II, pages 204 and 221; also to the story of Dr. Slade in the same volume; to the proceedings of the American S. P. R., Vol. II, part I, pages 17, 36-59; to Abbot's, "Behind the Scenes with Mediums," pages 114 to 192; to "Revelations of a Spirit Medium," page 121-157; to "Bottom Facts," pages 143-159; to the Report of the Seybert Commission; "Spirit Slate Writing," by Wm. E. Robinson, and newspaper exposures without number.

[69] According to "The Medium and Daybreak," October 6, 1876, Slade *"discovered"* the phenomena of slate-writing while experimenting at the private house of Mr. Gardiner Knapp, New Albany, Indiana, where Slade was visiting.

summonses for Slade and his manager, Simmons, they both skipped across the channel into France, thus closing the doors of England against Slade for all time as he never dared to set foot on her unfriendly shores again. He made ready for a Paris performance but a friend of Sir Lankester's sent an account of the court proceedings to the Paris press so the French people had the whole story before Slade was able to begin.

While touring Europe in 1920 I had the pleasure of meeting Sir Ray Lankester and hearing from him an account of Dr. Slade's undoing. Both he and Donkin were physicians. They had been laying their plans to expose two other mediums, Herne and Williams, but Slade's unexpected arrival in London changed these plans and instead they plotted the séance which proved to be Slade's downfall. Donkin was away from London at the time but Sir Lankester wired him and while waiting for his return attended one of Slade's séances. He pretended to Slade that he came to see if the Spirits would write a message on the slates if he held them himself. Slade assured him that they would and arrangements were made for a second sitting. Before Sir Lankester left Slade asked him if he had been in communication with any departed relatives.

"No, but I have an Uncle John," Sir Lankester replied.

Consequently at the second sitting the following message was received:

"I am glad to see you here again.--John." "But have you an Uncle John?" I asked. "No, Houdini," he replied smiling, "that is why everyone laughed in the courtroom at the time of the trial. You see, Slade thought I was a firm believer, and I allowed him to distract my attention. He said to me 'You have a great deal of mediumistic power about you. I see them over you behind your head.' "

As he said this Sir Lankester raised his head with seeming credulity acting the part splendidly.

"What made you suspect Slade?" I asked him. "At the first séance I noticed the tendons move on Slade's wrist as he held his hand outstretched under the table," Sir Lankester replied, "and while making a number of suspicious moves he scratched the slates a number of times with his finger nail to simulate the noise made by a slate pencil when writing on a slate."

On the return of Sir Donkin it was arranged that he and Sir Lankester should attend a séance together and that Sir Donkin was to watch for the "suspicious move" and when he saw it signal Sir Lankester. Everything worked as planned. On receiving the agreed signal from Donkin, Lankester seized the slate containing the finished message proving that a skillful exchange of slates had been made by Slade and this was the *real evidence which caused the downfall of Henry Slade* in England.

Blocked in Paris from working his tricks because of the publication of an account of his exposure in England Slade seems to have gone to Germany for it was during the next year, 1877, that he so successfully deluded Professor Zollner. "Zollner" is one of the names on which Spiritualistic enthusiasts bank most heavily for proof of their claims. Even Sir Arthur Conan Doyle to this day quotes Zollner as indisputable authority. Nevertheless Zollner is discredited by Mr. George S. Fullerton, Secretary of the Seybert Commission. While in Germany Mr. Fullerton made a special business of investigating the value of this Zollner endorsement, and at the time all of the men who participated in the Slade investigation were alive with the exception of Zollner himself. Mr. Fuller-ton in the summary of his report to the Commission said:

"Thus it would appear that of the four eminent men whose names have made famous the investigation, there is reason to believe one, Zollner, was of unsound mind at the time, and anxious for experimental verification of an already accepted hypothesis; another, Fechner, was partially blind and *believed* because of Zollner's observation; a third, Scheibner, was also afflicted with defective vision and not entirely satisfied in his own mind with the phenomena; and a fourth, Weber, was advanced in age, and did not even recognize the disabilities of his associates. None of the men named had any previous experience or knowledge of the possibilities of deception."

The Seybert Commission, in 1884, seems to have made the first systematic, organized effort to fathom the so-called phenomena of Spiritualism, and this Commission sent for Slade, who was then operating in New York, and had him give a number of séances under their observation, but in spite of the fact that Slade gave the Commission a personal letter thanking them for their courtesies and expressing his willingness to sit with them again, the Commission considered his work fraudulent throughout.

At a very early stage of the sittings, the Commission noticed two kinds of communications. Those in answer to questions were slovenly written, often illegible, while those which came as voluntary contributions from the Spirits, were more carefully written, even to punctuation. It was very evident that this writing on the slates had been prepared previous to the sitting, while that written under the restraint of observation was the crude scrawl, abrupt in composition, and often almost or quite illegible. It was evident that where the nicely written communications were used an exchange of slates had been effected, whereas the other writing was the result of such skill as could be brought to bear without detection under the unfavorable conditions. It was also noticed that all of the long messages most suspiciously resembled the handwriting of the medium. Every test to which Slade submitted proved to be transparent to the Commission and some of his efforts to mystify it were referred to as:

"Several little tricks which he imputed to Spiritual agency, but which were almost puerile in the simplicity of their legerdemain, and which have been repeated with perfect success by one of our number."

After all the slate-writing mediums who came in answer to an advertisement broadcasted by the Seybert Commission had been examined by it, the acting Chairman of the Commission, Mr. Horace Howard Furness, invited the late Harry Kellar to exhibit his slate-writing skill before it, not with any claim to supernatural phenomena but as a magician openly admitting his purpose to baffle by purely natural means. Mr. Kellar submitted to a series of tests far more complicated and difficult of execution than any produced by Slade or any other medium; nevertheless the Commission was unable to detect his methods and admitted itself completely baffled.

Mr. Kellar told me that when Mr. Furness, and Coleman Sellers, another member of the Commission who was himself an amateur entertainer, applied to him for an exhibition of his skill as a slate-writer they expected him to do the stock tricks of Slade. But someone tipped Kellar off that Sellers had told the members of the Commission what Kellar was to do and his probable method of doing it and for them to watch out for his *modus operandi*. So, not to be "caught napping," Kellar, like the skillful mystifier that he was, determined to out-do Slade and beat Sellers. As he told me about it he laughed heartily, saying:

"If you could have seen Mr. Sellers' face at the time of the unfolding of the mystery, it would have done your heart good."

When Kellar arrived for the demonstration he insisted that the Commission furnish its own slates, so a boy was sent out who brought back about a dozen of various kinds. Then all sat down around the table with hands resting, palm down, on its top. The Commission opened the sitting by writing questions on the slates. Kellar held them under the table with the thumb on top and when he withdrew them in a few moments they had answers to the questions written in a clear round hand. The questions gradually became longer and longer, but the replies kept pace with them, sometimes covering a whole side of the slate. Although the slates were all different and could not possibly be mistaken for one another, the Commission began to put identifying marks on them. Once no pencil was put on the top of the slate but the reply came just the same. This fact was commented upon and Kellar replied:

"Oh, my Spirits can write *without* pencils," a statement which puzzled the members of the Commission all the more.

Finally the magician asked them to write a question on a slate and cover it with another, placing the pencil between the two. Even this did not bother the "Spirits," for when the slates were returned, both sides were found covered with writing.

The following extract from the Preliminary Report of the Seybert Commission, originally published in 1887, describes this performance of Harry Kellar before members of the Commission and shows the impression which it made on them.

"An eminent professional juggler performed, in the presence of three of our Commission, some independent slate-writing far more remarkable than any of which we have witnessed with mediums. In broad daylight, a slate perfectly clean on both sides, was, with a small fragment of slate pencil, held under a leaf of a small, ordinary table, around which we were seated; the fingers of the juggler's hand pressed the slate tight against the underside of the leaf, while the thumb completed the pressure and remained in full view clasping the leaf of the table. Our eyes never for the fraction of a second lost sight of that thumb; it never moved; and yet in a few minutes the slate was produced, covered with writing. Messages were there, and still are there, for we preserved the slate, written in French, Spanish, Dutch, Chinese, Japanese, Gujorati, and ending with *'ich bin ein Geist, und lieb, mein Lagerbier.'* For one of our number the juggler subsequently repeated the trick and revealed its every detail."

The method which Kellar used, and which he described to me, was this. With the consent of the owner of the hotel, whom he agreed to pay for any damage, he had a small trap made in the floor of the room, about as large as a hot air register, with the necessary means of opening and closing it. A plush rug with rectangular designs was placed over this trap, and one of the designs, which was just the size of the trap, was cut out with a razor, these cuts being imperceptible. The piece of rug was glued firmly to the top of the trap. In addition to these preparations, Kellar bought a specimen of every variety of slate to be found in the downtown section of Philadelphia.

When the time for the "séance" arrived, Barney, Kellar's clever young assistant, was seated on a platform in the room underneath the trap with the assortment of slates by his side. As soon as the Commission was seated around the table he opened the trap and could then hear all that was said in the room above. When the exhibition commenced he simply took the slate Kellar put under the table leaf, selected one from his assortment to match it, wrote on it the answer, and then slipped it under Kellar's fingers. In the case of a marked slate he used that instead of a duplicate. Of course it was perfectly easy for Kellar to do his part without removing his thumb from the top of the table.

"A fake, pure and simple, you will say," Kellar remarked to me, and then added, "but that's what all Spiritualistic manifestations are."

In point of time John W. Truesdell was probably the first exposer of Slade as he investigated him as early as 1872, but the results of his investigation were not made public until he published his book, "Bottom Facts," in 1883. In this book he tells of setting a trap for Slade and proving that he substituted slates.

As Sam Johnson of Rome, N. Y., Truesdell arranged for a séance with Slade. Knowing that his overcoat would be searched, he left it hanging on the hall rack with an unsealed letter in the pocket and while waiting in the Spirit room he made the most of his opportunity to look around. Under the sideboard he found a slate with a message written on the lower side which read:

"We are happy to meet you in this atmosphere of Spirit research. You are now summoned by many anxious friends in the Spirit life, who desire to communicate with you, but who cannot until they learn more of the laws which govern their actions. If you will come here often, your Spirit friends will soon be able to identify themselves and to communicate with you as on earth life.

"Allie."

In a bold hand Truesdale added:

"Henry, look out for this fellow. He is up to snuff.

"Alcinda."

This was the name of Slade's deceased wife, a fact which Truesdell happened to know. He replaced the slate as he had found it. Slade presently appeared and the séance began with the general phenomena of moving chairs, etc., preceding the slate-writing. When the name "Mary Johnson" appeared plainly written on the slate Slade said it was Truesdell's sister. Upon being told that this was incorrect, Slade, pretending to change the light, drew the table over by the sideboard. As usual he *lost control* of the slate, letting it fall to the floor, and as he stooped over to pick it up took the prepared one instead. When he read the two messages he became livid with rage and turning to Truesdell demanded to know what it meant and who had been meddling with the slate.

"Spirits," was Truesdell's reply.

There were a few tense seconds and then the séance continued serenely.

I was too young in Slade's time to seek an audience with him but I have the good fortune to know Mr. Frederick E. Powell, a prominent magician and a member of the Society of American Magicians.

He is one of the very few persons now living who had séances with Slade and with his permission I quote the following description of his experiences with Slade.

"In the Autumn of 1881 or 82, Henry Slade, the famous Spirit medium, came to Philadelphia and took quarters at the Colonade Hotel, where he opened a room, in which to hold séances. At that time I was instructor of Mathematics in the Pennsylvania Military College at Chester, Pa. Reading the announcement of Slade's séances in a Philadelphia paper, I wrote to him, and made an appointment for myself and Capt. R. K. Carter, to be present at one of them. Capt. Carter was at that time our instructor in Civil Engineering. Reaching the Colonade at the appointed time, we were ushered into Slade's presence, in a room, bare of furniture, save a rather long table and several chairs, placed in the center of the room, while at the side and just back of where Slade was to sit, was a smaller table on which were piled a number of ordinary looking school slates, of various sizes. The center table had no cloth on it. Several small articles were on the mantelpiece, such as a smoker might use, viz.: a match box, etc.

"According to my recollection, Slade was rather tall and slim, and of an ingratiating presence. He was expecting us and at once placed me at a long table.

"The séance began, with Slade holding two slates of rather large size, and showing all their surfaces devoid of writing, placed them on the top of the table, and while rubbing their surfaces kept up a running fire of conversation. He then told us to place our hands on the table as near the center as possible with our little fingers touching. Slade placed the slates together, and after a moment or two separated them, saying he had forgotten to put a piece of pencil between. This he did, and holding them together placed them under the table with one hand, while he placed the other on the table so that his fingers touched our hands. This position was held for several minutes, when he said he would see if he had gotten any results. Bringing the slates from under the table he laid them on top and after a moment told Capt. Carter to look at them. Following this direction, Capt. Carter separated them, when one was found to have its entire surface covered with writing. This message, according to Slade, came from a man who had just died. (Notice of the man's death had been published in the morning paper.) The message was signed with the full name, but as neither Capt. Carter nor I knew the man, we could not affirm or deny the correctness of the handwriting, nor the truth of the signature.

"Capt. Carter asked Slade if he might copy the message, but Slade demurred, saying he did not know if the Spirits would like the message copied. I found it difficult to account for the reticence of the Spirit or Spirits since the message had been written for our information. Its purport was, as far as I can recall, that everything was very glorious in the Spirit World, and that he, the writer, was very happy. There was nothing in the message that was above the mentality of Slade or that was, in any sense, descriptive of Spirit Life. All was vague and unsatisfactory, where real information was desired.

"During this demonstration and indeed throughout the entire séance, Slade sat sidewise to the table, his left hand resting generally on its top and his right hand free. Several short messages were next produced on a small slate held by Slade, under the table, and out of sight, a short piece of slate pencil always being placed on the upper surface of the slate. Two points were made very emphatic by Slade. First, that the piece of pencil was always found just at the end of the last word of the message, and second, that the messages were found on the upper side of the slate, which according to Slade was held close against the under surface of the table top. However, as we could not see the slate when placed under the table, since we were reaching as far as we could to get our hands on the center of its top, and the slate was only shown to us when being brought from under its surface, it would have been an easy thing to lower the slate after placing it under the table and writing with a single finger of Slade's right hand, then bringing the slate to the under surface of the table, bring it slowly into sight.

"Once when the small slate was laid on top of the table the sound of writing was distinctly heard. During this time Slade had both hands on the upper surface of the table and in full sight. This was quite startling at the time, but later I discovered how to produce this sound of writing myself and without the aid of Spirits.

"Once, while we were having our attention directed to a slate held by Slade, the unoccupied chair on the side opposite to Slade and almost at the side of Capt. Carter, suddenly rose so that its seat struck the under side of the table, and then fell back with quite a thud.

"Another telling effect was carried out, when Slade gave me one of the small slates telling me to hold it under the table. I did so and felt it suddenly snatched from my hand (I was holding it with one hand, my other hand was on the top of the table) and carried with a scraping noise to the very end of the table and there it rose above the surface enough to disclose about a third or possibly a half its length. Then it was carried swiftly back and put in my hand.

"This concluded the first séance; when Slade, after a moment, said he thought that was all he could get at the time.

"On our second visit I need recount but three effects: First, difference in the method of obtaining writing on the large slates which began the séance, as in the first visit. Slade showed one slate and cleaned it thoroughly, then while keeping up a running fire of conversation, he casually reached to the small table, spoken of as having several piles of slates on it, and taking one as though at hazard, placed it flat on the big table. Rubbed its upper surface with his fingers, and placed a piece of pencil on it, held it under the table. After a pause he brought it out and taking the upper slate off the under, showed both surfaces without writing. He remarked that perhaps a different piece of pencil would be better and he placed another pencil on the upper surface of the top slate and then placed the lower slate over it, without at any time having shown its under surface. This surface was found covered with writing, the purport of which I do not now recall.

"The second variation of the first séance was when Slade asked me if I had ever seen the 'dematerialization of a solid object?' I said I had not, whereupon Slade took a small slate and, looking around as though to find a proper object for his test, picked up a match box from the mantelpiece, and put it on the upper surface of the slate rather close to where he would hold it. He then placed the slate and its superimposed object carefully under the table and after a moment brought out the slate, without the match box. I looked under the table but found nothing suspicious there.

"In a moment Slade replaced the slate under the table and on bringing it out, we saw the match box in its former place. This disappearance did not impress me greatly as I concluded the whole secret of dematerialization consisted in turning the slate over and holding the box in place by a finger, then after showing the surface empty, the slate was again turned over on being replaced under the table, and so the materialization of the box was realized.

"The last test was quite startling. Slade drew his chair close to mine, placed one of his hands on the chair back and the other on the table. My hands were resting on the table top. Suddenly I felt the chair rise, and I was tipped forward, but kept my balance by pushing back with my hands, which, as I have said, were resting on the table top. Then the force was quickly withdrawn and my chair and I came back to the floor with a grand thud. This concluded the second séance. I never saw Slade again."

Powell explains the levitation thus:

"When Slade drew his chair close to mine he crossed his legs and was thus enabled to bring his foot under the rung of my chair. The leg resting over the knee gave considerable leverage to the limb having a foot under the rung of my chair. Now he exerted the necessary strength by pressing upward with his foot, and holding the chair back with his hand while the other hand steadied the whole, by bearing against the table. Slade took his hand away from the back of my chair for the fraction of a second *before he released his foot.* I was thus naturally tilted forward and had to exert some force to keep myself from sliding off the chair. This effort kept me from seeing Slade free himself and get his limbs back to their normal position, viz., one hand on the table, and his feet and legs fairly under it. Slate was rather tall and, though somewhat slim, was very muscular. Of course I did not actually see Slade use his foot to do the lifting, but his position and all the circumstances surrounding the effect tend to prove my claim as to what I believe he did. Further, while I was far from being as strong as Slade, I succeeded in duplicating this 'Levitation' by the means I have described."

While searching for material about Slade I heard of an old medium living in Philadelphia by the name of Remigius Weiss, known as Remigius Albus, who had testified before the Seybert Commission regarding Slade's manipulation of the slates. I went over to Philadelphia to his home and there met the only man who had tangible evidence of Dr. Slade. This he thoroughly explained to me. I asked him why he had never exposed it to the world and he told me that he held back at first because of pity for Slade's condition and afterwards figured that if the fraud mediums and other potential criminals knew Slade's methods they might make use of the methods to gain control of poor human beings who wished to get in touch with loved ones who had passed away. He did not hesitate to give me full details and at my request wrote me a letter describing his experience with Slade. I quote it because I believe it to be the best expose ever written of Slade's slate writings.

"August 18, 1923.

"My dear Houdini:--

"Please accept, from me, this Lock-book, and the locked double-slate--as a small token of comradeship-- in combating Spiritualistic deception, popular superstition and Delusion.

"The book and the slate were my own. I put the lock and hinges on the slate, and prepared the book, and a number of other, different objects--(such as Professor Zollner had, when he, in his foolishness, was pleased to be deceived by Dr. Slade's Humbug).

"In order to gain the perfect, full confidence of Dr. Slade, and to have him give a séance in my home, and in order to counteract and overcome his explicit aversion as to do writing on or between a sealed slate or a locked book--I showed him letters from (two eminent and confiding Spiritist Authors)--Dr. Heinrich Tiedemann and Tiedemann's intimate friend Hudson Tuttle, promising to me that they would be present at that séance (at 148 Fairmount Avenue).

"Dr. Slade had handled and inspected that Book and Slate, during a Séance, at my residence (at 148 Fair-mount Avenue, Phila., Pa.), where I, together with Mr. Wertheimer (then a student of Jurisprudence)--and in presence of other witnesses (who were concealed and not seen, nor suspected by Dr. Slade, nor his 'Spirits') detected the manipulations, pedalations (foot, leg and other bodily movements)--and the general *modus operandi* of his simple Legerdemain at the séance. I had ready, for that séance, three different suites of Furniture, and thus, I found out that he would, or could, perform only at, or on a certain kind of plain, square or drop-leaf table and ordinary wooden chairs or cane seat chairs.

"Each person present at the Séance, wrote, *independent* of and *before* communicating with, the others, a personal, individual report of the Séance and signed it within the next few days. A day or two after, I put these papers in my pocket and also another paper I had prepared, to serve or use as Dr. Slade's confession to be signed by him. I went to the Girard Hotel, Room 24 (N. W. corner of 9th and Chestnut Streets, Philadelphia, Pa.), to have Dr. Slade arrested for obtaining money under false pretense,--or to get him to sign his own confession. There, in his room, No. 24, in the Girard Hotel, I had another, a different Séance, with Dr. Slade. He again carefully scrutinized the book and the slate, and then, holding the book under the table, secretly and carefully, attempted to open the lock, with a small key, hidden in his handkerchief.

"Dr. Slade and his pretended *'Spirits'* could not write in the book. While holding it under the table, he attempted to pull out of the book that thin, wooden, square frame, I had put there at the edges of the leaves so that the small piece of lead pencil could move about.--Then. in a similar attempt, he worked and perspired, on, and over the double slate. His 'Spirits' could not write in the locked slate and he could not open it.

"He said, 'The Spirits seem to be angry at your skepticism, it's no use to lose more time by trying. My guide don't want to have anything more to do with you.'

"Then upon Dr. Slade's request I unlocked the slate, and he wrote in the ordinary way, as writing generally is done in schools, two short sentences in the slate. Then he worked the sponge,[70] and turning the written on side downward, sleight-of-hand trick, tried to palm this off, claiming that this is 'Genuine, independent, Spirit slate writing.'

"Up to this time, November the 4th, 1882, I had shown to Dr. Slade friendly, joyful attentiveness. We talked about some of my newspaper articles I had published some weeks before he consented to give me a séance.

"In these newspapers I had described him (Dr. Slade) as 'The Modern Cagliostro, a celebrated necromancer, martyr or a charlatan, of radical free-religious proclivities, fine manners and a humistic, witty and forceful public lecturer and most powerful Spiritistic Medium, who again and again has been and is challenging exposures, and calling special attention to the fact that Dr. Slade has, in his lectures, and otherwise, again and again publicly announced that he is prepared to pay a thousand dollars ($1000.00) to any person that can prove that he (Dr. Slade) is a humbug, or that Dr. Slade's "manifestations" are trickery, legerdemain, humbug or in any way fraudulent.'

"Dr. Slade seemed to be pleased by my description. After some pleasant talk as to his appearance with Scientists, Kings and other royal persons and Rulers in Europe and his success as a lecturer and his way of living, he gave me his address, No. 221 West 22nd Street, *New York.*

"Then I asked Dr. Slade that we change 'roles,' he to take my place and be the Investigator,--and I to play the 'medium,' there, in his room, as an 'experiment.'

"Dr. Slade also said that if I could overcome my skepticism I would be a good 'psychic,' having 'mediumistic' gifts.

"I suggested that he should watch me carefully and then honestly tell me, as to the effect and 'impression' my 'manifestations' could (or would) be producing on his mind, and eventually on the outcome of the 'Spiritualistic, the Harmonial, Philosophy, or so-called, Scientific Religion of the Spiritists.'

"Then, to his consternation, I, earnestly, by actual demonstration, reproduced every one of his manifestations, *exactly* (and by the same *modus operandi,* as I, and my witnesses had seen and detected) as *Dr. Slade had performed them.* He asked me, how, and by what means we detected his 'occult' or secret mode, or 'process of wonder working' or miracle?--I mentioned that he had positively refused to try any 'experiment' on the first and second sets of tables and chairs, and had requested me to substitute them by a plain kitchen table and chairs of a certain construction.

"I told him that I had bored observation-holes in the *corners* of the panels (particularly so through the *lower* corners) in the parlor doors, the floor, ceiling and other places from where my concealed witnesses observed, and have seen exactly all the movements of his feet, hands, etc., *below* and above the table,--saw how he raised ('floated') Mr. Wertheimer sitting in the chair, saw how he (Dr. Slade) with his foot upset chairs, kicked a book (extending over the edge of the table) tossed a slate pencil from the edge of the table from a slate held under and at the edge of the table, etc, etc.

"Dr. Slade, now turned very pale and wiping off the thick perspiration from his forehead and face, said:-- 'Well, what of it?' and rashly asked:--'Where were Hudson Tuttle and Dr. H. Tiedemann?' I reminded him of the fact that they had sent an excuse, being unable (by reason of unforeseen circumstances) to attend that séance in my house.

"Then I sternly gave him the alternative:--That either he *sign his own confession* (as to the fact)--that he has (during the many years in his career as a professional Spirit medium and in everything he had professed or pretended to be 'genuine' Spiritistic or Spiritualistic) deceived and defrauded the public.--I read the confession to him and sternly demanded, 'Either you sign this or you will be put behind the bars.'--

---

[70] As he reached for the sponge, which had been placed purposely on centre of table, he held slate just below range of vision and with the reaching for sponge, twisted slate around, blank side on top and pretended to wipe off the sentence he had "read"—when in fact he had written something entirely different.

SKETCH SHOWING SLADE'S SEAT AT THE TABLE, DIFFERENT POSITIONS OF SLATES, LOCATION OF SPONGE, AND METHOD OF MOVING BOOK.

CONFESSION

"The undersigned, Henry Slade, known professionally as Dr. Henry Slade,--the powerful Spiritistic medium-- by reason of the force of unfavorable circumstances, years ago became a Spiritualistic slate writing (etc., etc.) medium, and Spiritistic lecturer and he herewith confesses that all his pretended Spiritualistic manifestations were and are deceptions, performed through tricks.

(Signed) H. Slade."

"I (R. Weiss) had also stipulated that he (Dr. Slade) promises to discontinue his present dishonest, criminal method of gaining a livelihood by preying on the superstition of Spiritualists and through the gullibility of the public,--Dr. Slade then remonstrated and said:--that I could not affect his standing in the eyes of those who had seen and believed his manifestations, mentioning the Czar of Russia and others of world prominence.

"I then walked to the door, signifying that *my part* of the interview and argument was ended--and also conveying the 'impression' as to my intention to have him arrested.

"He then changed his attitude and in a cringing manner he pleaded with me to have mercy on him, as he had only this one method of earning a livelihood. All of this, and his pleading, was so strenuous that he fell in a 'dead' faint. --

"Then, after I 'revived' him out of a *'genuine'* fainting spell, he begged me to desist from having him arrested and then *he signed the confession.*

(Signed) "Remigius Weiss."

Dr. Henry Slade

Unexplained Spirit Photo - Arthur Conan Doyle? (Center)

Chapter 7
Slate Writing And Other Methods

A REMARKABLY large number of methods have been used at one time and another by the numerous mediums of lesser repute than Slade who prospered on slate writing. Slade himself, like any skilled prestidigitator, had a variety of ways which he used to produce his effects. His usual method was very simple. A common kitchen table with the leaves extended was used, the Doctor being seated at the end and the client on the side against the leaf, at the Doctor's right.

After the slate had been thoroughly washed on both sides he placed it under the leaf at the left of the sitter, holding it in position with the fingers of his right hand, with his thumb above the table. The sitter was requested to hold the left end of the slate with one hand and with the other to grasp the Doctor's left hand near the center of the table. In such a position it was impossible for the sitter to see the slate or the fingers of the medium.

On the forefinger of his right hand Slade had a sort of thimble or ring to which was attached a bit of slate pencil. With this he wrote a short message on the bottom side of the slate, the scratching of the pencil being quite audible to the sitter. When this scratching ceased the Doctor would be seized with a series of nervous spasms during which the slate was snatched from the sitter's hand for the fraction of a second and, unknown to him, turned over, thus bringing the message to the top so that when a few minutes later it was shown the message appeared as though written between the slate and the table leaf.

A second method, which produced longer messages, was the substitution of slates. If this message was of a general character the slate was *switched* for one bearing a previously written message concealed about a nearby piece of furniture. If a special message was required it was written by an assistant listening in the next room. When the slate had been cleaned ready for the message the Doctor gave the cue and the assistant rapped on the door. The Doctor answered the knock in person, taking the slate with him, and while listening to some commonplace report the slates were exchanged. On resuming his seat the slate was placed under the table leaf as before. No sound of writing being heard, he would examine the top of the slate several times but of course find no writing. Finally, claiming that the influence did not seem powerful enough, he would lay the slate on the top of the table, message side down with a piece of pencil under it, and then take both the hands of the sitter in his. Soon a sound of writing would be heard and on examination the message would be found. It was possible for Slade to produce the sound of writing while his hands were holding those of his client by slipping a piece of pencil through threads on the side of his knee and rubbing it against another piece held to the table leg by a wooden clip.

One of the most common methods of slate writing is known as the "flap slate." The message is written beforehand and concealed with a flap of silicated gauze, or thin slate, which fits closely within the slate frame. One side of this flap is covered with cloth to match that used on the top of the table and when it is dropped is unnoticed. A better way is to cover the back of the flap with newspaper and by dropping it on a newspaper it becomes invisible.

There is an ingenious double form of this flap slate with which it is possible to make a message appear on both inside surfaces of a pair of locked slates without having them leave the sight of the sitter for an instant. The two slates are hinged together like the old-fashioned school slates but with the hinges on the outside of the slates. The slabs of slate are very thin and the ends of the frames bevel toward them slightly. One end of each frame is so made that by pressing on one of the hinge screws the frame end is released and can be drawn out about a quarter of an inch. A very thin slab of slate called the "flap" is arranged to fit snugly over the real slate when the frame ends are in place but drops out as soon as they are released and drawn out. In working these slates the medium writes a message on the inside of one of them, say the left, and also on one side of the flap. The end of the slate with the message is then drawn out and the flap inserted, message side down, and the frame fastened back in place. A secret mark on the outside of the frame shows which slate is written upon. The slates can then be shown and will appear clean on all four sides, and it is possible to either seal or lock them without interfering with the success of the demonstration. They are then placed on the table with the fake ends nearest the medium and while he leans on their ends with half-folded arms, engaging the sitter in conversation, he at the same time with the fingers of his concealed hand pulls out the frame ends, allowing the flap to fall from one slate to the other, and then secures it in place by putting the ends back. Of course when the slates are opened a closely written message is found on both.

Another sort of double slate intended for producing a similar effect in dark séances or cabinet work also has a loose end which instead of moving a quarter of an inch draws out to any length, bringing the slab with it. After the lights are out or the cabinet closed it is an easy matter to draw out the slab and write a message on it.

WRITING ON "HONEST SLATES" BY MEANS OF WEDGE AND WIRE.

Writing is sometimes produced between two perfectly honest slates which have been fastened together at the corners by inserting a wedge of hard wood between the frames, thus separating them enough to slip between them a piece of wire with a bit of slate pencil fastened to its tip. By this means a message can be produced at a dark séance in a few minutes without breaking the seals.

There is a form of slate where the slab is invisibly hinged on the side so that it opens like a door and is held shut by a secret catch. This slate can be used in a dark séance or under the table at a light one. It can also be used on a cloth-top table with an invisible trap. The trap and the hinged slate drop down together and the medium is able to write on the slate by reaching under the table.

Still another scheme used with a pair of hinged slates is to have a hole through both frames at one end and locking them with a padlock. In working this the pins are pushed out of the hinges and the frames, moving easily on the shackle of the padlock, permit the medium to write on the inside of the slates without difficulty, afterwards fastening the slates together again by simply replacing the pins in the hinges.

A method of concealing an extra slate is to have it a trifle smaller than the rest and then hidden in some convenient place, say the seat of a chair. A large slate is first examined and laid on the chair. Later it is picked up with the extra one under it. Sometimes the extra one is hidden under the edge of a rug on the floor and worked in the same way. At other times it is hidden on the medium's body and slipped under a large slate when the medium stands with his right side on a line with the sitter's vision.

An entirely different method is employed to some extent by mediums who are very rapid and interesting talkers. Throughout the séance the medium walks nervously about the room, keeping up a continual flow of conversation. He passes two slates to the sitter for examination. A third, the same size, with a previously written message on one side, being concealed in a large pocket inside the breast of his coat. While the slates are being examined he walks about the room sometimes behind and sometimes in front of the sitter, tapping him on the shoulder to emphasize his remarks. As soon as the slates are examined he takes them and, passing behind the sitter, places them on his head and asks him to hold them there and at the same time continuing his walk and talk. Of course when the slates are examined there is a message on the inside of one of them. When the medium steps behind the sitter with the slates in his hand he quickly changes the slate with a message which he has hidden for one of the blank ones. This is no more bold or difficult than many mediumistic tricks but it requires a particularly fluent conversationalist to successfully produce the needed amount of misdirection when the slates are switched. Women mediums effect a similar exchange sometimes by the aid of a special pocket in the dress.

A very effective method of getting a direct answer to a question on the inside of a sealed double slate is as follows. The slates are thoroughly cleansed by the sitter, who writes a question on a slip of paper, folds it and places it between the slates, with a bit of pencil. The medium keeps at a distance during the writing and cannot see what has been written. The slates are then sealed with strips of paper and placed on the table and the sitter holds both hands of the medium. After a time, as no sound of writing is heard, the medium shows some concern as to the possibility of failure and *suggests* that the sitter hold the slates at the top of his own head. Still there is no sound and the slates are returned to the table, where they remain for some time without any sign of writing. The medium becomes very much worried and suggests that the slates be placed on the sitter's head again, remarking that if no sound is heard he will be obliged to postpone that test till a future sitting. This time the writing is heard almost as soon as the slates touch the head and when it ceases and the slates are unsealed a complete answer is found written on the inner surface of one or both slates.

This seeming marvel is produced in the following simple manner. The medium's assistant steals into the room with a duplicate pair of sealed slates and stands behind the sitter. In the act of placing the slates on the head a switch is made, and the sitter holds the duplicates while the originals are taken into an adjoining room by the assistant. He lifts the seals with a hot table knife and after reading the question he writes an appropriate answer, reseals the slates and returns to his position behind the sitter. Another exchange is made when the slates are placed on the sitter's head the second, time. The sound of writing is made by the medium under the table with a piece of slate pencil and a bit of slate, but it is so faint that the sitter cannot locate it.

In Bohemia, Province of Prague, I ran across a medium who was especially good in slate writing. At first I could not "get" his work. When I was playing in Berlin, at the Wintergarten, he came in one night and wanted to give a performance to the directors. I was guest but went prepared for him. His work was so designed that he walked behind us and in so doing he baffled me. I asked for a private sitting and he readily consented.

When he did the slate writing at this sitting I felt someone's presence, and, sure enough, when he took the slates away there was an almost imperceptible hesitation. In this fraction of a second the slates were switched through a *trap in the panel* behind me. I had a mirror on a rubber elastic fastened to my vest and as I took my seat I pulled the elastic so I could sit on it. I managed to secure this mirror and keep it palmed in my hand, and with it saw the panel slide open, the arm extended with the duplicate slates, and the exchange made.

S. S. Baldwin, an acknowledged expert in Spiritualistic and Telepathic tomfoolery, was bamboozled by a Dr. Fair, according to his own story which he told to me in December, 1920. He received a message on a slate held by himself under a table, and afterwards, at the suggestion of the Doctor, made a thorough examination of the table, the room, and everything in sight, but failed to discover a concealed door in the wainscot of the wall through which a man in black garments could find his way to space under a sofa and thence to the table, which was a rather large one, do the Spirit writing and then make his exit while Mr. Baldwin was fully occupied holding the slate under the table with his eyes fixed on space above it.

One of the very best mediumistic tricks, and one that has made the reputation of more than one well-known medium, is done with a number of small slates and one large one. The size of the slates is immaterial but the large one should be three or four inches larger each way than the others. The manner of presentation differs somewhat with different performers but in general is as follows.

When the sitters arrive the slates are piled near one corner of the table, the larger one at the bottom and eight or nine smaller ones on top of it. The medium stands at the end of the table nearest the slates and after a few casual remarks he picks up the top slate with his left hand, changes it to his right and passes it to the sitter to be examined and cleaned if desired. When he is quite satisfied the medium takes it back, glances at both sides, and then places it on the table directly in front of the sitter. This is repeated with the remaining small slates, which are not stacked up evenly but left in a haphazard pile. While the last small slate is being placed on the pile with the medium's right hand he picks up the large slate with his left and rests it on top of the others, at the same time passing the sitter a pencil and asking him to write a few lines on it requesting the Spirits to favor him with a message and to sign his name to it. He is at liberty to examine this slate also and to write his message on either side.

The large slate is then placed at the right of the sitter and he is asked to place his right hand on it. The small slates are then evened up by the medium, secured by a heavy rubber band and then placed in the center of the table. The medium then takes a seat at the table opposite the sitter and they clasp hands at the sides of the slates. After a sufficient pause the slates are unbound by the sitter and on a slate near the center of the stack a message is found written in chalk or slate pencil and signed by a departed friend.

The secret of this startling effect is extremely simple. Concealed beneath the big slate at the beginning of the séance is a smaller slate with the message already written on it. This is picked up with the larger one when the latter is placed on the stack for the sitter to write on it and dropped on the others, written side down. The extra slate is never noticed as the pile has not been counted and the business of passing the slate pencil occupies the sitter's attention so that he does not realize that the large slate rests on the small ones before he examines it.

The medium then takes about half the small slates, evens them up and lays them to one side and repeats with the remaining ones, laying them evenly on the others. This is a perfectly natural move as the whole stack makes more than a handful and by means of it the slate with the message is placed in the middle of the stack. The stack is then set on end, the rubber band placed around it, and it is then ready to be placed in the middle of the table for conclusion of the séance.

Two methods of writing between locked or sealed double slates when only one or two words were needed puzzled the investigators for a long time. The first was worked with a strong magnet. The bit of slate pencil which was put between the slates was specially prepared with either powdered soapstone mixed with iron filings, water, and glue, or a small piece of iron was used covered with a paste of soapstone, water, and mucilage. By holding the magnet under the slates and tracing the words *backwards* the prepared pencils would follow the magnet and write the words. The other method was worked with an electro magnet set in the table, the necessary wires running down one leg and making contact with a copper plate in the floor under the rug by means of a sharp metal point on the end of the leg.

Since the introduction of "raps"[71] by the Fox Sisters various methods have been devised for producing them. One of the simplest expedients is for the medium to slightly moisten the fingers and slide them very gently on the top of the table. A little experimenting soon shows the amount of pressure necessary to produce the desired amount of sound and of course the medium is cautious to let the fingers move only the desired distance and that too when no one is looking.

---

[71] In regard to involuntary and subconscious table rapping and tapping: Some people rap and tip table in all seances of table tipping and rapping. I have attended seances where I have caught some one obligingly cheating to relieve the monotony, and the imposition once started is forced to be kept up.

Another simple method is to place the thumbs close together in such a manner that the nail of one overlaps the other a trifle. Then while the thumbs are pressed hard on the table if one nail is slipped up or down distinct raps are produced which seem to come from the top of the table.

Some mediums produce raps by slipping a knee up and down against a table leg. Others have been known to fasten blocks of wood to the knee under the skirt and rap on the table leg with a sidewise motion of the knee. Still others strike the table leg with the heel of the shoe or press the side of the heel against the table leg and by moving the heel up and down the friction of the leather against the wood produces raps.

TUBE AND PISTON ARRANGEMENT FOB MAKING RAPS.

RAPPING MECHANISM IN HEEL OF MEDIUM'S SHOE.

Many mediums will not depend on these methods but use more complicated ones which produce the raps by means of mechanical devices which they conceal about their person. One of these consists of a small hollow metal tube in which a long, heavy burlap needle is arranged to move up and down like a piston, and attached to it to operate it a stout black thread. The tube is fastened to the inner side of a trouser leg. The free end of the thread is brought out through a seam and an inconspicuous little hook attached. After being seated at the séance table the medium attaches the little hook to the opposite trouser leg and draws on it until the needle point comes through the cloth. He then watches an opportunity to press on to the point of the needle a cork to which has been attached a piece of lead. This accomplished, all he has to do is to place the knee in the proper relation to the table and by moving the other back and forth the piston is made to work up and down, causing the leaded cork to rap out all sorts of messages.

Another ingenious mechanical contrivance is built into the heel of the medium's shoe and operated electrically by running a wire from it up through the sole of the shoe and passing it between the back of the shoe and the foot and so on up the leg to batteries concealed in a pocket. By placing this heel against a table leg the raps can be made to sound as though coming from the middle of the table and with a proper amount of "suggestion" the sitters can be made to believe that the mysterious taps are produced in turn under each pair of hands on the table.

Table levitating is easily accomplished in the dark, through the aid of a confederate, by several different methods. If the medium and his assistant are seated opposite, by raising their knees at a signal they can lift the table from the floor without difficulty. By slightly rocking or tipping the table the medium and assistant can simultaneously slip a foot under table legs diagonally opposite, lift the table and keep it balanced by the pressure of the hands on its top. These and many similar methods are perfectly practical in dark séances but for manifestations where there is any danger of the sitters being able to see mechanical contrivances are resorted to. The oldest form is simply a light, though powerfully strong, length of blue steel riveted to a stout leather wrist strap. When not in use the whole thing is concealed in the medium's sleeve. Sometimes both the medium and the assistant are thus equipped.

This has been somewhat superseded by a chamois-covered flat steel hook concealed under the vest and riveted to a tight-fitting leather belt encircling the medium's body. With this hook under the table edge great power can be exerted upon the table with very little strain upon the operator. The lifting strength of a human hair is not generally known, yet by means of one freshly taken from the head, long enough to span a small light table, the table can be lifted. One of the more modern contrivances is a steel belt which the operator wears and to the front of which is attached a short metal arm which can be engaged under the table top in such a way that the operator can take his hands off the table and still support it in the air. When releasing the table the metal arm is slipped back and the steel belt shifted to another position on the body, the medium's coat concealing both.

Just as advances are made in other lines of work, so too mediums advance in their methods of deceiving their subjects. Few would resort to the old-time methods of releasing a foot from under the foot of an investigator. They have devised a new and baffling method. The medium's shoes are especially made for her in such a way that by a certain pressure on the sole it is possible to withdraw the greater portion of the shoe with the foot from a false front. This front is made of metal and padded. When the medium asks the committee to place their feet on hers she makes sure that they do not overreach the portion she can withdraw from. In the full glare of the light the investigator thinks he feels the medium's foot securely held under his own and as he cannot see under the table the medium has the full use of her foot to produce manifestations.

I once gave a séance while I was touring in England. It was a dark séance and just at the psychological moment a Spirit came through the window and walked around on the wall and ceiling of the room and then out of another window. The explanation is simple. On the bill with me were two acrobats, hand to hand balancers. One took off his shoes and stockings and the other sneaked up to him. He pulled down the window and then did a hand-to-hand balance with his partner and walked around the room. He then went back to his seat, put on his shoes, and looked as innocent and meek as possible under the circumstances when the lights were turned on. I told every one present that it was only a trick but as usual they insisted that I was a medium.

A rope trick which always causes astonishment and helps to create a belief in supernatural aid is done by a- woman medium who enters a cabinet with a rope bound around her neck. The loose ends of the rope are forced through opposite sides of the cabinet and held tightly by two members of the committee. Nevertheless the manifestations take place just the same and when the cabinet is opened afterwards the medium is found bound just as she was before the séance. As a matter of fact when the curtains have been closed and the committee have a grip on the ends of the rope the medium cuts the specially tied loop around her neck. When she is ready to come out she simply ties another loop, using a duplicate piece of rope which she had concealed on her person. When the committee release the ends of the rope she slips the mutilated piece into her bloomers and appears with the duplicate, which looks like the original one.

There are various methods of producing Spirit photographs. One is to have a table prepared so that a developing pan is placed where an X-ray penetrates to the negative. This produces a "Spirit light." Another is to fix the side of the plate with some luminous substance, shape, or flash, and it is astonishing what these things look like. You get forms and frequently recognize faces in the splotches. Father de Heredia has palmed a figure in his hand and as the investigator signed the negative remarked: "I might as well sign it myself." In so doing he rested the left hand over the plate while signing with his right and the phosporous figure in his hand was photographed on the negative. A simple method is to have something concealed in the hand and hold it over the lens instead of a cap, and still another is to get the camera out of focus and snap it secretly, then when the regular exposure is made there is an additional hazy something on the plate.

One of the most startling swindles I ever heard of a medium working was called "finger-printing a Spirit." In this test the medium shows the sitter finger prints of the departed soul. I hesitated at first about including this fake, fearing to add to the stock of unscrupulous mediums but I finally concluded that the public should know about it. The scheme was first discovered by a sculptor who dabbled some in Spiritualism. One day, several years ago, a workman fell from the top of the building, in which this man had his studio, and was killed. The body was carried into the studio and while alone with it the sculptor conceived the idea of fooling some guests who were to hold a séance that night. He hurriedly made a plaster of Paris mould of the dead man's fingers and later filled it with a rubber-like substance used in his work. When this had hardened and the plaster had been removed it resembled, even to the most minute detail, the dead hand.

During the séance that night he produced finger prints with it on a trumpet which he had lampblacked and upon investigation it was found that these finger prints corresponded exactly with those of the man in the morgue. No one was able to explain the mystery and he kept the secret for some time but later another medium learned it and obtained a position in an undertaking establishment where he found an opportunity after a while to secure the finger prints of several of the dead who belonged to the wealthy class. In due time he arranged séances with the relatives and convinced them of his genuineness. There are two cases on record where fortunes were at stake because of this sort of fraud. In one case five hundred thousand dollars changed hands upon the recognition of the finger prints of a man who had died two years before. His hand had been maimed in an accident and all the scars showed in the impression on the Spirit slate. Fortunately a confession was wrung from the medium and the money went to the rightful heirs.

A "manifestation" which seems mysterious but which is in reality ridiculously simple is worked as follows. A glass is filled with water and placed on the table in a cabinet. Ribbons or bands of tape are then drawn over it at right angles and the ends fastened to the table with nails. Thus secured the glass cannot be lifted and the top is entirely covered except some small openings. The medium is then locked into the cabinet for a few minutes, during which he keeps up a continual clapping of his hands, but when the cabinet is unlocked the glass is empty of water and the general impression is that the Spirits drained it. As a matter of fact the medium had worked his hands up near his face and shifted from slapping his hands to slapping his face with one hand. This left a hand free and with it he had no difficulty in producing a straw from his pocket and sucking the water from the glass.

Of course these examples are only a few of the many means employed by mediums to produce their "manifestations" and take advantage of the credulity of the average sitter, but they are enough to show the reader the sort of methods practiced and the lengths to which they will go in their deceptions.

Mr. & Mrs. Jack London - Mr. & Mrs. Harry Houdini

Chapter 8
Spirit Photography

WITH what is perhaps pardonable pride we point to the genius of American enterprise in scientific advancement but it is with decided chagrin that I repeat that, as modern Spiritualism was born in America, so also have been most of the phenomena that under the mask of Spiritualism have unbalanced so many fine intellects the world over. Spirit photography, the most prominent of mediumistic phenomena, had its beginning in Boston, "Hub" of intellectual development, its coming being announced by Dr. Gardner, a devout Spiritualist, who discovered a photographer that "in taking a photograph of himself, obtained on the same plate a likeness of a cousin dead some twelve years before."

This was in 1862, but a little more than a decade after the original demonstration of so-called Spirit power at Hydesville. Fortunately for the success of the new art the photographer selected by the inhabitants of "Summer-land"[72] to use for the demonstration of the new phenomena was a medium and of all the hosts in heaven the spirit chosen to be photographed was (singular coincidence) a cousin of his who had passed the border some years previous.

No sooner had the discovery been announced than spiritual enthusiasts in large numbers began flocking to the studio of the medium, Mr. William H. Mumler, and this kept up until evil spirits (?) began to create an atmosphere of doubt and skepticism, whereupon he abruptly took himself and his new enterprise to New York City, a precipitous plunge presumably prompted by his Spiritual guides.

The change proved to be of great financial benefit to Mumler until the ire of the evil Spirits was once more aroused and he was arrested on a charge of fraudulent transactions. A most interesting and sensational trial followed with many noted people appearing as witnesses, among them being that prince of showmen, Phineas Taylor Barnum, who testified for the prosecution, and Judge John W. Edmonds, of the Supreme Court Bench, for the defence.[73]

Mr. Barnum testified to having spent much time and study in the detection of humbugs and had recently written a book called "The Humbugs of the World." He knew Mumler only through reputation but had had some correspondence with him in regard to his pictures, wishing to learn his process and expose it in his book, and some pictures which Mumler sent him Barnum paid ten dollars apiece for and put in his museum labelled as "Spiritualistic Humbugs."

Barnum's testimony was attacked by Mumler's lawyer who characterized it as being a "very pretty illustration of humbug" and added that even if it were true Barnum violated the "great precept relating to honor among thieves," but I want to go on record as believing that Mr. Barnum told the truth in the Mumler case.

Judge Edmonds declared on the stand that he had seen Spirits although many Spiritualists could not and recalled an instance when he was on the bench trying a case in which the payment of an accident insurance policy was the issue. He told the court that the whole aspect of the case was changed after he saw the spirit of the suicide and several questions which this Spirit had suggested were put to the witness, the decision being reversed on the testimony thus brought out. He also testified to his belief that Mumler's pictures were genuine photographs of Spirits.

During the trial many methods[74] of producing Spirit "extras" were shown in court by expert photographers and the possibilities of the effect being produced by natural means proven. The

---

[72] Coined by Andrew Jackson Davis, in 1845, and meaning the hereafter. Now used frequently by Sir Arthur Conan Doyle.

[73] See Appendix F.

[74] In those days there were no dry plates and with the old "wet" plates it was quite possible to expose a plate, develop it, and then prepare it again and expose it the second time. When this was done both pictures appeared in the print. Such a plate could be used under the strictest test conditions without detection.

investigators, however, did not have their case in good shape. There were strong grounds for suspicion but they were unable to present positive proof and though the court was morally convinced that fraudulent methods had been practiced sufficient evidence to convict Mumler was lacking.

Although acquitted, it is significant that Mumler refused an offer of five hundred dollars to reproduce his pictures in another studio under test conditions and while free to resume his business so far as the court was concerned, with a full harvest of dupes waiting to be fleeced, he was nevertheless soon lost to view and seems to have vanished entirely after the publication of his book in 1875.

Spiritualistic mediumship is not immune to the flattery of imitation for even a casual examination of Spiritualistic history and development shows that just as soon as a medium forms a new alliance with the psychic power dispenser and produces phenomena unknown before, other mediums immediately begin to produce it also and the new manifestation soon becomes epidemic. It was so with Spirit photography. No one had thought of such a possibility before Mumler invented the mystery but talented mediums everywhere when they heard of his pictures began to produce them also. Stories of his success crossed the sea and Europe discovered equal talent there.

In the summer of 1874 a Parisian photographer by the name of Buguet went over to London and attracted considerable attention with his Spirit pictures. They were of much higher artistic quality than any preceding ones and Podmore in his "Modern Spiritualism" tells us that:

"The Spirit faces were in most cases clearly defined, and were, in fact, frequently recognized by the sitters, and even W. H. Harrison failed to detect any trickery in the operation."

After a short stay during which his demonstrations completely satisfied such men as Rev. Stainton Moses, who was liberal with his endorsements, Buguet returned to Paris, where the next year he was placed under arrest "charged with the fraudulent manufacture of Spirit photographs." Unlike Mumler, his conscience did not prove court-proof, or perhaps the evidence against him was such that a friendly Spirit advised confession, at any rate he told the court that all of his Spirit photographs were the result of double exposure. On the strength of this confession Buguet was convicted and sentenced to one year of imprisonment and a fine of five hundred francs. A like sentence was given to M. Leymaire, Editor of the *Revue Spirits,* who admitted suggesting to Buguet that he should enter the field of Spirit photography.

The police seized all the paraphernalia in the studio of Buguet and took it to court. Amongst it was a lay figure and a large stock of heads. These with dolls and assistants at the studio took turns as inspirations for Spirit extras. But the real interest of the trial was not these revelations, Podmore tells us, for after all Buguet did little to improve on the methods inaugurated by his predecessors. It is the effect produced on his dupes by Buguet's confession, and the display of his trick apparatus, which is really worthy of attention. Witness after witness--journalist, photographic expert, musician, merchant, man of letters, optician, ex-professor of history, Colonel of Artillery, etc., etc.--came forward to testify on behalf of the accused. Some had watched the process throughout, and were satisfied that trickery had not been practiced. Many had obtained on the plate unmistakable portraits of those dear to them, and found it impossible to relinquish their faith. One after another these witnesses were confronted with Buguet, and heard him explain how the trick had been done. One after another they left the witness-box, protesting that they could not doubt the evidence of their own eyes. Here, chosen almost at random from many similar accounts, is the testimony of M. Dessenon, picture-seller, aged fifty-five. After describing how he had obtained in the first instance various figures which he could not recognize, he continues:--

" 'The portrait of my wife, which I had especially asked for, is so like her that when I showed it to one of my relatives he exclaimed, "It's my cousin!"

"*The Court:* 'Was that chance, Buguet?'

"*Buguet:* 'Yes, pure chance. I had no photograph of Mme. Dessenon.'

"*The Witness:* 'My children, like myself, thought the likeness perfect. When I showed them the picture they cried, "It's mama." A very fortunate chance! . . . I am convinced it was my wife.'

"*The Court:* 'You see this doll and all the rest of the things?'

"*The Witness:* 'There is nothing there in the least like the photograph which I obtained.' "

Incidentally there were two or three curious bits of evidence on the value of recognition as a test. *A police officer stated that Buguet showed him a portrait which had done duty as the sister of one sitter, the mother of a second, and the friend of a third.* Again, it came out in the evidence that a very clearly defined head (reproduced as an illustration to Stainton Moses' articles in *Human Nature*) which had been claimed by M. Leymaire as the portrait of his almost life long friend, M. Poiret, was recognized by another witness as an excellent likeness of his father-in-law, *still living* at Breux, and much annoyed at his premature introduction to the Spirit world.

From Mumler's first pictures to the present day, Spirit photography has played a large part in the field of Spiritualistic devotion, and innumerable mediums have discovered that they possessed the same phenomenal power for producing the coveted likeness in the form of "extras" on the sensitized plate. The art has now advanced to such a stage that it is no longer necessary for one to sit but all that is needed is a relic of the departed one, something which either belonged or was of especial interest, to the person. This relic is photographed and when the plate is developed there appears beside it as an "extra" the face of the departed; that is, I should say, if your imagination is strong enough to see a resemblance to the person supposed to be represented.

Nor is a camera necessary in these days, according to Spiritualists. In fact, I am told that it is not necessary to even open a box of plates, but that they can be "magnetized" just as they come from the maker *provided* the box is in the possession of the medium a few days in advance of the sitting. This single condition fulfilled and the demonstration will follow if the sitters, including the nearest relative, pile their hands on top of the medium's. Then to create a solemn atmosphere the sitters are usually asked to join in some form of religious devotion such as singing "Nearer, My God, To Thee," or a fervent prayer.

This is the type of performance conducted by what is known as the "Crewe Photographers" and supported and defended by the present day leaders in Spiritualism. This Crewe combination of photographers is under the management of professional Spiritualists and is an organized effort to promulgate this particular phase of Spiritualistic phenomena. The group consists of Mr. William Hope and Mrs. Buxton, Crewe; Mrs. Deane of London; and Mr. Vearnacombe of Bridgewater.

My friend, Harry Price, attended a sitting given by Hope and tells of the religious exercises as follows:

"Mrs. Buxton sang several verses of 'Nearer, My God, to Thee,' after which Mr. Hope made a long impromptu prayer in which he thanked God for all our many mercies, and hoped He would continue His blessings at the present moment. He also craved blessings on our fellow creatures and friends on the other side and asked assistance in the attempt to link up with them, etc. Then Mrs. Buxton sang another hymn, after which Mr. Hope picked up the package of dry plates, put them between the hands of Mrs. Buxton, placed her hands on his, and others in the party piled their hands on top. Then we had another impromptu prayer by Mrs. Buxton. Then the Lord's Prayer was sung, and a short hymn concluded the service."

Can one imagine a sacrilege more revolting than singing hymns, saying prayers, and calling on the Almighty for help in such fraudulent work?

The combination evaded detection and were doing a most successful business when in the spring of 1921, Mr. Edward Bush, of the Society of Psychical Research, laid a snare into which Hope walked with his eyes wide open. Mr. Bush wrote for an appointment under the assumed name of "D. Wood," enclosing a photograph of a son-in-law who was alive. On the back of the photograph was written:

"Tell Dad, if anything happens to me, I will try and let him have a Spirit Photo. Tell him to shout up to let me know where he goes to.

"Jack Ackroyd."

Hope arranged a time for a sitting but returned the photo, saying he regretted that it had been sent as it subjected him to suspicion. When the time for the sitting arrived Hope went under control and Mr. Bush manipulated the plates as he directed but no "extras" appeared. On the next day, however, when the plate was developed after another sitting, there was an "extra" which proved to be a likeness of the son-in-law. Mr. Bush published the details of this exposure in a pamphlet and the London *Truth* said editorially:

"But not only have William Hope and his sister medium, Mrs. Buxton, cause to kick themselves at Mr. Bush's exposure, Sir Arthur Conan Doyle,[75] Lady Glen-Conner, the Rev. Walter Wynn, and many other leading lights of the movement have brought these products of faith and hope forward as conclusive proof of the continuation of existence and the possibility of communication with the next world."

Later in the same year, Mr. C. R. Mitchell, a former leader of the Hackney Spiritualistic Society and well known in mediumistic circles in London, was selected to "undertake certain tests of a scientific nature for the purpose of ascertaining the value of these Spirit phenomena." Mr. Mitchell was a photographer and wished to use his own plates in the experiment but Mrs. Deane, who was to conduct it, refused to let him unless he *first left them with her for a few days to be magnetized.* He objected to this and it was finally agreed that he could use his own plates provided he would magnetize them himself but the results were unsatisfactory. He then purchased from Mrs. Deane a package of fresh plates, which, it was claimed, had not been opened since it left the manufacturer. The likeness of a soldier appeared on one of these which Mr. Mitchell developed himself and he concluded that not only had the plates been "magnetized" but that they had been exposed in a camera as well.

The issue of *Truth* for June 28th, 1922, gives an account of the experience of an ex-Indian missionary, who, with three others, visited the Crewe photographers and sat for Spirit pictures. Four exposures were made and Spirit "extras" appeared on two of the plates but the men could not remember whether the plates had at any time been beyond their control so the missionary arranged for another sitting taking the precaution to have his plates marked on the comer with a glazier's diamond. At this second sitting one Spirit extra was produced but there was *no diamond mark* on the plate, positive proof that an exchange had been effected.

During 1922 the Occult Committee of the Magic Circle took up the investigation of Spirit photography first giving its attention to Mr. Vearncombe who produced Spirit extras in connection with some object once in possession of the deceased. Sir Arthur Conan Doyle put this committee in touch with the Honorary Secretary of the Society for the Study of Supernormal Pictures, Mr. Barlow, and at the latter's suggestion sent him an unopened package of plates for Mr. Vearncombe. Although Barlow objected, "for Vearncombe's satisfaction, though not essential," the package was enclosed in a lead case. Also at Barlow's suggestion a fee accompanied the package. After a month of waiting the committee received a photograph of the package and on the photograph was a spirit message which read: "Barred your side."

In order to remove the barrier a fresh package of plates was forwarded to Vearncombe, this time in an ordinary wrapper. Some months later, after the plates had been Spiritually treated by Vearncombe, they were returned to the committee. When developed "psychic extras" were found on two plates. There was evidence that the package had been tampered with and the same spirit had been seen on other photographs.

The committee sent Vearncombe a package of plates under an assumed name but received word from him that it was not necessary to send plates. That small objects which had belonged to the deceased would do and that if the proper fee were enclosed photographic prints showing the "psychic extras" obtained would be supplied. As a full compliance with this suggestion would have been useless as a test, a box of plates, a small object supposed to have belonged to the deceased, and the fee were sent.

Again Vearncombe protested that he did not treat unopened boxes of plates owing to many failures but offered to expose plates on the object which had been supplied. He was informed that such exposure would be unsatisfactory whereupon rather than disappoint his correspondent, he

---

[75] In speaking of Spirit photography, Sir Arthur Conan Doyle usually brings up as proof positive, that his fairy photographs are genuine. According to the *London Star,* December *20,* 1921, there were many interesting developments regarding these:

"Messrs. Price and Sons, the well known firm of candle makers, inform us that the fairies in this photograph are an exact reproduction of a famous poster they have used for years, to advertise their night lights.

" 'I admit on these fairies there are wings, whereas our fairies have no wings,' said a representative of the firm to a *Star* reporter, 'but, with this exception, the figures correspond line for line with our own drawing.'"

consented and forwarded the package with the statement that he had treated the plates as desired and hoped for success. On development a "psychic image" appeared on one of the plates but the committee found that the wrappers of the package had been unsealed and the plates disturbed in their arrangement.

In order to clinch the results of their trapping Vearncombe was informed that the experiment had been a "success" but in order to "avoid criticism" he was asked for an assurance that the package had not been tampered with. It soon came in the form of a written statement that the package had been treated by him and returned to the sender as originally sealed when he received it.

The committee has arranged fourteen tests, twelve of which had been violated, and as two or three violations would have been sufficient evidence of fraud it did not consider more necessary but reported that it had been established by the evidence that fraud-proof packages produced no results whereas it found "Spirit extras" in packages which had been tampered with and that "collectively the result is damning."

The committee next directed its attention to Mrs. Deane who, because of "complications from annoying sitters," had given up private practice at her residence and was working under engagement with the British College of Psychic Science. The Principal of the College, Mr. McKenzie, had vouched for her as being absolutely conscientious and straightforward in her work and one fully qualified to produce "psychic extras without resort to trickery." Mr. Harry Price and Mr. Seymour negotiated for a private sitting with her. She required that sealed plates should be sent several days in advance for "magnetization." Six plates were exposed at the sitting and on most of them "extras" appeared, but evidence was obtained that the package had been opened previous to the sitting and the plates *treated* but there had been no substitution of plates.

An effort was made to get more convincing evidence and after considerable difficulty a second sitting was arranged for. This time the committee went to a manufacturer, whose plates had been mentioned by the college people as being preferable, and had a special package made up and sealed. In this package each plate was so marked that substitution or manipulation were sure to be revealed. It was simply fraud-proof.

At the sitting the regular prayer and hymn singing were conducted as usual after which the plates were exposed and developed. It was found that the package had been opened previously, the top plate removed and another substituted for it and on this substituted plate, only, there was a "Spirit extra." At a third sitting a fresh box of secretly marked plates were opened in the presence of Mrs. Deane. Four plates were loaded into as many separate slides and Mrs. Deane carried them into the adjoining studio. On a table in the studio was a hand-bag and beside it a hymn book. The hand in which she held the four slides momentarily disappeared inside the bag while at the same time she picked up the hymn book with her other hand. With the hymn book she had picked up a duplicate slide which, with a perfectly natural movement, she added to the three in her other hand one of the four marked plates having been dropped in the bag where it was found later by one of the investigators who examined the bag while Mrs. Deane was absent for a moment.

Following the customary religious service the four plates were exposed and then developed. Three plates which had the identifying marks had no Spirit extra, but the fourth plate which had no identification mark did have a Spirit form.

As a result of this investigation the committee found that whenever there was an opportunity packages were opened and treated, plates substituted, and in the tests which followed "Spirit extras" were secured, but when the conditions were absolutely fraud-proof there were no "extras," and so far as it was able to discover all the so-called Spirit photography rested on the flimsy foundation of fraud.

In December 1921 I tried to visit Mr. Hope and have some Spirit photographs made but I was informed that his engagements would keep him busy for months and that I would have to wait my turn. I then got in touch with a friend of mine by the name of DeVega[76] who lives in Glasgow and asked him if he would not see Hope and arrange to sit for a photograph. After considerable

---

[76] I would like to say for the benefit of the reader that DeVega is a skilled magical entertainer; has invented a number of legerdemain feats; contributed a number of interesting articles to magical publications; is a skilled artist and a clever photographer. I was very fortunate in being able to secure a roan of his ability for the investigation.

correspondence between DeVega and Hope the latter agreed to make the photographs provided DeVega would go to Crewe. DeVega assented to this, and an appointment was made and the sitting took place. The following account of DeVega's experience is taken from a full report which he sent me.

"Dec. 16, 1921.--Arrived at No. 144 Market Street, the door was opened by an elderly lady. I asked if Mr. Hope was in and presently he came down. I told him that a well known member of the Spiritualist Society and a man known to be a collector of Spirit photographs sent me and that seemed to be sufficient for Mr. Hope.

"I had brought my own camera along and asked him whether the pictures could be taken with it. However, he said he used his own camera but would let me investigate it all I wanted to. He told me he could not possibly photograph me that forenoon as there was another gentleman coming but arranged for two o'clock.

"I watched Market Street, from a distance, all the forenoon but saw no one go in. I arrived there promptly but it was 2:30 before Mr. Hope arrived. A Mrs. Buxton joined us. She, Hope and myself sat around a small table. They sang hymns, said a prayer and asked the table if all was favorable.

"At his request I placed my packages of plates on the table. They placed their hands above them and sang again. Hope suddenly gave a quiver and said, 'Now we will try.' He showed me the dark room, which is a small arrangement of about six feet high, three feet wide and five feet long. There were two shelves and on these were dusters, cloths, bottles of chemicals, a lamp, etc. The lamp is an old affair lit by a candle. The room is so very small that when two people are in it there is no room to move about.

"He next showed me the camera and asked me to examine it. I gave a glance at it and told him I did not doubt his word, which seemed to please him a great deal. I thought if it was a fake he would not allow me to examine it as closely as he asked me to. It was an old make, one fourth plate, studio camera and had no shutter, but worked with a cap over a lens (the cap was missing). He next showed me the dark slide. It was an old-fashioned, double wood end slide. I examined it very closely but it was unprepared.

"The studio itself is a little glass hot-house arrangement built on to the side of the house. A green curtain is hung at the one end at which the sitter sits.

"We went again into the dark room to load the plates. He gave me his slide and told me to leave two of my own dark slides down in front of the light as he would try my camera too. I opened my plates and placed two in his dark slide and closed it. It was placed on the under shelf where I could see it faintly. He then asked me to open my own two slides slightly and sign my name on them. (I signed J. B. Gilchrist.) As I signed them he moved the lamp to let me see better. This threw the one fourth plate in the shadow. After that he handed me the one fourth plate slide to sign the two plates in the same way.

"*I am sure, although I did not actually see him, that the slide I loaded, was changed for another one.* It was too dark to see under the level of the shelf. I, for a moment, considered letting my pencil slip and spoil the plate and load in another from my packet but I thought it advisable to let things go on as I would then see just what his usual procedure was. I wondered at the time *Why I could not have been told to take the plates from the package, sign them and then place the plates in the slide and place the slide in my pocket until they were to be exposed. Why was it necessary to sign my own plates in my dark slide at all? In fact, there was no necessity for me to take my slide in the dark room.*

"We went back into the studio, again I was asked to examine the camera. However, I took up my position in front of the camera. Mrs. Buxton stood at one side and Mr. Hope at the other. The dark focusing cloth was low over the lens (the cap being missing) and the slide open.

Mrs. Buxton and Hope sang a hymn and each took an end of the cloth, uncovering the lens. This was repeated with other plates as well.

"Now my camera was set up. I was asked to open the slide and show them how the shutter worked. The exposure was made. He placed his hand in front of the camera, covering the lens and asked me to open the slide myself as he did not want to touch it. *Now why did he close the lens in that way?* It would have been simpler to have pushed down the open front of the slide, closing it, but I believe that on his hand was a spot of some radiant salt or some such substance that would cause a bright spot to appear on the negative, such as appeared on that plate when it was developed. Holding his hand in front of the lens while an exposure was being made is such an unnatural action that I believe that was the cause of what he called 'a Spirit Light,' when it was developed. The next photograph I told him to press the release again to close the shutter. He did so.

"We then adjourned into the dark room to develop the plates. The two, one fourth plates were placed by me, side by side, in a dish and the two three and a half by two and a half in another dish and developed. By pouring the developer from one dish to another, one of the one quarter plates flashed up dark. I remarked that one was coming up very quickly and he replied that 'when they come up like that it is a good sign for it is very likely there is an "extra" on them.' I said no more but in my experience and knowledge of photography, such an occurrence is impossible unless the plates have been previously exposed.

"The two plates were taken from the same packet, loaded into the dark slide at the same time, with the same dark room light and the same distance from the light.

They were then exposed on the same subject immediately after each other; the same length of exposure being given (I counted them mentally) with the same aperture of lens. The plates were then placed side by side in the same dish of developer and I contend that the image must come up at a uniform speed on both plates and that it is impossible for one to flash up before the other and darken all over unless it was previously exposed, especially when there was no variation in the light when the exposure was made, it being three P.M., December 16, clear sky, no sunshine.

"An 'extra' did appear on this (one fourth plate). It is a clean shaven face above mine and drapery hanging from it. On my own three and a half by two and a half a light splotch is over my face. Mrs. Buxton informed me that it was a 'Spirit light' but Mr. Hope believed he saw the faint features of a face in it."

While in Denver, Colorado, in May, 1923, I called one morning on Mr. Alexander Martin, whom Sir Arthur Conan Doyle had told me was a noted psychic photographer and a very wonderful man in his particular line. Doyle himself had called on Martin the day before but as Martin did not feel in the mood there had been no demonstration. In this Sir Arthur was no more unfortunate than Hyslop, the eminent Psychic investigator, who, according to Sir Arthur, had made a special journey from England to Denver in order to have a séance with Martin but had not been successful.

Martin lived about fifteen minutes out of town by taxi. I took with me my chief assistant, James Collins, so I would have a witness if anything of a psychic nature occurred. Collins had my camera as I wanted at least to get a picture of Martin. We found him standing in the doorway of a rear building and after I introduced myself he seemed cordial. I showed him some Spirit photographs which I had with me and after a few minutes talk I asked him if he was willing that Collins should take a snap-shot at us. He thought I was asking for a sitting and replied that he did not feel good and besides had been engaged to take the pictures of the children in two schools. I kept on talking in my most entertaining manner and before long he invited us into the house saying he would photograph both of us. Meanwhile Collins had secured five snap-shots at close range without Martin knowing it.

When we went into the house I walked right into the dark room but Martin called me saying:

"Now don't you go in there, just wait a minute."

While we waited outside Martin spent about eight minutes in the dark room. Then he came out and we went into his studio, a simple room with a black background. He had me sit down and placed Collins behind me on my right. As a test I told Collins to step over to the other side as it might look better. Then when he had done so I turned to Martin and asked:

"Is that all right or is it better to have him take the original position?"

"I think it would be nicer if he stood where he was in the first place," Martin replied.

This led me to think he was keeping that side of the plate clean for something to appear. There was considerable light in the room and Martin pulled a dark screen on our right explaining that he did not need much light for the psychic stuff, then putting a shade on his eyes he turned to us and said:

"Now keep quiet and I will try and do something."

When he uncovered the lens I counted the time of the exposure which was about fifteen seconds. As he covered it again he said to us:

"That is all I can do to-day. Now I must hurry away."

We thanked him and as we were going out I asked him if he had any photographs we could see. He went into an adjoining room but closed the door so we had no opportunity to look in. When he came out he had four photographs which he allowed me to keep but he would not write on them who they were of.

The next day I went to see him again and he gave me another séance. This time he said he would have to cut a plate and he gave me a book to read while I waited. In looking for a piece of paper on which to write my address he picked up a lot of newspapers and I noticed some scientific publications systematically inserted between the leaves which led me to think he was trying to hide his knowledge and wished to appear as a simple minded old man who knew but little about photography.

I have not the slightest doubt that Mr. Martin's Spirit photographs were simply double exposures. I think his method was to cut out various pictures, place them on a background and make an exposure. His plates were then ready for his next sitter, which in the above instance was myself. Being an expert photographer he might have used the original wet plate method of making an exposure, developing it, washing the emulsion off the plate and refinishing it with a new emulsion but I am convinced that the two Spirit photos which he made of me were simply double exposures.

The technique of photography does not trouble the psychic operator. He has no regard for the laws of light or chemistry. The fact that in all of his pictures the Spirits appear to be perfectly conscious of posing does not disconcert him, nor is he disturbed because they always appear as they were in life. How much more interesting it would be and how much more such photographs would add to our knowledge and aid the advancement of science if once in a while the Spirits would permit themselves to be snapped while engaged in some Spiritual occupation.

From a logical, rational point of view, Spirit photography is a most barefaced imposition and stands as evidence of the credulity of those who are in sympathy with the superstitions of occultism. It is also evidence of how unscrupulous mediums become and how calloused their consciences.

Pierre Louie Ormand Augustus Keeler

In this country there is no such organized group of Spirit photographers as the Crewe photographers in England. Since Mumler's narrow escape from deserved punishment and his disappearance there have been few who had the courage to operate as boldly as he did. The most conspicuous one practicing at the present time is Dr. (?) W. M. Keeler, who according to Spiritualistic publications has a nerve and conscience equal to any psychic undertaking.

With Spirit photography as with all other so-called psychic marvels, there never has been, nor is now, any proof of genuineness beyond the claim made by the medium. In each and every case it is a simple question of veracity, and when the most sincere believers in Spiritualism unhesitatingly admit, as they do, that all mediums at times resort to fraud and lying, what dependence can possibly be placed in any statement they make?

There can be no better evidence of rottenness in the whole structure than the fact that for upwards of forty years there have been standing offers of money in amounts ranging from five hundred to five thousand dollars for a single case of so-called phenomena which could be proven actually psychic. Knowing the character of mediums as I do I claim if proof were possible there is not a single medium, including Spirit photographers, who would not have jumped at the chance to win such a prize. If there are any who are operating honestly let them come forward with proof and take the reward.

Chapter 9
Sir Arthur Conan Doyle

SPIRITUALISM has claimed among its followers numbers of brilliant minds--scientists, philosophers, professionals and authors. Whether these great minds have been misdirected, whether they have followed the subject because they were convinced fully of its truth, or whether they have been successfully hoodwinked by some fraudulent medium, are matters of conjecture and opinion; nevertheless they have been the means of bringing into the ranks of Spiritualism numbers of those who allow themselves to be led by minds greater and more powerful than their own.

Such a one is Sir Arthur Conan Doyle. His name comes automatically to the mind of the average human being to-day at the mention of Spiritualism. No statistician could fathom the influence he has exerted through his lectures and his writings or number the endless chain he guides into a belief in communication with the Realm Beyond. His faith and belief and confidence in the movement have been one of the greatest assets of present-day believers and whatever one's views on the subject, it is impossible not to respect the belief of this great author who has wholeheartedly and unflinchingly thrown his life and soul into the conversion of unbelievers. Sir Arthur *believes.* In his great mind there is *no* doubt.

He is a brilliant man, a deep thinker, well versed in every respect, and comes of a gifted family. His grandfather, John Doyle, was born in Dublin in 1797. He won popularity and fame in London with his caricatures of prominent people. Many of his original drawings are now preserved in the museum under the title "H. B. Caricatures." He died in 1868. An uncle of Sir Arthur's was the famous "Dicky Doyle," the well-known cartoonist of *Punch* and designer of the familiar cover of that magazine. In his later years he became prominent as an illustrator, making drawings for *The Newcomes* in 1853, and becoming especially successful in illustrating such fairy stories as Hunt's "Jar of Honey," Ruskin's "King of the Golden River," and Montelbas' "Fairy Tales of all Nations." The fact that he leaned toward Spiritualism is not generally known. Sir Arthur's father, Charles A. Doyle, was also an artist of great talent though not in a commercial way. His home life is beautiful and Lady Doyle has told me on numerous occasions that he never loses his temper and that his nature is at all times sunshiny and sweet. His children are one hundred per cent children in every way and it is beautiful to note the affection between the father, mother and the children. He is a great reader who absorbs what he reads but he believes what he sees in print *only* if it is favorable to Spiritualism.

The friendship of Sir Arthur and myself dates back to the time when I was playing the Brighton Hippodrome, Brighton, England. We had been corresponding and had discussed through the medium of the mail, questions regarding Spiritualism. He invited Mrs. Houdini and myself to the Doyle home in Crowborough, England, and in that way an acquaintanceship was begun which has continued ever since. Honest friendship is one of life's most precious treasures and I pride myself in thinking that we have held that treasure sacred in every respect. During all these years we have exchanged clippings which we thought might be of mutual interest and on a number of occasions have had an opportunity to discuss them in person. Our degree of friendship may be judged best from the following letter of Sir Arthur's.

"15 Buckingham Palace Mansion, S.W. 1,

"March 8, 1923.

"My dear Houdini:--

For goodness' sake take care of those dangerous stunts of yours. You have done enough of them. I speak because I have just read of the death of the "Human Fly."[77] Is it worth it?

"Yours very sincerely,
(Signed) A. CONAN DOYLE."

It would be difficult to determine just when Sir Arthur and I first discussed Spiritualism, but from that talk to the present we have never agreed upon it. Our viewpoints differ; we do not believe the same thing. I know that he treats Spiritualism as a religion. He believes that it is possible and that he can communicate with the dead. According to his marvellous analytical brain he has had proof positive of this. There is no doubt that Sir Arthur is sincere in his belief and it is this sincerity which has been one of the fundamentals of our friendship. I have respected everything he has said and *I have always been unbiased,* because at no time have I refused to follow the subject with an open mind. I cannot say the same for him for he has refused to discuss the matter in any other voice except that of Spiritualism and in all our talks quoted only those who favored it in every way, and if one does not follow him sheep-like during his investigations then he is blotted out forever so far as Sir Arthur is concerned. Unfortunately he uses the reasoning, so common among Spiritualists, that no matter how often mediums are caught cheating he believes the only reason for it is that they have overstepped their bounds and resorted to trickery in an effort to convince. I wonder if some day Sir Arthur will forget that he is a Spiritualist and argue a case of trickery with the sound logic of an outsider. I firmly believe that if he ever does he will see and acknowledge some of his errors. I am ready to believe in Sir Arthur's teachings if he can convince me beyond the shadow of a doubt that his demonstrations are genuine.

There is no doubt in my mind, Sir Arthur believes implicitly in the mediums with whom he has convened and he knows positively, in his own mind, they are all genuine. Even if they are caught cheating he always has some sort of an alibi which excuses the medium and the deed. He insists that the Fox Sisters were genuine, even though both Margaret and Katie confessed to fraud and explained how and why they became mediums and the methods used by them to produce the raps.

"Like Caesar's wife--always above suspicion," Hope and Mrs. Dean pass in his category as genuine mediums. He has often told me that Palladino[78] and Home some day would be canonized for the great work they did in the interest of Spiritualism, even though they were both exposed time and time again. In all gravity he would say to me, "Look what they did to Joan of Arc." To Sir Arthur it is a matter of most sacred moment. It is his religion, and he would invariably tell me what a cool observer he was and how hard it would be to fool him, or in any way deceive him.[79] He told me that he did not believe any of "the nice old lady mediums" would do anything wrong and it was just as unlikely for some old gentleman, innocent as a child unborn, to resort to trickery. But there comes to my mind the notorious Mrs. Catherine Nicol and her two daughters who were continuously getting in and out of the law's net, usually breaking the heads of a few detectives in the process. Among the "nice old lady" mediums might be mentioned a prominent medium of Boston who was accused of taking unlawfully from one of her believers over eight thousand dollars in cash.

---

[77] On March 5, 1923, Harry F. Young, known as "The Human Fly," fell ten stories from a window ledge of the Hotel Martinqiue, New York City. He succumbed before he reached the hospital.

For the benefit of those who do not know, "A Human Fly" is an acrobat who makes a specialty of scaling tall buildings, simply clinging to the apertures or crevices of the outward architecture of such building for the edification of an assembled throng, for which he receives a plate collection, a salary or is engaged especially for publicity purposes. It is not a very lucrative profession and its dangers are many.

[78] On April 14, 1923, in New York City, Sir Arthur, according to his book, "Our American Adventure," attended a seance given by a young Italian by the name of Pecoraro. During the seance the name Palladino was given and he was told that the famous medium was present. A voice from the cabinet, supposedly Palladino's, said, "I, who used to call back the Spirits, now come back as a Spirit myself," to which Sir Arthur answered, "Palladino, we send you our love and our best encouragement." However, the force was broken by "the absurd and vile dancing of the table," and there was no physical manifestation. This shows Sir Arthur's will to excuse even Palladino, who was on numerous occasions exposed as a fraudulent medium.

[79] *ALL* Spiritualists say that.

Another case was that of a medium who received $1,000 from a man in Baltimore for the privilege of a few minutes' chat with the Spirit of his dead wife. He later sued her for fraud. Later she was exposed while giving a séance in Paris, but after a few years she appeared in New York City.

At this time Asst. District Attorney Krotel asked that she be brought into court to answer to a charge of selling California mining stock to her followers through the advice of certain disembodied Spirits. The stock was found to be worthless.

There was also a woman, who was arrested and convicted for vagrancy in Seattle and numerous other cases, such as that of Katie King of Philadelphia in 1875; however, no matter how many cases I cited, it did not seem to make any impression on Sir Arthur.

I had known for some time that a number of people wanted to draw Doyle into a controversy. When I saw Sir Arthur I told him to be careful of his statements and explained a number of pitfalls he could avoid. Nevertheless, despite my warnings, he would say: "That's all right, Houdini, don't worry about me, I am well able to take care of myself. They cannot fool me." To which I would reply he had no idea of the subtleness of some of the people who were trying to draw his fire.

When I called Sir Arthur's attention to the number of people who have gone crazy on the subject because of persistent reading, continuous attendance at séances and trying automatic writing, his answer would be: "People have been going mad[80] for years, and you will find on investigation that many go mad on other subjects besides Spiritualism." On being reminded that most of these people hear voices and see visions, he denied that they were hallucinations, and insisted that he had spoken to different members of his family,[81]

I recall several flagrant instances in which Sir Arthur's faith has, I think, misguided him. One particular time was when he attended a public séance by a lady known as "The Medium in the Mask." Among those present at the time was Lady Glenconner, Sir Henry Lunn and Mr. Sidney A. Mosley, a special representative of a newspaper.

According to reports, the medium wore a veil like a "yashmak." She appeared very nervous. A number of articles, including a ring that had belonged to Sir Arthur's deceased son, were put in a box, and the medium correctly gave the initials on the ring, although Sir Arthur said that they could hardly be discerned, even in a good light, they were so worn off.[82]

Later in describing another article, the medium said the words, "Murphy" and "button" and it was afterwards explained that "Murphy's button" was a surgical operation term. She said that the person described would die as a result of the operation. Unfortunately, for the medium, no one present knew of such a case and yet, *Sir Arthur described this séance as very clever.*[83]

The "Masked Lady" was sponsored by a theatrical agent and illusionist and all proceedings of the séances were brought to light in a suit against Mr. George Grossman and Mr. Edward Laurillard, theatrical producers, to recover damages for breach of agreement to place a West End theatre at his disposal.

Accounts of mediums by the name of "Thompson" have misled several people. There is a Thompson of New York and a Thomson of Chicago. Sir Arthur had a séance with the Thompsons of

---

[80] Dr. A. T. Schofield wrote in the *Daily Sketch,* February 9, 1920, that thousands of persons were estimated by a famous mental specialist to have been driven to the asylum through Spiritualism. A truly pitiful record.

[81] Letter from Sir Arthur to H. H. (dated April 2, 1920): "I have had very conclusive evidence since my two books were written. Six times I have spoken face to face with my son, twice with my brother and once with my nephew, all beyond doubt in their own voices and on private matters, so for me there Is not, nor has been for a long time, any doubt. I *know* it is true, but we can't communicate that certainty to others. It will come—or not, according to how far we work for it. It is the old axiom, 'Seek and ye shall find.'"

[82] Report of trial before Mr. Justice Darling—*Morning Post,* July 16, 1920.

[83] I have it on the positive word of Stuart Cumberland, who was at one of the seances of the "Masked Medium" and he gave me definite specifications and positive facts of the reading of the initials in the ring submitted by Sir Arthur Conan Doyle to the "Masked Medium" whom he said possessed remarkable powers. Stuart Cumberland told me a number of ways this feat could be done. Among them, the black boxes were exchanged surreptitiously in the dark, and then brought back. It is an easy thing to present a box for inspection and yet have false compartments in it so that the contents will fall out. It was only after the methods were told innumerable times to Sir Arthur that he condemned it as a fraud.

New York and according to all the news clippings I have had they claimed to have brought back his mother. In fact it was stated that he asked permission to kiss his mother's hand.

The Thomsons got into trouble in Chicago and New Orleans also.[84] As a matter of fact I was in Chicago when their trial took place. I had been present at two of their séances. The first was in New York at the Morosco Theatre and I had all I could do to keep J. F. Rinns from breaking up the performance. The second was in Chicago. It was a special séance given after my performance at the Palace Theatre. I was accompanied by H. H. Windsor, Publisher and Editor of *Popular Mechanics;* Oliver R. Barrett, a prominent member of the bar; Mr. Husband Manning, author; and Leonard Hicks, a well-known hotel proprietor. Among others present at the séance were Cyrus McCormick, Jr., Muriel McCormick, and Mrs. McCormick McClintock. We witnessed a number of unsatisfactory phenomena and afterwards adjourned to the home of Cyrus McCormick and discussed the séance, being unanimously of the opinion that it was a glaring fraud just as I had believed the one in New York to be.

At the Morosco Theatre, New York City, the Thomsons made the broad statement that they had been tested by Stead and Sir Oliver Lodge and at a special séance he had come out and publicly endorsed Mrs. Thomson as being genuine. The following letter not only disproves this but explains the feeling of an active Spiritualist toward the Thomsons.

"Normanton, Lake, Salisbury.

"7th January 1921.

"Dear Mr. Houdini:--

"It is a pleasure to hear from you, and I thank you for asking the question about the Thomsons. I have replied to one or two other queries of the same kind, but I would be grateful if you would make it known that any statement that I have vouched for their genuineness, is absolutely false.

"I only saw them once, at a time when they called themselves Tomson. It was at Mr. Stead's house, at his urgent request. I considered the performance fraudulent, but the proof was not absolutely complete because the concluding search was not allowed, and the gathering dispersed in disorder, or at least with some heat.

"I felt sorry at this termination, and it is just possible that Thomson genuinely thought I was favourably impressed. That is the charitable view to take, but it is not the true view, and Mr. Stead was annoyed with me because of my skeptical attitude. (He has since admitted to me, from the other side, that he was wrong and I was right; bringing the subject up spontaneously. This latter statement, however, is not evidence.)

"What I should like the public to be assured of, is that I was *not* favourably impressed, and never vouched for them in any way.

"I am afraid I must assume that Thomson is aware of that, and therefore is not acting in good faith, because once in England the same sort of statement was made, either at Leicester or at Nottingham I think, and I wrote to a paper to contradict it.

"With all good wishes believe me,

"Faithfully yours,
(Signed) "OLIVER LODGE."

Sir Arthur personally told me that he was convinced of the genuineness of the Welsh miners of Cardiff, or Thomas Brothers. Stuart Cumberland who was infinitely my superior in investigation (he had a start of 20 years) told me that there wasn't a chance of the Thomas Brothers being genuine, and related how, owing to the great interest of Sir Arthur in them, the *London Daily Express* eventually induced them to hold a séance before a committee of investigators. Cumberland was to have been one of the committee, but the mediums refused to allow him to be "Among those present." As they refused to proceed if Cumberland was admitted, it was thought advisable to eliminate him. Before

---

[84] According to the *New Orleans Times-Picayune,* March 9, 1923, Clarence Thomson, self-styled missionary, President and member of the Board of Directors of the International Psychical Association, was fined $35 and sentenced to serve 30 days in jail. He admitted he had been arrested in Chicago and Kansas City for conducting seances, but said he had been honorably discharged.

leaving, Cumberland arranged the musical instruments that were used and instructed the investigating committee how to detect fraud. The feature of the séance was the passing along in the circle, of a button and a pair of suspenders, which were thrown on the knees of a news Editor present. I ask the common-sense reader what benefit this would be--to project a button clear across the room and to find a pair of suspenders on a sitter's knee? If there is any object lesson in this, please let me know!

At the séance, Lady Doyle was asked whether she was cold, on answering in the affirmative a holland jacket which had been worn by the medium was dropped in her lap. The Thomas Brothers claimed this had been done by the Spirits. When the séance was over, the medium was found bound but minus his coat.

When I quizzed Sir Arthur about the manner in which the Thomas Brothers of Cardiff were bound during a séance which he attended, he told me that they were secured so tightly that it was impossible for them to move as they were absolutely helpless. I told him that did not make it genuine, for any number of mediums had been tied the same way and had managed to free themselves. He replied that I might be able to release myself by natural means, but that mediums do not have to, as they always receive Spiritual help. Maybe so, but I should like, sometime, to tie them myself and see whether the Spirits could release them under test conditions.[85]

I reminded Sir Arthur of the Davenport Brothers and called to his attention the fact that they were able to release themselves. Sir Arthur feels very strongly in the matter of the Davenport Brothers and although I have told him and proven to him that I was a pupil of Ira Erastus Davenport[86] and that Ira personally told me that they did not claim to be Spiritualists and their performances were not given in the name of Spiritualism, Sir Arthur insists that they *were* Spiritualists and has strongly said that if they did their performances under any other name, then Ira was "not only a liar, but a blasphemer as he went around with Mr. Ferguson, a clergyman, and mixed it all up with religion."

I want to go on record that to the best of my knowledge and belief I never stated that Sir Arthur endorsed the mediumship of the New York Thompsons. I did say there were full page articles[87] where he was illustrated as accepting the genuineness of the materialization of his mother. I never claimed that Sir Arthur's son or brother came through the Thomas mediums in Cardiff. I did state that Sir Arthur said they were genuine and that they, the mediums, were helpless to move because he had tied them and in his judgment if they were tied in my presence I would be convinced of their genuineness. I wish to call attention to the fact that in a letter written by the late Stuart Cumberland he agreed with me that there was not a vestige of truth in the mediumship of the Thomas Brothers, and regarding Sir Arthur's endorsement of the "Masked Lady," I did not say he endorsed her although I should judge from newspaper[88] accounts he seemed very much impressed.

Sir Arthur has rarely given me an opportunity to deny or affirm any statement. In fact one of our sore points of discussion has been the matter of being quoted, or misquoted,[89] in newspapers or periodicals and it seems that Sir Arthur always believes everything I have been quoted as having said. When I was in Oakland, California, I was interviewed by a Mr. Henderson of the *Oakland Tribune.* I gave him some material to work on, enough for one article from which, to my surprise, he wrote a series of eight articles enlarging and misquoting to an "nth" degree. Sir Arthur took exception to a number of statements which I was supposed to have made and he replied to them caustically through the press and then sent me the following letter in explanation.

"THE AMBASSADOR, Los Angeles, May 23, 1923.

"My dear Houdini:--

---

[85] Other performers are doing this feat. I have performed it regularly for thirty years without any supernatural power whatever.

[86] Sec Davenport chapter.

[87] These articles were syndicated, *New York American,* Sept. 3rd, 1923.

[88] *Morning Post,* July 16, 1920.

[89] See Appendix G.

"I have had to handle you a little roughly in the *Oakland Tribune* because they send me a long screed under quotation marks, so it is surely accurate. It is so full of errors that I don't know where to begin. I can't imagine why you say such wild things which have no basis in fact at all. I put the Thompsons down as humbugs. I never heard of my son or brother through the Thomas brothers. They were never exposed. I never said that Masked Medium was genuine. I wish you would refer to me before publishing such injurious stuff which I have to utterly contradict. I would always tell you the exact facts as I have done with the Zancigs.

"Yours sincerely,
"A. Conan Doyle."

"I hate sparring with a friend in public, but what can I do when you say things which are not correct, and which I have to contradict or else they go by default. It is the same with all this ridiculous stuff of Rinn's. Unless I disprove it, people imagine it is true.

"A. C. D."

At the written invitation of Sir Arthur and Lady Doyle Mrs. Houdini and I visited them while they were stopping at the Ambassador Hotel in Atlantic City. One day as Sir Arthur, Mrs. Houdini and I were sitting on the sand skylarking with the children Sir Arthur excused himself saying that he was going to have his usual afternoon nap. He left us but returned in a short time and said "Houdini, if agreeable, Lady Doyle will give you a special séance, as she has a feeling that she might have a message come through. At any rate, she is willing to try," and turning to Mrs. Houdini he said, "we would like to be alone. You do not mind if we make the experiment without you." Smilingly, my good little wife said, "Certainly not, go right ahead, Sir Arthur; I will leave Houdini in your charge and I know that he will be willing to go to the séance." Doyle said, "You understand, Mrs. Houdini, that this will be a test to see whether we can make any Spirit come through for Houdini, and conditions may prove better if no other force is present."

Before leaving with Sir Arthur, Mrs. Houdini cued me. We did a second sight or mental performance years ago and still use a system or code whereby we can speak to each other in the presence of others, even though to all outward appearances we are merely talking, pointing or doing the most innocent looking things, but which have different meanings to us.

In that manner Mrs. Houdini told me that on the night previous she had gone into detail with Lady Doyle about the great love I bear for my Mother. She related to her a number of instances, such as, my returning home from long trips, sometimes as far away as Australia, and spending months with my Mother and wearing only the clothes that she had given me, because I thought it would please her and give her some happiness. My wife also remarked about my habit of laying my head on my Mother's breast, in order to hear her heart beat. Just little peculiarities that mean so much to a mother and son when they love one another as we did.

I walked with Sir Arthur to the Doyles' suite. Sir Arthur drew down the shades so as to exclude the bright light. We three, Lady Doyle, Sir Arthur and I, sat around the table on which were a number of pencils and a writing pad, placing our hands on the surface of the table.

Sir Arthur started the séance with a devout prayer. I had made up my mind that I would be as religious as it was within my power to be and not at any time did I scoff at the ceremony. I excluded all earthly thoughts and gave my whole soul to the séance.

I was *willing* to believe, even *wanted* to believe. It was weird to me and with a beating heart I waited, hoping that I might feel once more the presence of my beloved Mother. If there ever was a son who idolized and worshipped his Mother, whose every thought was for her happiness and comfort, that son was myself. My Mother meant my life, her happiness was synonymous with my peace of mind. For that reason, if no other, I wanted to give my very deepest attention to what was going on. It meant to me an easing of all pain that I had in my heart. I especially wanted to speak to my Mother, because that day, *June 17,* 1922, was her birthday.[90] I was determined to embrace Spiritualism if there was any evidence strong enough to down the doubts that have crowded my brain for the past thirty years.

---

[90] This was not known to Lady Doyle. If it had been my Dear Mother's Spirit communicating a message, she, knowing her birthday was nay most holy holiday, surely would have commented on it.

Presently, Lady Doyle was "seized by a Spirit." Her hands shook and beat the table, her voice trembled and she called to the Spirits to give her a message. Sir Arthur tried to quiet her, asked her to restrain herself, but her hand thumped on the table, her whole body shook and at last, making a cross at the head of the page, started writing. And as she finished each page, Sir Arthur tore the sheet off and handed it to me. I sat serene through it all, hoping and wishing that I might feel my mother's presence. There wasn't even a semblance of it. Everyone who has ever had a worshipping Mother and has lost earthly touch, knows the feeling which will come over him at the thought of sensing her presence.

The letter which follows, purported to have come from my Mother, I cannot, as much as I desire, accept as having been written or inspired by the soul or Spirit of my sweet Mother.

"Oh, my darling, thank God, thank God, at last I'm thorough--I've tried, oh, so often--now I am happy. Why, of course I want to talk to my boy--my own beloved boy--Friends, thank you, with all my heart for this."--

"You have answered the cry of my heart--and of his-- God bless him--a thousandfold for all his life for me-- never had a Mother such a son--tell him not to grieve-- soon he'll get all the evidence he is so anxious for--Yes we know--tell him I want him to try and write in his own home. It will be far better."

"I will work with him--he is so, so dear to me--I am preparing so sweet a home for him in which some day in God's good time he will come to it, is one of my great joys preparing for our future."

"I am so happy in this life--it is so full and joyous-- my only shadow has been that my beloved one hasn't known how often I have been with him all the while, all the while--here away from my heart's darling--combining my work thus in this life of mine."

"It is so different over here, so much larger and bigger and more beautiful--so lofty--all sweetness around one --nothing that hurts and we see our beloved ones on earth--that is such a joy and comfort to us--Tell him I love him more than ever--the years only increase it-- and his goodness fills my soul with gladness and thank-fulness. Oh, just this, it *is* me. I want him only to know that--that--I have bridged the gulf--that is what I wanted, oh, so much--Now I can rest in peace--how soon--"

"I *always* read my beloved son's mind--his dear mind --there is so much I want to say to him--but--I am almost overwhelmed by this joy of talking to him once more--it is almost too much to get through--the joy of it--thank you, thank you, friend, with all my heart for what you have done for me this day--God bless you, too, Sir Arthur, for what you are doing for us--for us, over here--who so need to get in touch with our beloved ones on the earth plane--"

"If only the world knew this great truth--how different life would be for men and women--Go on let nothing stop you--great will be your reward hereafter--Good-by--I brought you, Sir Arthur, and my son together--I felt you were the only man who might help us to pierce this veil --and I was right--Bless him, bless him, bless him, I say, from the depths of my soul--he fills my heart and later we shall be together--Oh so happy--a happiness awaits him that he has never dreamed of--tell him I am with him--just tell him that I'll soon make him know how close I am all the while--his eyes will soon be opened-- Good-by again--God's blessing on you all."

In the case of my séance, Sir Arthur believed that due to the great excitement it was a direct connection.

The more so do I hesitate to believe and accept the above letter because, although my sainted mother had been in America for almost fifty years, she could not speak, read nor write English but Spiritualists claim that when a medium is possessed by a Spirit who does not speak the language, she automatically writes, speaks or sings in the language of the deceased; however, Sir Arthur has told me that a Spirit becomes more educated the longer it is departed and that my blessed Mother had been able to master the English language in Heaven.

After the purported letter from my Mother had been written and I had read it over very carefully, Sir Arthur advised me to follow out the advice, given by my Mother, --to try to write when I reached home.

I picked up a pencil in a haphazard manner and said, "Is there any particular way in which I must hold this pencil when I want to write, or does it write automatically?" *I then wrote the name of "Powell" entirely of my own volition.* Sir Arthur jumped up excitedly and read what I had just written. He saw the word "Powell" and said, "The Spirits have directed you in writing the name of my dear fighting partner in Spiritualism, Dr. Ellis Powell, who has just died in England. I am the person he is most likely to signal to, and here is his name coming through your hands. Truly Saul is among the Prophets."

I must emphatically state that this name was written entirely of my own volition and in full consciousness. I had in mind, my friend Frederick Eugene Powell, the American Magician, with whom at the time I was having a great deal of correspondence regarding a business proposition which has since been consummated. There is not the slightest doubt of it having been more than a deliberate mystification on my part, or let us say a kindlier word regarding my thoughts and call it "coincidence."

A few days later Sir Arthur sent me the following letter in reference to my explanation of the writing of the name, "Powell."

"The Ambassador, New York, June 20th, 1922.

"My dear Houdini:--

". . . No, the Powell explanation, won't do. Not only is he the one man who would wish to get me, but in the evening, Mrs. M., the lady medium, got, "there is a man here. He wants to say that he is sorry he had to speak so abruptly this afternoon." The message was then broken by your Mother's renewed message and so we got no name. But it confirms me in the belief that it *was* Powell. However, you will no doubt test your powers further.

(Signed) "A. Conan Doyle."

I had written an article for the *New York Sun,* October 30, 1922, which gave my views in reference to Spiritualism and at the same time answered the challenge offered by the General Assembly of Spiritualists of New York State. This had been called to the attention of Sir Arthur, who wrote as follows:

"Windlesham, Crowborough, Sussex., November 19, 1922.

"My dear Houdini:--

"They sent me the *New York Sun* with your article and no doubt wanted me to answer it, but I have no fancy for sparring with a friend in public, so I took no notice.

"But none the less, I felt rather sore about it. You have all the right in the world to hold your own opinion, but when you say that you have had no evidence of survival, you say what I cannot reconcile with what I saw with my own eyes. I know, by many examples, the purity of my wife's mediumship, and I saw what you got and what the effect was upon you at the time. You know also you yourself at once wrote down, with your own hand, the name of Powell, the one man who might be expected to communicate with me. Unless you were joking when you said that you did not know of this Powell's death, then surely that was evidential, since the idea that out of all your friends you had chanced to write the name of one who exactly corresponded, would surely be too wonderful a coincidence.

"However, I don't propose to discuss this subject any more with you, for I consider that you have had your proofs and that the responsibility of accepting or rejecting is with you. As it is a very real lasting responsibility. However, I have it at last, for I have done my best to give you the truth. I will, however, send you my little book, on the fraud perpetrated upon Hope, but that will be my last word on the subject. Meanwhile, there are lots of other subjects on which we can all meet in friendly converse.

"Yours very sincerely,
(Signed) "A. Conan Doyle."

To which I replied:--

"December 15, 1922.

"Sir Arthur Conan Doyle, Windlesham, Crowborough, Sussex.

"My dear Sir Arthur:--

"Received your letter regarding my article in the *New York Sun.* You write that you are very sore. I trust that it is not with me, because you, having been truthful and manly all your life, naturally must admire the same traits in other human beings.

"I know you are honorable and sincere and think I owe you an explanation regarding the letter I received through the hands of Lady Doyle.

"I was heartily in accord and sympathy at that séance but the letter was written entirely in English and my sainted Mother could not read, write or speak the English language. I did not care to discuss it at the time because of my emotion in trying to sense the presence of my

Mother, if there was such a thing possible, to keep me quiet until time passed, and I could give it the proper deduction.

"Regarding my having written the name 'Powell." Frederick Eugene Powell is a very dear friend of mine. He had just passed through two serious operations. Furthermore Mrs. Powell had a paralytic stroke at that time. I was having some business dealings with him which entailed a great deal of correspondence; therefore, naturally, his name was uppermost in my mind and I cannot make myself believe that my hand was guided by your friend. It was just a coincidence.

"I trust my clearing up of the séance, from my point of view is satisfactory, and that you do not harbor any ill feelings, because I hold both Lady Doyle and yourself in the highest esteem. I know you treat this as a religion but personally I cannot do so, for up to the present time I have never seen or heard anything that could convert me.

"Trusting you will accept my letter in the same honest, good faith feeling as it has been written.

"With best wishes to Lady Doyle, yourself and the family, in which Mrs. Houdini joins,

"Sincerely yours,
(Signed) "Houdini."

In January 1923, the *Scientific American* issued a challenge of $2500. to the first person to produce a psychic photograph under test conditions. An additional $2500. was offered to the first person who, under the test conditions, defined, and to the satisfaction of the judges named, produced an objective psychic manifestation of physical character as defined, and of such sort that permanent instrumental record may be made of its occurrence.

The committee named were: Dr. William McDougall, D.Sc., Professor of Psychology at Harvard; Daniel Frisk Comstock, Ph.D., former member of the Faculty of the Massachusetts Institute of Technology; Walter Franklin Prince, Ph.D., Principal Research Officer for the S. P. R.; Hereward Carrington, Ph.D., Psychic Investigator; J. Malcolm Bird, Member of the Scientific American Staff; and myself.[91]

Sir Arthur's letter is self-explanatory.

"Windlesham, Crowborough, Sussex, January 1, 1923.

"My dear Houdini:

"... I see that you are on the Scientific American Committee, but how can it be called an Impartial Committee when you have committed yourself to such statements as that some Spiritualists pass away before they realize how they have been deluded, etc? You have every possible right to hold such an opinion, but you can't sit on an Impartial Committee afterwards. It becomes biased at once. What I

---

[91] So far, all of the several seances of investigation held under the auspices of the Scientific American, have failed in proving the existence of supernatural power or force, such as might with logical consistency be conceded as psychic.

Valentine, the Wilkesbarre medium, proved to be a failure. Rev. (?) Jessie K. Stewart the same. Mrs. Elizabeth Allen Tomson of Chicago, a complete fiasco, not possessing sufficient courage to attempt a sitting other than under conditions and in a place prescribed by herself. And lastly the Italian lad, Nino Pecoraro, has accomplished nothing beyond the possibility of human exertion, and failed utterly in so doing when securely fettered, as proved to be the case, when I personally did the tying. See also Appendix H.

And from the results gotten thus far from the series of sittings with this "medium" it is safe to predict that the final analysis will place him in the same category as all others to date.

wanted was five good clear-headed men who can push to it without any prejudice at all, like the Dialectical Society[92] of London, who unanimously endorsed the phenomena.

"Once more all greetings,

(Signed) "A CONAN DOYLE."

On May 21, 22 and 24 the *Scientific American* held their first test séances. The permanent sitters were Mr. Walker, Mr. Lescurboura, Mr. J. Malcolm Bird of the Editorial staff of the *Scientific American*, Mr. Owen of the *Times,* Mr. Granville Lehrmann of the American Telephone and Telegraph and Richard I. Worrell, *a friend* of the medium. Drs. Carrington and Prince of the Committee of Judges sat on Monday. Dr. Prince and myself on Thursday. On Tuesday the Committee was represented by Mr. Frederick Keating, conjuror.

The medium, a man by the name of George Valentine of Wilkes-Barre, Penn., claimed to be genuine. He was trapped by being seated on a chair which was so arranged that when he arose an electric light arrangement was fixed in the room adjoining, together with dictographs and a phosphorous button. In the estimation of the Committee, Mr. Valentine was just a common, ordinary trickster.

Lady Doyle, Miss Juliet Karcher, Mrs. Houdini, Sir Arthur and I were lunching at the Royal Automobile Club in London, May 11, 1920, and Sir Arthur called attention to the fact that a few days previously they had been sitting at the same table with a powerful medium, and he told me in a very serious tone, which was corroborated by Lady Doyle, that the table started to move all around the place to the astonishment of the waiter, who was not aware of the close proximity of the medium.

All the time he was relating it, I watched him closely and saw that both he and Lady Doyle were most sincere and believed what they had told me to be an actual fact.

There are times when I almost doubt the sincerity of some of Sir Arthur's *statements,* even though I do not doubt the sincerity of his belief.

I have been over a number of letters which I have received from Sir Arthur during the last few years and selected the following excerpts which show his viewpoint regarding many of the matters we have discussed.

"I do not wonder that they put you down as an occult. As I read the accounts I do not see how you do it. You must be a brave man as well as exceptionally dexterous."

"How you get out of the diving suits beats me, but the whole thing beats me completely."

"I spoke of the Davenport Brothers. Your word on the matter knowing, as you do both the man and the possibilities of his art, would be final."

"You are to me a perpetual mystery. No doubt you are to everyone."

"In a fair light I saw my dead Mother as clearly as I ever saw her in life. I am a cool observer and I do not make mistakes. It was wonderful--but it taught me nothing I did not know before."

"Our best remembrances to your wife and yourself. For God's sake be careful in those fearsome feats of yours. You ought to be able to retire now."

"These clairvoyants whose names I have given you are passive agents in themselves and powerless. If left to themselves they guess and muddle--as they sometimes do, when the true connection is formed, all is clear. That connection depends on the forces beyond, which are repelled by frivolity or curiosity but act under the impulse of sympathy."

"I see that you know a great deal about the negative side of Spiritualism."

---

[92] According to Spiritualistic publications The Dialectical Society never made a full report. The "Reports" of sub-committees only were published by Spiritualist papers used by writers in books but such *reports* were based on "hear-say" evidence taken from Spiritists. They told their ghost stories to Committees and they were believed. There never was a unanimous report or conclusion. The non-Spiritual (?) members of the Dialectical Society refused to have anything to do with the investigation. The great majority of the Committee were full-fledged Spiritualists, and the few whom they claimed to have convinced were simply credulous,

"If you think of a lost friend before going to a séance and breathe a prayer that you may be allowed to get in touch you will have a chance--otherwise none. It really does depend upon psychic or mental vibrations and harmonies."

"I fear there is much fraud among American mediums where Spiritualism seems to have deservedly fallen into disrepute. Even when genuine it is used for stock exchange, and other base worldly purposes. No wonder it has sunk low in the very land that was honored by the first Spiritual manifestations of the series."

"You certainly have very wonderful powers, whether inborn or acquired."

"I envy you the privilege of having met Ira Davenport."

"Most of our great mediums at present are unpaid amateurs, inaccessible to any but Spiritualists."

"Something *must* come your way if you really persevere and get it out of your mind that you should follow it as a terrier follows a rat."

"Mental harmony does not in the least abrogate common sense."

"I heard of your remarkable feat in Bristol. My dear chap, why do you go around the world seeking a demonstration of the occult when you are giving one all the time?"

"I *know* Hope to be a true psychic and will give you my reasons when I treat it, but you can give no man a blank check for honesty on every particular occasion, whether there is a temptation to hedge when psychic power runs low is a question to be considered. I am for an uncompromising honesty-- but also for thorough examination based on true knowledge."

"I am amused by your investigation with the Society for Psychical Research. Have they never thought of investigating you?"

"It was good of you to give those poor invalids a show and you will find yourself in the third sphere alright with your dear wife, world without end, whatever you may believe."

"Incredulity seems to me to be a sort of insanity under the circumstances." This was in reference to some photographs of ectoplasm which I questioned.

"This talk of 'fake' is in most cases nonsense and shows our own imperfect knowledge of conditions and of the ways of Controls, who often take short cuts to their ends, having no regard at all to our critical idea."

"Our opponents talk of one failure and omit a great series of successes. However, truth wins and there is lots of time."

"I never let a pressman (newspaper man) get away with it with impunity if I can help it."[93]

"Our relations are certainly curious and likely to become more so, for as long as you attack what *I know* from experience to be true I have no alternative but to attack you in turn. How long a private friendship can survive such an ordeal I do not know, but at least I did not create the situation."

---

[93] Sir Arthur Conan Doyle seems to imagine that all the newspapers in the world are against him. After his Australian tour he accused the Australian papers of refusing to publish the truth about his seances. Writing about American newspapers in his book, "An American Adventure," he says: "The editors seem to place the intelligence of the public very low, and to imagine that they cannot be attracted save by vulgar, screaming headlines.

"The American papers have a strange way also of endeavoring to compress the whole meaning of some item into a few words of headline, which, as often as not, are slang."

Even in Canada Sir Arthur claims to have badly used by the newspapers. In "Our American Adventure" he writes: "There were some rather bitter attacks in the Toronto papers, including the one leader in the *Evening Telegram,* which was so narrow and illiberal that I do not think the most provincial paper in Britain could have been guilty of it.

"It was to the effect that British lecturers took money out of the town, that they did not give the money's worth, and that they should be discouraged.

" 'Poking Them in the Eye' was the dignified title.

"It did not *seem* to occur to the writer that a comic opera or a bedroom comedy was equally taking the money out of the town, but that the main purpose served by lectures, whether one agreed with the subject or not, was that they kept the public in first hand touch with the great current questions of mankind. I am bound to say that no other Toronto paper sank to the depth of the *Evening Telegram* but the general atmosphere was the least pleasant that I had met with in my American travels."

"You have a reputation among Spiritualists of being a bitterly prejudiced enemy who would make trouble if it were possible--I know this is not so."

On page 150 of Sir Arthur's book "Our American Adventure" he says:

"Houdini is not one of those shallow men who imagine they can explain away Spiritual phenomena as parlor tricks, but he retains an open--and ever, I think, a more receptive--mind toward mysteries which are beyond his art. He understands, I hope, that to get truth in the matter you have not to sit as a Sanhedrim of Judgement, like the Circle of Conjurors in London, since Spiritual truth does not come as a culprit to a bar, but you must submit in a humble spirit to psychic conditions and so go forth, making most progress when on your knees."

Sir Arthur has told me time and time again that his whole life is based upon the subject of Spiritualism and that he has sacrificed some of the best years of his life to the betterment and spread of the cause, which, due to his sincerity, is a beautiful faith.[94] But in my opinion it is no "sacrifice" to convince people who have recently suffered a bereavement of the possibility and reality of communicating with their dear ones. To me the poor suffering followers eagerly searching for relief from the heart-pain that follows the passing on of a dear one are the "sacrifice."

Sir Arthur thinks that I have great mediumistic powers and that some of my feats are done with the aid of spirits. Everything I do is accomplished by material means, humanly possible, no matter how baffling it is to the layman. He says that I do not enter a séance in the right frame of mind, that I should be more submissive, but in all the séances I have attended I have never had a feeling of antagonism. I have no desire to discredit Spiritualism; I have no warfare with Sir Arthur; I have no fight with the Spiritists; but I do believe it is my duty, for the betterment of humanity, to place frankly before the public the results of my long investigation of Spiritualism. I am willing to be convinced; my mind is open, but the proof must be such as to leave no vestige of doubt that what is claimed to be done is accomplished only through or by supernatural power. So far I have never on any occasion, in all the séances I have attended, seen anything which would lead me to credit a mediumistic performance with supernatural aid, nor have I ever seen anything which has convinced me that it is possible to communicate with those who have passed out of this life. Therefore I do not agree with Sir Arthur about what Spiritism has done, and is still doing, to fill our lunatic asylums all over the world. There are over thirty thousand lunatics in England alone who lost their mind through this modern necromancy. Doyle does not even hint at the countless cases of insanity and suicide, of blasphemy and obscenity, of lying and deception, of broken homes and violated troth, all caused by Spiritism. To suppose that a God of truth and sanctity is giving a new message through such sources and with such consequences, is blasphemy pure and simple. Furthermore, to assert that this New Revelation is to supersede a worn-out creed is both gratuitous and absurd. Christianity will last till the crack of doom, when titled prophets shall have ceased to cross the Atlantic in quest of American shekels."

---

[94] In an article in Truth, April, 1923, entitled "The New Revelation," by Rev. P. J. Cormican, S. J., he asks:

"Does the knighted prophet of the New Revelation (Sir Arthur Conan Doyle) tell the whole truth about Spiritism? We think not. He says nothing about the evil consequences, physical, intellectual and moral, to those who dabble in Spiritism. He gives a one-sided account of the matter. He says nothing

Chapter 10
Why Ectoplasm?

YEARS have passed since my first meeting with the Hon. Everard Feilding! Many times during those years I have discussed Spiritualism with him and no one has ever been more interested than he in the results of my investigations and study of it and it was through his help that I was able to investigate personally the famous Eva Carriere, better known perhaps as Mlle. Eva.

One evening in the spring of 1920 during a quiet dinner at his home in London the conversation drifted toward Ectoplasm. I told Mr. and Mrs.[95] Feilding about attending a Sunday meeting of the London Psychical College through the courtesy of Hewat McKenzie. At this meeting Mme. Bisson and Mlle. Eva were introduced by Fornieur d'Albe and Mme. Bisson while delivering an impromptu talk seized the opportunity to resent the attack of a French magician and to explain in unmistakable tones her antagonism toward prestidigitators.

Mr. Feilding assured me I was correct about her antipathy towards magicians and suggested that the only way I could ever hope to attend one of her séances was to convince the medium that I was not one of the biased prestidigitator class, and proposed as a means to attain this end a theatre party to see my performance and thus enable Mme. Bisson and Mlle. Eva to judge for themselves. This was arranged and the night they came to the theatre to see me I did the Torture Cell Mystery, in which I am completely submerged, head foremost, in a tank of water, and it is a physical impossibility to obtain air while locked in the device. They were so much mystified that they expressed a desire to attend another performance of mine sometime in the near future. I had just accepted a challenge to escape from a packing case which was to be built on the stage by experienced carpenters and thinking that it would be an interesting performance for Mme. Bisson to witness I extended her an invitation and received the following letter in reply.

"May 19, 1920.

"Dear Mr. Houdini:

"We, Mlle. Eva and I, shall be charmed to see you at the performance of which you have spoken to me, on next Wednesday. Since you have had the great kindness to offer us several tickets, it gives me great pleasure to accept, and if you wish, you may send us four, as we expect to join in the applause with Mr. and Mrs. Feilding.

"I also wish to tell you something else!

"You know that we give séances here, showing the phenomena of materialization. These are not spirit studies. They are scientific.

"It would interest Mr. Feilding and ourselves to have at our séances a master in the art of prestidigitation, but I have always refused to admit to my house, an ordinary prestidigitator, or even one of better rank. Our work is serious and real, and the gift of Mlle. Eva might disappear forever, if some awkward individual insists on thinking there is fraud involved, instead of real and interesting facts, which especially interest the scientific.

"For you this does not hold! You are above all this.

You are a magnificent actor, who can not call himself a prestidigitator, a title beneath a man of your talent.

"I shall therefore, (rather we shall) be proud to see you attend our séances and hear you tell us all, after you have been thoroughly convinced yourself, that their merit is far beneath your own, for these manifestations depend merely upon allowing the forces of nature to act, and lie simply in truth of fact.

---

[95] Mrs. Feilding is Mme. Tomchik, the Polish medium examined by Professor Ochorowiz, and is the best known medium who "levitates" things without physical contact.

Whereas with you, it is your merit, your talent, and your personal valor that have enabled you to attain the place of King in your art.

"With kind and esteemed regards to Mme. Houdini and yourself, (Signed) Juliette Bisson."

(Translated.)

When I showed this letter to Mr. Feilding he was both surprised and pleased for it gave him an opportunity to invite me to become one of the Committee which was to investigate Mme. Bisson and Mlle. Eva's séances to be held by the Society for Psychical Research, and so at the combined invitations of the mediums and Mr. Feilding I attended eight. Each of them lasted three hours and I firmly believe that a description of them and their results is important.

At these séances my word was pledged to give full and sacred thoughts and I tried to control my thoughts so that my whole attention could be given to the medium. There was no scoffing and there was the will to believe. I felt that if anything was manifested by the Spirits my conscience would be clear. However, I sat with my eyes open, taking in even the most minute details and keeping on my guard against any trickery. A number of times I occupied a "control" chair at the medium's left with her left limb between mine and both of my hands holding her left hand and wrist, while Eric Dingwall had the Committee seat on her right. Eva was accompanied at all of the séances by Mme. Bisson and the method of procedure was always the same. After Eva had been stripped and searched[96] in an adjoining room by the lady members of the Committee, she returned dressed in tights and Mme. Bisson would then put her into a mesmeric sleep. There is no doubt in my mind that the girl was really put to sleep. We were requested to all join in asking her in unison for about fifteen minutes at each crisis to "give"-- "donnez"--then, after about three hours, she would bring forth this alleged ectoplasm.

At one of the séances the Hon. Feilding did insist on Eva's eating crackers and drinking coffee, so that if she had anything concealed in her stomach, which she might by regurgitation expel, the coffee would discolor it.

The séance of June 22, 1920, was held at 20 Hanover Square, London. Mme. Bisson and Eva retired to another room and Eric Dingwall sewed a black lace veil to the tights which Eva wore. This veil completely enshrouded her and looked like a sort of bag or net. The object of this was to prevent her from placing anything in her mouth or get anything from her tights to the neck--in fact, it was a double security against fraud. We sat and waited and finally she expelled from her mouth a great deal of foam.

Feilding and Baggley stated that it looked as though it had come from her nose. I saw distinctly that it was a heavy froth and was adhering to her veil on the inside. Dingwall, who sat next to the medium, agreed with me it had emanated from her mouth, but when she leaned forward it looked as though it was coming from her nose. She produced a white plaster and eventually managed to juggle it over her eye. There was a face in it which looked to me like a colored cartoon and seemed to have been unrolled.

The last thing she produced that evening was a substance which she said she felt in her mouth and asked permission to use her hands to show. This was granted and she took a load from her mouth behind the veil which was wet and looked soaked. It appeared to be inflated rubber. No one saw a face painted on it. Presently it seemed to disappear. They all said it "vanished suddenly," but my years of experience in presenting the Hindoo needle trick[97] convinced me that she "sleight-of-

---

[96] At no time, to my knowledge, did the search include the orifices of her body.

[97] In this trick I swallow (if one's eyes are to be trusted) anywhere from fifty to a hundred and fifty needles and from ten to thirty yards of thread; then after a few seconds I bring up the needles all threaded. The length of thread is governed by the size of my audience. For instance, at the Hippodrome, in New York, I used one hundred and ten feet of thread and two hundred needles; at the Berlin Winter Garden one hundred feet of thread and one hundred needles. In the regular large size theatres I use about eighty feet of thread and a hundred needles but for ordinary purposes thirty-five feet of thread and seventy-five needles are sufficient.

So far this trick has never been properly explained but that does not prove that I have abnormal powers. This needle mystery has been examined by a great many physicians and surgeons and in Boston at Keith's Theatre it was presented at a special performance to over a thousand physicians and they were unable to explain it. However, there is nothing abnormal in it. It is nothing more than a clever and natural mystification.

handed" it into her mouth while pretending to have it between her fingers. I know positively that the move she made is almost identical with the manner in which I manipulate my experiment. Dingwall was very confident and told Mme. Bisson that he was *nearly* satisfied with Eva's experiments. She showed her peevishness to Feilding so plainly that I could scarcely conceal my smiles.

In the course of conversation after the séance, Mme. Bisson told the Committee that at one time Eva had materialized on the top of her knees the head of an American soldier with a heavy mustache and blue eyes. It caused some merriment when Dingwall asked her how she could tell the color of a man's eyes in the dark.

Mme. Bisson, perplexed and in grieved tones, asked whether they were suspicious or simply did not believe her. They tried hard to pacify her but to no avail.

At the séance of June 24th, held in the same place, I arrived somewhat late but the Committee allowed me to come in. That evening I felt that there was something wrong in the air and after the lapse of two hours Mme. Bisson told us that she was in grief and greatly disheartened because there was so much suspicion aimed at her. She was especially peeved at Dingwall, who had told her that he was only "almost" convinced. At no time was I antagonistic but, on the contrary, willing to help along.

Presently Feilding in a rather jovial mood left the room for a breath of fresh air. When he came back he was very serious and asked that they continue. Mme. Bisson thought he was trying to tease her and became very angry. She was wrong, in my opinion, but they argued and expostulated for half an hour and then the séance broke up. During the argument Eva, who was in a cabinet in a "trance state," spoke out as though she had not been in a trance. I afterwards asked Mr. Feilding if this was not suspicious, but he told me that it was possible for a human being while in a trance or hypnotic state to carry on a conversation consciously. When Mme. Bisson left us Mr. Feilding told me that he was very sorry about the unpleasantness and would make all possible amends to her.

After a number of sittings with Eva during which nothing startling occurred I made up my mind to be lenient with the medium and help her, so I held her hands for some time and gradually withdrew both of mine, giving her all the leeway she needed in case there was any desire on her part to use the hand which I was supposed to be holding, but she made no move whatever.

I was not in any way convinced by the demonstrations witnessed. I believe that Eva's feats are accomplished by regurgitation. If not, the work she is reputed to do is an "inside job."[98] I regret that I do not believe Mme. Bisson entitled to a clean bill of health. During the séances which I attended she kept up a quasi hypnotic work full of gestures and suggestions as to what could be seen, putting into the minds of those present "shadowy forms and faces." In my estimation she is a subtle and gifted assistant to Eva whom I do not believe to be honest. On the contrary, I have no hesitation in saying that I think the two simply took advantage of the credulity and good nature of the various men with whom they had to deal.

In this conclusion I am not alone, for in reviewing the Villa Carmine séances of Mlle. Eva, Mr. Heuze states in the *London Telegraph* of September 4th, 1922:

"The whiteness supposed to have come from the 'world beyond' was nothing but a Communicant's veil rolled up in the medium's pocket."

He also quotes Mlle. Eva as saying:

"Monsieur, I never made any confession."

"In that case," he comments, "all I can say is that M. Carborrnel, M. Coulom, Maitre Marsault, Maitre Jourman, Dr. Demis, Mlle. Mare, M. Verdier, Cochet M. Portal, Mme. Portal and others must have all lied in a body to persecute Mlle. Eva."

Also the Sorbonne scientists at Paris, according to a report in the *New York Times*, stated officially that during fifteen séances with Mlle. Eva there was nothing beyond the simple act of regurgitation. In two instances there was no ectoplasm seen at any time in spite of the fact that Mme. Bisson suggested that two little discs produced by Mlle. Eva were assuming forms and faces. None of the professors, however, were able to see anything of the kind, but on the contrary declared that:

---

[98] That is, has a secret accomplice. One who does things to help along "unknown." One who is in the "click."

"The substance was absolutely inert, only moving as movement was given it by the medium's mouth. The substance having been reabsorbed the medium seemed to be chewing for some seconds and then apparently swallowed it."[99]

W. J. Crawford, Doctor of Science, and a lecturer on Mechanical Engineering, of Belfast, Irleand, became very much interested in a family of mediums consisting of a father, four daughters, a son, and a son-in-law and known as the Goligher Circle. Of the seven, the most successful was Miss Kathleen Goligher.[100]

While at Mr. Feilding's home in London I had the pleasure of meeting this Dr. Crawford and talking with him for several hours. During the talk he showed me pictures of what he claimed was ectoplasm exuding from different parts of Kathleen Goligher's body and told me he was going to use them in a forthcoming book.

"Do you honestly believe that everything you have experienced through your contact and experiments with the girl is absolutely genuine?" I asked him.

"I am positive in my belief," he answered.

After he had gone Mr. Feilding turned to me and asked:

"What do you think of Dr. Crawford?"

"He seems mad to me," I answered.

"Houdini, you are mistaken," he replied.

Nevertheless I do not think that Dr. Crawford was the right man or had the right sort of a mind for an investigation. To me his credulity seemed limitless. E. E. Fournier d'Albe's report of Dr. Crawford's séance with the Goligher Circle coincides with my judgment. In a communication addressed to "Light" in August, 1922, d'Albe referring to his own tenth séance says:

"I found to my surprise that I could myself with some little management, produce the phenomena with my feet exactly as I had observed them."

Dr. Von Schrenk-Notzing[101] charged d'Albe with entering his investigation with "prejudice against the genuineness of the Goligher phenomena." This d'Albe denied, saying:

"I had gone to Belfast fresh from Eva C's séance with a strong conviction of reality and with firm faith in Dr. Crawford's reliability and accuracy. I expected a gifted medium surrounded by her honest folks, but then came the blows: first, the contact photographs, then the evidences of trickery. The sight of the 'medium' raising a stool with her foot, filled me with bitter disappointment. *The simple, honest folks all turned out to be an alert, secretive, troublesome group of well-organized performers.*"

Here is the experience of a man, who, with a mind *prejudiced in favor,* entered upon a series of tests expecting full confirmation of impressions already gotten from his experiences with Eva C., but though ready to believe, not biased against the conclusions or rational deduction. His summary, though brief, is worthy of note:

"The Goligher Circle has repeatedly been urged, by myself and others, to submit to further investigations by a fresh investigator, but so far without success. If it does consent, I can predict two things with confidence:

I. No genuine psychic phenomena will be observed.

---

[99] After my last seance with Mlle. Eva Mr. Feilding discovered by accident that I was writing a book on the subject. He begged me not to say a word or publish anything about the seances until after the Society for Psychical Research had published a full report. Now that it has done so there is nothing to keep me from writing my experiences.

[100] The result of his investigations are published in three books: "Reality of Psychic Phenomena," "Psychic Structures at Goligher Circle," and "Experiments in Psychical Science."

[101] It would be difficult to convince me that the many things photographed and described by Baron Schrenck-Notzing could be presented under rigid test conditions

II. No evidence of fraud will be obtained, as the members of the Circle are exceedingly wary, and the evidence of trickery which I obtained was gathered under conditions which they had not foreseen, but which they will doubtless avoid in the future.

"I also feel safe in predicting that if Miss Goligher's feet and hands are controlled, *and the cooperation of the other sitters eliminated,* there will be no levitation of any kind.

(Signed) E. E. Fournier d'Albe,
21 Gower Street, W.C.I

Poor Dr. Crawford! He committed suicide in Belfast in 1920 and left a note saying that his research into Spiritualism had nothing to do with his self-murder. I am very sorry indeed that this sincere investigator became his own judge because what he had written had been done in good faith.

A short time after Dr. Crawford's death his literary executor requested Dr. d'Albe, early in 1921, to undertake a further series of researches with the same medium and circle in order, if possible, to obtain an independent confirmation of his results and theories and to collect more data concerning the nature of these manifestations. d'Albe tells in his book how he caught Katie Goligher manipulating and how he saw against the dim, red background of the wall the stool held by Katie's foot and a portion of her leg. In some of these manipulations the people around the table assisted.

When he left Belfast he wrote a very nice letter in which he intimated that the result of his three months' experience with the Goligher Circle did not furnish any definite proofs of the psychic origin of the numerous phenomena witnessed by him, and as they were of no scientific value he had decided to have no more sittings. It was suggested that Katie Goligher give twelve more sittings under test conditions, but she refused on the ground that her health would not permit her to entertain such a proposal for at least a year.

I sat with d'Albe at one of Mlle. Eva's séances. I liked his methods and believe him to be a sincere investigator. I have the following note from him in answer to a letter of mine.

Kingston-on -Thames, October 10, 1922.

"Dear Houdini:

"Yours of the 26th ult. just received. Yes, the Goligher legend has lost its glamour. I must say I was greatly surprised at Crawford's blindness. . . . "

Sincerely yours,
"d'Albe."

In 1920, Capt. C. Marsh Beadnell, of London, published a pamphlet in which he offered twenty pounds if Dr. Crawford's mediums would produce a single levitation under conditions which would preclude trickery. I am certain that any magician with a circle of six of his own choosing and with only one observer of the Crawford type could, under the same conditions, produce effects much more startling than any of those recounted by the trustful doctor.

The book to which Dr. Crawford referred when he showed me the photographs he intended to use in it has, since his death, been published by David Gow, Editor of the Spiritualistic paper *Light*. In a prefatory note he writes:

"I could say much about the present book with its remarkable elucidation of many problems connected with the psychical phenomena of Spiritualism, but I content myself with a reference to such experiments as those with the soft clay and the methylene blue, which finally clear away certain suspicions which have always attached to psychical mediums in connection with materialization phenomena amongst uninstructed investigators. This is not the least valuable part of a valuable book."

The above statement raises the question of what bearing any of these experiments, supposing every detail claimed were a fact, has on a future state. What possible information could impressions in clay, or stockings soiled by dye, furnish concerning the future state of a soul?

Ejner Nielson, of Copenhagen, was sponsored by Dr. Oscar Jaeger, Professor of Economics at the University of Christiania, Norway, and President of the Norwegian Society for Psychical Research. Professor Jaeger was invited by the Editor of the *Politikon,* at Copenhagen, to hold a séance with

Neilson. He accepted and it took place in January, 1922, before a specially selected committee[102] appointed by the president of the Norwegian University, Professor Frederick Stange. A few weeks later the committee reported that Nielson had not been capable of producing any so-called teleplasma or phenomena of materialization. Subsequently the Society for Psychical Research reported that teleplasma had been "artificially brought into the body of the medium."

Paul Heuze, writing of the Polish medium, in the *London Daily Telegraph* of September 18, 1922, says:

"S. D. Stamislaski arrived in Paris on April 7th. On the 10th he had an interview at the Sorbonne with Professor Pieron and on the 11th I went, at his request, to take part in the initial séance which was held in a bedroom of his hotel. This was, of course, merely a preparatory séance. My impression was not at all favorable."

In speaking of the subsequent séances of this medium he declares:

"The whole thing may be summed up in a single sentence; the result was pitiable. Suffice it to say that in spite of inadequate control, not only did I never see any of the luminous phenomena of the first séances but that hardly anything took place at all and when it did it was merely one of those clumsy pieces of deception that are practiced in the most ordinary Spiritualistic séances: --Articles moved, thrown forward, touchings, slaps, books dropped on the head, etc. The whole thing carried out in such a manner that there could not be the slightest doubt as to the gross trickery with which it was performed."

I have personally attended séances held by two of the ectoplasmic mediums, Mlle. Eva and Mrs. Thompson, and I have no doubt that it is only a question of time when all such mediums, as well as these two, including Stamislawa, P. Frank Kluski, S. G. Stamislaski, Jean Guzek,[103] Kathleen Goligher, Ejner Nielson, Frau Siebert and Willy Sch, will be authentically classified as questionable.

Bear in mind, I am not a skeptic. It is my will to believe and if convincing evidence is brought forward I will be the first to acknowledge my mistake, but up to the present day nothing has crossed my path to make me think that the Great Almighty will allow emanations from a human body of such horrible, revolting, viscous substances as Baron Von Schrenk Notzing claims, hideous shapes, which, like "genii from the bronze bottle," ring bells, move handkerchiefs, wobble tables, and do other "flap-doodle" stunts.

---

[102] Dr. Troup, Professor of Psychology; Dr. Stormer, Professor of Mathematics; Dr. Scheldrup, Professor of Physics; Dr. Monrad Krhn, Professor of Neurology; Dr. (med.) Leegaard, and Mr. Johs Dammann, a prominent expert of conjuring tricks.

[103] Guzek was exposed in Paris *as* I predicted, the exposure occurring sooner than expected.

Chapter 11
By-Products of Spiritualism

IT has come to my attention in talking to numbers of laymen that the general public thinks of Spiritualism only in terms of mediums and séances and that the average man does not seem to realize the suffering, losses, misfortunes, crimes and atrocities of which it is the underlying cause and must bear the primary responsibility. During the more than thirty years in which I have been investigating Spiritualism I have industriously collected all possible data on the subject and in the thousands of clippings, dating from 1854 to the present time, which are filed away in my library, there are hundreds which tell of crimes attributable to Spiritualism. In my great collection of books there are many by world-renowned writers, men of science, physicians, and philosophers, each dealing with the curse of Spiritualism. It touches every phase of human affairs and emotions, leaving in its wake a crowd of victims whose plight is frequently pathetic, sometimes ludicrous, oftener miserable and unfortunate, and who are always deluded. It is to these effects of Spiritualism which are seldom considered that I wish to call the reader's attention in this chapter.

The *New York Herald* on June 16, 1923, told under a Syracuse date line the following incident:

"William H. Burr of Rochester, speaking to-day at the business session of the New York State Assembly of Spiritualists, of which he is President, said he could prove scientifically and conclusively the fact of communication with the Spirit world. Mr. Burr appealed for the abolition of capital punishment. He explained that he had communicated with Spirits from the bodies of murderers and realized their sufferings, as those skeptical of psychic communication never can."

The *New York Evening World* of March 8, 1922, reports that:

"Thurs Bergen Vigelius, a student in chemistry, of Brooklyn, N. Y., with faith that a Spiritual 'glimpse' of the hereafter and power to write a book thereof would be a distinct contribution to science and literature if he could 'project himself into a comatose condition simulating death,' drugged himself frequently into experimental sleep, but on his last experiment his consciousness not only deserted him, but breath and life accompanied it. He was regarded as an exceptionally bright student with every prospect of a promising career, had he not been susceptible to a fallacious belief."

One of the saddest cases of modern times is that of the young Barnard College student, Miss Marie Bloom-field, who declared herself in love with a Spirit and finally was driven to suicide in order to join him. The young lady had been an ardent student of Spiritualism and very active in its cause. All the newspapers of February 9, 1923, carried an account of her death, which attracted so much attention that a law was proposed in the New York Assembly to prevent séances but it failed of being passed.

The *Washington Times* (D. C.) of January 14, 1923, tells of an Earl L. dark who secured a divorce on the grounds that his wife claimed that she had a "Spirit affinity" named Alfred and that this Alfred through Clark's wife made his life unbearable, even predicting his death so that she might marry some man who would "accept Alfred's Spiritual guidance."

According to an account in the *New York World,* John Slater, chief medium of the National Spiritualists Association, claims that there were over five hundred Spiritualists who served with the American Expeditionary Force, none of which were wounded or afflicted with "cooties." The freedom from wounds he attributed to the influence of Spirits.

The *New York Times* on April 27, 1922, told of a John Cornyn, in San Francisco, who shot and killed two of his boys, one seven and the other eight, because, according to the police, he had been in "communication" with his wife who had been dead a year and she "had asked him to send all of their five children to her."

The following story in the *New York Times* of April 22, 1887, comes from Philadelphia:

"The jury in the case of Mrs. Sarah Patterson, an alleged medium, charged by the County Medical Society with practising medicine and surgery without being registered as a physician, this afternoon returned a verdict of guilty. The defence set up by the defendant's counsel was that Mrs. Patterson was a medium and under the control of Spirits, and was not therefore responsible for what she did in a trance. The defendant's counsel are both Spiritualists and the case has attracted considerable interest, the court room being crowded since the trial began."

These are the sort of things for which Spiritualism is responsible that are being told of in the papers frequently. To these few examples I could add hundreds from my files and they are constantly growing.

A hoax which usually creates a sensation, but which is apt, ultimately, to have a decidedly bad effect on believers' nerves, consists in allowing some person to touch or even fondle a materialized Spirit. One such demonstration occurred in a Southern city, where there lived a medium known as Mrs. M------. Her séances were always well attended and largely made up of the elite of the town. On one particular night a Spirit came forth and called for Andrew, saying in the most austere tones:

"I am the Spirit of 'Josie' and I want to see my beloved whom I left twenty years ago. I know that he is present and that he wants to hear from me, and more important, I know he still loves me, for in those twenty years he has never married."

With trembling knees and shaking hands the man climbed to the stage and in the midst of sobs recognized and embraced his sweetheart. It was a very touching and pathetic scene and the believers were greatly affected, and at some one's suggestion an ex-minister and editor of a Spiritualistic magazine, who was present, married the Spirit bride to the live groom. It was a sensational proof of mediumship and Mrs. M------ was headlined in all the local papers. Unfortunately, however, for the cause of Spiritualism, my old friend, Professor Harry Cook, happened to be in the neighborhood and on hearing about it hired a hall, challenged the medium to a test, and with a lady assistant performed and exposed the miracle.

I recall another instance where one of my friends was investigating a materialization séance. It was claimed that the Spirit of his deceased wife was manifesting and he asked permission to kiss her. This was graciously granted and he told me later that she must have forgotten to shave for she had a stubble beard. Incidentally I might add that while he attended the séance his real wife waited for him at a nearby theatre.

Such an eminent scientist as Sir William Crookes evidently fell for the materialization hoax, judging from what he tells us about his experience at a séance where Florence Cook was the medium and Katie King the phantom. I will quote the story in his own words as he tells it in his hook "Researches in Spiritualism."

"Several times she took my arm and the impression I received that it was a living woman at my side and not a visitor from the other world was so strong that the temptation to repeat a recent and curious experiment became almost irresistible.

"Realizing then that if it were not a Spirit beside me it was in any case a lady, I asked her permission to take her in my arms in order to verify the interesting observation that a bold experimenter had recently made known. This permission was graciously given, and I took advantage of it respectfully, as any gentleman would have done in the same circumstances. The 'ghost,' which made no resistance, was a being as material as Miss Cook herself.

"Katie then declared that on this occasion she felt able to show herself at the same time as Miss Cook. I lowered the gas and with my phosphorus lamp entered the room which served as a cabinet. It was dark and I groped for Miss Cook, finding her crouched upon the floor. Kneeling down, I let the air enter my lamp and by its light saw the young woman dressed in black velvet, as she had been at the beginning of the séance, and appearing completely insensible.

"She did not stir when I took her hand and held the lamp near her face, but she continued to breathe quietly. Raising my lamp, I looked around me and saw Katie, who was standing close behind Miss Cook. She was clad in flowing white drapery, as we had already seen her in the séance. Holding one of Miss Cook's hands in mine, and still kneeling, I raised and lowered the lamp, as much to illuminate the whole figure of Katie as to convince myself fully that I really saw the true Katie, whom I had held in my arms a few moments ago, and not the phantom of a disordered brain.

"She did not speak but nodded her head in recognition. Three different times I carefully examined Miss Cook, crouching before me, to assure myself that the hand I held was indeed that of a living woman, and thrice turned my lamp toward Katie to scrutinize her with sustained attention, until I had not the slightest doubt that she was really there before me."

Another instance of this sort is told of by Florence Marryat in her book "There Is No Death."

"I opened the curtains of the cabinet and there stood John Powles himself, stalwart and living. He stepped up brusquely and took me in his arms and kissed me, four or five times, as a long departed brother might have done; and strange to say, I did not feel the least surprised at it, but clung to him like a sister. John Powles had never once kissed me during his life time. Although we had lived for four years in the closest intimacy, often under the same roof, we had never indulged in any familiarity."

Unfortunately mere deception is not the only or the worst evil in these Spiritualistic materializations. Frequently they are made the means of accomplishing criminal designs. There came to my attention a case of a very peculiar nature in which a widow was robbed of a large fortune. It appears that there was a wealthy old widower, a devoted Spiritualist, who was easily influenced by certain mediums. These same mediums also had among their clients a rather weak-minded widow. At a séance they got the old man to propose marriage to this widow who, in turn, was being advised through them by the Spirit of her husband to marry the old man. The old man did not live very long after the wedding and on his death bed promised the woman that he would come back to aid her and give her financial advice. He had previously made a will giving her absolute control of his estate.

The body was taken to an undertaking establishment to be cared for until the funeral and on the day before the service the widow attended a séance at which her husband told her:

"You go to my coffin to-morrow morning before the ceremony and I will speak to you, giving you my final instructions from my mortal body."

The next morning, accompanied by a nurse, the woman went to the undertaker's and was taken to the room where the body lay in its casket. She spoke and to her astonishment the corpse opened its eyes and said:

"I want you to give half of the fortune I willed you to B------ and M------, the mediums. They have helped me for years and I would like to show them my appreciation. Farewell, I will speak to you at séances but never again from the body."

The astounded widow threw herself on the body crying:

"I promise! I will! I promise!"

"Promise?" asked the corpse.

"I promise faithfully," she replied.

True to her word, the widow divided the fortune with the mediums, who are now in foreign countries living a peaceful life unless troubled by their consciences.

The deception was worked as follows: the mediums, taking advantage of the undertaker's weakness, kept him intoxicated and were thus free to do whatever they cared to around his establishment. The casket was arranged with a false bottom which ran in and out on ball bearings and one end was made to open. Just before the widow's visit to the undertaking establishment this false bottom with the old man's body was run out of the casket and hidden in an adjoining room and one of the mediums, made up to represent the dead man, was placed in the casket. As soon as the act was over the corpse was put back in its proper place.

This is not the only instance of this sort by any means. I have known of two other instances in which corpses have been used for purposes of fraud. In one a man was dying. A lawyer was sent for and the nurse gotten out of the way on some plausible excuse. After the man died, but before the lawyer arrived, his body was hidden under the bed. One of the gang took his place in the bed and dictated a will with gasping breath and afterwards made his mark in the presence of a perfectly honest attorney and witness. Before the nurse got back the corpse had been placed in the bed and there was nothing to show that a fraud had been committed.

To show that such things are possible and that exchanging bodies in a coffin can be accomplished, I want to call attention to the coffin act which I did for the Boston Athletic Association. A solid oak coffin was furnished by the National Casket Company and delivered to the Association. Six-inch screws were used to fasten down the lid but I managed to escape nevertheless, leaving no traces.

It is not generally known that Charles J. Guiteau, the assassin of President Garfield, was a pronounced Spiritualist. He claimed that he was inspired by the Spirits four times. Once in connection with his entering the Oneida community. Once preceding his attempt to establish a newspaper called "The Theocrat." Again when writing his book "The Truth a Companion to the Bible," and still again when he was inspired to kill the President.

Another case in which Spirits were claimed to have been responsible for diverting funds is told in "The Fallacies of Spiritualism."

"In September, 1920, an action was brought in the New York Courts against a medium named Mrs. Mabelle Hirons, for the recovery of twelve thousand four hundred dollars, alleged to have been obtained by 'Spiritualistic' means from Dr. J. B. Hubbell, of Rockville, Maryland. Dr. Hubbell declared that after the death of Clara Barton,[104] founder of the American Red Cross, to whom he had been secretary, it was intended to erect a memorial to that lady, to which he proposed contributing twelve thousand four hundred dollars of his own money, including nine hundred dollars bequeathed him by Clara Barton herself. In 1914 he visited Mrs. Hirons, who, he said, went into a trance and gave him a 'message' that was supposed to come from Clara Barton and which directed him to give all the money to Mrs. Hirons for the memorial. Dr. Hubbell believed the 'message' to be genuine and gave her the money, but the memorial was never erected-- hence the action."

A few years ago the papers told of the case of a woman in the Middle West who was sensationally and cruelly deceived by a medium. When she lost her little girl it was feared that she would not recover from the intense grief with which she was overcome. On the woman's farm was a hired man whose wife was a medium. He talked sympathetically with her and got her to allow him to send for his wife, who was in Chicago. She began preaching Spiritualism as soon as she arrived, finding the woman a willing listener. When it was apparent to the medium that the woman thoroughly believed her doctrine she began to advise her to pray nightly for the restoration of her child and finally one night she announced to the credulous woman that at midnight four days later her child would be restored to her. She cautioned her that she must fast that day, dress her room and bed in white, and sleep alone that night. The instructions were followed to the letter. At midnight she heard the stairs creak. Then suddenly her door was pushed open and she saw something luminous approaching her bed. It carried a bundle and a voice announced that her daughter was coming back to her. After the apparition left the woman found a baby girl in the bed with her. Soon after the medium persuaded the woman and her husband to dispose of their property and go to a Spirit Colony in California. After nearly three years they came back to their home with practically no means but with the knowledge that the baby girl came from a foundling society in Chicago.

Not the least of the evils of Spiritualism is the insanity which it causes. A mental specialist of high standing in Birmingham, England, issued a warning in 1922 quoting numerous cases which came under his observation and were the result of Spiritualistic teaching. An English doctor has estimated the number of such cases at a million. It is a well-established fact that the human reason gives way under the exciting strain of Spiritualism. The list is not limited to European countries; we have a goodly share of baneful results right at home. Not long ago Dr. Curry, Medical Director of the State Insane Asylum of New Jersey, issued a warning concerning the "Ouija-board" in which he said:

---

[104] One of the greatest women born in America.—H. H.

"The 'Ouija-board' is especially serious because it is adopted mainly by persons of high-strung neurotic tendency who become victims of actual illusions of sight, hearing and touch at Spiritualistic séances."

He predicted that the insane asylums would be flooded with patients if popular taste did not swing to more wholesome diversions.

In March, 1920, it was reported in the papers that the craze for the Ouija-boards, with which it was thought spirit messages could be received, had reached such a pitch in the little village of Carrito, across San Francisco Bay, that five people had been driven mad.

The available amount of evidence of this sort is almost unbelievable, but enough has been given to show the extent of the evil. The average medium works only for the money he or she can extract from the public; money obtained by moving the deepest sentiments in the human soul. Is it right to legally sanction the medium, to allow him to prey on the public--not only allowing him to take the earthly possessions of his victims, but their soul, and oftentimes their mind as well? Spiritualism is nothing more or less than mental intoxication, the intoxication of words, of feelings and suggested beliefs. Intoxication of any sort when it becomes a habit is injurious to the body but intoxication of the mind is always fatal to the mind. We have prohibition of alcohol, we have prohibition of drugs, but we have no law to prevent these human leeches from sucking every bit of reason and common sense from their victims. It ought to be stopped, it must be stopped, and it would seem that the multiplicity of exposures and the multitude of prosecutions that have followed rational investigation should be sufficient to justify, yes, demand legislation for the complete annihilation of a cult built on false pretence, flimsy hearsay evidence, and the absurdity of accepting an optical *illusion* as a fact.

Sir William Crookes & Katie King

Sir William Crookes (left) & Katie King

Harry Kellar & Harry Houdini

Chapter 12
Investigations -- Wise and Otherwise

SPIRITUALISM has been the cause of much discussion between men of science, men of magic, and believers in the "Spirit World." Countless investigations, wise and otherwise, have been held in most of the countries of the globe. Many of them have been made by fair-minded, unbiased men; men who delved deep into the unknown with a clear conscience and whether successful or not were willing to give the world the result of their probings. Men who were not afraid to admit that their experience was not sufficient to cope with the medium's skill and years of training and that they had been fooled. But there have been other so-called investigators who have attended séances wishing to be fooled and as "the wish is father of the thought" they have been misled.

What these investigators *see* done and what they *think* they see done are in reality two entirely different things and by the time they start to write their experiences there are usually complications. I rarely believe a full hundred per cent the explanations I hear or read. It is to be said to the credit of the investigators that they do not deliberately make misstatements but the nature of the brain is such that it is almost impossible to avoid mal-observation and these mal-observations are the curse of investigation.

Investigations under conditions favorable to the medium cannot be termed "investigations." They are nothing more than a demonstration of the medium's power to divert the attention, carrying it at will to any place they wish and numbing the subconscious mind. Under such conditions they are not only able to delude the innocent and simple-minded but also men whose accomplishments have proven their intellects to be above the average.

When a medium is subjected to conditions which are, to say the least, disconcerting, and the usual effects are not obtained, almost invariably the claim is made that there are antagonistic waves and that the "auras" are bad, and if, as often happens, the result is an unqualified expose and the medium's fall from power the followers of Spiritualism usually put forth a statement saying the medium overstepped the bounds in trying to give results and resorted to trickery, but that the majority of previous séances were genuine.

Perhaps my ideas on the subject of how to conduct an investigation are wrong; I am fully convinced, however, that the only way to conduct a successful one is to get the committee together previous to the séance, discuss the expected manifestations, formulate some plan for concerted action and if possible assign each member some specific part as was done in the case of Palladino's fall. These parts should be rehearsed and then when the séance is held there is a much greater possibility of the committee being able to judge intelligently. But when scientists report some feat of legerdemain as being abnormal simply because they cannot detect the deception, I think it is time to add to each investigating committee a successful and reputable professional mystifier, and I might add that all mediums hate to have a magician attend a séance.

Of the many investigations, since the beginning of modern Spiritualism, I have selected a few of the most important and will try and show the reader the necessity of placing on investigating committees men who cannot be prejudiced or influenced by subdued lights or weird and mystifying sounds; men who use their God-given gift of reason to the best of their ability; men whose attention cannot be diverted by the medium; men whose brain cells are versatile and not overdeveloped in one particular direction; men who can pay strict attention to their commission and not be led astray by the glib-tongued medium's misdirection. Then we will have real investigations and the world at large will benefit.

A short time before his death Henry Seybert, an enthusiastic Spiritualist with a conscientious desire that Spiritualism should be authentically established, gave the University of Pennsylvania sufficient money to establish a chair of Philosophy on condition that a commission should be appointed to investigate "all systems of morals, Religion or Philosophy which assume to represent the *truth* and particularly modern Spiritualism." Accordingly there were selected from among the doctors and professors of the University ten men to be known as the "Seybert Commission." A fairer-minded and more impartial commission could not have been appointed. Each man had declared himself holding an open mind and ready to accept whatever there was evidence to prove, but realizing "that men eminent in intelligence and attainment yield to Spiritualism an entire credence," they felt that one could not "fail to stand aside in tender reverence when crushed and bleeding hearts are seen to seek it for consolation and for hope." In order to be amply prepared to do their work in an intelligent and understanding manner they provided themselves with the best literature of the day on the subject and such records of previous investigations as were available. After a careful digest of all this information the Commission was ready to begin its actual work in March, 1884. *The entire ten men* of the Commission *were willing to believe,* and their adviser, Mr. Thomas R. Hazard, had been a personal friend of Mr. Seybert and was known throughout the land as an *uncompromising Spiritualist."*

The first medium to which the Commission gave its attention was Mrs. S. E. Patterson, a slate writing mystifier and automatic writer. The result of this first case was *nil.* After waiting patiently an hour and a half for the spirits to move the meeting adjourned to the disappointment of all. Mr. Hazard was especially chagrined, for the medium was considered "one of the very best in the world." She had given him a private sitting the evening before at which "messages from the Spirit of Henry Seybert came thick and fast," but they declined to manifest for the Commission.

This séance proved to be typical of all that fell to the lot of the Seybert Commission to investigate. It continued its work for three years and investigated every case of importance which came before it. One of these was Margaret Fox, with whom the Commission had two sittings and became convinced that the raps came from her person. When she was told of its conclusion she admitted that the séances were not satisfactory but declined further sittings on the ground of ill health and because she doubted if more satisfactory results would follow and admitting that they might result in a *"confirmation9* of the Commission's belief as to the cause of the raps.

Many of the most prominent mediums of the day appeared before the Commission during its three years of work. Some of them underwent a whole series of tests and the phenomena covered the whole gamut from simple rapping to spirit photography, automatic and slate writing, materialization, etc. In every case with but one exception the result was either a blank séance, a positive failure, or a deliberate cheat. The exception was when Mr. Harry Kellar was called in as a magician to demonstrate his power as a slate writer. The Commission was successfully baffled, not a single member being able to fathom his method until he explained it.

The Commission carefully weighed all the evidence placed before it and formed its conclusions with such deliberation and thoroughness that the most critical on either side found no cause for objecting or saying that it was swayed or biased by any undue influence whatever. It pursued its work on purely rational, scientific lines, strenuously avoiding all conditions which might be construed as conducive to doubtful conclusions. It was looking for facts in a matter-of-fact way and as there was no opportunity for screening artifices no occult or psychic phenomena were proven to have existed. As an evidence of the fairness with which the Commission was considered to have done its work, I quote the following letter to the Commission from Dr. Henry Slade.

"No. 11E. 13th Street, N. Y., Feb. 4, 1885. "Dear Mr. Furness:--I take this opportunity to express to you, and through you to the other members of the Seybert Commission, my hearty approval of the course pursued by them in their investigation of phenomena occurring in my presence. Fully realizing that I am only the instrument or channel through which these manifestations are produced, it would be presumption on my part to undertake to lay down a line to be followed by the unseen intelligence, whose servant I am. Hence I did say their conditions must be acceded to or I would return to New York. That they did so, is evident to my mind from the results obtained, which I regard as a necessary preliminary to a continuation, when other experiments may be introduced with better prospects of success. It may be well not to insist on following the exact course followed by Professor Zollner, but leave it open to original or impromptu suggestions that may be adopted without previous consideration, which, if successful, would be of equal value as evidence of its genuineness, at the same time give greater breadth to the experiments. In conclusion, allow me to say that in the event the Committee desires to continue these experiments through another series of sittings with me, it will give me pleasure to enter into arrangements for that purpose.

"Very truly yours,
Henry Slade."

If all the investigators were to adopt the rational methods of the Seibert Commission they might easily discover the truth and no longer submit to imposition by charlatans nor aid and abet them by accepting as true the claims made by a class which they admit is of a low type, dishonest, and otherwise disreputable. If sincere, they would assist in all reasonable attempts to detect fraud and not accept the irrational pretext that light and touch are detrimental to the health or life of a medium.

Following in the footsteps of the Seybert Commission the Society for Psychical Research was organized in America and England for the purpose of investigating all so-called phenomena and freak occurrences not easily accountable for by natural law and in spite of the following message which it is claimed was sent by the spirit of the late William Walker, President of the Buxton Camera Club, to the Crewe Circle, I believe they are doing good work.

"Dear Friends of the Circle,[105]

"I would not spend a moment with the Psychical Research Society, because they are nothing more or less than fraud hunters and I want you to come to Buxton for a sitting with Mrs. Walker, 3, Palace Rd., about the 8th, 9th, of Aug. Then the spirit friends can further demonstrate the wondrous powers which to-day are needed more than ever. Peace be with you.

"Yours faithfully,
W. Walker."

The membership of these societies is made up of men and women who have a certain degree of scientific training, all classes of scholarship and all professions being represented. As a consequence the investigations have been most exhaustive and carried out by persons especially qualified for the work, but the results have been most emphatically against a belief in the return of a soul after death in the guise of a spirit or the occurrence of anything supernatural at the bidding of a medium.

Naturally, we might not expect a general agreement among a group of scientific scholars who had entered the field of research from different points of view, but I believe I can say without fear of contradiction, that of all who have undertaken the task without prejudice the majority agree in the opinion that all phenomena ascribed to spirit power developed through, and presented by, a medium, are without foundation in fact, and that the result of their investigations has agreed perfectly with the findings of the Seybert Commission.

In January, 1869, the London Dialectical Society appointed a committee with thirty-three members to investigate the phenomena alleged to be Spiritual manifestations and to report on its findings. Professor Huxley, Professor John Tyndall, and Mr. George Henry Lewes, were invited to co-operate with the Committee. Professor Huxley refused to have anything to do with the investigation and in the following letter, written in answer to the Committee's invitation, he terms Spiritualism a "gross imposture."[106]

"Sir,--I regret that I am unable to accept the invitation of the Council of the Dialectical Society to co-operate with a Committee for the investigation of 'Spiritualism', and for two reasons. In the first place, I have no time for such an inquiry, which would involve much trouble and (unless it were unlike all inquiries of that kind I have known) much annoyance. In the second place, I take no interest in the subject. The only case of 'Spiritualism' I have had the opportunity of examining into for myself was as gross an imposture as ever came under my notice. But supposing the phenomena to be genuine-- they do not interest me. If anybody would endow me with the faculty of listening to the chatter of old women and curates in the nearest cathedral town, I would decline the privilege, having better things to do.

"And if the folk in the Spiritual world do not talk more wisely and sensibly than their friends report them to do, I put them in the same category.

---

[105] This Spirit Message is taken from Doyle's book, "The Case for Spirit Photography," English Edition.
[106] This and letters of Tyndall and Lewes, from "Report on Spiritualism," by J. Burns, pp. 229, 230, 265.

"The only good that I can see in a demonstration of the truth of 'Spiritualism' is to furnish an additional argument against suicide. Better live a crossing-sweeper than die and be made to talk twaddle by a 'medium' hired at a guinea a *séance*.

"I am, Sir, &c., T. H. Huxley, 29th January, 1869."

A few days later Mr. Lewes declined the Committee's invitation as follows:

"Dear Sir,--I shall not be able to attend the investigation of 'Spiritualism'; and in reference to your question about suggestions would only say that the one hint needful is that all present should distinguish between facts and inferences from facts. When any man says that phenomena are produced by *no* known physical laws, he declares that he knows the laws by which they are produced.

"Yours, &c.,
G. H. Lewes.

"Tuesday, 2nd February, 1869."

Under date of December 22, 1869, Professor Tyndall wrote the following in response to his invitation to aid the Committee.

"Sir--You mention in your note to me three gentlemen, two of whom are personally known to me, and for both of whom I entertain a sincere esteem.

"The house of one of these, namely Mr. Wallace, I have already visited, and made there the acquaintance of the lady who was the reputed medium between Mr. Wallace and the supernatural.

"And if earnestly invited by Mr. Crookes, the editor of the 'Chemical News,' to witness phenomena which in his opinion 'tend to demonstrate the existence of some power (magnetic or otherwise) which has not yet been recognized by men of science,' I should pay due respect to his invitation.

"But understand my position: more than a year ago Mr. Cromwell Varley, who is, I believe, one of the greatest modern Spiritualists, did me the favor to pay me a visit, and he then employed a comparison which, though flattering to my spiritual strength, seems to mark me out as unfit for spiritual investigation. He said that my presence at a *séance* resembled that of a great magnet among a number of small ones. I throw all into confusion. Still he expressed a hope that arrangements might be made to show me the phenomena, and I expressed my willingness to witness such things as Mr. Varley might think worth showing to me. I have not since been favored by a visit from Mr. Varley.

"I am now perfectly willing to accept the personal invitation of Mr. Crookes, should he consider that he can show me phenomena of the character you describe. "I am, sir, your obedient servant,

"John Tyndall."
"G. W. Bennett, Esq."

Unlike the Seybert Commission, which made a formal report to the University of Pennsylvania immediately on the completion of its work, the Committee of the Dialectical Society which was appointed in 1869 did not make any report until 1877 and then only what seems to be a garbled report of sub-committees. The *Spiritual Magazine* in 1870 commented on this lack of a report as follows:

"Where is the report of the Dialectical Society? This is the question which many people are asking, but to which no one seems prepared to give a satisfactory reply. Has this Report, which was to settle the question of Spiritualism, only unsettled the Dialectical Society-- causing, as we learn, some of its principal officers and members to secede from it on finding that the investigations of the Committee pointed in a different way to what they anticipated, and to which they had committed themselves? People ask--Have the Committee come to an opinion on the subject or have they too many opinions?"

The only information I have come in contact with referring to the Dialectical Committee and its work has been from Spiritualistic publications, most of them under authorship of Mr. James Burns, and I copy the following from "The Medium and Daybreak" of November 16, 1877:

"Objection has been taken in some quarters to the fact that the Society itself did not publish the Report, but left the matter of the publication as an open question to its Committee." Again: on the 20th of July, 1870, the council passed a resolution--"that the request of the Committee, that the Report be printed under the authority of the Society, be not acceded to."

The exact nature of the work done by the Dialectical Society's Committee can be summed up by another extract from the same issue of "The Medium and Daybreak":

"In due time the Committee presented to the Council the General and Sub-Reports, supplementing the same by a voluminous mass of evidence taken directly from the *lips of Spiritualists practically acquainted with the subject --persons of the highest respectability and representing nearly every grade of society.*" (The italics are mine.)

Another element of discord in the Dialectical investigation is shown by the following:

"Attempt has been made, of course, to undervalue these telling researches. The non-successful Committees have been brought gleefully into prominence, in hope that *positive* results obtained by the successful Committees might thereby be discredited."

It seems to be a published fact that this movement on the part of the Dialectical Society resulted in much discord amounting to a split in the Society. Mr. Burns in his editorial column of the "Medium and Daybreak" says:

"Our present issue affords an important and valuable addition to the cheap literature of Spiritualism. It is filled with useful matter for investigators, *judiciously extracted from the Report of the London Dialectical Society.*" (My italics.)

The supporters of Spiritualism lay great stress and importance on the fact that a few of their co-workers are men prominent in scientific and literary circles, but these are in such a minority, when compared with men of the same time who do not co-operate, that the Spiritualists in order to give force and dignity to their argument "ring the changes" on these few names and keep them prominently to the front, notwithstanding that it has been proven beyond question, time and again, that these sages themselves have frequently been the victims of fraudulent mediums, sometimes knowingly.

Doyle in his book "The New Revelation" says:

"The days are surely passing when the mature and considerate opinions of such men . . . can be dismissed with the empty 'all rot' or 'nauseating drivel' formulae."

Perhaps the most prominent man in this respect and whose conclusions, especially in his later years, were pointed to by Spiritualists as being beyond dispute was the eminent chemist, Sir William Crookes. He became intensely interested in Spiritualistic research work as early as 1870 and for the first four years devoted most of his attention to D. D. Home, who seemed successful in baffling Crookes' super-knowledge of scientific investigation. In 1874 he turned his attention to Florrie Cook, a fifteen year old medium who had been commanding attention for about three years. She seems to have captivated him within the first month to such an extent that he went to her defense in print after a *"disgraceful occurrence"* had given rise to a *"controversy,"* after which he entertained her at his house. The most convincing test, though, took place at her home in Hackney. In February, 1874, he wrote:

"These *séances* have not been going on many weeks but enough has taken place to thoroughly convince me of the perfect truth and honesty of Miss Cook, and to give me every reason to expect that the promises so freely made to me by Katie will be kept. All I now ask is that your readers will not hastily assume that everything which is *prima facie* suspicious necessarily implies deception, and that they will suspend their judgment until they hear from me again on this subject."

It was not long, evidently, before the scientist awoke from his dream, for on August 1st, 1874, he wrote to a Russian lady that after four years of investigation, including months of experience with Home, Katie Fox, and Florence Cook, he found "no satisfactory proof that the dead can return and communicate." A copy of this letter was sent by Aksakoff to *Light,* and was published in that journal on May 12, 1900. "Sir W. Crookes did not dissent."[107] Sometime along about 1875 forty-four photographic negatives which he had made of Katie King and her medium, Florrie Cook, together with what prints he had, were, for some reason not given, accidentally destroyed and he forbade

---

[107] "Spiritism, a Popular History," by Joseph McCabe.

friends who had copies to reproduce them. He must have made some sort of a discovery for he "buried himself in a sulky silence which he would not break" for forty years. "No one knew whether he was a Spiritualist or not," his only statement being that "in all his Spiritualistic research he had 'come to a brick wall.'"[108] In 1914 when asked plainly if he were a Spiritualist "he evaded the question." Perhaps the change in his opinions came over him when he learned that Florence Cook (who became Mrs. Corner) was exposed[109] on a continental tour and sent back disgraced. But in 1916, notwithstanding his statement in 1900 and other previous statements, he went on record in the December 9th issue of *Light* as accepting Spiritualism.

All of this stands as proof that Professor Crookes, even after he was knighted, was of a vacillating mind and for some reason seemed to be deficient in rational methods of discovering the truth, or at least disinclined to put them in force outside of his particular line of science. Possibly, one of the convincing proofs to him may have been the "tricks" played on him by Annie Eva Fay, for if I am not in error his failure to detect her trickery was the turning point which brought him to a belief in Spiritualism. She told me that when Maskelyne, the magician, came out with an expose of her work she was forced to resort to strategy. Going to the home of Professor Crookes she threw herself on his mercy and gave a series of special tests. With flashing eyes she told of taking advantage of him. It appears that she had but one chance in the world to get by the galvanometer[110] but by some stroke of luck for her and an evil chance for Professor Crookes, the electric light went out for a second at the theatre at which she was performing, and she availed herself of the opportunity to fool him. One of the tests was duplicated by Professor Harry Cooke, a magician.

There is not the slightest doubt in my mind that this brainy man was hoodwinked, and that his confidence was betrayed by the so-called mediums that he tested. His powers of observation were blinded and his reasoning faculties so blunted by his prejudice in favor of anything psychic or occult that he could not, or would not, resist the influence.[111] This seems more difficult to comprehend when one remembers that he did not accept Spiritualism in full until he was nearing the end of his earthly career. The weakness and unreliability of Sir William's judgment as an investigator is further proved by the fact that he admitted that many of the tests he proposed were rejected by the mediums he was investigating. Such conditions made the test impossible and he did not seem to realize it, but notwithstanding all this he is one of the most quoted authorities in Spiritualistic realms, particularly by Sir Arthur Conan Doyle.

Another who was misled by the chicanery of mediums which he investigated during many years of research is Sir Oliver Lodge. He failed to find sufficient evidence to prompt him to spread the teachings of Spiritualism until 1904, after which he occasionally sent a "glow through the Spiritualistic world by some bold profession of belief." In 1905 he was not quite ready to endorse but strongly commended mediums. But by 1916 he had become "the great scientist of the movement, the link between the popular belief and scientific theory." It is extremely difficult, however, to understand how a leading scientist can permit his pen to lay before a thinking world such inconsistent impossibilities as the following:

"A table can exhibit hesitation, it can seek for information, it can welcome a newcomer, it can indicate joy or sorrow, fun or gravity, it can keep time with a song as if joining in the chorus and most notably of all it can exhibit affection in an unmistakable manner."

What has all this to do with the spirit of the departed? How is it possible to accept such silly nonsense? Think of it! A *table* with intelligence, brains--a *table* with consciousness--a *table* with emotion. Yet that is the sort of reasoning used by Sir Oliver in his book "Raymond" and it is

---

[108] "Master Workers," McCabe.

[109] Florence Cook was repeatedly exposed.

[110] The "galvanometer" is an instrument used to control the medium. It is an electric device provided with a dial and two handles, so constructed that if the medium were to let go of either handle the contact would be broken and the dial fail to register. The medium in fooling the sitter simply placed one of the handles on the bare flesh under her knee and gripping it there with her leg kept the circuit intact and left one hand free to produce "spirits."

[111] An honest scientist does not dream that his confidence is being betrayed and that the bland innocence, the "stalling" for breath, or the almost fainting scenes are only camouflages to help malobservation so that the medium can successfully ply her trade.

acceptable to all enthusiastic advocates of occult teaching. When we read of a mind of such high culture being overcome by such misfortune we are moved to compassion rather than censure and can only conjecture that the loss of his beloved son, Raymond, in an accursed war was the cause of it.

Margaret Deland wrote:

"As for the scientific value of the evidence submitted by Sir Oliver, one must not lose sight of the fact that by far the greater part of it is from the experience of others and accepted by him as established facts, in many cases with little or no investigation as applied to telepathy. By following his career, one familiar with the psychology of deception will see that he has been an exceptionally 'easy mark.'"

In describing a private performance of what is known among magicians as "long-distance second-sight," after detailing the tests in full, Sir Oliver writes:

"As regards collusion and trickery, no one who has witnessed the absolutely genuine and artless manner in which the impressions are described, but has been perfectly convinced of the transparent honesty of all concerned.

"This, however, is not evidence to those who have not been present, and to them I can only say that to the best of my scientific belief, no collusion or trickery was possible under the varied circumstances of the experiments."

From the above, the reader may form his own opinion as to the value of Sir Oliver Lodge's investigation, and at the same time should bear in mind that his so-called investigation is typical of all the investigations by scientists and sages who have accepted Spiritualism as a fact or a religion (?).

The remaining figure of this type most conspicuously in the spotlight on the Spiritualistic stage at the present time is my esteemed friend, Sir Arthur Conan Doyle. Very much like Sir Oliver, his opinion hung in the balance during many years of *investigation,* some thirty or thirty-five, and it is significant that he did not manifest his deep concern in the cult until he too, like Sir Oliver, had lost a son in the late war and his heartstrings had been wrung by a similar grief.

In "The New Revelation," which was written after he had lost his son, he tells us that for thirty years he had studied the subject of Spiritualism *"carelessly," then suddenly in a crisis of emotion,*[112] he sees a possible balm in it, but instead of realizing that this was, or should be, the time for real investigation, he threw up his hands with the cry:

"The objective side of it ceased to interest, for having made up one's mind that it was true there was an end of the matter."[113]

It is evident from his own confession that he decided to accept Spiritualism regardless of any real revelation that might present itself at a future time and the fact that he did cease intelligent investigation is proved by his own published statements quoted below.

In a letter in the *New York Evening Mail,* Dec. 29, *1921,* he says:

"I don't need scientific proof of what I hear with my own ears, see with my own eyes. Nobody does. This is one of the fine things about Spiritualism. Each person can prove it for himself. It proves immortality and the better you live here, the further you'll go there, progressing finally to the perfect state."

In the *New York World,* June 22, 1922, he says:

"That mediums I have recommended have been convicted of fraud; any medium may be convicted, because the mere fact of being a medium is illegal by our benighted laws, but no medium I have ever recommended has been shown to be fraudulent in a sense which would be accepted by any real psychic student.[114] *This same applies I believe to mediums recommended by Sir Oliver Lodge"*[115]

---

[112] The italics are mine.

[113] The reader will do well to read Tuke's "Influence of the Mind upon the Body" (or similar work) and he will find an explanation of what grief will do to a sensitive mind.

[114] Perhaps so, but would not be accepted as evidence before any court of equity.

[115] He has personally repeated the same thing to me.

In connection with his corroboration of Sir Oliver's opinion about mediums Sir Arthur is reported to have said:

"Sir Oliver is too damn scientific."

And the *New York World* of June 3rd, 1922, quotes him as saying:

"Most mediums take their responsibilities very seriously and view their work in a religious light. A temptation to which several great mediums have succumbed is that of drink. This comes about in a very natural way, for overworking leaves them in a state of physical prostration and the stimulus of alcohol affords a welcome relief and may tend at last to become a custom and finally a curse.[116] Alcoholism always weakens the moral sense, so that these degenerate mediums yield themselves more readily to fraud. Tippling and moral degeneration are by no means confined to psychics.

"Far from being antagonistic to religion, this psychic movement is destined to revivify religion. We come upon what is sane, what is moderate, what is reasonable, what is consistent with gradual evolution and the benevolence of God. This new wave of inspiration has been sent into the world by God."

I will not, at this time, dissect and analyze the above statements, preferring to let the reader decide for himself after reading them over carefully and digesting their literal meaning. It is sufficient to direct attention to the various contradictory statements and variance in the subjects of law, morality, and religion, and their application to the subject of Spiritualism.

Sir Arthur is reported as saying that mediumship is like an ear for music and might exist in "some vulgar person," but that the medium is only a carrier of messages comparable to the boy who delivers telegrams. From the foregoing excerpts of Sir Arthur's own statements it will be seen that he depends solely on his *senses* of *seeing* and *hearing* (the two weakest and most easily deceived) for his evidence. When once a medium has his confidence he believes implicitly what the medium tells him, accepts their "hearsay evidence" as gospel truth, notwithstanding that he admits they are possibly of a vulgar, dishonest class, often addicted to alcoholism to a degree of debauchery. It is extremely difficult to harmonize these statements.

As to the sense of sight coupled to the sense of hearing: while at Washington, D. C., Sir Arthur had a "sitting" with the Zancigs and after witnessing phenomena at their expert hands and minds, he gave them a letter of which the following is a transcript:

"I have tested Professor and Mrs. Zancig to-day and am quite assured that their remarkable performance, as I saw it, was due to psychic causes (thought transference) and not to trickery.

(Signed) "Arthur Conan Doyle."

Mr. Jules Zancig is a magician, a member of the Society of American Magicians of which I have been the President for the past seven years. I believe he is one of the greatest second-sight artists that magical history records. In my researches for the past quarter of a century I have failed to trace anyone his superior. His system seems to be supreme. He never at any time claimed telepathy and as he has not, to my knowledge, obtained money by pretending telepathy or spirit presentations, it would not be fair to disclose his methods despite the fact that Sir Arthur Conan Doyle put the stamp of genuineness on his work. Undoubtedly it *appeared* unfathomable to Sir Arthur and he therefore concluded that it was psychic and that there could be no other solution.

Mal-observation is responsible for a lot of misunderstanding, consequently misrepresentation, and as a result much investigation is rendered valueless. Such misrepresentation is not intended to deceive but is an honest expression of a conviction based on supposed facts by persons unaware that they are victims of illusion. One of the most, if not the most, flagrant instances of mal-observation I have ever known of is told of in a book by J. Hewat McKenzie, President of the British College of Psychic Science, entitled "Spirit Intercourse." On page 107 he says:

"Houdini, called the 'Handcuff King,' who has so ably demonstrated his powers upon public-hall platforms is enabled by psychic power (though this he does not advertise), to open lock, handcuff, or bolt that is submitted to him. He has been imprisoned within heavily barred cells, doubly and trebly locked, and from them all he escaped with ease. This ability to unbolt locked doors is undoubtedly

---

[116] Drink is no excuse for crime.

due to his mediumistic powers, and not to any normal mechanical operation on the lock. The force necessary to shoot a bolt within a lock is drawn from Houdini the medium, but it must not be thought that this is the only means by which he can escape from his prison, for at times his body has been dematerialized and withdrawn, but this will be treated in another part of this chapter."

As I am the one most deeply concerned in this charge I am also the best equipped to deny such erroneous statements. I do claim to free myself from the restraint of fetters and confinement, but positively state that I accomplish my purpose purely by physical, not psychical means. The force necessary to "shoot a bolt within a lock," is drawn from Houdini the living human being and not a medium. My methods are perfectly natural, resting on natural laws of physics. I do not *dematerialize* or *materialize* anything; I simply control and manipulate material things in a manner perfectly well understood by myself, and thoroughly accountable for and equally understandable (if not duplicable) by any person to whom I may elect to divulge my secrets. But I hope to carry these secrets to the grave as they are of no material benefit to mankind, and if they should be used by dishonest persons they might become a serious detriment.

On page 112 of his book Mr. McKenzie again refers to me saying:

"Houdini of world wide fame, previously mentioned, has for years demonstrated dematerialization, and the passage of matter through matter upon the public platform, while Mrs. Thompson of America, has demonstrated materialization. Mrs. Zancig has, with her husband, publicly exhibited her psychic gift, called 'thought transference,' which is purely soul projection, in all the leading world centres. Miss Fay, and several well known Japanese mediums, for years demonstrated the passage of matter through matter, and also materialization. These are only a few of the many who might be mentioned, who demonstrate psychic gifts before the public. Such public mediums do not, of course, advertise themselves as performing their wonders by occult powers, or through the help of spirits, and the public are therefore left in ignorance of how they perform their marvelous tricks, as they are called. The author has tested each of those mentioned, by a personal experiment from the stage, and several also in private, and can testify that they are mediums, performing most, if not all of their great wonders by spirit agency. They are naturally reluctant to acknowledge the fact, for the music-hall public would instantly resent any claims they might make that they performed their wonders by spirit power. Their audiences would regard such claims as 'bunkum,' and probably subject them to insult, if not to ill treatment, for the general public are entirely ignorant of such possibilities in the manipulation of psychical matter as related in this book, which a medium can develop with the co-operation of spirit entities. It can be left to the reader's imagination to picture the face of a music-hall manager if he were asked to allow upon the stage a demonstration of spirit powers. Horrors! The poor man would not be able to sleep for nights if he thought ghosts were working around his buildings or upon his stage. Thus, knowing the attitude of men toward such things these wonders of wonders are produced upon the music-hall stage as clever 'mystery' tricks. The author does not wish his readers to suppose that the mechanical sleight-of-hand tricks carried out by Maskelyne and Devant and similar operators, have anything to do with the mediumistic gift, for they are a mechanical copy of true magic. These tricks are performed with tons of machinery, whereas the genuine medium can produce his wonders, if necessary, naked and in an empty room.

"The last occasion on which the author, under strict test conditions saw Houdini demonstrate his powers of dematerialization, was before thousands, upon the public stage of the Grand Theatre, Islington, London. Here a small iron tank, filled with water, was deposited upon the stage, and in it Houdini was placed, the water completely covering his body. Over this was placed an iron lid with three hasps and staples, and these were securely locked. The body was then completely dematerialized within this tank within one and a half minutes, while the author stood immediately over it. Without disturbing any of the locks, Houdini was transferred from the tank direct to the back of the stage in a dematerialized state. He was there materialized, and, returned to the stage front, dripping with water, and attired in the blue jersey suit in which he entered the tank. From the time that he entered it to his appearance on the stage only one and a half minutes had expired. While the author stood adjacent to the tank, during the dematerialization process, a great loss of physical energy was felt by him, such as is usually experienced by sitters in materializing séances, who have a good stock of vital energy, as in such phenomena, a large amount of energy is required. Dematerialization is performed by methods similar in operation to those in which the psycho-plastic essence is drawn from the medium. The body of the medium may be reduced to half its ordinary weight in the materializing room, but in the case of dematerialization the essence continues to be drawn until the whole physical body vanishes, and the substance composing it is held in suspension within the atmosphere, much in the same way as moisture is held by evaporation. While in this state, Houdini was transferred from the stage to the retiring room behind, and there almost instantaneously materialized. The speed with which this dematerialization was performed is much more rapid than is possible in the materializing séance room, where time is required for the essence to be crystallized into psycho-plastic matter. Not only was Houdini's body dematerialized, but it was carried through the locked iron tank, thus demonstrating the passage of matter through matter. This startling manifestation of one of nature's profoundest miracles was probably regarded by most of the audience as a very clever trick."

With the indulgence of the reader, I may be pardoned perhaps, if I insist that it is just what I claim it to be-- *simply a superior trick*. The effect is original with me and was invented in the course of my professional career as a public entertainer, for the sole purpose of *entertaining* audiences by mystifying them. My success seems to be attested by Mr. McKenzie in his acknowledgment that he was deceived into the belief as to my mediumistic powers; that I dematerialized my body and material substance, and materialized these things, so restoring them to a normal condition.

In rebuttal of this misconception I can only say that it is a demonstration of mal-observation; there was nothing supernatural in my performance. If I really possessed such abnormal powers as Mr. McKenzie credits me with, I should be only too ready to prove it for the enlightenment of a waiting world. I disagree with Mr. McKenzie that such acknowledgment would displease the "music-hall" or theatrical managers; on the contrary I am sure they would gladly open their stages to the demonstration and regard it as good management and showmanship. As to the performance of Mrs. Thompson of America, and Miss Fay their work is no more psychic than mine. It is simply another phase of magical deception, and I stand ready to reproduce such performances in an emergency.

Regarding the personally conducted tests of my work, by Mr. McKenzie, he did no more or less than all my committees are privileged to do while on the stage during my acts. Just as all Spiritualist believers do, so Mr. McKenzie relied on what he *thought* he saw, and therefore failed to affirm or negative his misguided and misdirected vision by rational application of his conscious intelligence. Had he brought his reasoning faculties to bear, as all sincere, unbiased investigators should, he would have discovered the utter inconsistency of his deductions and never have gone on record as the author of such folly, without a particle of real evidence with which to substantiate his claim.

Dr. Crawford, whose life was devoted to scientific pursuit and research, gave the last three years of his life to *investigating* occult or psychic phenomena, and failed utterly. His mind became impaired and he ended his own life by suicide, acknowledging that his brain was overtaxed with abstruse problems. He was so completely nonplussed and befuddled by the tricks of the Goligher family, that he gave them publicity as being genuine mediums; and the unfortunate man died without discovering his own weakness and error. Had he retained his mental balance a year or two longer, he would have been disillusioned by his co-worker in science, my friend Mr. E. E. Fournier d'Albe, the result of whose investigation is to be found elsewhere in this volume.

The unsuccessful investigations of those I have referred to are typical of all I have come in contact with or have learned of, and the barrier to their success has been their perfect willingness to be deceived. They agree to and tolerate the most absurd propositions as to the conditions under which the so-called investigations are conducted; just as they are *fixed* by the mediums themselves. They acquiesce in and assist the medium to produce results, and accept such results as conclusive evidence of the supernatural.

What does it all mean?

What importance can be attached to any one of these supposed phenomena as proof of the return of departed spirits?

Chapter 13
How Mediums Obtain Information

WE read in the newspapers of some payroll bandit who holds up the paymaster of a big concern and steals thousands of dollars, or of burglars entering homes and stores and breaking open safes and taking valuable loot, but these cases which we read of are nothing in comparison to some of the news which never reaches our ears, news of mediums who, because resourceful in obtaining information have made millions of dollars; blood money made at the cost of torture to the souls of their victims.

Suppose a medium comes to your town. He advertises a private séance. Like the average person you are curious and wish to be told things about yourself which you honestly believe no one in the world knows not even your most intimate friend. Perhaps you would like to learn some facts about a business deal, or know what is to be the outcome of a love affair, or it may be that you seek the comfort and solace that one is hungry for after the death of a near one. You go to this medium and are astounded by the things which are told you about yourself.

I do not claim that I can explain all the methods used by mediums to obtain this knowledge. A reader might attend a séance where the medium would use altogether different means to get the facts, but I am familiar with a great many of the methods of these human vultures. I think though that it is an insult to that scavenger of scavengers to compare such human beings to him but there is, to my mind, no other fit comparison.

The stock-in-trade of these frauds is the amount of knowledge they can obtain. It is invaluable and they will stop at nothing to gain it. They will tabulate the death notices in the newspapers; index the births and follow up the engagement and marriage notices; employ young men to attend social affairs and mix intimately with the guests, particularly the women.

It is seldom that one of these mediums will see a person the day he calls but will postpone the séance from a day or two to a week or more. As the person leaves the building he is followed by one of the medium's confederates who gathers enough information about him to make the medium's powers convincing when the séance is held.

It is a common occurrence for mediums of this stamp to hunt through the court records of property and mortgages. Cases have been known where they have employed men to read proof sheets in the press rooms of newspapers to find material with which to "foretell" events at séances. They frequently tap telephone wires. It is customary for these mediums to search letter boxes, steam open the letters, and make copies for future use. They have been known to buy the old letters sold to paper mills by big concerns, one useful letter, out of a ton of rubbish, being enough to pay them a great profit. It is also a common thing for mediums to "plant" assistants as waiters in restaurants for the purpose of overhearing conversation, especially in restaurants of the better class, business clubs, and luncheon clubs, where men of note freely discuss their plans and secrets, and in the "gilded lobster palaces" of Broadway and many hotel cabarets in other towns there are men who check and tabulate the good spenders and who in one way or another, usually when the victims are under the influence of drink, get into their confidence and secure information which is sold for money.

My attention was called to a case where it was said that a medium "planted" clerks in a Metropolitan hotel who would open, read, and re-seal the letters of guests. The medium was also able to get girls at the switchboard who intercepted messages and made a typewritten record of telephone conversations for him.

In many apartment houses the elevator boys, superintendents and servants are bribed to make a daily report of the inside happenings of the house. Most of the mediums work in the dark and many of them have employed expert pickpockets who cleverly take from the sitters' pockets letters, names, memorandums, etc., while they are being interviewed. These are passed to the medium who tells the sitter more or less of their contents. Having served their purpose they are returned to the pockets of the sitter who, none the wiser, goes out to help spread reports of the medium's wonderful ability. Mediums' campaigns are planned a long time ahead. They make trips on steamers gathering, tabulating and indexing for future reference the information to be overheard in the intimate stories and morsels of scandals exchanged in the smoking rooms, card rooms, and ladies' salons.

A man in a confidential moment told some very intimate secrets of his business to a chance traveling acquaintance while they sat in the smoking compartment of a Pullman car. Unfortunately for him this acquaintance belonged to an unscrupulous gang of mediums who used the information to blackmail him. These gangs of clairvoyant blackmailers will stop at nothing. They will move into the apartment house in which their victim lives and watch his habits. When sure of ample time they will break into his rooms, not to steal valuables, but information which nets them far more than the small amount of diamonds and cash which they might snatch. If it is possible to steal the records of great political parties how much easier to steal the secret papers of a family. If you doubt that information leaks out look up some of the cases that have been brought to the attention of the courts; cases where papers from secret organizations were missing; where the most intimate documents have been given publicity. Such information is far more difficult to obtain than the records of the dead. The Bar Association protects its reputation by weeding out lawyers who prey on clients but it cannot so easily discover a dishonest employee in a lawyer's office who takes advantage of information which he knows to be sacred and secret.

Mediums are especially desirous of keeping in touch with disgruntled employees. There is no limit to what they will do. They have been known to arrange for the employment of accomplices as domestics and chauffeurs in families where they were particularly anxious to get information and have frequently had dictagraphs placed in homes by fake or disloyal servants and after a month or so of tabulating secrets and information were prepared for a séance at which the sitters could only account for the amazing things told them by believing the medium had occult aid. The result was an unqualified confidence in the mediumistic powers which in the end cost the sitters an exorbitant sum.

I heard of a medium who employed a quiet couple for the express purpose of attending funerals, mixing with the mourners, and gathering information which was eventually turned into gold, and what is known as a "sure-fire" method is to dress some little woman demurely and place her in the reception room where she greets the visitors, telling them her troubles and naturally receiving their confidences in return.

I have even known of two cases in which these human wolves, apparently out of the kindness of their hearts, sent girls to a young ladies' seminary where they were able to wheedle from their roommates secrets which caused the loss of several fortunes.

One of the biggest scoops and one that is talked of in hushed tones even among the fraud fraternity is that of an old-time circus grafter who, having been cleaned out in Wall Street, was at his wits' ends to make a living. One evening, tired and weary from a day's unsuccessful efforts to find honest employment, he overheard his two daughters discussing a bit of scandal they had listened to in the hairdressing parlor where they were employed and which compromised a prominent society woman's name. The old man pricked up his ears, recognized the possibilities, and a very short time after invested what little capital he had and all he could borrow in a beauty parlor and with the information it furnished him through the aid of his wife and daughters he was able to set himself up as a medium, the venture yielding handsomely the first year.

A most novel method of obtaining information was devised by a man who decided after listening to the conversation in a Turkish bath to open one himself. Most of his attendants were accomplices and while the patrons were enjoying the bath their clothes were searched, letters opened and signatures traced. The end of the first year found him enjoying a country home in an aristocratic neighborhood.

During one of my engagements in Berlin, Germany, I made the acquaintance of the foreman of a safe factory who told me that he made a duplicate key[117] for every safe which passed through his hands and that he sold these keys to mediums but with the express understanding that there should

---

[117] The great majority of Continental safes are opened by keys and not by combination locks as in America

be nothing stolen. The mediums assured him that all they wanted was an opportunity to read the mail and private papers which the safes contained.

I have known of a number of cases in which the medium used a drug addict to secure information giving the poor tortured creature his necessary drug only in return for facts he wanted, knowing that when the addict was suffering for the drug's stimulus he would stop at nothing to secure it.

In small towns "Bible sellers" have sometimes been employed who were able to get exact dates, names, and birth places which were eventually used in some form. Men employed by mediums to gather information are often disguised as agents. One in particular I know of who goes from house to house trying to sell typewriters and washing machines on the installment plan. Even if he does not make a sale he can at least engage the lady of the house in conversation, drawing on her sympathy by telling of the trials and tribulations of a canvasser and a pitiful tale of how he was driven to such work and in return usually receiving the particulars of some similar case among her friends or relatives. Information which is carefully saved for use in the future.

It has been necessary for the United States Government to assign special men to break up a band of fake census enumerators, which, going from neighborhood to neighborhood, secures complete family histories which are later sold to mediums for large sums of money.

One of the most interesting cases I have heard of lately is that of a young man who was greatly in debt and sought the advice of a medium. The medium offered to pay his debts if he in return would take a position which the medium would secure for him in the Bureau of Records and in addition to his work furnish the medium with copies of certain documents. Fear of his debts becoming known to his parents forced him to accept the offer and the medium got the desired data but before an improper use could be made of it the young man's conscience led him to make a clean breast of the whole affair to the police and a gigantic fraud was "nipped in the bud."

The most dastardly and unscrupulous methods that I ever heard of, methods almost beyond belief, were those used by a medium who made arrangements with a ring, of "white slavers" by which he paid them a certain specified sum for any information which the "girls" in their "houses" were able to secure. In addition he also established a number of places where, under the direction of a woman, the girls drew out many secrets which would never have been told under any other circumstances.

One thing which makes the work of these mediums easier is the fact that many people tell things about themselves without realizing it. I have known people to deny emphatically that they had made certain statements or mentioned certain things in a séance although I had personally heard them say those very things not more than twenty minutes before. Under the excitement of the moment their subconscious mind[118] speaks while their conscious mind forgets. This does not escape the medium who takes advantage of everything which it is possible to.

An incident related to me by the late Harry Kellar shows in a striking way what can be done with information the possession of which is not suspected nor its source accounted for by the victim. He had met in Hong Kong a troupe of travelling players, known as the "Loftus Troupe" which was featuring Jefferson De Angelus. Among these players was one, Jim Mass, who, during a discussion of Spiritualism scoffed at anyone's belief in it. Kellar told him to visit his hotel the following night and he would be given a séance. Mass did and Kellar pretended to go into a deep trance rolling his eyes and imitating all the other effects. While in the trance he told Mass his history from the time he ran away from Newark, N. J., relating his trials and tribulations and his efforts to make a success on the stage up to the time when a young lady committed suicide in San Francisco because of his jealousy. Then Kellar turned to him and said:

"What is your name?"

"Jim Mass," was the answer.

"That is not your right name," Kellar retorted, "your right name is James Cropsey!"

"It is a lie," said Mass.

---

[118] I firmly believe In the workings of the subconscious mind.

"No, it is not a lie, for I see before me your name. I see that your father has just died of a broken heart because of your behaviour. I see your mother writing you a letter to that effect, begging you to come home and be her son again. I see the grave of your father and on the tombstone is inscribed, 'James Cropsey.'"

Kellar came out of the trance and Mass sprang up exclaiming:

"My God, you have told me things that only the Almighty and I know!"

Kellar claimed to Mass that he did not know anything which had transpired in the trance. The following day a letter came from Mass' mother telling him of the death of his father. This fully convinced him that Kellar had strong mediumistic powers, and to such an extent that when they met a few days later and Kellar told him that it was all a fake, Mass refused to believe it.

Kellar explained to me that while in Manila a few weeks previous he had met an American traveller who, while they were discussing the different theatrical companies in the Orient, had told him all the incidents he had repeated to Mass in the supposed trance. This traveller had written home to Mass' mother telling her of her son's whereabouts and therefore Kellar felt fairly safe in saying that a letter would arrive in a few days, but in spite of Kellar's confession Mass continued to believe firmly that he was a genuine psychic.

Mediums have been known after gaining the sitter's confidence sufficiently, to advise, through a Spirit, the purchase of certain stocks, bonds, or "swamp lands," and a certain group which I know has made over a million dollars by this system. One of the keenest and most unscrupulous of this class, a man who at present is abroad waiting for things to blow over, had a method which gained him a huge fortune. He would acquire the confidence of a widow whose husband had not been dead long and for months he would search into her private affairs without her knowledge. Then he would arrange for a meeting with her at which he would mention casually that he was a Spiritualist and that she could find solace and comfort in Spiritualism. At an impromptu séance he would tell her so many things of a most intimate character that she would be convinced. After a series of séances he would materialize and manifest what was supposedly the Spirit of her husband who would tell her to turn over certain property and deeds to this medium who would take care of them in a business-like manner. Invariably the poor deluded widow would surrender to his machinations and that would be the last she would ever hear of medium or money.

At a time when it was a British society fad to delve into the affairs of the beyond a house of clairvoyance was opened in London's most exclusive section, the fashionable West End. It was exquisitely furnished and the interior decorating was the show work of a well-known firm. Though known as "Madame _____" the proprietor was in reality the daughter of an English aristocrat. She had formed a partnership with a man known to society as "Sir _____" and thought of as being simply a "man about town," but was in reality the head of a desperate band of the underworld.

A rich clientele soon became accustomed to a rule which required sittings to be arranged for at least a week in advance which gave Madame _____ plenty of time for her confederates to investigate the client's affairs. After several sittings the Madame would tell her client that she was exhausted but could reveal more if allowed to enter the atmosphere of the home and come in personal contact with some of the intimate belongings of the client. This hint invariably secured the desired invitation. Once a guest in the client's home, she went from room to room selecting various things and finally suggesting, at the psychological moment, that she be shown all of the client's jewelry. While this was being brought out Madame _____ supposedly went into a trance but was in reality watching closely to see where the jewelry was kept. Back in her own home again she at once got in touch with Sir _____ giving him such detailed information about the client's house that it was easy for him to plan its successful robbery by his men, while the victims never suspected how their secret hiding places had been discovered. It only took the pair five years to acquire a fortune of three million dollars by these methods. Then Scotland Yard became suspicious of their actions and in a search for a more congenial climate they came to America and began working their system in New York.

Sir _____ learned through underworld channels of a rich eccentric who would have nothing to do with banks and safe deposit vaults but kept all his money and valuables in his home where he boasted so many burglar alarms and other protective devices as to practically dare thieves to rob him. After making sure that this man had very strong Spiritualistic tendencies Madame _____ wrote him a letter in which she told him that she had been requested by the spirit of his dead brother to get into communication with him. An interview followed and then a séance at which the brother's spirit was claimed to have been materialized. The man was so convinced that he had received a message from his brother that the instructions to safeguard his money and valuables by placing them in a certain bank were followed implicitly even to the extent of taking them to the president (?) of the bank at his home instead of going to the bank with them. It is needless to say that the "bank president" was none other than Sir _____. This exploit netted them about four hundred thousand dollars. Not long after they appeared in Paris. Madame _____ proceeded to dupe a jeweler out of a quantity of valuable jewels and with Sir _____ succeeded in escaping to Germany where they tried to repeat the performance but were arrested.

The majority of the people who are fleeced do not blame the medium but really believe that the Spirit of their departed one prescribed the loss and that the medium simply acted as an agent. It is only when the mediums fall out; when there ceases to be "honor among thieves" that the cases are brought to the attention of the police. Although I realize that it would be difficult to enforce, there should be a law to prevent these frauds, for as the result of investigation I know that this particular line has netted many millions of dollars from unwary, trusting, and believing people. An end ought to be put to it.

Chapter 14
What You Must Believe To Be A Spiritualist

THERE is an old adage that "truth is stranger than fiction" but some of the miraculous things attributed to the Spirits would not be told, could not be told, even by such a famous writer of wild fiction as Baron Munchausen, but under the protecting mantle of Spiritualism these vivid tales are believed by millions. The conglomerated things you are asked to accept in good faith are almost inconceivable. If you do not then you are not a real Spiritualist. There must not be the shadow of a doubt in your mind as to the truth of the extravagant feats claimed to be performed by the Spirits through their earthly messengers the mediums.

Among the spirits who have come back and written stories, according to the Spiritualists, are no less personages than Shakespeare, Bacon, Charles Dickens who completed his "Mystery of Edwin Drood," Jack London, Edgar Allan Poe, Mark Twain, and lately Oscar Wilde. Magazines have been published by the "Spirits"[119] and there are numbers of cases where entire books have been claimed to be their work. I ask the reader if he believes the following incidents which I have selected from various Spiritualistic publications in my library. If so he is entitled to join the cult.

The "Medium and Daybreak" of June 9, 1871, tells of an instance where "The Spirits 'floated' Mr. Herne to Mrs. Guppy's in open day as was reported by us two weeks ago. . . . This has been speedily followed by other cases some of which are exceedingly well substantiated. On Saturday evening, as a circle consisting of about nine persons, sat within locked doors, with Messrs. Herne and Williams, at these mediums' lodgings, 61 Lambs' Conduit Street, after a considerable time an object was felt to come upon the table, and when a light was struck, their visitor was found to be Mrs. Guppy. She was not by any means dressed for an excursion, as she was without shoes, and had a memorandum book in one hand and a pen in the other.

"The last word inscribed in the book was 'onions.' The writing was not yet dry and there was ink on the pen. When Mrs. Guppy regained her consciousness she stated that she had been making some entries of expenses, became insensible and knew nothing until she found herself in the circle. A party of gentlemen accompanied Mrs. Guppy home; a deputation went in first and questioned Miss Neyland as to how or when Mrs. Guppy had been missed. She said that she had been sitting in the same room; Mrs. Guppy was making entries in her book, and Miss Neyland was reminding her of the items to put down. Miss Neyland was reading a newspaper in the intervals of conversation, and when she raised her head from her reading Mrs. Guppy could not be seen. It was intimated, through raps on the table, that the Spirits had taken her, and as Mrs. Guppy had every confidence in the beneficence of these agents, Mrs. Guppy's abduction gave no concern. Both Mr. Herne and Mr. Williams were 'floated' the same evening. Mr. Williams found himself at the top of the stairs, the doors being shut all the while.

"At the séance at the Spiritual Institution, a young lady who was a sceptic was levitated. At Messrs. Herne and Williams' séance, at the same place, a geranium in a pot was brought into the room from the staircase window above, while doors and windows were closed. Mrs. Burns had a knife taken out of her hand, which 'Katie' (the Spirit) said she would deposit at Lizzie's, meaning Mrs. Guppy. A gentleman had two spirit photographs taken from his hand. A cushion was carried from the front room to the back room, where the séance was held, the door being shut. Mr. Williams' coat was taken off while his hands were held. Mr. Herne was floated. Mr. Andrews, a gentleman who has not the use

---

[119] *The Spirit Messenger* and the *Star of Truth* were published in 1852 by R. P. Ambler of Springfield, Mass. They were *"edited and composed by spirits."* The Spirit of the Sixth Circle took entire charge of the *Spirit Messenger,* and not even the publisher was permitted to dictate in the least. There were elucidations by the Spirits on "Hope, Life, Truth, Initiation, Marriage Relations, Evils of Society, and Destiny of the Race." *The Northwestern Orient,* published in 1852 by C. H. White, contained communications from John Adams, Edgar Allan Poe, John Wesley, John Whitefield, Thomas Paine, *et al.* It also contained several poems by the Spirits. Copies are on file in my library.

of his limbs, held a very interesting conversation with 'Katie' who promised to try and benefit him. The generous sympathy of these good spirits was very apparent from their eagerness to help the distressed. A letter from Northampton intimates that similar phenomena are being produced in that town. These feats are doing a mighty work in convincing hundreds of the power.

"At a séance given by Mrs. Guppy ('Medium and Daybreak,' November 18, 1870), the Spirits knowing it was tea time, first of all brought through the solid wall the dishes and placed them on the table, then transported cake and hot tea, and in the center of the table was placed violets, mignonette, geranium leaves and fern leaves, all wet with rain, which had been gathered by the Spirits.

"Herne, with whom Williams was associated, made it his business to have his Spirits bring in the slates from the hallway through the closed door. He had books ooze through the solid floors, from the library overhead, and drop on the séance table. Williams would be entranced in the cabinet and the Spirits would disrobe him much to his 'entranced' embarrassment.

On the testimony of Orville Pitcher, John King at a séance stood in the full glare of the daylight for twenty minutes. He then retired and was followed by no less a personage than Oliver Cromwell, who walked around, embraced his medium and all the sitters. He afterwards controlled the medium and gave utterance to thoughts of a most elevated nature.

"Mrs. Catherine Berry goes on record ('Medium and Daybreak,' July 9, 1876) that through the mediumship of Mrs. Guppy she had seen the Sultan of Zanzibar on the previous day. "He had a handsome copper-colored face and a large black beard, on his head he had a white turban such as worn by the Spirit of John King."

"Dr. Monck, ex-preacher, disappeared one night from the bed in which he slept with another man in Bristol and to his surprise, when he awoke, found himself in Swindom." (*Spiritualism,* by Joseph McCabe.)

"Mr. Harris, his wife and a friend, who happened to be a medium, were just about to sit down to a mid-day meal when the medium, a man named Wilkinson, was suddenly 'controlled.' He fought hard against this unexpected behaviour of his Spirit control, but to no avail. In his unconscious state he jangled money in his pocket, then pointed to a cigarette box which was lying on a shelf in the opposite corner. In that box, it seemed, was the sum of 17s, 6d. Mr. and Mrs. Harris were wondering what this all meant, when suddenly the box virtually flew from the shelf, passed through the closed door, and was gone. Mrs. Harris immediately left the room and tried to find trace of the box. SHE FOUND IT UPSTAIRS UNDERNEATH THE PILLOW ON THE BED. The money was intact." (*An Amazing Séance and an Exposure, by* Sidney A. Mosley, page 21.)

At a séance held on February 15, 1919, at the home of Mr. Wallace Penylan at Cardiff, by Mr. Thomas, there were present Sir Arthur, Lady Doyle, and others, numbering about twenty in all. "Thomas, speaking from his chair (apparently still under control) then asked, 'Is Lady Doyle cold?' Then Lady Doyle said she felt 'a little bit shivery' and Thomas said, 'Oh, you'll be warm soon,' and in a second or two something fell on her lap. At the close of the séance, this was found to be the Holland jacket which somehow had been removed from the medium." (*An Amazing Séance,* page 51.)

Most mediums to-day have perfected the art of levitating tables and chairs and other pieces of furniture, though I doubt if any of them have ever reached the mark of perfection attained by Palladino with her years of experience, inscrutable face and uncanny knowing when to seize opportunities to fool her investigators, but you are also asked to believe that Daniel Dunglas Home, floated out of one window, over the street, and rushed through another one into a different room.

Col. Olcott asks in "Communication" What is this performance compared with the experience of Webster Eddy (a younger brother of the Eddy Brothers) when a grown man, in the presence of three reputable witnesses, was carried out of a window and over the top of a house and landed in a ditch a quarter of a mile distant?

"William Eddy was carried bodily to a distant wood and was kept there three days under control and was carried back again.

"Horatio Eddy was taken bodily three miles to a mountain top and was obliged to find his way home alone the next morning.

"In Lyceum Hall, Buffalo, Horatio was levitated for twenty-six consecutive evenings, while bound to a chair and he and the chair were hung on a chandelier hook in the ceiling. He was then lowered safely to his former position.

"Mary Eddy was raised to the ceiling in Hope Chapel, in New York City, and while there wrote her name. Her little boy, Warren, was floated many evenings in dark circles and squealed lustily all the while to be let down.

"Since 1347 authenticated reports prove that similar experiences occurred to Edward Irving, Margaret Rule, St. Philip of Neri, St. Catherine of Columbine, Loyola, Savonarola, Jennie Lord, Madame Hauffe and many others."

Col. Olcott omitted mentioning myself. I stand ready to vouch for the fact that I personally floated in the air and *levitated* many times and marvelled at the ease with which I did it, but I woke up later in the night.

Horatio Eddy in a personal letter to me under date of July 6, 1920, wrote:

"A book six inches thick would not hold my history. I cannot give any version of our floating in the air, but it is just as stated in 'Communication.' Webster Eddy is my youngest brother. My father did put live coals on William's head and poured hot water down his back. We all used to get horsewhipped by him to prove the devil was in us."[120]

In another letter dated July 3, 1922, he writes that he and his sister had been giving a joint exhibition with Ira Erastus Davenport, who had been ordered by the authorities in Syracuse to take out a juggler's license, but would not.

"The result was while we were holding a private séance we were handcuffed and taken to jail; on the way the handcuffs were taken off. We did not ride to jail but were dragged along through the snow for more than a mile. They did not put us in cells, as I told them if they did I would have every prisoner's door open before daylight, so two police sat up all night with us. In the morning a Mr. McDonald of 7 Beach Street went our bail for fifteen thousand dollars.

"Our trial was to be held in Schenectady in March. We arrived there and had to wait three weeks, then they put it over to Albany three months later and our bail was renewed. We stayed in Albany until court was almost through. The day our trial was to take place the judge stated we claimed it to be a phase of religion and ruled it out of court."

If you are to be a Spiritualist you must believe that fifteen persons, several of them reporters, met in Mrs. Young's parlors in 27th Street, New York City, and at the request of the Spirit several English walnuts were placed near the piano, and that the piano rose and descended on the walnuts without crushing them. Col. Olcott writes that seven of the heaviest persons in the room were asked to sit upon the instrument. The invitation being accepted Mrs. Young played a march and the instrument and the persons surmounting it were lifted several feet.

"A portfolio containing Eliza White's Katie King note and John's duplicate was at this time in my coat pocket, where it had been constantly since the preceding evening.

John broke in upon our expressions of surprise by rapping out 'Do you folks want me to commit forgery for you? I can bring you here the blank check of any National Bank and sign upon it the name of any president, cashier or other official.' I thanked his Invisible Highness and declined the favor upon the sufficient ground that the police did not believe in Spiritualism and I did not care to risk the chance of convincing them in case the forged papers should be found in my possession." *(People from the Other World,* Henry S. Olcott, page 458.)

"In a house on Ferretstone Road, Hornsey, London, explosions like bombs were heard, lumps of coal were propelled by some unknown agency in all directions. Brooms were thrown violently from a landing into the kitchen. Glass and china had been smashed and windows broken and to top it all off

---

[120] "When William was in a trance his father tried to bring him out by slapping, pinching and other cruelty, and finally tried to pour boiling water down his back. This failing, he took a blazing ember from the hearth and placed it on the young man's head, but William slept on, with only the scars as reminders of his parent's deep concern for his well being and safety."— "Eddy Brothers," by Henry S. Olcott

a boy sitting on a chair had been raised with the chair from the ground." (The *London Evening News,* Feb. 15, 1921.)

Vincenzo Gullots, a Sicilian violinist at Batavia, Ill., well known by reason of his Chautauqua concerts, decided to take a bride chosen for him after death "by the companion of my most thrilling hours, my departed wife. She died in August and I was almost frantic with grief but in the night I could sense her presence and I followed her guidance implicitly. My new mate will comfort her." (The *New York World,* May 17, 1922.)

Sir Arthur Conan Doyle in an interview at the Hotel Ambassador, New York City, as reported by the *New York World,* April 11, 1922, stated that "in 'Summer-land' marriage is on a higher and more spiritual plane than here and is merely the mating of affinities, who are always happy. No babies are born however. The spirits as they go about their daily tasks, keep a watchful eye on earthly matters and are extremely interested in the births here."

He stated that there is a plane called "Paradise" where "normally respectable" persons go after death and this "plane" is only slightly removed from this earthly sphere. Bad people when they die are transported to a plane considerably lower than that tenanted by respectable ones and they continue to sink lower and lower unless they repent. After a considerable probationary period they are able to climb into "Paradise." The average length of time they stay in "Paradise" is about forty years after which they float to higher and still higher planes. All mediums have guardian angels to whom they are especially subject, but they can communicate with other Spirits, the "guardian angel" acting as a sort of master-of-ceremonies upon such occasions.

Sir Arthur proclaimed that he once saw his dead mother's face in the ectoplasm of a medium. This was a few months after her death and he added, "There was not the slightest question about it. That was while I was in Australia. The face seemed as solid as in life. My mother wrote me a letter through the medium signing a pet name,[121] which could not have been known to the medium. There is no question about having been in communication with my son either."

An account in the *New York American,* April 5, 1923, says that Sir Arthur Conan Doyle told the reporters that he had recently hurt the ligaments in his right leg from the shin to the thigh, and that his son Kingsley who had died in the War had massaged the limb with beneficial results: "I was sitting with Evan Powell, a very unusual and powerful medium," he said, "when my son Kingsley appeared, saying 'it will be alright, Daddy; I will get you fixed up alright,' and began massaging my leg."

In an article in the *London Magazine,* August, 1920, Mr. C. W. Leadbeater, a prominent member of the Theosophical Society and an authority on occult theories, speaking of the apport of Spirits says: "living astrally as they do, the Fourth Dimension is a commonplace fact of their nature, and this makes it quite simple for them to do many little tricks which to us appear wonderful, such as the removal of articles from a locked box or an apport of flowers into a closed room."

Sir Arthur Conan Doyle, in his book "Wanderings of a Spiritualist," devotes seven pages to Charles Bailey, who was known as an "apport medium." Sir Arthur defends Bailey, notwithstanding that he has been exposed many times.[122] Among the things Bailey claims to have apported are birds, oriental plants, small animals, and a young shark eighteen inches long which he pretended the Spirit guides had brought from India and passed through the walls into the séance room.

Mrs. Johnson of Newcastle-on-Tyne, England, told me personally that the Spirit of her deceased son was very mischievous at times and caused her a great deal of embarrassment. One of his favorite jokes when she was on a journey was to open her travelling bag and allow all her belongings to be strewn about. She also told me that the boy's Spirit would light the fire for her to get breakfast.

A widow in Brooklyn, N. Y., became a mother and claimed that the Spirit of her husband was the father of the child.

---

[121] I gave a pseudo seance for Sophie Irene Loeb and had two slates which were examined by the Circle and marked. I asked if the Spirits would manifest and when the slates were opened there was a message containing a code word. Miss Loeb was astounded, for the message signed by Jack London contained a word which she claimed no one In the whole world knew about. I did it by trickery but she declared that if she had not known I was a magician she would have believed readily that I had psychic powers.

[122] A man by the name of Rider, professionally known as "Kodarz," exposed Bailey in New Zealand in 1910.

The celebrated Professor Hare, a professor of chemistry in the University of Pennsylvania, graduate of Yale and Harvard, and associated with the Smithsonian Institute of Washington, tells that when travelling with a boy and while in his room, after they had locked up the iron Balled Spiritscope, shaving case, etc., in his carpet bag, in some inscrutable manner all the contents were taken from the bag and fell about him in a shower.

Anna Stuart, a medium of Terre Haute, could produce Spirits that would weigh from practically nothing to more than a hundred pounds, and Spiritualists are expected to believe that one human being can go into a trance and bring forth three or four beings with his own Spirit form. W. T. Stead, one of the most brilliant Spiritualists, now dead, claimed to have seen the Spirit of an Egyptian who left the "earthly life" in the time of Semir-Amide, three thousand years ago. "For several minutes the Spirit was distinctly visible to us munching an apple, but I felt so exhausted by the loss of magnetism and nervous as well that I begged him to leave us. I will never forget his soulful expression."

Florence Marryat, the daughter of Capt. Marryat, the famous writer of sea stories, has written a number of books on Spiritualism. She wrote one of the best introductions in favor of Spiritualism that I ever read, nevertheless some of the things she claims to have witnessed and lived through are of such a nature that I will only give a brief mention of them without comment, letting the reader form his own opinion. They are taken from her book "There is no Death."

She tells of her brother-in-law coming into the room after rifle practice and while showing his rifle it was "accidentally discharged, the ball passing through the wall within two inches of my eldest daughter's head." She claims that she foresaw the occurrence the night previous.

She writes of having joined Mr. d-Oyley Carte's "Patience" company to play the part of Lady Jane, and tells that the different members of the company on different occasions mentioned the fact that although she was standing on the stage she appeared to be seated in the stalls. This always occurred at the same time, just before the end of the second act.

In another place she says: "We unanimously asked for flowers. It being December and a hard frost, simultaneously we smelt the smell of fresh earth, and we were told to light the gas again, when the following extraordinary sight met our eyes. In the middle of the sitters, still holding hands, was piled up on the carpet an immense quantity of mold, which had been torn up apparently with the roots that accompanied it. There were laurestenius, laurels and holly and several others, just as they had been pulled out of the earth and thrown in the midst of us. Mrs. Guppy looked anything but pleased at the sight of her carpet and begged the Spirits to bring cleaner things next time. They then told us to extinguish the lights again and each sitter was to wish mentally for something for himself. I wished for a yellow butterfly, knowing it was December, and as I thought of it a little cardboard box was put in my hand. Prince Albert whispered to me 'Have you got anything?' 'Yes,' I said, 'but not what I asked for. I expect they have given me a piece of jewelry.' When the gas was relit I opened the box and there lay *two yellow butterflies,* dead of course, but none the less extraordinary for that."

While talking of a séance with Katie King she said: "She told me to take the scissors and cut off her hair.

She had a profusion of ringlets flowing to her waist that night. I obeyed religiously, hacking the hair wherever I could whilst she kept on saying *'Cut more! cut more! not for yourself you know, because you cannot take it away.'* So I cut off curl after curl and as fast as they fell to the ground, *the hair grew again on her head.* When I had finished, 'Katie' asked me to examine her hair and see if I could detect any place where I had used the scissors, and I did so without any effect. Neither was a severed hair to be found. It had vanished out of sight."

In another place she says: "Once a conductor spoke to me. 'I am not aware of your name,' he said (and I thought 'No, my friend, and won't be aware of it just yet either!') 'but a Spirit here wishes you would come up to the cabinet.' I advanced, expecting to see some friend, and there stood a Catholic priest, with his hand extended in blessing. I knelt down and he gave me the usual benediction, and then closed the curtain. 'Did you know the Spirit?' the conductor asked me. I shook my head and he continued, 'He was Father Hayes, the well known priest in this city. I suppose you are a Catholic?' I told him 'Yes' and went back to my seat. The conductor addressed me again 'I think Father Hayes must have come to pave the way for some of your friends,' he said. 'Here is a Spirit who says she has come for a lady by the name of Florence, who has just crossed the sea. Do you answer to that description?' I was about to say yes when the curtain parted again and my daughter 'Florence' ran across the room and fell into my arms. 'Mother,' she exclaimed, 'I said I would come with you and look after you, didn't I?' I looked at her. She was exactly the same in appearance as when she came to me in England under the different mediumships of Florence Cook, Arthur Coleman, Charles Williams and William Ellington."

She tells of a business man who attended a séance. every night and presented a white flower to the Spirit of his wife who had died on her wedding day eleven years before.[123] The book is full of such incidents as these but I think enough have been repeated to show the reader what it is necessary to believe to be a good Spiritualist.

[124]In Judge Edmonds' book "Spiritualism," we read that it was customary to receive on blank sheets of paper messages from the Spirits of well-known men; that Benjamin Franklin came in accompanied by two other Spirits; that a pencil got up of its own accord and wrote five lines of ancient Hebrew; that books were levitated from a table numerous times, and a number of other incidents which drew upon the reader's imagination.

Daniel Dunglas Home in testifying in July, 1869, as reported in the *London Times,* told of an incident which had occurred several years previous. "We were," he said, "in a large room in the Salon de Quatorze. The Emperor and Empress were present,--I am now telling the story as I heard the Emperor tell it,--a table was moved, then a hand was seen to come. It was a very beautifully formed hand. There were pencils on the table. It lifted, not the one next to it, but the one on the far side. We heard the sound of writing, and saw it writing on fine note paper. The hand passed before me and went to the Emperor, and he kissed the hand. It went to the Empress; she withdrew from its touch, and the hand followed her. The Emperor said, 'Do not be frightened,' and she kissed it too. The hand seemed to be like a person thinking and as if it were saying, 'Why should I?' It came back to me. It had written the word 'Napoleon' and it remains written now. The writing was the autograph of the Emperor Napoleon I, who had an exceedingly beautiful hand." Mr. Home also said that the Emperor of Russia as well as the Emperor Napoleon, had seen hands and had taken hold of them, "when they seemed to float away into thin air."

Such are the things Spiritualists are expected to believe and do believe. I could continue to recite incidents *ad infinitum, ad nauseam,* but I believe the reader can form his own judgment from the above. It is the kind of material which drives people insane for when some poor, sick, human being is just on the verge of recovery such nonsensical utterances often overthrow reason. Is it any wonder that the population of our insane asylums is swelled with "followers" who have attempted to believe these things?

---

[123] Without any reservation she says she has investigated the majority of mediums and given them a hundred per cent clean bill. She writes that Eglinton actually materialized the spirit of Grimwaldi, the great clown. Eglinton was detected on four different occasions and so far as I have been able to learn, almost every medium she mentions in her books has, at some time or other, been detected and exposed.

[124] See Appendix F.

Chapter 15
Magicians As Detectors of Fraud

THE alacrity with which Spiritualists seize upon letters or other statements of magicians that they believe the so-called spirit manifestations which they have witnessed were not accomplished by means of legerdemain but were attributable to supernatural or occult powers has astonished me and while I intend to refute them I want to call attention at the same time to the incompetence of the opinion of the ordinary magician with a knowledge of two or three experiments in Spiritualism who stands up and claims that he can duplicate the experiments of any medium who ever lived.

My personal opinion is that notwithstanding the fact that innumerable exposures have been successfully made, such fact is no proof that any investigator, legerdemain artist or otherwise, is fully capable of fathoming each and every effect produced.

Some magicians with a knowledge of pseudo-Spiritualistic effects imagine that they have all they need to qualify them as investigators, and should anything transpire at a séance which they cannot explain they are mystified into temporary belief and write letters or make statements which they are quite likely to regret as the years roll on.[125]

A good card "shark" or "brace game"[126] gambler can cheat and fleece the slickest sleight-of-hand performer that ever lived, unless the performer has made a specialty of gambling tricks. It seems strange, but it is true, that card magicians are poor gamblers, and mediums, like the gamblers, resort to deception and take advantage of the sitters at all angles.

It is manifestly impossible to detect and duplicate all the feats attributed to fraudulent mediums who do not scruple at outraging propriety and even decency to gain their ends. A slick medium will even resort to drawing on the sitters[127] for desired information by recourse to what may be palmed off for a mere lark, and if the bait is swallowed by the sitter the circumstance is turned to good account for the perpetration of deliberate fraud to his consternation and bewilderment.

Again many of the effects produced by mediums are impulsive, spasmodic, done on the spur of the moment, inspired or promoted by the attending circumstances, and could not be duplicated by themselves. Because the circumstances of their origin and performance are so peculiar detection and duplication of Spiritualistic phenomena is sometimes a most complex task. Not only are mediums alert to embrace every advantage offered by auto-suggestion but they also take advantage of every accidental occurrence. For instance, my greatest feat of mystery was performed in 1922 at Seacliffe, L. I., on the Fourth of July, at the home of Mr. B. M. L. Ernest. The children were waiting to set off their display of fireworks when it started to rain. The heavens fairly tore loose. Little Richard in his dismay turned to me and said:

"Can't you make the rain stop?"

"Why certainly," I replied and raising my hands said appealingly, "Rain and Storm, I command you to stop."

This I repeated three times and, as if by miracle, within the next two minutes the rain stopped and the skies became clear. Toward the end of the display of fireworks the little fellow turned to me and with a peculiar gleam in his eyes said:

---

[125] Maskelyne, Kellar, and Hoffmann were all three magicians who changed their minds.

[126] Any prepared gambling device or game, like electrically controlled steel dice, roulette; pointer and arrow revolving artifice; prepared cards, either marked, concave or convex cut, which gives the dealer the advantage at all times. Brace games include everything from a put and take to the changing of a black bag on the top of an innocent looking chiffonier. The games, while appearing to be governed by the law of chance, are secretly controlled by the gambler, or his confederate, in so subtle a manner that it is impossible for the poor dupe, who wagers on the result, to detect it.

[127] Known as fishing.

"Why, Mr. Houdini, it would have stopped raining anyway."

I knew I was risking my whole life's reputation with the youngster but I said:

"Is that so? I will show you."

Walking out in front I raised my hands suppliantly toward the heavens and with all the command and force I had in me called:

"Listen to my voice, great Commander of the rain, and once more let the water flow to earth and allow the flowers and trees to bloom."

A chill came over me for as if in response to my command or the prayer of my words another downpour started, but despite the pleading of the children I refused to make it stop again. I was not taking any more chances.

I am also aware of the fact that there are effects produced by magicians which they declare are accomplished by natural agencies, which other magicians are entirely unable to account for or satisfactorily explain. A notable case was a card performance by Dr. Samuel C. Hooker which included the levitation of a life-sized head of an animal, possessed of life-like movement while in a state of suspension and still there were no visible means of support. A number of these séances were given to groups of magicians only. On one occasion a dozen or more of the most expert professional magicians were in attendance, but no one could offer a satisfactory solution.

Many magical mysteries as practised for entertainment are just as incomprehensible as so-called Spiritualistic Phenomena and it is not to be wondered at that even minds trained to analytical thinking are deceived and misguided. Were I at a séance and not able to explain what transpired it would not necessarily be an acknowledgment that I believed it to be genuine Spiritualism. The fact that I have mystified many does not signify that what I have done, though unexplainable to them, was done by the help of the Spirits. Mr. Kellar frequently, particularly during the last two years of his appearance on the stage, said to the audience:

"Do not be ashamed if I mystify you; I have seen Houdini and his work and I do not know how he does it."

The simple fact that a thing looks mysterious to one does not signify anything beyond the necessity of analytic investigation for a fuller understanding. But to return to possibilities; I believe that the great majority of so-called manifestations can be duplicated but I am not prepared to include all, because, as before explained, some are spontaneous, and cannot be reproduced by the mediums themselves unless the identical opportunity should present itself, which is as uncertain as lightning striking twice in the same place--possible but improbable.

It would be extremely difficult, if not out of the question, to reproduce much of the "phenomena" by description as given by those who have witnessed it. The lapse of time and the fact that a story twice told never loses, renders such reproduction extremely doubtful. Were I to be challenged to duplicate any particular phase as presented by a medium, permission would have to be granted to allow me not less than three demonstrations. At the first, not wishing to accept any one's word as to what happened I should want to see the manifestation so that there would be no surprise attack on my mind afterwards. At the second sitting I would be prepared to watch what I had seen at the first sitting and the third time I would try to completely analyze for duplication. It might be that some peculiar formation or years of special practice enabled the medium to do a certain action and naturally it would require at least three séances to become thoroughly cognizant of the *modus operandi,* or the manipulative process used. If there were no fraud, then there could be no objection to the demonstrations.

Let us dissect a few of the magician's statements. First: Belachini, conjuror to the imperial German Court, is claimed by Spiritualists as a great magician countenancing and acknowledging the genuineness of Spiritualism, but by no possible stretch of imagination could he be so classed despite the efforts of modern Spiritualists to prove that he was, for the very nature of his tricks belie his statement. No present day magician would permit him to be mentioned as an authority on. Spiritualism notwithstanding the fact that Spiritualists are trying to prove from his letters that he was, just as they have ever since the letters were written.

I have received reports from Karl Wilmann, of Hamburg; A. Herman, of Berlin, and Rosner of Haisenhaid, to the effect that Belachini was solely an apparatus or mechanical conjuror with an adroit and daring address. In fact, his unbounded self-confidence won him the position for which he is famous. He was performing for Kaiser Wilhelm I. who sat amazed at his suave dexterity. The climax of the performance came when Belachini, bowing, proffered a pen to Wilhelm.

"Take this, your Majesty," he requested, "and attempt to write with it. I warn you it is a magical pen and subject only to my control; I can write anything with it or cause anything to be written; you cannot."

Wilhelm laughingly took the pen with a confident mien, hiding his real awe of Belachini. He applied it to the paper before him but in spite of his most careful efforts, the pen balked, spluttering and splashing ink, while Belachini stood by smiling.

"Well," said the Kaiser, "tell me what to write."

Belachini reflectively caressed his chin, then replied with a dry smile:

"Write this. I hereby appoint Belachini Court Conjuror."

The monarch chuckled at the wit and without difficulty wrote and signed the order.

A second, famous in his day, was "Herr Alexander," a magician whose full name was Alexander Heinberger. He gave séances at the White House for President Polk who sent him to South America once on a man-of-war. The President was willing to believe that Heinberger was guided and aided by the Spirits but Heinberger would neither affirm nor deny the suspected origin of his feats but like a good showman left his observers to their own deductions as was the practice of the Davenport Brothers. He lived to be ninety years old, and was a most remarkable old man. I visited him at his home in Munster, Westphalia.

Sometimes a misunderstanding entangles a magician with Spiritualism. The following instance comes to my mind. It is a popular belief among Spiritualists that certain letters and statements bearing the signature of Robert Houdin are acknowledgments of his belief in Spiritualism. On the contrary they refer simply to certain acts of clairvoyance purported to have taken place at the instance of one Alexis Didier. The first statement has been translated as an interview of considerable length which is concluded as follows:

"Ah, Monsieur (Alexis Didier, as addressed by Houdin), that may seem so to a man of no experience in these matters, to the ordinary person,--though even then such a mistake is hardly admissible,--but to the expert! Just consider, Monsieur, that all my cards are faked, marked, often of. unequal sizes, or at least artistically arranged. Again I have my signals and telegraphs. But in this case a fresh pack was used which I had just taken out of its wrapper, and which the somnambulist cannot have studied. There is another point, where deception is impossible, namely, in the handling of the cards: in the one case, the entire artlessness of the performance, in the other, that tell-tale air of effort which nothing can entirely disguise. Add to this his total blindness, for need I insist on the impossibility--the absolute impossibility--of his having seen. *Besides, even supposing he could see, how can we account for the other phenomena?* With regard to my own 'second-sight' performances, without being able to divulge my secret to you now, bear in mind that I am careful to tell you every evening, that I only promise a *second* sight! Consequently in my case a first sight is indispensable.

"The following day Robert Houdin gave me (Alexis Didier) the following signed statement:

" 'While I am by no means inclined to accept the compliments which M_____ is kind enough to pay me, and while I am particularly anxious that my signature should not be held to prejudice in any way my opinion, either for or against magnetism, still I cannot refrain from affirming that the incidents recorded above are ABSOLUTELY CORRECT, *and that the more I think about them the* more impossible I find it to class them with those which form the subject of my profession and of my performances.

" 'Robert Houdin.' "
" 'May 4th, 1847.' "

It will be seen at a glance that the signature in this case refers to a mystification by card handling, clairvoyance, forecasting, etc. His second letter was written a fortnight later and is as follows:

"Monsieur, (Alexis Didier) as I informed you, I was anxious to have a second sitting. This sitting which was held at Marcillet's house yesterday proved even more extraordinary than the first, and has left me without a shadow of a doubt as to the clairvoyance of Alexis. I went to this séance, fully determined to keep a careful watch on the game of *ecarte,* which had astounded me so much before. This time I took much greater precautions than at the first séance, for distrusting myself I took a friend, whose natural imperturbability enabled him to form a cool judgment and helped me to steady mine. I append an account of what took place, and you will see that trickery could never have produced such results as those which I am about to recount.

"I undo a pack of cards, which I had brought with me in a marked wrapper to guard against another pack being substituted for it. I shuffle and it is my deal. I deal with every precaution known to a man well up in all the dodges of his profession. It is all of no use, Alexis stops me, and pointing to one of the cards that I had just placed in front of him on the table, says:

" 'I've got the King.'

" 'But you can't possibly know yet; the trump card has not been turned up.'

" 'You will see,' he replies. 'Go on.'

"As a matter of fact I turn up the eight of Diamonds and his was the King of Diamonds. The game was continued in an odd enough manner, for he told me the cards I had to play, though my cards were hidden under the table and held close together in my hands. To each lead of mine he played one of his own cards without turning it up, and it was always the right card to have played against mine. I left this séance then in the greatest possible state of amazement, and convinced of the utter impossibility of chance or conjuring having been responsible for such marvellous results.--Yours, etc.,

(Signed) "Robert Houdin,
"16th May, 1847."

I here embrace the opportunity to make a correction of a statement in "The Unmasking of Robert Houdin" (page 287). The record and source of information at that time was published in Berlin, Germany. It gave the impression that the "letters" cited above referred to Spiritualistic phenomena, but now, having come into possession of a true translation of these documents complete, as published by the Society for Psychical Research,[128] I am of the opinion that Houdin did treat the subject of Spiritualism with conservative prudence and impartiality, as recorded by Professor Hoffmann.

But I wish to say that in my estimation of Robert Houdin, despite his wonderful reputation and record as mentioned in Larousse's Encyclopedia, I cannot agree with his statements, because he misrepresented so much in his "Memoirs of a Magician." In "The Unmasking of Robert Houdin" I devoted a whole chapter to his ignorance of magic and by investigating I have found that he was not competent as an investigator of the claims of Spiritualists.

It came quite as a shocking surprise to me to find that the letters which were supposed to refer to Spiritualistic séances, and which have been quoted so often as being such, refer only to his experience with Alexis the clairvoyant. It must be apparent, even to the casual observer, that they have no bearings whatsoever on Spiritualism, but refer only to sittings with a clairvoyant in a game of sharp card practice. Knowing, as I do now, what it all meant, the fact that he wrote the letters does not surprise me in the least. I believe a lot of things transpired in that room which he could not see, or know whether there was confederacy, for clairvoyants as well as mediums often get information from the most unexpected sources. Clairvoyance, like Spiritualism, was not in the direct line of professional observation to Robert Houdin. What would he or any of his confreres, who were supposed to be adepts at that time, say if they could visit a séance of some of our present day clairvoyants who are appearing before the public and making use of radio, wireless, induction coils, etc.? What a wonderful bunch of letters they might write because of the simple fact that they could not tell how the effects were produced. It is ridiculous for any magician to say that the work he witnesses is not accomplished by conjuring or legerdemain simply because he cannot solve the problem.

---

[128] *Society for Psychical Research Proceedings,* Vol. XIV, pp. 380, 381.

As to his qualifications for adjudging the work of a clairvoyant, we have but to revert to his own narration of the origin and development of second-sight as used by himself. This account can be found in the English edition of his Memoirs:

"My two children were playing one day in the drawing-room at a game they had invented for their own amusement; the younger had bandaged his elder brother's eyes and made him guess the objects that he touched, and when later he guessed right they changed places. This simple game suggested to me the most complicated idea that ever crossed my mind. Pursued by the notion, I ran and shut myself in my workshop, and was fortunately in that happy state when the mind follows easily the combinations traced by fancy. I rested my head in my hands, and in my excitement laid down the first principles of second sight."

It is hard to reconcile this statement with truth in view of the fact that memory training, as he describes it, was in vogue and practised long before[129] his time and is not the way second sight is learned. It could not have been discovered or invented by him except coincidentally by his utter lack of knowledge bearing on the methods of seership and clairvoyance as practised either in his time or antiquity. Let me explain clearly, and I hope once for all, the valuelessness of his letters as far as they relate to Spiritualism and clairvoyance.

In the first place the blindfold test[130] as produced by Alexis Didier to mystify Houdin. Putting cotton on the eyes and covering it with a handkerchief is now used by amateurs in the cheapest kind of what we term "muscle reading." There is not the slightest difficulty in seeing beneath such a bandage, sometimes over it, and the range of vision can easily be determined by a test. In Paris I saw a mysterious performer, named Benoval, who had his eyes glued together with adhesive paper, on top of it cotton was placed, and over the cotton a handkerchief, but he danced around bottles and burning candles without any difficulty.

Regarding the information given clairvoyantly to Madame Robert Houdin during another séance with Alexis; Houdin at that time was one of the best known characters of Paris, a public person, and it was the easiest thing in the world for Alexis to gather information concerning him and his family. Houdin may not have been acquainted with the subtlety of what we now term "fishing," "stalling," or "killing time," in order to get information or put something over. He might have been mystified but his knowledge of Spiritualism and clairvoyance was nil according to his own statement.

One of the demonstrations presented by Alexis to mystify Houdin was the reading from a book, by the seer, several pages in advance of a page designated by the person holding the book at the time. There does not seem to be any really authentic details reported regarding the exact performance of this man, Alexis, consequently much must of necessity be left to conjecture and a knowledge of the orthodox methods for doing such things. Such information as there is available seems to have passed through several hands and in all probability was first presented to the public through a Spiritualistic publication. However, the particular effect referred to is neither new nor strange but has always been a feature in second sight acts and with clairvoyants. The reading of a book from memory is quite possible to persons of abnormal mind or special training in co-relative memorizing; a very clever system with surprising possibilities. There are many cases on record of persons who, having read a book once, could repeat every word and even tell where the punctuation was. The ability to recite entire chapters or parts of them is much more common, and is not difficult for trained minds such as are possessed by members of theatrical stock companies, who are oftentimes obliged to commit to memory simultaneously three or four plays, and this too while on the road. In order to be prepared to play one part in the afternoon and an entirely different one the same night, stock actors frequently have to do some marvellous memorization work on short notice. It is not an exception but the rule. They get long parts with from fifty to a hundred and fifty "sides," each side containing from one to ten speeches. The foster-mother's speech in "Common Clay" is over three pages, and the Duchess' in the first act of Oscar Wilde's "Lady Wild-mere's Fan" is about four pages. The well-known actress, Miss Beatrice Moreland, told me that she memorized them both in an hour and was almost letter perfect. The actor's rule for memorizing parts is to take ten pages first and when they have been committed to

---

[129] "Second sight" was presented by Pinetti, the celebrated Italian magician, at the Haymarket Theatre, London, England, Dec. 1, 1784.

[130] A girl named Shireen is holding a similar seance to-day and is able to hit a bulls-eye with a rifle.

memory take ten more. If such feats can be done as the result of training how easy it must be for an abnormal mind to memorize a book.

There comes to my mind a phenomenal memory feat by a blind slave boy called "Blind Tom." He would listen while a composer played an original composition. As soon as the composer finished Tom seated himself at the piano and reproduced the entire piece with all the composer's delicacy of shading and technique.

There is a case on record of a memory performance, I think in Rousseau's time, where a poet read a piece of poetry, a long monody, to the King. At its conclusion the King said:

"Why, that is quite an old story, I have heard it before. As a matter of fact the man who related it to me is in my palace now; I will send for him and have him recite it for you."

He spoke to a servant who left the room and returned in a few minutes with the memory man who stood in the center of the room and recited the entire poem. It appears that the King, wishing to mystify the poet, had the memory man hidden in a closet where he could hear the poem read.

Inaudi, a Frenchman, has given performances both in America and Europe in which he looks at a blackboard covered with figures written by a committee, then turns around and immediately tells correctly every figure on the board and its position; adds, subtracts, and multiplies them, with lightning-like rapidity, and all without looking at the board a second time. He makes no claim to psychic or clairvoyant powers but simply explains his wonderful performance as being the result of a photographic memory.

I might repeat such instances indefinitely but I think I have given enough to substantiate my claim of precedence for God's natural laws and their marvellous, even incomprehensible working, over any so-called supernatural endowment of a class of people so thoroughly disqualified by all known laws of moral sociology, as many professional mediums are admitted to be by their most ardent supporters.

Even such an eminent mystifier as Robert Houdin can misjudge when it comes to fathoming the so-called manifestations of the professional medium. As I have explained in "The Unmasking of Robert Houdin," page 291. he makes two flagrant errors in attempting to explain the Davenport Brothers' trick. First he claims that "by dint of special practice on the part of the mediums, the thumb is made to lie flat in the hand, when the whole assumes a cylindrical form of scarcely greater diameter than the *wrist.*" Secondly, he declares that the Davenport Brothers possessed the power of seeing in the dark as the result of practice or training.

Releasing myself from fastenings of all sorts, from ropes to straightjackets, has been my profession for over thirty-five years, therefore I am in a position to positively contradict Houdin's first statement. I have met thousands of persons who claimed that the rope trick as well as the handcuff trick was accomplished by folding the hand together or by making the wrist larger than the hand, but I have never met the man or woman who could make the hand smaller than the wrist. I have even gone so far as to have iron bands made to press my hands together, hoping to make them smaller than my wrists eventually, but it was no use. Even if the thumbs were cut away I believe it would be impossible to slip a rope that is properly bound around the wrist. Furthermore I know that Houdin was wrong in regard to the Davenports because of what Ira Erastus Davenport himself told me.

Equally preposterous is the gift of seeing in the dark with which Houdin endowed the Davenports. Professor Hoffmann defends Houdin by citing instances of prisoners who had been confined in a dungeon for an indefinite period and had learned to see in the dark. Ira Erastus Davenport laughed at the idea and Morelle, who was confined in a dungeon for a number of years, told me that all the years he had spent in darkness did not accustom his eyesight at all and that to have seen an article plainly he would have been forced to hold it close to his eyes and even then would have had to stretch his imagination.

Baggally, an investigator, a member of the Society for Psychical Research, London, England, emphatically records that he believes the Zancigs are *genuine telepathists,* and my friend, Sir Arthur Conan Doyle, though he says that Zancig has given proof numerous times that he works with a code, nevertheless has stated in writing that he believed the Zancigs to be genuine. I want to go on record that the Zancigs never impressed me as being anything but clever, silent and signal codists. Zancig has admitted freely to members of the Society of American Magicians, of which he is a member, that they were not telepathists but, as we term it, "second sight artists." They simply have a wonderful code which the public cannot detect. It is interesting to know that after Mrs. Zancig's death, Zancig took a street-car conductor from Philadelphia and broke him in to do the act. This young man soon quit his teacher, married, and began presenting the act with his wife. Then Zancig took young David Bamberg, an intelligent son of Theodore Bamberg, one of our well-known magicians. The boy proved exceptionally clever but on account of unexpected circumstances he left and went abroad. Zancig came to me for an assistant and I introduced him to an actress. He said he would guarantee to teach her the code inside of a month, but they never came to an agreement on financial matters. Zancig has now married again, this time a school teacher, and they are doing a very clever performance. In passing I would note that in 1906 or 1907 I engaged Zancig to go with my show. I had ample opportunity to watch his system and codes. They are swift, sure, and silent, and I must give him credit for being expertly adept in his chosen line of mystery, but I have his personal word, given before a witness, that telepathy does not enter into it.

Charles Morritt has a code for second sight which is very simple and can be taught to anyone in thirty minutes. He has given me the secret. He gave this code to a banker who performed it with his sister, and Morritt, although he had taught the signals, could not follow or detect them once they began to work smoothly. Of course he knew what they were doing but simply could not follow them.

Regarding the possibility of using codes and cues before others without being detected I can say positively that it is not only possible but simple and practical. I had a fox terrier by the name of "Bobby" that I trained to pick up cards by a cue. On May 31, 1918, I performed with this dog before the Society of American Magicians and I do not believe that there was one in the audience who detected my silent cue. I spoke about this to a number of expert professionals who thought, to all intents and purposes, that Bobby was listening to my speech, whereas I was silently cueing him all the time. I do not wish to expose the silent cue as I know that the great dog trainers of the world use it and it would not be fair to them to make it public. I was able to give Bobby his silent cue in any room or even a newspaper office and the spectators could watch me closely all the time because I never made a move they could see or a sound they could hear.

William Eglinton

It is common to train other animals in a similar way. During one of my tours in Germany I saw a horse called "Kluge Hans" that was able to spell, add, subtract, pick out cards, and with his feet make one tap for yes and two taps for no. Kluge Hans fooled the professors for a long time but finally it came out that he got his cues from the trainer's assistant. It is not generally known that, owing to the position of his eyes, a horse can look backwards to a certain degree and the investigators did not notice the assistant who stood just back of the horse's head.

At one time William Eglington, an English medium, was undoubtedly considered by Spiritualists the most powerful professional psychic not only in England but throughout a greater part of Europe. In 1876 he held the palm as a successor to Slade in slate writing tricks. He was a strong card for the cause and was extolled and lauded to the skies by the Spiritualistic press. He produced varied phenomena in addition to his slate writing effects, such as the movement of articles, production of Spirit lights, and materialization. The Spiritualists have told that "he was so skillful that several practised conjurors as well as many investigators" were at a loss to detect or account for his methods. That may have been so. Half a century ago conjurors were not up on Spiritualism as they are to-day, and besides, it must be conceded that even conjurors are not immune to being deceived. Nevertheless there were conjurors and lay investigators fully qualified to discover and expose his frauds.

In 1876, while in his prime as a medium, he was exposed in the materialization of an Arab. This Arab's flowing beard and draperies were very familiar to English Spiritualists and as proof of the actual materialization sitters were permitted to cut fragments from the beard and robes. Archdeacon Colley, an interested member of a circle of sitters, suspecting fraud, secured some clippings and a few days later when opportunity offered "he *found* in Eglinton's portmanteau a false beard and a quantity of muslin to which the detached relics perfectly corresponded." He was also exposed several other times but this did not prevent the Spiritualist paper, *Light,* from publishing in October, 1886, a mass of testimony given by more than a hundred observers, including persons of high culture and social standing, to show that the phenomena at his séances were not due to any deliberate action on the part of the medium but to "conclusively establish the existence of some objective, intelligent force, capable of acting externally to the medium and in contravention of the recognized laws of matter."

The publication of such statements inspired Professor H. Carvill Lewis[131] to visit Eglinton for the purpose of investigation and arrangements were made for him to have a first sitting in November just a month after the extravagant statement in *Light.* Aware of the frailty of memory Professor Lewis made notes during the séance and wrote out his deductions and conclusions immediately after. He discovered at an early stage that close scrutiny did not produce an atmosphere sufficiently wholesome for desired results. While his attention was concentrated on the medium the *"objective intelligent force"* seemed totally inoperative, but whenever he turned his attention from the medium and apparently became absorbed in making notes the *"intelligent force"* became active instanter. Under the observation of Professor Lewis, Eglinton failed utterly at times and at others simply *declined* to work when conditions were against him. Professor Lewis quotes him as claiming that he had converted Kellar to Spiritualism but refutes such a claim in the following words:

"So far is this from being the case that Mr. Kellar, whom I know personally, is nightly offering in America twenty pounds to anyone who will produce Spiritualistic phenomena that he cannot imitate by conjuring."

The facts are that Kellar had a sitting with Eglinton in Calcutta to see if he could reproduce his effects by natural means. His mind was unbiased, and failing to detect Eglinton's method he remarked, "If my senses are to be relied on the writing is in no way the result of trickery or sleight-of-hand." But note the qualification in his remark: "If my senses are to be relied upon." Evidently he had his misgivings then and he must have worked out the problem soon after for two years later, as Professor Lewis told, he was producing the effect in America, and not long after performed both the Slade and Eglinton slate tricks before the Seybert Commission in Philadelphia to its complete amazement.

It was not strange that Kellar did not detect Eglinton's method instantly nor is it strange that he acknowledged that he was baffled. No magician is immune from being deceived and it is no way beneath a magician's dignity or demeaning to professional reputation to openly admit that he cannot always account for what he thinks he sees.

Ernst Basch, of the famous Basch family, who made the major apparatus for the magicians of the world, told me that he made hundreds of wireless tables before wireless was so well known under the name of "The Bewitched Table." He was a great illusion inventor and builder with a wonderful knowledge but in all his experience and contact with mediums he had never seen anything which would make him believe in Spiritualism. Neither has Francis J. Martinka, who traveled around the world with Haselmeyer, the magician, and who has sold magical apparatus in New York City for over forty years. 1 have the following letter from him in regard to Spirit-communication.

"146 East 54th Street, New York City, March 23rd, 1921.

"Dear Mr. Houdini:

"In answer to your question if I believe in Spiritualism, or the possibility of the return to this earth after death, how can I believe in such a thing as Spiritualism, when for more than two score years as the prominent magical dealer and manufacturer of mysterious effects I have supplied almost every known and thousands of unknown tricks or apparatus to the great majority of magicians, and indirectly to well-known mediums (one instance you may remember owing to the hullabaloo it raised

---

[131] A full detailed account of the clever work done by Professor Lewis will be found in *Proceedings of the Society for Psychical Research,* Vol. IV, pp. 338-352.

at the time, when I sold luminous paint to Heyward Carrington, at the exact time when he was manager of the celebrated medium, E. Palladino, who had baffled the scientists of the world), also to all the managers of magician supply houses in existence.

"No, I must say positively I do not believe in Spiritualism and it has always amused me to see how easy it is to deceive the human beings who seek solace for their grief or those who delve into the mysteries of which they know nothing.

"In the forty years experience I have never seen anything that could convince me that such a thing as Spiritualism existed.

"And to show you that I wish my letter to be positively authentic, have two friends sign as witnesses. "Regards.

"Sincerely yours,
(Signed) "Francis J. Martinka,

Witnesses.
(Signed) Jean A. Leroy,
133 3rd Ave.
(Signed) Billy O'Connor,
Magicians' Club, London."

Another who finds nothing but "gross fraud" in Spiritualism after sixty years of study is A. M. Wilson, M. D., of Kansas City, Mo., Editor and Publisher of *The Sphinx*. He wrote me as follows:

1007 Main St., Kansas City, Mo.

My dear Houdini:--

For almost sixty-one years I have been witnessing and investigating Spiritualism and Spiritism as propagated by mediums through their so-called communications with the dead. Up to this time I have not met a medium, celebrated or obscure, that was not a gross fraud, nor seen a manifestation that was not trickery and that could not be duplicated by any expert magician and that without the conditions and restrictions demanded by the mediums or explained by perfectly natural mental or physical methods.

Sure there are certain mental and psychic phenomena peculiar to a few persons who use their special gift to delude believers (as well as other credulous persons) with the belief that their work is supernatural, but even these phenomena can be analyzed and explained by any competent psychologist.

The thing that first aroused my suspicion and disbelief and started me to thinking and investigating, was, why could not the dear departed communicate direct with their relatives and friends? why talk, or rap, or write or materialize through a medium, the majority of whom are ignorant men and women, though shrewd and cunning; and if through a medium why should the medium need a control, especially of an old Indian chief or prattling Indian maiden? Why a control at all?

True there are a few well educated, intelligent and refined mediums in the business and which advantage makes them the more dangerous but none the less fraudulent than their more ignorant confreres.

I repeat, that from my first séance in Aurora, Ind., February, 1863, until this date of 1923 I have never met a medium that was not a fraud or seen a manifestation of any kind or character that was not fraudulent. In other words was a more or less crude or skillful magical performance by a clever trickster or tricksteress.

(Signed) A. M. Wilson, M. D.,
Editor *The Sphinx*.

A William Eglinton Spirit Photo

Chapter 16
Conclusion

IT has been my desire in this book to convey to the reader my views regarding Spiritualism which are the result of study and investigation, the startling feature of which has been the utter inability of the average human being to describe accurately anything he or she has witnessed. Many sitters, devoid of the sense of acute observation, prefer to garnish and embellish their stories with the fruits of their fertile imaginations, adding a choice bit every time the incident is reported, and eventually, by a trick of the brain, really believing what they say. It is evident, therefore, that by clever misguidance and apt misdirection of attention, a medium can accomplish seeming wonders. The sitter becomes positively self-deluded and actually thinks he has seen weird phantoms or has heard the voice of a beloved one.

To my knowledge I have never been baffled in the least by what I have seen at séances. Everything I have seen has been merely a form of mystification. The secret of all such performances is to catch the mind off guard and the moment after it has been surprised to follow up with something else that carries the intelligence along with the performer, even against the spectator's will. When it is possible to do this with a highly developed mind like Mr. Kellar's, one trained in magic mystery, and when scientific men of the intelligence of Sir Oliver Lodge, Sir Arthur Conan Doyle, the late William Crookes and William T. Stead, can be made to believe by such means how much easier it must be in the case of ordinary human beings.

I cannot accept nor even comprehend the intelligence which justifies the conclusion, so often put in print as the opinion of brainy men supporting Spiritualism, that admits the possibility of a result being accomplished by natural means but nevertheless assert their sincere belief that the identical performance by a professional medium is solely of supernatural origin and guidance, nor can I understand the reasoning that, acknowledging the disreputable character of certain practitioners or mediums, deliberately defends the culprits in the performance of what has been proven a crime. Is it true logic, logic that would stand either in court or club room, to say that a medium caught cheating ninety-nine times out of a hundred was honest the hundredth time because not caught? Would the reader trust a servant who stole ninety-nine articles and then professed innocence when the hundredth article was missing?

Sir Conan Doyle asks in all innocence, "Is it really scientific to deny and at the same time refuse to investigate?" My answer is most emphatically "no." Nevertheless, they absolutely oppose all honest efforts at investigation, and justify the mediums in refusing to work when the conditions are not just as they want them. When one is invited to a dark séance for the purpose of investigation and finds the conditions so fixed as to bar him from enquiring too closely and compel him to be content with merely looking on he stands a poor chance of getting at the facts, and should he dare to disregard the "rules of the circle" and the séance results in a blank, the investigator is charged with having brought an atmosphere of incredulity to bear which prevents manifestation.

I do not affirm that the claims of Spiritualism are disproved by such failures but I do say that if under such circumstances one dared to investigate properly and sanely, and to cross-examine, as he most certainly would do in any other form of investigation, scientific, or in the other walks of life, Spiritualism would not be so generously accepted. In justification the psychic says that darkness or excessively dim light is perfectly legitimate and that tangible investigation might result in *injury* or even *death* to the medium. The folly of any such fear has been proven time and again by the unexpected play of a flash light. Even the ardent supporters who lay emphasis on such an absurdity have, according to their own confession, made, or had made, flashlight photographs and there has never been a single case of harm or disaster reported. This necessity for darkness seems but the grossest invention of the medium to divert, even to the point of intimidation, the attention of the sitters. Such a necessity cannot be accorded a logical reason for existing under test conditions to demonstrate a scientific subject. It can be supported only as a visionary, speculative superstition; an instrument to foster hallucinatory illusion and as an admirable subterfuge to cover fraud.

Sir Arthur says:

"If you want to send a telegram you must go to a telegraph office. If you want to telephone you must first pick up the receiver and give your message to either an operator or a waiting automaton."

Very we'll, I have gone to the operator between the Beyond and this earthly sphere, I have gone to the telegraph office that receives the message in code, to the so-called *medium*. What would be more wonderful to me than to be able to converse with my beloved mother? Surely there is no love in this world like a mother's love, no closeness of spirit, no other heart throbs that beat alike; but I have not heard from my blessed Mother, except through the dictates of the inmost recesses of my heart, the thoughts which fill my brain and the memory of her teachings.

Would not my private secretary, John William Sargent, come back to me and tell me the secrets of the beyond if it were possible? Did he not, just before he died, tell me that he would come to me if there was any way of doing it? More than being a private secretary, he was my friend,--true, loyal, sacrificing,--knew me for thirty years. He has not come back to me and he would if it were possible.

I had compacts with a round dozen. Each one promised me faithfully to come back if it were possible. I have even gone so far as to create secret codes and handgrips. Sargent had a certain word he was to repeat to me; William Berol, the eminent mental expert, gave me the secret handshake a few hours before he died and did not regain consciousness after silently telling me that he remembered our compact; Atlanta Hall, niece of President Pierce, a woman ninety years of age, who had had séances with the greatest mediums that visited Boston, called for me just before her death, clasped my hand and gave me our agreed-upon grip which she was to give me through a medium. They have never come back to me! Does that prove anything? I have attended a number of séances since their death, the mediums have called for them, and when their spirit forms were supposed to appear not one of them could give me the proper signal. Would I have received it? I'll wager I would have. There was love of some kind between each of these friends who are gone and myself. It is needless to point out the love of a mother and son; the love of a real friend; the love of a a woman of ninety toward a man who held her dear; the love of a philosopher toward a man who respected his life study,--they were all loves, each strong, each binding. If these persons, with all the love they bore in their heart for me and all the love I have in my heart for them, did not return, what about those who did not hold me close, who had no interest in me? Why should they come back and mine not?

Sir Arthur Conan Doyle has repeatedly told the Spiritualists that I will eventually see the light and embrace Spiritualism. If the memory of a loved one, gone to the protection of the hands of the Great Mystifier means Spiritualism, then truly I do believe in it. But if Spiritualism is to be founded on the tricks of exposed mediums, feats of magic, resort to trickery, then I say unflinchingly I do not believe, and more, I will not believe. I have said many times that I am willing to believe, want to believe, will believe, if the Spiritualists can show any substantiated proof, but until they do I shall have to live on, believing from all the evidence shown me and from what I have experienced that Spiritualism has not been proven satisfactorily to the world at large and that none of the evidence offered has been able to stand up under the fierce rays of investigation.

It is not for us to prove that the mediums are dishonest, it is for them to prove that they *are* honest. They have made a statement, the most serious statement in recent times, for it affects the welfare, the mental attitude and means a complete revolution of age-old beliefs and customs of the world. If there is anything to Spiritualism then the world should know it. If there is nothing to it, if it is, as it appears, built on a flimsy framework of misdirection, then too the universe must be told. There is too much at stake for a flighty passing, for unsubstantiated truths.

Appendix

A
Statement of Margaret Fox

"Do you know that there is something behind the shadowy mask of Spiritualism that the public can hardly guess at? I am stating now what I know, not because I actually participated in it, for I would never be a party to such promiscuous nastiness, but because I had plenty of opportunity, as you may imagine, of verifying it. Under the name of this dreadful, this horrible, hypocrisy--Spiritualism--everything that is improper, bad and immoral is practiced. They go even so far as to have what they call 'Spiritual children.' They pretend to something like the immaculate conception! Could anything be more blasphemous, more disgusting, more thinly deceptive than that? In London I went in disguise to a quiet séance at the house of a wealthy man, and I saw a so-called materialization. The effect was produced with the aid of luminous paper, the luster of which was reflected upon the operator. The figure thus displayed was that of a woman, virtually nude, being enveloped in transparent gauze, the face alone being concealed. This was one of those séances to which the privileged non-believing friends of believing Spiritualists could have access. But there are other séances where none but the most tried and trusted are admitted, and where there are shameless goings on that vie with the secret Saturnalia of the Romans. I could not describe these things to you, because I would not."

From "The Death Blow to Spiritualism," by Ruben Briggs Davenport. Page 50.

B
Irving's Speech

Speech of Henry Irving preceding his imitation of the Davenports February 25, 1865, at the Manchester Athenaeum, Manchester, England.

"Ladies and gentlemen:--In introducing to your notice the remarkable phenomena which have attended the gentlemen, who are not brothers, who are about to appear before you, I do not deem it necessary to offer my observations upon their extraordinary manifestations. I shall therefore at once commence a long rigmarole for the purpose of distracting your attention, and filling your intelligent heads with perplexity. I need not tell this enlightened audience that the manifestations they are about to witness are produced by occult power, the meaning of which I don't clearly understand; but, we simply bring before your notice facts, and from these you must form your own conclusions. Concerning the early life of these gentlemen, columns of the most uninteresting description could be written; I will mention one or two interesting facts connected with these remarkable men, and for the truth of which I personally vouch. In early life, one of them to the perfect unconcern of everybody else, was constantly and most unconsciously floating about his peaceful dwelling in the arms of his amiable nurse, while, on other occasions, he was frequently tied with invisible hands to his mother's apron strings. Peculiarities of a like nature were exhibited by his companion, whose acquaintance with various Spirits commenced many years ago, and has increased to the present moment with pleasure to himself and profit to others. These gentlemen have not been celebrated throughout the vast continent of America, they have not astonished the civilized world, but they have travelled in various parts of this glorious land--the land of Bacon--and are about to appear in a phase in your glorious city of Manchester. Many really sensible and intelligent individuals seem to think that the requirement of darkness seems to infer trickery. So it does. But I will strive to convince you that it does not. Is not a dark chamber essential to the process of photography? And what would we reply to him who would say 'I believe photography is a humbug, do it all in the light and we will believe otherwise'? It is true that we know why darkness is essential to the production of a sun picture; and if scientific men will subject these phenomena to analysis, they will find why darkness is essential to our manifestations. But we don't want them to find out, we want them to avoid a common-sense view of the mystery. We want them to be blinded by our puzzle, and to believe with implicit faith in the greatest humbug in the nineteenth century."

C
Lord Adare's Story.

That is the way Spiritualistic chroniclers tell this story, but Lord Dunraven, in a letter to the Editor of *The Weekly Dispatch,* London, Eng., March 21, 1920, gives quite a different version of the occurrence, and because of its intrinsic worth as refutation of the loud claim made by Spiritualists I am reproducing the entire article including head lines;

"MEDIUM'S ENTRY BY WINDOW

"WHAT I SAW AT ASHLEY HOUSE

"By Lord Dunraven.

"My attention has been drawn to accounts of a debate on 'Spiritualism' on March 11 between Sir Arthur Conan Doyle and Mr. Joseph McCabe, in which the latter is reported to have described the alleged wafting of Mr. D. D. Home from window to window as one of the greatest pieces of trickery to be found in the whole Spiritualistic movement.

"Assuming the substantial accuracy of the report, I, as the sole survivor of those present on the occasion, think it my duty, in justice to the dead, to mention the facts as recorded by me at the time.

"They are extracted from a long letter descriptive of the evening to my father, who was much interested in the subject. Whether my letter was submitted to the others present I cannot now say for certain. I have no doubt that it was, for my custom was always to ask others present to test the accuracy of any record that I kept.

"The date was December 16, 1868. Those present were myself (then Lord Adare), the late Lord Crawford, (then Master of Lindsay), a cousin of mine, Mr. Wynne (Charlie) and Mr. D. D. Home.

"ON THE THIRD FLOOR

"The scene was Ashley House (in Ashley-place). Speaking from memory, it consisted of two rooms facing the front--that is, looking on Ashley-place--a passage at the back running the length of the two rooms, a door in each room connecting it with the passage. The locality is thus described in the letter to my father:

" 'Outside each window is a small balcony or ledge, 19 in. deep, bounded by stone balustrade, 18 in. high. The balustrades of the two windows are 7 ft. 4 in. apart, measuring from the nearest points. A string-course, 4 in. wide, runs between the windows at the level of the bottom of the balustrade, and another, 3 in. wide, at the level of the top. Between the window at which Home went out and that at which he came in the wall recedes 6 in. The rooms are on the third floor.'

"The following account of the incident is extracted from the letter to my father:

"He (Home) then said to us, 'Do not be afraid, and on no account leave your places;' and he went out into the passage.

"FROM ROOM TO ROOM

"Lindsay suddenly said, 'Oh, good heavens! I know what he is going to do; it is too fearful.' Adare: 'What is it?' Lindsay: 'I cannot tell you; it is too horrible! Adah says that I must tell you; he is going out of the window in the other room, and coming in at this window.'

"We heard Home go into the next room, heard the window thrown up, and presently Home appeared standing upright outside our window. He opened the window and walked in quite cooly. 'Ah,' he said, 'you were good this time,' referring to our having sat still and not wished to prevent him. He sat down and laughed.

"Charlie: 'What are you laughing at?' Home: 'We are thinking that if a policeman had been passing and had looked up and seen a man turning round and round along the wall in the air he would have been much astonished. Adare, shut the window in the next room.'

"I got up, shut the window, and in coming back remarked that the window was not raised a foot, and that I could not think how he had managed to squeeze through.

"OUT, HEAD FIRST

"He arose and said 'Come and see.' I went with him; he told me to open the window as it was before, I did so; he told me to stand a little distance off; he then went through the open space, head first, quite rapidly, his body being nearly horizontal and apparently rigid. He came in again, feet foremost, and we returned to the other room.

"It was so dark I could not see clearly how he was supported outside. He did not appear to grasp, or rest upon, the balustrade, but rather to be swung out and in."

"Such are the facts as narrated at the time. I make no comment except this. Rigorously speaking, it is incorrect to say, as I think has been said, that we *saw* Mr. Home wafted from one window to the other.

"As to whether he was or was not, I am concerned only to state the facts as observed at the time, not to make deductions from them."

In view of this publication, it is quite natural to infer that Sir Arthur Conan Doyle was cognizant of it at the time of its appearance, because of his controversy with Mr. Joseph McCabe, on that subject; therefore, it is difficult to reconcile that thought with the fact of Sir Arthur's unmitigated praise and endorsement of a man such as all adduced evidence has branded a charlatan.

D
Luther R. Marsh and the Huylers

In 1903, Luther R. Marsh again fell into the hands of charlatans as Mr. Isaac K. Funk tells in his book "The Widow's Mite and Other Psychic Phenomena." A court set aside the assignment of several insurance policies which Marsh had made to a medium known as Mrs. Huyler. Mr. Funk tells the story as follows:

"On the day Mr. Marsh transferred the policies he (Huyler) and his wife had gone to Mr. Marsh's room, where Mrs. Huyler claimed to hold communication with the Spirits and told Mr. Marsh there was a terrible uproar in Spiritland because be declined to transfer the policies. She told him that his Spiritualistic wife, Adelaide Neilson, was tearing her hair and weeping, and heaping reproaches upon him. His wife, Mrs. Marsh, was acting in the same fashion, and his father-in-law, 'Sunset,' Alvin Stewart, was exceedingly wroth.

"Mr. Marsh was alarmed at this manifestation of Spiritualistic displeasure, and agreed to transfer the policies. At the last moment he hesitated and claimed that because his will was made out he thought it better to postpone the matter a little while; but Mrs. Huyler insisted that he go across the way to a lawyer's office, and he did so.

"While he was gone Mrs. Huyler admitted that the trance was a 'fake' and said that she wanted to get all she could from the 'old fool' before he died.

"Mr. Marsh returned to the room presently and assured her that the transfer had been made as she desired. As soon as this evidence had been given by Huyler, Justice Marean ended the proceedings.

" 'This man is a thief and a fraud,' he said turning to Huyler, 'and he acted the part of a thief when he and his wife conspired to secure those policies by the means he has just related.' "

E
Police Record of Ann O'Delia Diss Debar.

Editha Loleta, Jackson, alias The Swami--5--3 1/2--sallow.

Hair brown, turning gray. Blue eyes. Occupation, authoress.

Sentence:

6 mos.. New York. 19.6.88. Swindling. Ann O'Delai Diss Debar.

2 years, Geneva. 25.3.93. Larceny. Vera P. Ava.

Expelled from New Orleans. 7.5.99. Swindling, Susp. Person. Edith Jackson.

30 days, New Orleans. 16.5.99. Susp. Person. Edith Jackson.

7 years penal servitude, Central Criminal Court, London. 16.12.01. Aiding and abetting the commission of rape. Editha Loleta Jackson.

F
Judge Edmonds

Judge Edmonds was born in Hudson, N. Y., in 1799, received a college education and studied law. In 1819 he entered the law office of President Van Buren. In 1828 he was appointed Recorder of Hudson and in 1831 was elected to the State Senate by an unprecedented majority. In 1843 he was appointed Inspector of the State Prison at Sing Sing holding the position until 1845 when he resigned to become a Circuit Judge of the First Judicial District. Later he was elected Judge of the State Supreme Court and finally in 1851 became a member of the Court of Appeals. These various offices gave him experience in the widest range of judicial duties; he had a greatly developed mentality and was known as the shrewdest judge of his time.

In 1850 he lost his wife with whom he had lived for over thirty years. He was very much affected by her death and his mind became occupied with inquiries concerning the nature and conditions of death, frequently spending the greater part of the night reading and reflecting on the subject. One midnight he seemed to hear the voice of his wife speaking a sentence to him. It was his doom. He started as though shot and from that time on devoted all his time, money and energy to Spiritualism. His faith did not waver to the end. On his death bed he claimed to be surrounded by Spirit forms and declared that by reason of entering their sphere in an advanced state of spiritual development he would be able to send back messages and proofs of Spiritualism at once. He died April 5th, 1874 (the very date of my birth). I doubt if the history of Spiritualism can point out a man of greater brilliancy who ruined his life following up this "will-o-the-wisp" to relieve his grief.

G
Doyle and the "Denver Express."

This reminds me of a conversation which we had in Denver in May, 1923, when he admitted to me that he was frequently misquoted and made to say things which he never even thought of.

By some prank of fate, Sir Arthur was booked to lecture in Denver at the same time I was performing there.

Lady Doyle, Sir Arthur, Mrs. Houdini and myself went out motoring in the morning and when we returned to the hotel Sir Arthur excused himself. About two hours later on my way to the Orpheum Theatre, Sir Arthur came dashing through the lobby of the hotel excitedly looking around for someone. I walked up to him saying, "Anything I can do for you?" He put his arm around me and said, "Houdini, there is a challenge of $5,000 in this paper which I am purported to have issued. I want you to know that I would never dream of doing such a thing, to you above everyone else."

I replied, "Sir Arthur, this is just another case, where you have been misquoted. No doubt you are thinking that I am going to believe it, for I know that if conditions were reversed you would have believed it; therefore, you see it is best to investigate before giving credence to anything as being a fact. I am not even upset about it--things happen that way. Will you please remember this incident the next time you read an interview supposedly issued by me?" Sir Arthur left for Salt Lake City the next morning.

I walked into the Editorial Department of the *Denver Express,* saw Mr. Sydney B. Whipple, the Managing Editor, and told him that I had met Sir Arthur the night before and that he was very indignant at the challenge which the paper reported he issued. I said, "You see, Mr. Whipple, Sir Arthur, Lady Doyle, Mrs. Houdini and myself were out motoring all yesterday afternoon, and when Sir Arthur returned he saw the "scare head-line" to the effect that he had challenged me for $5,000! Whipple asked, "You mean to say that Sir Arthur Conan Doyle denies having challenged you?" I replied, "Most emphatically,--he said that it was not true and he never made such a statement and added he had written to the Editor to let him know what he thought of him for misrepresenting and misquoting what he said." Mr. Whipple asked me to wait a moment until he got to the bottom of the matter.

Whipple called over Mr. Sam Jackson and said, "Regarding this challenge of Sir Arthur Conan Doyle, did he or did he not challenge Houdini during your interview?" Jackson answered, "Why he positively did. You do not think, Mr. Whipple, that I would come in with a story which is not true? Sir Arthur distinctly made his statement in terms positive, that he was willing to challenge Houdini for $5,000. Miss Jeanette Thornton was there at the time interviewing Lady Doyle, and she overheard the conversation. Will you please call her and have her confirm my statement."

Miss Thornton came over and upon being questioned, answered, "Most assuredly I heard Sir Arthur's challenge yesterday. I thought it was a very interesting incident so I paid particular attention. I am surprised that Sir Arthur now denies having made it."

Whipple turned to me saying, "There you are--any further proof you want, is there anything we can do for you to contradict this? Do you wish us to make a statement?" To which I replied, "No, just let it go, we will let it pass."

The following letters which I received from Mr. Whipple are self-explanatory:

"THE 'DENVER EXPRESS'

"THE TRUTH--QUICK.

"May 11, 1923.

"Dear Mr. Houdini:--

"I am enclosing a letter from Sir Arthur Conan Doyle complaining that the report of his challenge regarding mediumistic appearances was garbled in this paper.

"I must also say that our reporter, who talked with Doyle insists that his report of the conversation was absolutely correct, and that Doyle said what we printed.

"Cordially yours,
(Signed) "Sydney B. Whipple.

"THE BROWN PALACE HOTEL

Denver, Colo., "May 9, 1923.

"Sir:--

"The report in the *Denver Express* that I offered to bring back the spirit of my mother for five thousand dollars, in order to confute Mr. Houdini, is a monstrous fabrication, and I cannot imagine how you dare to print such a thing, which is on the face of it so blasphemous and absurd.

"What actually occurred was that your reporter said that my friend Mr. Houdini had wagered $5,000 that he could do anything any medium could do, to which I answered "To do that he would have to show me my mother." This is surely very different.

"Yours faithfully,
(Signed) "A. Conan Doyle."

H
Exposure of Mrs. Stewart

It is significant to note that on December 28, 1923, at St. Louis, Mo., I was fortunate in forming acquaintance with Judge Daniel G. Taylor, who presided over Division No. 2 of the Circuit Court, to which division Josie K. Folsom-Stewart, as President, Charles W. Stewart, Secretary, and Phoebe S. Wolf, as Treasurer, made application for incorporation of the "Society of Scientific and Religious Truthseekers," who claimed that they had associated themselves by articles of agreement in writing, as a "Society for religious and mutual improvement purposes." "The articles of agreement and association are signed by some forty persons." As was customary in such cases, Judge Taylor "appointed J. Lionberger Davis, then a practicing attorney, now President of Security National Bank, as amicus curiae to examine into the matter and report whether or not the charter should be granted." The outcome of which was evidence of guilt of fraudulent manifestations of mediumship. In the course of investigation, Miss Martha Grossman, a member of Mrs. Folsom's "Development Class," testified that Mr. Stewart and Mrs. Folsom were conducting meetings which she had attended for six months, at which time she saw writing on cards which Mrs. Folsom said was done by Spirits.

Miss Grossman testified that what Mrs. Folsom claimed to be spirit photographs were mere transfers from prints in the *Post-Dispatch,* advertising "Syrup of Figs" and "Lydia Pinkham's" concoction. It also developed that Miss Alice C. Preston confessed to having been a confederate and in that capacity "assisted Mrs. Folsom in producing, physically, and by natural means, the supposed supernatural demonstrations." A reference to this testimony is contained in the memorandum document on the evidence which is signed by the attorney for the petitioners and which is in the court files.

As a conclusion, Judge Taylor denied the petition for incorporation, which in any event could have been granted for the purpose of holding real estate only, and not for promulgating teachings of a cult.

The Judge acknowledged that he himself was convinced that Mrs. Folsom was a fraud; and this is the same *Mrs. Stewart,* who appeared before the Scientific American Committee of Investigation in 1923, wherein she was detected in her card-trick.

Mrs. Folsom was forced to acknowledge to the court in 1905 that she was the author of a small book under title of "Non-Godism," a copy of which together with documentary evidence bearing on the court proceedings referred to above are now in my possession.

JOHN D. FOX AND HIS WIFE

.THE FOX HOME AT HYDESVILLE

LEAH FOX FISH

KATIE FOX JENCKEN

MARGARET FOX KANE

ELISHA KENT KANE, M.D.

An Expose By Sir Arthur Conan Doyle

This photo taken at a church on April 1923 by Nathan Moss (a funeral). No explanation has ever been reached as to what the image is that appears in the photo. Even Houdini said this one could not be explained nor was it a fraud. (From The Mystery of Houdini's Death by Vincent Gaddis- Fate Magazine / August 1963)

One of Harry Houdini's Escape Acts

Mayville Jan 19th 1909.

Mr Harry Houdini
  Dear Sir,
      I was most agreeably surprised on my return to Mayville from Buffalo by receiving your letter of Dec 12" mailed at Liverpool. I had been several weeks in Buffalo

- - - - - - - - - - - - - - - - - -

You must not fail to do me the honor of a visit when you return to America, although two years is quite a long time, and in the meantime please let me hear from you whenever the spirit moves you, regarding the future, I think the possibilities within your grasp are almost boundless, Splendid new Territory, all South and Central America, Mexico, Australia, New Zealand, India, Spain, Portugal and Africa.

- - - - - - - - - - - - - - - - - -

We never in public affirmed our Belief in spiritualism, that we regarded as no business of the public, nor did we offer our entertainments as the result of slight of hand, nor on the other hand as spiritualism, we let our friends and foes settle that as best they could between themselves, but unfortunately we were often the victims of their disagreements. You will find enclosed in this letter a few clippings referring to my daughter also a poem on the death of my Brother.
Hoping to hear from you soon and wishing you all kinds of good luck I remain
              Yours Truly
                  Ira E Davenport

FACSIMILE OF PORTIONS OF A LETTER WRITTEN TO HOUDINI BY IRA E. DAVENPORT

DANIEL DUNGLAS HOME

HENRY SLADE

ANN O'DELIA DISS DEBAR

EUSAPIA PALLADINO AND HER SÉANCE TABLE

"LOCKED SLATE" USED BY DR. HENRY SLADE
IN HIS WRITING TESTS AT PHILADELPHIA

HOUDINI, MRS. HOUDINI, AND MR. TEALE DEMONSTRATING
A METHOD OF SWITCHING SLATES OVER A SITTER'S HEAD

SO-CALLED "SPIRIT EXTRA" ON PHOTOGRAPH OF HARRY PRICE
MADE BY WILLIAM HOPE OF THE CREWE CIRCLE

HOUDINI AND ALEXANDER MARTIN

PHOTOGRAPH OF HOUDINI MADE BY ALEXANDER MARTIN,
AT DENVER, COLORADO, ON MAY 10, 1933,
SHOWING SO-CALLED "SPIRIT EXTRAS"

MME. BISSON, MRS. FEILDING (TOMCHICK), AND MLLE. EVA

KELLAR AND HOUDINI

Appendix – Sir Arthur Conan Doyle: Research and Rebuttal to Houdini's Debunking of Famous Mediums

The Fox Sisters

The Davenport Brothers

Eusapia Palladino

Henry Slade

The Career of Daniel D. Home

Publishers Note:
It should be noted that much of this material is from long out of print and hard to find sources, thus some of the scanning of clippings might have modified or altered some of the names, places, but certainly not events. We apologize for anything that has inadvertently been changed without our knowledge.

Harry Houdini & Arthur Conan Doyle

The Fox Sisters
by Sir Arthur Conan Doyle

The Hydesville Episode

We have now traced various disconnected and irregular uprushes of psychic force in the cases which have been set forth, and we come at last to the particular episode which was really on a lower level than those which had gone before, but which occurred within the ken of a practical people who found means to explore it thoroughly and to introduce reason and system into what had been a mere object of aimless wonder. It is true that the circumstances were lowly, the actors humble, the place remote, and the communication sordid, being based on no higher motive than revenge. When, however, in the everyday affairs of this world one wishes to test whether a telegraphic wire is in operation, one notices whether a message comes through, and the high or low nature of that message is quite a secondary consideration. It is said that the first message which actually came through the Transatlantic cable was a commonplace inquiry from the testing engineer. None the less, kings and presidents have used it since. So it is that the humble spirit of the murdered peddler of Hydesville may have opened a gap into which the angels have thronged. There is good and bad and all that is intermediate on the Other Side as on this side of the veil. The company you attract depends upon yourself and your own motives.

Hydesville is a typical little hamlet of New York State, with a primitive population which was, no doubt, half-educated, but was probably, like the rest of those small American centres of life, more detached from prejudice and more receptive of new ideas than any other set of people at that time. This particular village, situated about twenty miles from the rising town of Rochester, consisted of a cluster of wooden houses of a very humble type. It was in one of these, a residence which would certainly not pass the requirements of a British district council surveyor, that there began this development which is already, in the opinion of many, by far the most important thing that America has given to the commonweal of the world. It was inhabited by a decent farmer family of the name of Fox-a name which, by a curious coincidence, has already been registered in religious history as that of the apostle of the Quakers. Besides the father and mother, who were Methodists in religion, there were two children resident in the house at the time when the manifestations reached such a point of intensity that they attracted general attention. These children were the daughters-Margaret, aged fourteen, and Kate, aged eleven. There were several other children out in the world, of whom only one, Leah, who was teaching music in Rochester, need come into this narrative.

The little house had already established a somewhat uncanny reputation. The evidence to this effect was collected and published very shortly after the event, and seems to be as reliable as such evidence can be. In view of the extreme importance of everything which bears upon the matter, some extracts from these depositions must be inserted, but to avoid dislocation of the narrative the evidence upon this point has been relegated to the Appendix. We will therefore pass at once to the time of the tenancy of the Fox family, who took over the house on December 11, 1847. It was not until the next year that the sounds heard by the previous tenants began once more. These sounds consisted of rapping noises. A rap would seem to be the not unnatural sound to be produced by outside visitors when they wished to notify their presence at the door of human life and desired that door to be opened for them. Just such raps (all unknown to these unread farmers) had occurred in England in 1661 at the house of Mr. Mompesson, at Tedworth.[132] Raps, too, are recorded by Melancthon as having occurred at Oppenheim, in Germany, in 1520, and raps were heard at the Epworth Vicarage in 1716. Here they were once more, and at last they were destined to have the closed door open.

---

[132] "Saducismus Triumphatus," by Rev. Joseph Glanvil.

The noises do not seem to have incommoded the Fox family until the middle of March, 1848. From that date onwards they continually increased in intensity. Sometimes they were a mere knocking; at other times they sounded like the movement of furniture. The children were so alarmed that they refused to sleep apart and were taken into the bedroom of their parents. So vibrant were the sounds that the beds thrilled and shook. Every possible search was made, the husband waiting on one side of the door and the wife on the other, but the rappings still continued. It was soon noticed that daylight was inimical to the phenomena, and this naturally strengthened the idea of trickery, but every possible solution was tested and failed. Finally, upon the night of March 31 there was a very loud and continued outbreak of inexplicable sounds. It was on this night that one of the great points of psychic evolution was reached, for it was then that young Kate Fox challenged the unseen power to repeat the snaps of her fingers. That rude room, with its earnest, expectant, half-clad occupants with eager upturned faces, its circle of candlelight, and its heavy shadows lurking in the corners, might well be made the subject of a great historical painting. Search all the palaces and chancelleries of 1848, and where will you find a chamber which has made its place in history as secure as this little bedroom of a shack?

The child's challenge, though given with flippant words, was instantly answered. Every snap was echoed by a knock. However humble the operator at either end, the spiritual telegraph was at last working, and it was left to the patience and moral earnestness of the human race to determine how high might be the uses to which it was put in the future. Unexplained forces were many in the world, but here was a force claiming to have independent intelligence at the back of it. That was the supreme sign of a new departure.

Mrs. Fox was amazed at this development, and at the further discovery that the force could apparently see as well as hear, for when Kate snapped her fingers without sound the rap still responded. The mother asked a series of questions, the answers to which, given in numerals, showed a greater knowledge of her own affairs than she herself possessed, for the raps insisted that she had had seven children, whereas she protested that she had borne only six, until one who had died early came back to her mind. A neighbor, Mrs. Redfield, was called in, and her amusement was changed to wonder, and finally to awe, as she also listened to correct answers to intimate questions.

The neighbors came flocking in as some rumors of these wonders got about, and the two children were carried off by one of them, while Mrs. Fox went to spend the night at Mrs. Redfield's. In their absence the phenomena went on exactly the same as before, which disposes once for all of those theories of cracking toes and dislocating knees which have been so frequently put forward by people unaware of the true facts.

Having formed a sort of informal committee of investigation, the crowd, in shrewd Yankee fashion, spent a large part of the night of March 31 in playing question and answer with the unseen intelligence. According to its own account he was a spirit; he had been injured in that house; he rapped out the name of a former occupant who had injured him; he was thirty-one years old at the time of death (which was five years before); he had been murdered for money; he had been buried in the cellar ten feet deep. On descending to the cellar, dull, heavy thumps, coming apparently from under the earth, broke out when the investigator stood at the centre. There was no sound at other times. That, then, was the place of burial! It was a neighbor named Duesler who, first of all modern men, called over the alphabet and got answers by raps on the letters. In this way the name of the dead man was obtained-Charles B. Rosma. The idea of connected messages was not developed until four months later, when Isaac Post, a Quaker, of Rochester, was the pioneer. These, in very brief outline, were the events of March 31, which were continued and confirmed upon the succeeding night, when not fewer than a couple of hundred people had assembled round the house. Upon April 2 it was observed that the raps came in the day as well as at night.

Such is a synopsis of the events of the night of March 31, 1848, but as it was the small root out of which sprang so great a tree, and as this whole volume may be said to be a monument to its memory, it would seem fitting that the story should be given in the very words of the two original adult witnesses. Their evidence was taken within four days of the occurrence, and forms part of that admirable piece of psychic research upon the part of the local committee which will be described and commented upon later. Mrs. Fox deposed:

On the night of the first disturbance we all got up, lighted a candle and searched the entire house, the noises continuing during the time, and being heard near the same place. Although not very loud, it produced a jar of the bedsteads and chairs that could be felt when we were in bed. It was a tremulous motion, more than a sudden jar. We could feel the jar when standing on the floor. It continued on this night until we slept. I did not sleep until about twelve o'clock. On March 30th we were disturbed all night. The noises were heard in all parts of the house. My husband stationed himself outside of the door while I stood inside, and the knocks came on the door between us. We heard footsteps in the pantry, and walking downstairs; we could not rest, and I then concluded that the house must be haunted by some unhappy restless spirit. I had often heard of such things, but had never witnessed anything of the kind that I could not account for before.

On Friday night, March 31st, 1848, we concluded to go to bed early and not permit ourselves to be disturbed by the noises, but try and get a night's rest. My husband was here on all these occasions, heard the noises, and helped search. It was very early when we went to bed on this night-hardly dark. I had been so broken of my rest I was almost sick. My husband had not gone to bed when we first heard the noise on this evening. I had just lain down. It commenced as usual. I knew it from all other noises I had ever heard before. The children, who slept in the other bed in the room, heard the rapping, and tried to make similar sounds by snapping their fingers.

My youngest child, Cathie, said: "Mr. Splitfoot, do as I do," clapping her hands. The sound instantly followed her with the same number of raps. When she stopped, the sound ceased for a short time. Then Margaretta said, in sport, "Now, do just as I do. Count one, two, three, four," striking one hand against the other at the same time; and the raps came as before. She was afraid to repeat them. Then Cathie said in her childish simplicity, "Oh, mother, I know what it is. To-morrow is April-fool day, and it's somebody trying to fool us."

I then thought I could put a test that no one in the place could answer. I asked the noise to rap my different children's ages, successively. Instantly, each one of my children's ages was given correctly, pausing between them sufficiently long to individualize them until the seventh, at which a longer pause was made, and then three more emphatic raps were given, corresponding to the age of the little one that died, which was my youngest child.

I then asked: "Is this a human being that answers my questions so correctly?" There was no rap. I asked: "Is it a spirit? If it is, make two raps." Two sounds were given as soon as the request was made. I then said "If it was an injured spirit, make two raps," which were instantly made, causing the house to tremble. I asked: "Were you injured in this house?" The answer was given as before. "Is the person living that injured you?"

Answered by raps in the same manner. I ascertained by the same method that it was a man, aged thirty-one years, that he had been murdered in this house, and his remains were buried in the cellar; that his family consisted of a wife and five children, two sons and three daughters, all living at the time of his death, but that his wife had since died. I asked: "Will you continue to rap if I call my neighbours that they may hear it too?" The raps were loud in the affirmative.

My husband went and called in Mrs. Redfield, our nearest neighbour. She is a very candid woman. The girls were sitting up in bed clinging to each other, and trembling with terror. I think I was as calm as I am now. Mrs. Redfield came immediately (this was about half-past seven), thinking she would have a laugh at the children. But when she saw them pale with fright, and nearly speechless, she was amazed, and believed there was something more serious than she had supposed. I asked a few questions for her, and was answered as before. He told her age exactly. She then called her husband, and the same questions were asked and answered.

Then Mr. Redfield called in Mr. Duesler and wife, and several others. Mr. Duesler then called in Mr. and Mrs. Hyde, also Mr. and Mrs. Jewell. Mr. Duesler asked many questions, and received answers. I then named all the neighbours I could think of, and asked if any of them had injured him, and received no answer. Mr. Duesler then asked questions and received answers. He asked: "Were you murdered?" Raps affirmative. "Can your murderer be brought to justice?" No sound. "Can he be punished by the law?" No answer. He then said: "If your murderer cannot be punished by the law, manifest it by raps," and the raps were made clearly and distinctly. In the same way, Mr. Duesler ascertained that he was murdered in the east bedroom about five years ago and that the murder was committed by a Mr. on a Tuesday night at twelve o'clock; that he was murdered by having his throat cut with a butcher knife; that the body was taken down to the cellar; that it was not buried until the next night; that it was taken through the buttery, down the stairway, and that it was buried ten feet below the surface of the ground. It was also ascertained that he was murdered for his money, by raps affirmative.

"How much was it-one hundred?" No rap. "Was it two hundred?" etc., and when he mentioned five hundred the raps replied in the affirmative.

Many called in who were fishing in the creek, and all heard the same questions and answers. Many remained in the house all night. I and my children left the house.

My husband remained in the house with Mr. Redfield all night. On the next Saturday the house was filled to overflowing. There were no sounds heard during day, but they commenced again in the evening. It was said that there were over three hundred persons present at the time. On Sunday morning the noises were heard throughout the day by all who came to the house.

On Saturday night, April 1st, they commenced digging in the cellar; they dug until they came to water, and then gave it up. The noise was not heard on Sunday evening nor during the night. Stephen B. Smith and wife (my daughter Marie), and my son David S. Fox and wife, slept in the room this night.

I have heard nothing since that time until yesterday. In the forenoon of yesterday there were several questions answered in the usual way by rapping. I have heard the noise several times to-day.

I am not a believer in haunted houses or supernatural appearances. I am very sorry that there has been so much excitement about it. It has been a great deal of trouble to us. It was our misfortune to live here at this time; but I am willing and anxious that the truth should be known, and that a true statement should be made. I cannot account for these noises; all that I know is that they have been heard repeatedly, as I have stated. I have heard this rapping again this (Tuesday) morning, April 4. My children also heard it.

I certify that the foregoing statement has been read to me, and that the same is true; and that I should be willing to take my oath that it is so, if necessary."

(SIGNED) MARGARET FOX.
APRIL 11, 1848.

Statement By John D. Fox

I have heard the above statement of my wife, Margaret Fox, read, and hereby certify that the same is true in all its particulars. I heard the same rappings which she has spoken of, in answer to the questions, as stated by her. There have been a great many questions besides those asked, and answered in the same way. Some have been asked a great many times, and they have always received the same answers. There has never been any contradiction whatever.

I do not know of any way to account for those noises, as being caused by any natural means. We have searched every nook and corner in and about the house, at different times, to ascertain, if possible, whether anything or anybody was secreted there that could make the noise, and have not been able to find anything which would or could explain the mystery. It has caused a great deal of trouble and anxiety.

Hundreds have visited the house, so that it is impossible for us to attend to our daily occupations; and I hope that, whether caused by natural or supernatural means, it will be ascertained soon. The digging in the cellar will be resumed as soon as the water settles, and then it can be ascertained whether there are any indications of a body ever having been buried there; and if there are, I shall have no doubt but that it is of supernatural origin.

(SIGNED) JOHN D. FOX.
APRIL 11, 1848

The neighbours had formed themselves into a committee of investigation, which for sanity and efficiency might be a lesson to many subsequent re searchers. They did not begin by imposing their own conditions, but they started without prejudice to record the facts exactly as they found them. Not only did they collect and record the impressions of everyone concerned, but they actually had the evidence in printed form within a month of the occurrence. The author has in vain attempted to get an original copy of the pamphlet, "A Report of the Mysterious Noises heard in the House of Mr. John D. Fox," published at Canandaigua, New York, but he has been presented with a facsimile of the original, and it is his considered opinion that the fact of human survival and power of communication was definitely proved to any mind capable of weighing evidence from the day of the appearance of that document.

The statement made by Mr. Duesler, chief of the committee, gives important testimony to the occurrence of the noises and jars in the absence of the Fox girls from the house, and disposes once and for ever of all suspicion of their complicity in these events. Mrs. Fox, as we have seen, referring to the night of Friday, March 31, said: "I and my children left the house." Part of Mr. Duesler's statement reads:

I live within a few rods of the house in which these sounds have been heard. The first I heard anything about them was a week ago last Friday evening (March 31st). Mrs. Redfield came over to my house to get my wife to go over to Mrs. Fox's. Mrs. R. appeared to be very much agitated. My wife wanted me to go over with them, and I accordingly wentÉ. This was about nine o'clock in the evening. There were some twelve or fourteen persons present when I left them. Some were so frightened that they did not want to go into the room.

I went into the room and sat down on the bed. Mr. Fox asked a question and I heard the rapping, which they had spoken of, distinctly. I felt the bedstead jar when the sounds were produced.

The Hon. Robert Dale Owen,[133] a member of the United States Congress, and formerly American Minister to Naples, supplies a few additional particulars in his narrative, written after conversations with Mrs. Fox and her daughters, Margaret and Catharine. Describing the night of March 31, 1848, he says ("Footfalls, etc.," p. 287):

The parents had had the children's beds removed into their bedroom, and strictly enjoined them not to talk of noises even if they heard them. But scarcely had the mother seen them safely in bed and was retiring to rest herself when the children cried out, "Here they are again!" The mother chid them, and lay down. Thereupon the noises became louder and more startling. The children sat up in bed. Mrs. Fox called in her husband. The night being windy, it suggested itself to him that it might be the rattling of the sashes. He tried several, shaking them to see if they were loose. Kate, the youngest girl, happened to remark that as often as her father shook a window-sash the noises seemed to reply. Being a lively child, and in a measure accustomed to what was going on, she turned to where the noise was, snapped her fingers, and called out, "Here, old Splitfoot, do as I do." THE KNOCKING INSTANTLY RESPONDED. That was the very commencement. Who can tell where the end will be?. Mr. Mompesson, in bed with his little daughter (about Kate's age) whom the sound seemed chiefly to follow, "observed that it would exactly answer, in drumming, anything that was beaten or called for." But his curiosity led him no further. Not so Kate Fox. She tried, by silently bringing together her thumb and forefinger, whether she could still obtain a response. Yes! It could see, then, as well as hear! She called her mother. "Only look, mother!" she said, bringing together her finger and thumb as before. And as often as she repeated the noiseless motion, just so often responded the raps.

In the summer of 1848 Mr. David Fox, with the assistance of Mr. Henry Bush, Mr. Lyman Granger, of Rochester, and others, resumed digging in the cellar. At a depth of five feet they found a plank, and further digging disclosed charcoal and quicklime, and finally human hair and bones, which were pronounced by expert medical testimony to belong to a human skeleton. It was not until fifty-six years later that a further discovery was made which proved beyond all doubt that someone had really been buried in the cellar of the Fox house.

This statement appeared in the BOSTON JOURNAL (a non-Spiritualistic paper) of November 23, 1904, and runs as follows:

Rochester, N.Y., Nov. 22nd, 1904: The skeleton of the man supposed to have caused the rappings first heard by the Fox sisters in 1848 has been found in the walls of the house occupied by the sisters,

---

[133] Author of "Footfalls on the Boundary of Another world" (1860), and "The Debatable Land" (1871)

and clears them from the only shadow of doubt held concerning their sincerity in the discovery of spirit communication.

The Fox sisters declared they learned to communicate with the spirit of a man, and that he told them he had been murdered and buried in the cellar. Repeated excavations failed to locate the body and thus give proof positive of their story.

The discovery was made by school-children playing in the cellar of the building in Hydesville known as the "Spook House," where the Fox sisters heard the wonderful rappings. William H. Hyde, a reputable citizen of Clyde, who owns the house, made an investigation and found an almost entire human skeleton between the earth and crumbling cellar walls, undoubtedly that of the wandering peddler who, it was claimed, was murdered in the east room of the house, and whose body was hidden in the cellar.

Mr. Hyde has notified relatives of the Fox sisters, and the notice of the discovery will be sent to the National Order of Spiritualists, many of whom remember having made pilgrimage to the "Spook House," as it is commonly called. The finding of the bones practically corroborates the sworn statement made by Margaret Fox, April 11, 1848.

There was discovered a peddler's tin box as well as the bones, and this box is now preserved at Lilydale, the central country head-quarters of the American Spiritualists, to which also the old Hydesville house has been transported.

These discoveries settle the question for ever and prove conclusively that there was a crime committed in the house, and that this crime was indicated by psychic means. When one examines the result of the two diggings one can reconstruct the circumstances. It is clear that in the first instance the body was buried with quicklime in the centre of the cellar. Later the criminal was alarmed by the fact that this place was too open to suspicion and he had dug up the body, or the main part of it, and reburied it under the wall where it would be more out of the way. The work had been done so hurriedly, however, or in such imperfect light, that some clear traces were left, as has been seen, of the original grave.

Was there independent evidence of such a crime? In order to find it we have to turn to the deposition of Lucretia Pulver, who served as help during the tenancy of Mr. and Mrs. Bell, who occupied the house four years before. She describes how a peddler came to the house and how he stayed the night there with his wares. Her employers told her that she might go home that night.

I wanted to buy some things off the peddler but had no money with me, and he said he would call at our house next morning and sell them to me.

I never saw him after this. About three days after this they sent for me to come back. I accordingly came back.

I should think this peddler of whom I have spoken was about thirty years of age. I heard him conversing with Mrs. Bell about his family. Mrs. Bell told me that he was an old acquaintance of theirs- that she had seen him several times before. One evening, about a week after this, Mrs. Bell sent me down to the cellar to shut the outer door. In going across the cellar I fell down near the centre of it. It appeared to be uneven and loose in that part. After I got upstairs, Mrs. Bell asked me what I screamed for and I told her. She laughed at me being frightened, and said it was only where the rats had been at work in the ground. A few days after this, Mr. Bell carried a lot of dirt into the cellar just at night and was at work there some time. Mrs. Bell told me that he was filling up the rat-holes.

A short time after this Mrs. Bell gave me a thimble which she said she had bought of this peddler. About three months after this I visited her and she said the peddler had been there again and she showed me another thimble which she said she had bought from him. She showed me some other things which she said she had bought from him.

It is worth noting that a Mrs. Lape in 1847 had claimed to have actually SEEN an apparition in the house, and that this vision was of a middle-sized man who wore grey pants, a black frock-coat and black cap. Lucretia Pulver deposed that the peddler in life wore a black frock-coat and light-colored pants.

On the other hand, it is only fair to add that the Mr. Bell who occupied the house at that time was not a man of notorious character, and one would willingly concede that an accusation founded entirely upon psychic evidence would be an unfair and intolerable thing. It is very different, however, when the proofs of a crime have actually been discovered, and the evidence then centres merely upon which tenant was in possession at that particular time. The deposition of Lucretia Pulver assumes vital importance in its bearing upon this matter.

There are one or two points about the case which would bear discussion. One is that a man with so remarkable a name as Charles B. Rosma should never have been traced, considering all the publicity which the case acquired. This would certainly at the time have appeared a formidable objection, but with our fuller knowledge we appreciate how very difficult it is to get names correctly across. A name apparently is a purely conventional thing, and as such very different from an idea. Every practising Spiritualist has received messages which were correct coupled with names which were mistaken. It is possible that the real name was Ross, or possibly Rosmer, and that this error prevented identification. Again, it is curious that he should not have known that his body had been moved from the centre of the cellar to the wall, where it was eventually found. We can only record the fact without attempting to explain it.

Again, granting that the young girls were the mediums and that the power was drawn from them, how came the phenomena when they had actually been removed from the house? To this one can only answer that though the future was to show that the power did actually emanate from these girls, none the less it seemed to have permeated the house and to have been at the disposal of the manifesting power for a time at least when the girls were not present.

The Fox family were seriously troubled by the disturbances- Mrs. Fox's hair turned white in a week-and as it became apparent that these were associated with the two young daughters, these were sent from home. But in the house of her brother, David Fox, where Margaret went, and in that of her sister Leah, whose married name was Mrs. Fish, at Rochester, where Catharine was staying, the same sounds were heard. Every effort was made to conceal these manifestations from the public, but they soon became known. Mrs. Fish, who was a teacher of music, was unable to continue her profession, and hundreds of people flocked to her house to witness the new marvels. It should be stated that either this power was contagious, or else it was descending upon many individuals independently from some common source. Thus Mrs. Leah Fish, the elder sister, received it, though in a less degree than Kate or Margaret. But it was no longer confined to the Fox family. It was like some psychic cloud descending from on high and showing itself on those persons who were susceptible. Similar sounds were heard in the home of Rev. A. H. Jervis, a Methodist minister, living in Rochester. Strong physical phenomena also began in the family of Deacon Hale, of Greece, a town close to Rochester. A little later Mrs. Sarah A. Tamlin and Mrs. Benedict, of Auburn, developed remarkable mediumship. Mr. Capron, the first historian of the movement, describes Mrs. Tamlin as one of the most reliable mediums he had ever met, and says that though the sounds occurring in her presence were not so loud as those with the Fox family, the messages were equally trustworthy.

It speedily became evident, then, that these unseen forces were no longer attached to any building, but that they had transferred themselves to the girls. In vain the family prayed with their Methodist friends that relief would come. In vain also were exorcisms performed by the clergy of various creeds. Beyond joining with loud raps in the Amens, the unseen presences took no notice of these religious exercises.

The danger of blindly following alleged spirit guidance was clearly shown some months later in the neighboring town of Rochester, where a man disappeared under suspicious circumstances. An enthusiastic Spiritualist had messages by raps which announced a murder. The canal was dragged and the wife of the missing man was actually ordered to enter the canal, which nearly cost her her life. Some months later the absentee returned, having fled to Canada to avoid a writ for debt. This, as may well be imagined, was a blow to the young cult. The public did not then understand what even now is so little understood, that death causes no change in the human spirit, that mischievous and humorous entities abound, and that the inquirer must use his own instincts and his own common sense at every turn. "Try the spirits that ye may know them." In the same year, in the same district, the truth of this new philosophy upon the one side, and its limitations and dangers on the other, were most clearly set forth. These dangers are with us still. The silly man, the arrogant inflated man, the cocksure man, is always a safe butt. Every observer has had some trick played upon him. The author has himself had his faith sorely shaken by deception until some compensating proof has come along to assure him that it was only a lesson which he had received, and that it was no more fiendish or even remarkable that disembodied intelligences should be hoaxers than that the same intelligence inside a human body should find amusement in the same foolish way.

The whole course of the movement had now widened and taken a more important turn. It was no longer a murdered man calling for justice. The peddler seemed to have been used as a pioneer, and now that he had found the opening and the method, a myriad of Intelligences were swarming at his back. Isaac Post had instituted the method of spelling by raps, and messages were pouring through. According to these the whole system had been devised by the contrivance of a band of thinkers and inventors upon the spirit plane, foremost among whom was Benjamin Franklin, whose eager mind and electrical knowledge in earth life might well qualify him for such a venture. Whether this claim was true or not, it is a fact that Rosma dropped out of the picture at this stage, and that the intelligent knockings purported to be from the deceased friends of those inquirers who were prepared to take a serious interest in the matter and to gather in reverent mood to receive the messages. That they still lived and still loved was the constant message from the beyond, accompanied by many material tests, which confirmed the wavering faith of the new adherents of the movement. When asked for their methods of working and the laws which governed them, the answers were from the beginning exactly what they are now: that it was a matter concerned with human and spirit magnetism; that some who were richly endowed with this physical property were mediums; that this endowment was not necessarily allied to morality or intelligence; and that the condition of harmony was especially necessary to secure good results. In seventy odd years we have learned very little more; and after all these years the primary law of harmony is invariably broken at the so-called test séances, the members of which imagine that they have disproved the philosophy when they obtain negative or disordered results, whereas they have actually confirmed it.

The Davenport Brothers
by Sir Arthur Conan Doyle

The TIMES, the DAILY TELEGRAPH, and other newspapers published long and honest reports. We omit quotations from them because the following important statement from Mr. Dion Boucicault, which appeared in the Daily News as well as in many other London journals, covers all the facts. It describes a later séance at Mr. Boucicault's house on October 11, 1864, at which were present, among others Viscount Bury, M.P., Sir Charles Wyke, Sir Charles Nicholson, the Chancellor of the University of Sydney, Mr. Robert Chambers, Charles Reade, the novelist, and Captain Inglefield, the Arctic explorer.

SIR,

A séance by the Brothers Davenport and Mr. W. Fay took place in my house yesterday in the presence of_____ (here he mentions twenty-four names including all those already quoted).

At three o'clock our party was fully assembled. We sent to a neighbouring music-seller for six guitars and two tambourines, so that the implements to be used should not be those with which the operators were familiar.

At half-past three the Davenport Brothers and Mr. Fay arrived, and found that we had altered their arrangements by changing the room which they had previously selected for their manifestations.

The séance then began by an examination of the dress and persons of the Brothers Davenport, and it was certified that no apparatus or other contrivance was concealed on or about their persons. They entered the cabinet, and sat facing each other. Captain Inglefield then, with a new rope provided by ourselves, tied Mr. W. Davenport hand and foot, with his hands behind his back, and then bound him firmly to the seat where he sat. Lord Bury, in like manner, secured Mr. I. Davenport. The knots on these ligatures were then fastened with sealing-wax, and a seal was affixed. A guitar, violin, tambourine, two bells, and a brass trumpet were placed on the floor of the cabinet. The doors were then closed, and a sufficient light was permitted in the room to enable us to see what followed.

I shall omit any detailed account of the babel of sounds which arose in the cabinet, and the violence with which the doors were repeatedly burst open and the instruments expelled; the hands appearing, as usual, at a lozenge-shaped orifice in the centre door of the cabinet. The following incidents seem to us particularly worthy of note:

While Lord Bury was stooping inside the cabinet, the door being open and the two operators seen to be sealed and bound, a detached hand was clearly observed to descend upon him, and he started back, remarking that a hand had struck him. Again, in the full light of the gas chandelier and during an interval in the séance, the doors of the cabinet being open, and while the ligatures of the Brothers Davenport were being examined, a very white, thin, female hand and wrist quivered for several seconds in the air above. This appearance drew a general exclamation from all the party.

Sir Charles Wyke now entered the cabinet and sat between the two young men-his hands being right and left on each, and secured to them. The doors were then closed, and the babel of sounds recommenced. Several hands appeared at the orifice-among them the hand of a child. After a space, Sir Charles returned amongst us and stated that while he held the two brothers, several hands touched his face and pulled his hair; the instruments at his feet crept up, played round his body and over his head-one of them lodging eventually on his shoulders. During the foregoing incidents the hands which appeared were touched and grasped by Captain Inglefield, and he stated that to the touch they were apparently human hands, though they passed away from his grasp.

I omit mentioning other phenomena, an account of which has already been rendered elsewhere.

The next part of the séance was performed in the dark. One of the Messrs. Davenport and Mr. Fay seated themselves amongst us. Two ropes were thrown at their feet, and in two minutes and a half they were tied hand and foot, their hands behind their backs bound tightly to their chairs, and their chairs bound to an adjacent table.

While this process was going on, the guitar rose from the table and swung or floated round the room and over the heads of the party, and slightly touching some. Now a phosphoric light shot from side to side over our heads; the laps and hands and shoulders of several were simultaneously touched, struck, or pawed by hands, the guitar meanwhile sailing round the room, now near the ceiling, and then scuffling on the head and shoulders of some luck less Wight. The bells whisked here and there, and a light thrumming was maintained on the violin. The two tambourines seemed to roll hither and thither on the floor, now shaking violently, and now visiting the knees and hands of our circle-all these foregoing actions, audible or tangible, being simultaneous. Mr. Rideout, holding a tambourine, requested it might be plucked from his hand; it was almost instantaneously taken from him. At the same time, Lord Bury made a similar request, and a forcible attempt to pluck a tambourine from his grasp was made which he resisted. Mr. Fay then asked that his coat should be removed. We heard instantly a violent twitch, and here occurred the most remarkable fact. A light was struck before the coat had quite, left Mr. Fay's person, and it was seen quitting him, plucked off him upwards. It flew up to the chandelier, where it hung for a moment and then fell to the ground. Mr. Fay was seen meanwhile bound hand and foot as before. One of our party now divested himself of his coat, and it was placed on the table. The light was extinguished and this coat was rushed on to Mr. Fay's back with equal rapidity. During the above occurrences in the dark, we placed a sheet of paper under the feet of these two operators, and drew with a pencil an outline around them, to the end that if they moved it might be detected. They of their own accord offered to have their hands filled with flour, or any other similar substance, to prove they made no use of them, but this precaution was deemed unnecessary; we required them, however, to count from one to twelve repeatedly, that their voices constantly heard might certify to us that they were in the places where they were tied. Each of our own party held his neighbor firmly, so that no one could move without two adjacent neighbors being aware of it.

At the termination of this séance, a general conversation took place on the subject of what we had heard and witnessed. Lord Bury suggested that the general opinion seemed to be that we should assure the Brothers Davenport and Mr. W. Fay that after a very stringent trial and strict scrutiny of their proceedings, the gentlemen present could arrive at no other conclusion than that there was no trace of trickery in any form, and certainly there were neither confederates nor machinery, and that all those who had witnessed the results would freely state in the society in which they moved that, so far as their investigations enabled them to form an opinion, the phenomena which had taken place in their presence were not the product of legerdemain. This suggestion was promptly acceded to by all present.

There is a concluding paragraph in which Mr. Dion Boucicault states that he is not a Spiritualist, and at the close of the report his name and the date are affixed.

This wonderfully full and lucid account is given without abbreviation because it supplies the answer to many objections, and because the character of the narrator and the witnesses cannot be questioned. It surely must be accepted as quite final so far as honesty is concerned. All subsequent objections are mere ignorance of the facts.

In October, 1864, the Davenports began to give public séances at the Queen's Concert Rooms, Hanover Square. Committees were appointed from the audience, and every effort made to detect how it was all done, but without avail. These séances, interspersed with private ones, were continued almost nightly until the close of the year. The daily Press was full of accounts of them, and the brothers' names were on everyone's lips. Early in 1865 they toured the English provinces, and in Liverpool, Huddersfield, and Leeds they suffered violence at the hands of excited mobs.

At Liverpool, in February, two members of the audience tied their hands so brutally that blood flowed, and Mr. Ferguson cut the rope and released them. The Davenports refused to continue, and the mob rushed the platform and smashed up the cabinet. The same tactics were resorted to at Huddersfield on February 21, and then at Leeds with increased violence, the result of organized opposition. These riots led to the Davenports cancelling any other engagements in England. They next went to Paris, where they received a summons to appear at the Palace of St. Cloud, where the Emperor and Empress and a party of about forty witnessed a séance. While in Paris, Hamilton, the successor of the celebrated conjurer., Robert Houdin, visited them, and in a letter to a Paris newspaper, he said: "The phenomena surpassed my expectations, and the experiments are full of interest for me. I consider it my duty to add they are inexplicable." After a return visit to London, Ireland was visited at the beginning of 1866. In Dublin they had many influential sitters, including the editor of the IRISH TIMES and the Rev. Dr. Tisdal, who publicly proclaimed his belief in the manifestations.

In April of the same year the Davenports went to Hamburg and then to Berlin, but the expected war (which their guides told them would come about) made the trip unremunerative. Theatre managers offered them liberal terms for exhibitions, but, heeding the advice of their ever-present spirit monitor, who said that their manifestations, being supernatural, should be kept above the level of theatrical entertainments, they declined, though much against the wish of their business manager. During their month's stay in Berlin they were visited by members of the Royal family. After three weeks in Hamburg they proceeded to Belgium, where considerable success was attained in Brussels, and all the principal towns. They next went to Russia, arriving in St. Petersburg on December 27, 1866. On January 7, 1867, they gave their first public séance to an audience numbering one thousand. The next séance was at the residence of the French Ambassador to a gathering of about fifty people, including officers of the Imperial Court, and on January q they gave a séance in the Winter Palace to the Emperor and the Imperial family. They afterwards visited Poland and Sweden. On April 11, 1868, they reappeared in London at the Hanover Square Rooms, and received an enthusiastic welcome from a crowded audience. Mr. Benjamin Coleman, a prominent Spiritualist, who arranged their first public séances in London, writing at this time of their stay of close on four years in Europe, says[134]:

I desire to convey to those of my friends in America who introduced them to me, the assurance of my conviction that the Brothers' mission to Europe has been of great service to Spiritualism; that their public conduct as mediums-in which relation I alone know them-has been steady and unexceptionable.

He adds that he knows no form of mediumship better adapted for a large audience than theirs. After this visit to London the Davenports returned home to America. The brothers visited Australia in 1876, and on August 24 gave their first public séance in Melbourne. William died in Sydney in July, 1877.

Throughout their career the Davenport Brothers excited the deep envy and malice of the conjuring fraternity. Maskelyne, with amazing effrontery, pretended to have exposed them in England. His claims in this direction have been well answered by Dr. George Sexton, a former editor of the SPIRITUAL MAGAZINE, who described in public, in the presence of Mr. Maskelyne, how his tricks were done, and comparing them with the results achieved by the Davenports, said: "The two bear about as much resemblance to each other as the productions of the poet Close to the sublime and glorious dramas of the immortal bard of Avon." Still the conjurers made more noise in public than the Spiritualists, and with the Press to support them they made the general public believe that the Davenport Brothers had been exposed.

As is to be remarked that the Davenports themselves, as contrasted with their friends and travelling companions, never claimed any preternatural origin for their results. The reason for this may have been that as an entertainment it was more piquant and less provocative when every member of the audience could form his own solution. Writing to the American conjurer Houdini, Ira Davenport said in his old age, "We never in public affirmed our belief in Spiritualism. That we regarded as no business of the public, nor did we offer our entertainment as the result of sleight-of-hand, or, on the other hand, as Spiritualism. We let our friends and foes settle that as best they could between themselves, but, unfortunately, we were often the victims of their disagreements."

Houdini further claimed that Davenport admitted that his results were normally effected, but Houdini has himself stuffed so many errors of fact into his book, "A Magician Among the Spirits," and has shown such extraordinary bias on the whale question, that his statement carries no weight. The letter which he produces makes no such admission. A further statement quoted as being made by Ira Davenport is demonstrably false. It is that the instruments never left the cabinet. As a matter of fact, The Timer representative was severely struck in the face by a floating guitar, his brow being cut, and on several occasions when a light was struck instruments dropped all over the room. If Houdini has completely misunderstood this latter statement, it is not likely that he is very accurate upon the former.

It may be urged, and has been urged, by Spiritualists as well as by sceptics that such mountebank psychic exhibitions are undignified and unworthy. There are many of us who think so, and yet there are many others who would echo these words of Mr. P. B. Randall:

The fault lies not with the immortals, but in us; for, as is the demand, so is the supply. If we cannot be reached in one way, we must be, and are, reached in another; and the wisdom of the eternal world gives the blind race just as much as it can bear and no more. If we are intellectual babes, we must put up with mental pap till our digestive capacities warrant and demand stronger food; and, if people can best be

---

[134] SPIRITUAL MAGAZINE, 1868, p. 321.

convinced of immortality by spiritual pranks and antics, the ends resorted to justify the means. The sight of a spectral arm in an audience of three thousand persons will appeal to more hearts, make a deeper impression, and convert more people to a belief in their hereafter, in ten minutes, than a whole regiment of preachers, no matter how eloquent, could in five years.

The Career of Eusapia Palladino
by Arthur Conan Doyle

THE MEDIUMSHIP of Eusapia Palladino marks an important stage in the history of psychical research, because she was the first medium for physical phenomena to be examined by a large number of eminent men of science. The chief manifestations that occurred with her were the movement of objects without contact, the levitation of a table and other objects, the levitation of the medium, the appearance of materialized hands and faces, lights, and the playing of musical instruments without human contact. All these phenomena took place, as we have seen, at a much earlier date with the medium D. D. Home, but when Sir William Crookes invited his scientific brethren to come and examine them they declined. Now for the first time these strange facts were the subject of prolonged investigation by men of European reputation. Needless to say, these experimenters were at first sceptical in the highest degree, and so-called "tests" (those often silly precautions which may defeat the very object aimed at) were the order of the day. No medium in the whole world has been more rigidly tested than this one, and since she was able to convince the vast majority of her sitters, it is clear that her mediumship was of no ordinary type. It is little use pointing out that no psychic researcher should be admitted to the séance room without at least some elementary knowledge of the complexities of mediumship and the right conditions for its unfoldment, or without, for instance, an understanding of the basic truth that it is not the medium alone, but the sitters equally, who are factors in the success of the experiment. Not one scientific man in a thousand recognizes this, and the fact that Eusapia triumphed in spite of such a tremendous handicap is an eloquent tribute to her powers.

The mediumistic career of this humble, illiterate Neapolitan woman, of surpassing interest as well as of extreme importance in its results, supplies yet another instance of the lowly being used as the instrument to shatter the sophistries of the learned. Eusapia was born on January 21, 1854, and died in 1918. Her mediumship began to manifest itself when she was about fourteen years of age. Her mother died at her birth, and her father when she was twelve years old. At the house of friends with whom she went to stay she was persuaded to sit at a table with others. At the end of ten minutes the table was levitated, the chairs began to dance, the curtains in the room to swell, and glasses and bottles to move about. Each sitter was tested in turn to discover who was responsible for the movements, and in the end it was decided that Eusapia was the medium. She took no interest in the proceedings, and only consented to have further sittings to please her hosts and prevent herself from being sent to a convent. It was not until her twenty-second or twenty-third year that her Spiritualistic education began, and then, according to M. Flammarion, it was directed by an ardent Spiritualist, Signor Damiani.

In connexion with this period Eusapia relates a singular incident. At Naples an English lady who had become the wife of Signor Damiani was told at a table séance by a spirit, giving the name of John King, to seek out a woman named Eusapia, the street and the number of the house being specified. He said she was a powerful medium through whom he intended to manifest. Madame Damiani went to the address indicated and found Eusapia Palladino, of whom she had not previously heard. The two women held a séance and John King controlled the medium, whose guide or control he continued ever after to be.

Her first introduction to the European scientific world came through Professor Chiaia, of Naples, who in 1888 published in a journal issued in Rome a letter to Professor Lombroso, detailing his experiences and inviting this celebrated alienist to investigate the medium for himself. It was not until 1891 that Lombroso accepted this invitation, and in February of that year he had two sittings with Eusapia in Naples. He was converted, and wrote: "I am filled with confusion and regret that I combated with so much persistence the possibility of the facts called Spiritualistic." His conversion led many important scientific men in Europe to investigate, and from now onward Madame Palladino was kept busy for many years with test sittings.

Lombroso's Naples sittings in 1891 were followed by the Milan Commission in 1892, which included Professor Schiaparelli, Director of the Observatory of Milan; Professor Gerosa, Chair of Physics; Ermacora, Doctor of Natural Philosophy; M. Aksakof, Councillor of State to the Emperor of Russia; Charles du Prel, Doctor of Philosophy in Munich; and Professor Charles Richet, of the University of Paris. Seventeen sittings were held. Then came investigations in Naples in 1893; in Rome, 1893-4; in Warsaw, and France, in 1894 - the latter under the direction of Professor Richet, Sir Oliver Lodge, Mr. F. W. H. Myers, and Dr.

Ochorowicz; in 1895 at Naples; and in the same year in England, at Cambridge, in the house of Mr. F. W. H. Myers, in the presence of Professor and Mrs. Sidgwick, Sir Oliver Lodge and Dr. Richard Hodgson. They were continued in 1895 in France at the house of Colonel de Rochas; in 1896 at Tremezzo, at Auteuil, and at Choisy Yvrac; in 1897 at Naples, Rome, Paris, Montfort, and Bordeaux; in Paris in November, 1898, in the presence of a scientific committee composed of Mm. Flammarion, Charles Richet, A. de Rochas, Victorien Sardou, Jules Claretie, Adolphe Bisson, G. Delanne, G. de Fontenay, and others; also in 1901 at the Minerva Club in Geneva, in the presence of Professors Porro, Morselli, Bozzano, Venzano, Lombroso, Vassalo, and others. There were many other experimental sittings with scientific men, both in Europe and in America.

Professor Chiaia, in his letter to Professor Lombroso already referred to, gave this picturesque description of the phenomena occurring with Eusapia. He invited him to observe a special case which he considers worthy of the serious attention of the mind of a Lombroso, and continues:

"The case I allude to is that of an invalid woman who belongs to the humblest class of society. She is nearly thirty years old and very ignorant; her look is neither fascinating nor endowed with the power which modern criminologists call irresistible; but when she wishes, be it by day or by night, she can divert a curious group for an hour or so with the most surprising phenomena. Either bound to a seat or firmly held by the hands of the curious, she attracts to her the articles of furniture which surround her, lifts them up, holds them suspended in the air like Mahomet's coffin, and makes them come down again with undulatory movements, as if they were obeying her will. She increases their weight or lessens it according to her pleasure. She raps or taps upon the walls, the ceiling, the floor, with fine rhythm and cadence. In response to the requests of the spectators, something like flashes of electricity shoot forth from her body, and envelop her or enwrap the spectators of these marvellous scenes. She draws upon cards that you hold out, everything that you want - figures, signatures, numbers, sentences - by just stretching out her hand toward the indicated place.

"If you place in the corner of the room a vessel containing a layer of soft clay, you find after some moments the imprint in it of a small or a large hand, the image of a face (front view or profile) from which a plaster cast can be taken. In this way portraits of a face taken at different angles have been preserved, and those who desire so to do can thus make serious and important studies.

"This woman rises in the air, no matter what bands tie her down. She seems to lie upon the empty air, as on a couch, contrary to all the laws of gravity; she plays on musical instruments - organs, bells, tambourines - as if they had been touched by her hands or moved by the breath of invisible gnomes... This woman at times can increase her stature by more than four inches."

Professor Lombroso, as we have seen, was interested enough by this graphic account to investigate, with the result that he was converted. The Milan Committee (1892), the next to experiment, say in their report:

"It is impossible to count the number of times that a hand appeared and was touched by one of us. Suffice it to say that doubt was no longer possible. It was indeed a living human hand which we saw and touched, while at the same time the bust and arms of the medium remained visible, and her hands were held by those on either side of her."

Many phenomena occurred in the light supplied by two candles and an oil-lamp, and the same occurrences were witnessed in full light when the medium was in trance. Dr. Ochorowicz persuaded Eusapia to visit Warsaw in 1894, and the experiments there were in the presence of men and women eminent in scientific and philosophical circles. The record of these sittings says that partial and complete levitations of the table and many other physical phenomena were obtained. These levitations occurred while both the medium's feet were visible in the light, and when her feet were tied and held by a sitter kneeling under the table.

After the sittings at Professor Richet's house on the Ile Roubaud in 1894, Sir Oliver Lodge in the course of his report to the English Society for Psychical Research said:

"However the facts are to be explained, the possibility of the facts I am constrained to admit. There is no further room in my mind for doubt. Any person without invincible prejudice who had had the same experience would have come to the same broad conclusion, viz.: that things hitherto held impossible do actually occur... The result of my experience is to convince me that certain phenomena usually considered abnormal do belong to the order of nature, and, as a corollary from this, that these phenomena ought to be investigated and recorded by persons and societies interested in natural knowledge"[135].

At the meeting at which Sir Oliver Lodge's report was read, Sir William Crookes drew attention to the resemblance of the phenomena occurring with Eusapia to those that happened in the presence of D. D. Home.

Sir Oliver Lodge's report was adversely criticized by Dr. Richard Hodgson, then absent in the United States, and as a consequence Eusapia Palladino and Dr. Hodgson were invited to England, and a series of sittings were held at Cambridge at the house of Mr. F. W. H. Myers in August and September, 1895. These "Cambridge Experiments," as they were called, were for the most part unsuccessful, and it was claimed that the medium was repeatedly detected in fraud. A great deal has been written on both sides in the acute controversy that followed. It is enough to say that competent observers refused to accept this verdict on Eusapia, and that they roundly condemned the methods adopted by the Cambridge group of experimenters.

It is interesting to recall that an American reporter, on the occasion of Eusapia's visit to his country in 1910, bluntly asked the medium if she had ever been caught tricking. Here is Eusapia's frank reply: "Many times I have been told so. You see, it is like this. Some people are at the table who expect tricks - in fact, they want them. I am in a trance. Nothing happens. They get impatient. They think of the tricks - nothing but tricks. They put their mind on the tricks, and - I - and I automatically respond. But it is not often. They merely will me to do them. That is all." This sounds like Eusapia's ingenious adoption of a defence she has heard others make on her behalf. At the same time it has no doubt an element of truth in it, the psychological side of mediumship being little understood.

Two important observations may be made in this connexion. First, as Dr. Hereward Carrington pointed out, various experiments conducted with the object of duplicating the phenomena by fraudulent means resulted in complete failure in almost every case. Second, that the Cambridge sitters were apparently entirely ignorant of the existence and operation of what may be called the "ectoplasmic limb," a phenomenon observed in the case of Slade and other mediums. Carrington says: "All the objections Mrs. Sidgwick raises might be met if we could suppose that Eusapia materializes for the time being a third arm, which produces these phenomena, and which recedes into her body at the conclusion of a phenomenon." Now, strange as it may appear, this is just the conclusion to which abundant evidence points. As early as 1894 Sir Oliver Lodge saw what he describes as an "appearance as of extra limbs," continuous with Eusapia's body or very close to it. With that assurance which ignorance so often assumes, the editorial comment in the Journal of the Society for Psychical Research, wherein Sir Oliver's account was printed, says: "It is hardly necessary to remark that the continuity of the 'spirit' limbs with the body of the medium is prima facie a circumstance strongly suggestive of fraud."

But later scientific investigators amply confirm Sir Oliver Lodge's surmise. Professor Bottazzi states:

"Another time, later on, the same hand was placed on my right forearm, without squeezing it. On this occasion I not only carried my left hand to the spot, but I looked, so I could see and feel at the same time: I saw a human hand, of natural colour, and I felt with mine the fingers and the back of a lukewarm, nervous, rough hand. The hand dissolved, and (I saw it with my eyes) retreated as if into Madame Palladino's body, describing a curve. I confess that I felt some doubt as to whether Eusapia's left hand had freed itself from my right hand, to reach my forearm, but at the same instant I was able to prove to myself that the doubt was groundless, because our two hands were still in contact in the ordinary way. If all the observed phenomena of the seven séances were to disappear from my memory, this one I could never forget."

Professor Galeotti, in July, 1907, plainly saw what he called the doubling of the left arm of the medium. He exclaimed: Look, I see two left arms, identical in appearance One is on the little table, and it is that which M. Bottazzi touches, and the other seems to come out of her shoulder - to approach her, and touch her, and then return and melt into her body again. This is not an hallucination." At a séance in July, 1905, at the house of M. Berisso, when Eusapia's hands were thoroughly controlled and visible to all, Dr. Venzano and others present "distinctly saw a hand and an arm covered by a dark sleeve issue from the front and upper part of the right shoulder of the medium." Much similar testimony might be given.

Towards a study of the complexities of mediumship, especially with Eusapia, the following case is deserving of serious attention. In a sitting with Professor Morselli, Eusapia had been detected liberating

---

[135]) Journal, S.P.R., Vol. VI, Nov. 1894., pp. 334, 360.

her hand from the professor's grasp and stretching it out to reach a trumpet which was on the table. She was prevented, however, from doing this. The report then says:

"At this moment, while the control was certainly more rigorous than ever, the trumpet was raised from the table and disappeared into the cabinet, passing between the medium and Dr. Morselli. Evidently the medium had attempted to do with her hand what she subsequently did mediumistically. Such a futile and foolish attempt at fraud is inexplicable. There is no doubt about the matter; this time the medium did not touch, and could not touch, the trumpet; and even if she could have touched it she could not have conveyed it into the cabinet, which was behind her back."

It may be mentioned that a corner of the room was curtained off to form what is called a "cabinet" (i.e. an enclosure to gather "power") and that Eusapia, unlike most other mediums, sat outside it, about a foot distant from the curtains behind her.

The Society for Psychical Research in 1895 had decided that Eusapia's phenomena were all fraudulent, and would have no more to do with her. But on the Continent of Europe group after group of scientific inquirers, adopting the most rigorous precautions, endorsed Eusapia's powers. Then in 1908 the Society for Psychical Research decided to investigate this medium once more. It nominated three of its most capable sceptics. One, Mr. W. W. Baggally, a member of the Council, had been investigating psychic phenomena for more than thirty-five years, and during that time - with the exception, perhaps, of a few incidents at a séance with Eusapia a few years before - had never witnessed a single genuine physical phenomenon. "Throughout his investigations he had invariably detected fraud, and nothing but fraud." Also, he was an expert conjurer. Mr. Everard Feilding, the honorary secretary of the society, had been investigating for some ten years, but "during all that time he had never seen one physical phenomenon which appeared to him to be conclusively proved," unless, again, perhaps in the case of a séance with Eusapia. Dr. Hereward Carrington, the third of the nominees, though he had attended countless séances, could say, until he sat with Eusapia, "I had never seen one single manifestation of the physical order which I could consider genuine."

At first blush this record of the three investigators seems like a crushing blow to the assumptions of the Spiritualists. But in the investigation of Eusapia Palladino this trio of sceptics met their Waterloo. The full story of their long and patient research of this medium at Naples will be found in Dr. Hereward Carrington's book, "Eusapia Palladino and Her Phenomena" (1909).

As evidence of the careful investigation of scientific investigators on the Continent, we may mention that Professor Morselli noted no fewer than thirty-nine distinct types of phenomena occurring with Eusapia Palladino.

The following incidents may be mentioned because they can well be classed under the heading "Foolproof." Of a séance in Rome in 1894, in the presence of Professor Richet, Dr. Schrenck Notzing, Professor Lombroso, and others, the report says:

"Hoping to obtain the movement of an object without contact, we placed a little piece of paper folded in the form of the letter "A" under a glass, and upon a disc of light pasteboard ... Not being successful in this, we did not wish to fatigue the medium, and we left the apparatus upon the large table; then we took our places around the little table, after having carefully shut all the doors, the keys of which I begged my guests to put in their pockets, in order that we might not be accused of not having taken all necessary precautions.

"The light was extinguished. Soon we heard the glass resound on our table, and having procured a light, we found it in the midst of us, in the same position, upside down, and covering the little piece of paper; only the cardboard disc was wanting. We sought for it in vain. The séance ended. I conducted my guests once more into the antechamber. M. Richet was the first to open the doorwell bolted on the inside. What was not his surprise when he perceived near to the threshold of the door, on the other side of it, upon the staircase, the disc that we had sough for so long! He picked it up, and it was identified by all as the card placed under the glass."

A strong objective proof worth recording is the fact that M. de Fontenay photographed various hands appearing over Eusapia's head, and in one photograph the medium's hands can be seen to be securely held by the investigators. Reproductions of these photographs are given in the Annals of Psychical Science (April, 1908, p. 181 et seq.).

At the sixth and last séance of the series at Genoa with Professor Morselli in 1906-7, an effective test was devised. The medium was tied to the couch with a thick, broad band, of the kind used in asylums to fasten down maniacs, and capable of being tied very tightly without cutting the flesh. Morselli, with experience as an alienist, performed the operation, and also secured the wrists and ankles. After a red electric lamp of ten-candle power had been lighted, the table, which was free from all contact, moved from time to time, small lights were seen and a hand. At one stage the curtains in front of the cabinet opened, giving a view of the medium lying securely bound. "The phenomena," says an account, "were inexplicable considering that the position rendered movement on her part impossible."

Here, in conclusion, are two accounts, out of many, of convincing materializations. The first is related by Dr. Joseph Venzano in the Annals of Psychical Science (Vol. VI, p. 164, September, 1907). Light was provided by a candle, enabling the figure of the medium to be seen:

"In spite of the dimness of the light I could distinctly see Madame Palladino and my fellow sitters. Suddenly I perceived that behind me was a form, fairly tall, which was leaning its head on my left shoulder and sobbing violently, so that those present could hear the sobs: it kissed me repeatedly. I clearly perceived the outlines of this face, which touched my own, and I felt the very fine and abundant hair in contact with my left cheek, so that I could be quite sure that it was, a woman. The table then began to move, and by typtology gave the name of a close family connexion who was known to no one present except myself. She had died some time before, and on account of incompatibility of temperament there had been serious disagreements with her. I was so far from expecting this typtological response that I at first thought this was a case of coincidence of name, but while I was mentally forming this reflection I felt a mouth, with warm breath, touch my left ear and whisper, in a low voice in Genoese dialect, a succession of sentences, the murmur of which was audible to the sitters. These sentences were broken by bursts of weeping, and their gist was repeatedly to implore pardon for injuries done to me, with a fullness of detail connected with family affairs which could only be known to the person in question. The phenomenon seemed so real that I felt compelled to reply to the excuses offered me with expressions of affection, and to ask pardon in my turn if any resentment of the wrongs referred to had been excessive. But I had scarcely uttered the first syllables when two hands, with exquisite delicacy, applied themselves to my lips and prevented my continuing. The form then said to me, "Thank-you," embraced me, kissed me, and disappeared."

With other mediums there have been finer materializations than this one, and in better light, but in this case there was internal, mental evidence of identity.

The last example we shall give occurred in Paris, in 1898, at a sitting at which M. Flammarion was present, when M. Le Bocain addressed a materialized spirit in Arabic, saying: "If it is really thou, Rosalie, who art in the midst of us, pull the hair on the back of my head three times in succession." About ten minutes later, and when M. Le Bocain had almost completely forgotten his request, he felt his hair pulled three separate times, just as he had desired. He says: "I certify this fact, which, besides, formed for me a most convincing proof of the presence of a familiar spirit close about us." He adds that it is hardly necessary to say that Eusapia knows no Arabic.

Opponents and a section of psychic researchers contend that the evidence for phenomena occurring at séances is of little value because the usual observers have no knowledge of the resources of conjurers. In New York in 1910 Dr. Hereward Carrington took with him to a séance given by Eusapia, Mr. Howard Thurston, whom he describes as the most noted magician in America. Mr. Thurston who, with his assistant, controlled the hands and feet of the medium in a good light, wrote:

"I witnessed in person the table levitations of Madame Eusapia Palladino ... and am thoroughly convinced that the phenomena I saw were not due to fraud and were not performed by the aid of her feet, knees, or hands."

He offered to give a thousand dollars to a charitable institution if it could be proved that this medium could not levitate the table without resort to trickery or fraud.

It will be asked what has been the outcome of all the years of investigation conducted with this medium. A number of scientists holding with Sir David Brewster that "Spirit" is the last thing they will give in to have invented ingenious hypotheses to account for the phenomena, of the genuine nature of which they are fully convinced. Colonel de Rochas tried to explain them by what he called "exteriorization of motivity." M. de Fontenay spoke of a dynamic theory of matter; others believe in "ectenic force" and "collective consciousness," and the action of the subconscious mind, but those cases, well authenticated, where the operation of an independent intelligence is clearly shown, make these attempted explanations untenable. Various experimenters were forced to adopt the Spiritualist hypothesis as the only one that explained all the facts in a reasonable way. Dr. Venzano says:

"In the greater number of the materialized forms perceived by us either by sight, contact, or hearing, we were able to recognize points of resemblance to deceased persons, generally our relatives, unknown to the medium and known only to those present who were concerned with the phenomena."

Dr. Hereward Carrington speaks with no uncertain voice. Regarding Mrs. Sidgwick's opinion that it is useless to speculate whether the phenomena are Spiritualistic in character, or whether they represent "some unknown biological law," until the facts themselves have been established, he says: "I must say that before I obtained my sittings I, too, took Mrs. Sidgwick's view." And he continues: "My own sittings convinced me finally and conclusively that genuine phenomena do occur, and, that being the case, the question of their interpretation naturally looms before me... I think that not only is the Spiritualistic hypothesis justified as a working theory, but it is, in fact, the only one capable of rationally explaining the facts."[136]

The mediumship of Eusapia Palladino, as we said at the outset, was similar to that of others, but she had the advantage of enlisting the attention of men of influence whose published accounts of her phenomena have had a weight not given to the utterances of less well-known people. Lombroso in particular has recorded his convictions in his well-known book, After Death - What? (1909). Eusapia was the means of demonstrating the reality of certain facts not accepted by orthodox science. It is easier for the world to deny these facts than to explain them, and that is the course usually adopted.

Those who try to explain away all Eusapia's mediumship by alluding to her superficial habit of playing conscious or unconscious tricks upon the sitters are simply deceiving themselves. That such tricks are played is beyond all question. Lombroso, who entirely endorses the validity of her mediumship, describes the tricks thus:

"Many are the crafty tricks she plays, both in the state of trance (unconsciously) and out of it - for example, freeing one of her two hands, held by the controllers, for the sake of moving objects near her; making touches; slowly lifting the legs of the table by means of one of her knees and one of her feet; and feigning to adjust her hair and then slyly pulling out one hair and putting it over the little balance tray of a letter-weigher in order to lower it. She was seen by Faiforer, before her séances, furtively gathering flowers in a garden, that she might feign them to be "apports" by availing herself of the shrouding dark of the room ... And yet her deepest grief is when she is accused of trickery during the séances - accused unjustly, too, sometimes, it must be confessed, because we are now sure that phantasmal limbs are superimposed (or added to) her own and act as their substitute, while all the time they were believed to be her own limbs detected in the act of cozening for their owner's behoof."

In her visit to America, which was late in life when her powers were at a low ebb, she was detected in these obvious tricks and offended her sitters to such an extent that they discarded her, but Howard Thurston, the famous conjurer, narrates that he determined to disregard these things and continued the sitting, with the result that he obtained an undoubted materialization. Another well-known sitter deposed that at the very moment when he was reproaching her for moving some object with her hand, another object, quite out of her reach, moved across the table. Her case is certainly a peculiar one, for it may be most truthfully said of her that no medium has ever more certainly been proved to have psychic powers, and no medium was ever more certainly a cheat upon occasions. Here, as always, it is the positive result which counts.

Eusapia had a peculiar depression of her parietal bone, due, it is said, to some accident in her childhood. Such physical defects are very often associated with strong mediumship. It is as if the bodily weakness caused what may be described as a dislocation of the soul, so that it is more detached and capable of independent action. Thus Mrs. Piper's mediumship followed upon two internal operations, Home's went with the tubercular diathesis, and many other cases might be quoted. Her nature was hysterical, impetuous and wayward, but she possessed some beautiful traits. Lombroso says of her that she had "a singular kindness of heart which leads her to lavish her gains upon the poor, and upon infants in order to relieve their misfortunes, and which impels her to feel boundless pity for the old and the weak, and to lie awake at night thinking of them. The same goodness of heart drives her to protect animals that are being maltreated by sharply rebuking their cruel oppressors." This passage may be commended to the attention of those who think that psychic power savours of the devil.

---

[136] Eusapia Palladino and Her Phenomena. By Hereward Carrington Ph.D., pp. 250-1.

Daniel D. Home
By Arthur Conan Doyle

DANIEL DUNGLAS HOME was born in 1833 at Currie, a village near Edinburgh. There was a mystery about his parentage, and it has been both asserted and denied that he was related in some fashion to the family of the Earl of Home. Certainly he was a man who inherited elegance of figure, delicacy of feature, sensitiveness of disposition and luxury in taste, from whatever source he sprang. But for his psychic powers, and for the earnestness which they introduced into his complex character, he might have been taken as the very type of the aristocratic younger son who inherits the tendencies, but not the wealth, of his forbears.

Home went from Scotland to New England, at the age of nine years, with his aunt who had adopted him, a mystery still surrounding his existence. When he was thirteen he began to show signs of the psychic faculties he had inherited, for his mother, who was descended from an old Highland family, had the characteristic second-sight of her race. His mystical trend had shown itself in a conversation with his boy friend, Edwin, about a short story where, as the result of a compact, a lover, after his death, manifested his presence to his lady-love. The two boys pledged themselves that whoever died first would come and show himself to the other. Home removed to another district some hundreds of miles distant, and about a month later, just after going to bed one night, he saw a vision of Edwin and announced to his aunt his death, news of which was received a day or two after. A second vision in 1850 concerned the death of his mother, who with her husband had gone to live in America. The boy was ill in bed at the time, and his mother away on a visit to friends at a distance. One evening he called loudly for help, and when his aunt came she found him in great distress. He said that his mother had died that day at twelve o'clock; that she had appeared to him and told him so. The vision proved to be only too true. Soon loud raps began to disturb the quiet household, and furniture to be moved by invisible agency. His aunt, a woman of a narrow religious type, declared the boy had brought the Devil into her house, and turned him out of doors.

He took refuge with friends, and in the next few years moved among them from town to town. His mediumship had become strongly developed, and at the houses where he stopped he gave frequent séances, sometimes as many as six or seven a day, for the limitations of power and the reactions between physical and psychic were little understood at that time. These proved a great drain on his strength, and he was frequently laid up with illness. People flocked from all directions to witness the marvels which occurred in Home's presence. Among those who investigated with him at this time was the American poet Bryant, who was accompanied by Professor Wells, of Harvard University. In New York he met many distinguished Americans, and three - Professor Robert Hare, Professor Mapes, and Judge Edmonds, of the New York Supreme Court - had sittings with him. All three became, as already stated, convinced Spiritualists.

In these early years the charm of Home's personality, and the deep impression created by his powers, led to his receiving many offers. Professor George Bush invited him to stay with him and study for the Swedenborgian ministry; and Mr. and Mrs. Elmer, a rich and childless couple, who had grown to cherish a great affection for him, offered to adopt him and make him their heir on condition of his changing his name to Elmer.

His remarkable healing powers had excited wonder and, yielding to the persuasion of friends, he began to study for the medical profession. But his general delicate health, coupled with actual lung trouble, forced him to abandon this project and, acting under medical advice, he left New York for England.

He arrived in Liverpool on April 9, 1855, and has been described as a tall, slim youth with a marked elegance of bearing and a fastidious neatness of dress, but with a worn, hectic look upon his very expressive face which told of the ravages of disease. He was blue-eyed and auburn-haired, of a type which is peculiarly liable to the attack of tubercle, and the extreme emaciation of his frame showed how little power remained with him by which he might resist it. An acute physician watching him closely would probably have gauged his life by months rather than years in our humid climate, and of all the marvels which Home wrought, the prolongation of his own life was perhaps not the least. His character had already taken on those emotional and religious traits which distinguished it, and he has recorded how, before landing, he rushed down to his cabin and fell upon his knees in prayer. When one considers the astonishing career which lay before him, and the large part which he played in establishing those physical foundations which differentiate this religious development from any other, it may well be claimed that this visitor was among the most notable missionaries who has ever visited our shores.

His position at that moment was a very singular one. He had hardly a relation in the world. His left lung was partly gone. His income was modest, though sufficient. He had no trade or profession, his education having been interrupted by his illness. In character he was shy, gentle, sentimental, artistic, affectionate, and deeply religious. He had a strong tendency both to Art and the Drama, so that his powers of sculpture were considerable, and as a reciter he proved in later life that he had few living equals. But on the top of all this, and of an unflinching honesty which was so uncompromising that he often offended his own allies, there was one gift so remarkable that it threw everything else into insignificance. This lay in those powers, quite independent of his own volition, coming and going with disconcerting suddenness, but proving to all who would examine the proof, that there was something in this man's atmosphere which enabled forces outside himself and outside our ordinary apprehension to manifest themselves upon this plane of matter. In other words, he was a medium - the greatest in a physical sense that the modern world has ever seen.

A lesser man might have used his extraordinary powers to found some special sect of which he would have been the undisputed high priest, or to surround himself with a glamour of power and mystery. Certainly most people in his position would have been tempted to use it for the making of money. As to this latter point, let it be said at once that never in the course of the thirty years of his strange ministry did he touch one shilling as payment for his gifts. It is on sure record that as much as two thousand pounds was offered to him by the Union Club in Paris in the year 1857 for a single séance, and that he, a poor man and an invalid, utterly refused it. "I have been sent on a mission," he said. "That mission is to demonstrate immortality. I have never taken money for it and I never will." There were certain presents from Royalty which cannot be refused without boorishness: rings, scarf-pins, and the like - tokens of friendship rather than recompense; for before his premature death there were few monarchs in Europe with whom this shy youth from the Liverpool landing-stage was not upon terms of affectionate intimacy. Napoleon the Third provided for his only sister. The Emperor of Russia sponsored his marriage. What novelist would dare to invent such a career?

But there are more subtle temptations than those of wealth. Home's uncompromising honesty was the best safeguard against those. Never for a moment did he lose his humility and his sense of proportion. "I have these powers," he would say; "I shall be happy, up to the limit of my strength, to demonstrate them to you, if you approach me as one gentleman should approach another. I shall be glad if you can throw any further light upon them. I will lend myself to any reasonable experiment. I have no control over them. They use me, but I do not use them. They desert me for months and then come back in redoubled force. I am a passive instrument - no more." Such was his unvarying attitude. He was always the easy, amiable man of the world, with nothing either of the mantle of the prophet or of the skull-cap of the magician. Like most truly great men, there was no touch of pose in his nature. An index of his fine feeling is that when confirmation was needed for his results he would never quote any names unless he was perfectly certain that the owners would not suffer in any way through being associated with an unpopular cult. Sometimes even after they had freely given leave he still withheld the names, lest he should unwittingly injure a friend. When he published his first series of "Incidents in my Life," the Saturday Review waxed very sarcastic over the anonymous "evidence of Countess O , Count B , Count de K , Princess de B and Mrs. S ," who were quoted as having witnessed manifestations. In his second volume, Home, having assured himself of the concurrence of his friends, filled the blanks with the names of the Countess Orsini, Count de Beaumont, Count de Komar, Princess de Beauveau, and the well known American hostess, Mrs. Henry Senior. His Royal friends he never quoted at all, and yet it is notorious that the Emperor Napoleon, the Empress Eugenie, the Tsar Alexander, the Emperor William the First of Germany, and the Kings of Bavaria and Wurtemberg were all equally convinced by his extraordinary powers. Never once was Home convicted of any deception, either in word or in deed.

On first landing in England he took up his quarters at Cox's Hotel in Jermyn Street, and it is probable that he chose that hostelry because he had learned that through Mrs. Hayden's ministry the proprietor was already sympathetic to the cause. However that may be, Mr. Cox quickly discovered that his young guest was a most remarkable medium, and at his invitation some of the leading minds of the day were asked to consider those phenomena which Home could lay before them. Among others, Lord Brougham came to a séance and brought with him his scientific friend, Sir David Brewster. In full daylight they investigated the phenomena, and in his amazement at what happened Brewster is reported to have said: "This upsets the philosophy of fifty years." If he had said "fifteen hundred" he would have been within the mark. He described what took place in a letter written to his sister at the time, but published long after[137]. Those present were Lord Brougham, Sir David Brewster, Mr. E. W. Cox and the medium.

"We four," said Brewster, "sat down at a moderately sized table, the structure of which we were invited to examine. In a short time the table struggled, and a tremulous motion ran up all our arms; at our bidding these motions ceased and returned. The most unaccountable rappings were produced in various parts of the table, and the table actually rose from the ground when no hand was upon it. A larger table was produced, and exhibited similar movements...

"A small hand-bell was laid down with its mouth upon the carpet, and after lying for some time, it actually rang when nothing could have touched it." He adds that the bell came over to him and placed itself in his hand, and it did the same to Lord Brougham; and concludes: "These were the principal experiments. We could give no explanation of them, and could not conjecture how they could be produced by any kind of mechanism."

The Earl of Dunraven states that he was induced to investigate the phenomena by what Brewster had told him. He describes meeting the latter, who said that the manifestations were quite inexplicable by fraud, or by any physical laws with which we were acquainted. Home sent an account of this sitting in a letter to a friend in America, where it was published with comments. When these were reproduced in the English Press, Brewster became greatly alarmed. It was one thing to hold certain views privately, it was quite another to face the inevitable loss of prestige that would occur in the scientific circles in which he moved. Sir David was not the stuff of which martyrs or pioneers are made. He wrote to the Morning Advertiser, stating that though he had seen several mechanical effects which he could not explain, yet he was satisfied that they could all be produced by human hands and feet. At the time it had, of course, never occurred to him that his letter to his sister, just quoted, would ever see the light.

When the whole correspondence came to be published, the Spectator remarked of Sir David Brewster:

"It seems established by the clearest evidence that he felt and expressed, at and immediately after his séances with Mr. Home, a wonder and almost awe, which he afterwards wished to explain away. The hero of science does not acquit himself as one could wish or expect."

We have dwelt a little on this Brewster incident because it was typical of the scientific attitude of the day, and because its effect was to excite a wider public interest in Home and his phenomena, and to bring hundreds of fresh investigators. One may say that scientific men may be divided into three classes: those who have not examined the matter at all (which does not in the least prevent them from giving very violent opinions); those who know that it is true but are afraid to say so; and finally the gallant minority of the Lodges, the Crookes, the Barretts and the Lombrosos, who know it is true and who dare all in saying so.

From Jermyn Street, Home went to stay with the Rymer family in Ealing, where many séances were held. Here he was visited by Lord Lytton, the famous novelist, who, although he received striking evidence, never publicly avowed his belief in the medium's powers, though his private letters, and indeed his published novels, are evidence of his true feeling. This was the case with scores of well-known men and women. Among his early sitters were Robert Owen the Socialist, T. A. Trollope the author, and Dr. J. Garth Wilkinson the alienist.

In these days, when the facts of psychic phenomena are familiar to all save those who are wilfully ignorant, we can hardly realize the moral courage which was needed by Home in putting forward his powers and upholding them in public. To the average educated Briton in the material Victorian era a man who claimed to be able to produce results which upset Newton's law of gravity, and which showed invisible mind acting upon visible matter, was prima facie a scoundrel and an impostor. The view of Spiritualism pronounced by Vice-Chancellor Giffard at the conclusion of the Home-Lyon trial was that of the class to which he belonged. He knew nothing of the matter, but took it for granted that anything with such claims must be false. No doubt similar things were reported in far-off lands and ancient books, but that they could occur in prosaic, steady old England, the England of bank-rates and free imports, was too absurd for serious thought. It has been recorded that at this trial Lord Giffard turned to Home's counsel and said: "Do I understand you to state that your client claims that he has been levitated into the air?" Counsel assented, on which the judge turned to the jury and made such a movement as the high priest may have made in ancient days when he rent his garments as a protest against blasphemy. In 1868 there were few of the jury who were sufficiently educated to check the judge's remarks, and it is just in that

---

[137] Home Life of Sir David Brewster, by Mrs. Gordon (his daughter). 1869.

particular that we have made some progress in the fifty years between. Slow work - but Christianity took more than three hundred years to come into its own.

Take this question of levitation as a test of Home's powers. It is claimed that more than a hundred times in good light before reputable witnesses he floated in the air. Consider the evidence. In 1857, in a chateau near Bordeaux, he was lifted to the ceiling of a lofty room in the presence of Madame Ducos, widow of the Minister of Marine, and of the Count and Countess de Beaumont. In 1860 Robert Bell wrote an article, "Stranger than Fiction," in the Cornhill. "He rose from his chair," says Bell, "four or five feet from the ground... We saw his figure pass from one side of the window to the other, feet foremost, lying horizontally in the air." Dr. Gully, of Malvern, a well-known medical man, and Robert Chambers, the author and publisher, were the other witnesses. Is it to be supposed that these men were lying confederates, or that they could not tell if a man were floating in the air or pretending to do so? In the same year Home was raised at Mrs. Milner Gibson's house in the presence of Lord and Lady Clarence Paget, the former passing his hands underneath him to assure himself of the fact. A few months later Mr. Wason, a Liverpool solicitor, with seven others, saw the same phenomenon. "Mr. Home," he says, "crossed the table over the heads of the persons sitting around it." He added: "I reached his hand seven feet from the floor, and moved along five or six paces as he floated above me in the air." In 1861 Mrs. Parkes, of Cornwall Terrace, Regent's Park, tells how she was present with Bulwer Lytton and Mr. Hall when Home in her own drawing-room was raised till his hand was on the top of the door, and then floated horizontally forward. In 1866 Mr. and Mrs. Hall, Lady Dunsany, and Mrs. Senior, in Mr. Hall's house saw Home, his face transfigured and shining, twice rise to the ceiling, leaving a cross marked in pencil upon the second occasion, so as to assure the witnesses that they were not the victims of imagination.

In 1868 Lord Adare, Lord Lindsay, Captain Wynne, and Mr. Smith Barry saw Home levitate upon many occasions. A very minute account has been left by the first three witnesses of the occurrence of December 16[138] of this year, when at Ashley House Home, in a state of trance, floated out of the bedroom and into the sitting-room window, passing seventy feet above the street. After his arrival in the sitting-room he went back into the bedroom with Lord Adare, and upon the latter remarking that he could not understand how Home could have fitted through the window which was only partially raised, "he told me to stand a little distance off. He then went through the open space head first quite rapidly, his body being nearly horizontal and apparently rigid. He came in again feet foremost." Such was the account given by Lords Adare and Lindsay. Upon its publication Dr. Carpenter, who earned an unenviable reputation by a perverse opposition to every fact which bore upon this question, wrote exultantly to point out that there had been a third witness who had not been heard from, assuming without the least justification that Captain Wynne's evidence would be contradictory. He went the, length of saying "a single honest sceptic declares that Mr. Home was sitting in his chair all the time" - a statement which can only be described as false. Captain Wynne at once wrote corroborating the others and adding: "If you are not to believe the corroborative evidence of three unimpeached witnesses, there would be an end to all justice and courts of law."

To show how hard put to it the critics have been to find some loophole of escape from the obvious, they have made much of the fact that Lord Lindsay, writing some time after the event, declared that it was seen by moonlight; whereas the calendar shows that the moon was not at that time visible. Mr. Andrew Lang remarks: "Even in a fog, however, people in a room can see a man coming in by the window, and go out again, head first, with body rigid."[139] It would seem to most of us that if we saw so marvellous a sight we would have little time to spare to determine whether we viewed it by the light of the moon or by that of the street lamps. It must be admitted, however, that Lord Lindsay's account is clumsily worded - so clumsily that there is some excuse for Mr. Joseph McCabe's reading of it that the spectators looked not at the object itself and its shadow on the window-sill, but that they stood with their backs to it and viewed the shadow on the wall. When one considers, however, the standing of the three eye-witnesses who have testified to this, one may well ask whether in ancient or modern times any preternatural event has been more clearly proved.

So many are the other instances of Home's levitations that a long article might easily be written upon this single phase of his mediumship. Professor Crookes was again and again a witness to the phenomenon, and refers to fifty instances which had come within his knowledge. But is there any fair-minded person who has read the incident here recorded who will not say, with Professor Challis: "Either the facts must be

---

[138] The almanac shows it to be Sunday the 13th.

[139] Historical Mysteries, p. 236.

admitted to be such as are reported, or the possibility of certifying facts by human testimony must be given up."

"Are we, then, back in the age of miracles?" cries the reader. There is no miracle. Nothing on this plane is supernatural. What we see now, and what we have read of in ages past, is but the operation of law which has not yet been studied and defined. Already we realize something of its possibilities and of its limitations, which are as exact in their way as those of any purely physical power. We must hold the balance between those who would believe nothing and those who would believe too much. Gradually the mists will clear and we will chart the shadowy coast. When the needle first sprang up at the magnet it was not an infraction of the laws of gravity. It was that there had been the local intervention of another stronger force. Such is the case also when psychic powers act upon the plane of matter. Had Home's faith in this power faltered, or had his circle been unduly disturbed, he would have fallen. When Peter lost faith he sank into the waves. Across the centuries the same cause still produced the same effect. Spiritual power is ever with us if we do not avert our faces, and nothing has been vouchsafed to Judaea which is withheld from England.

It is in this respect, as a confirmation of the power of the unseen, and as a final answer to materialism as we now understand it, that Home's public career is of such supreme importance. He was an affirmative witness of the truth of those so-called "miracles" which have been the stumbling-block for so many earnest minds, and are now destined to be the strong solid proof of the accuracy of the original narrative. Millions of doubting souls in the agony of spiritual conflict had cried out for definite proof that all was not empty space around us, that there were powers beyond our grasp, that the ego was not a mere secretion of nervous tissue, and that the dead did really carry on their personal unbroken existence. All this was proved by this greatest of modern missionaries to anyone who could observe or reason. It is easy to poke superficial fun at rising tables and quivering walls, but they were the nearest and most natural objects which could record in material terms that power which was beyond our human ken. A mind which would be unmoved by an inspired sentence was struck into humility and into new paths of research in the presence of even the most homely of these inexplicable phenomena. It is easy to call them puerile, but they effected the purpose for which they were sent by shaking to its foundations the complaisance of those material men of science who were brought into actual contact with them. They are to be regarded not as ends in themselves, but as the elementary means by which the mind should be diverted into new channels of thought. And those channels of thought led straight to the recognition of the survival of the spirit. "You have conveyed incalculable joy and comfort to the hearts of many people," said Bishop Clark, of Rhode Island. "You have made dwelling-places light that were dark before." "Mademoiselle," said Home to the lady who was to be his wife, "I have a mission entrusted to me. It is a great and a holy one." The famous Dr. John Elliotson, immortalized by Thackeray under the name of Dr. Goodenough, was one of the leaders of British materialism. He met Home, saw his powers, and was able soon to say that he had lived all his life in darkness and had thought there was nothing in existence but the material, but he now had a firm hope which he trusted he would hold while on earth.

Innumerable instances could be quoted of the spiritual value of Home's work, but it has never been better summed up than in a paragraph from Mrs. Webster, of Florence, who saw much of his ministry. "He is the most marvellous missionary of modern times in the greatest of all causes, and the good that he has done cannot be reckoned. When Mr. Home passes he bestows around him the greatest of all blessings, the certainty of a future life."

Now that the details of his career can be read, it is to the whole wide world that he brings this most vital of all messages. His attitude as to his own mission was expressed in a lecture given in London in Willis's Rooms on February 15, 1866. He said: "I believe in my heart that this power is being spread more and more every day to draw us nearer to God. You ask if it makes us purer? My only answer is that we are but mortals, and as such liable to err; but it does teach that the pure in heart shall see God. It teaches us that He is love, and that there is no death. To the aged it comes as a solace, when the storms of life are nearly over and rest cometh. To the young it speaks of the duty we owe to each other, and that as we sow so shall we reap. To all it teaches resignation. It comes to roll away the clouds of error, and bring the bright morning of a never-ending day."

It is curious to see how his message affected those of his own generation. Reading the account of his life written by his widow - a most convincing document, since she of all living mortals must have known the real man - it would appear that his most utterly whole-hearted support and appreciation came from those aristocrats of France and Russia with whom he was brought into contact. The warm glow of personal admiration and even reverence in their letters is such as can hardly be matched in any biography. In

England he had a close circle of ardent supporters, a few of the upper classes, with the Halls, the Howitts, Robert Chambers, Mrs. Milner Gibson, Professor Crookes, and others. But there was a sad lack of courage among those who admitted the facts in private and stood aloof in public. Lord Brougham and Bulwer Lytton were of the type of Nicodemus, the novelist being the worst offender. "Intelligentzia" on the whole came badly out of the matter, and many an honoured name suffers in the story. Faraday and Tyndall were fantastically unscientific in their methods of prejudging a question first, and offering to examine it afterwards on the condition that their prejudgment was accepted. Sir David Brewster, as already shown, said some honest things, and then in a panic denied that he had said them, forgetting that the evidence was on actual record. Browning wrote a long poem - if such doggerel can be called poetry - to describe an exposure which had never taken place. Carpenter earned an unenviable notoriety as an unscrupulous opponent, while proclaiming some strange Spiritualistic thesis of his own. The secretaries of the Royal Society refused to take a cab-drive in order to see Crookes's demonstration of the physical phenomena, while they pronounced roundly against them. Lord Giffard inveighed from the Bench against a subject the first elements of which he did not understand.

As to the clergy, such an order might not have existed during the thirty years that this, the most marvellous spiritual outpouring of many centuries, was before the public. One cannot recall the name of one British clergyman who showed any intelligent interest; and when in 1872 a full account of the St. Petersburg séances began to appear in The Times, it was cut short, according to Mr. H. T. Humphreys, "on account of strong remonstrances to Mr. Delane, the editor, by certain of the higher clergy of the Church of England." Such was the contribution of our official spiritual guides. Dr. Elliotson the Rationalist, was far more alive than they. The rather bitter comment of Mrs. Home is: "The verdict of his own generation was that of the blind and deaf upon the man who could hear and see."

Home's charity was among his more beautiful characteristics. Like all true charity it was secret, and only comes out indirectly and by chance. One of his numerous traducers declared that he had allowed a bill for £50 to be sent in to his friend, Mr. Rymer. In self-defence it came out that it was not a bill but a cheque most generously sent by Home to help this friend in a crisis. Considering his constant poverty, fifty pounds probably represented a good part of his bank balance. His widow dwells with pardonable pride upon the many evidences found in his letters after his death. "Now it is an unknown artist for whose brush Home's generous efforts had found employment; now a distressed worker writes of his sick wife's life saved by comforts that Home provided; now a mother thanks him for a start in life for her son. How much time and thought he devoted to helping others when the circumstance of his own life would have led most men to think only of their own needs and cares."

"Send me a word from the heart that has known so often how to cheer a friend!" cries one of his protégés.

"Shall I ever prove worthy of all the good you have done me?" says another letter.

We find him roaming the battlefields round Paris, often under fire, with his pockets full of cigars for the wounded. A German officer writes affectionately to remind him how he saved him from bleeding to death, and carried him on his own weak back out of the place of danger. Truly Mrs. Browning was a better judge of character than her spouse, and Sir Galahad a better name than Sludge.

At the same time, it would be absurd to depict Home as a man of flawless character. He had the weakness of his temperament, and something feminine in his disposition which showed itself in many ways. The author, while in Australia, came across a correspondence dating from 1856 between Home and the elder son of the Rymer family. They had travelled together in Italy, and Home had deserted his friend under circumstances which showed inconstancy and ingratitude. It is only fair to add that his health was so broken at the time that he could hardly be called normal. "He had the defects of an emotional character," said Lord Dunraven, "with vanity highly developed, perhaps wisely to enable him to hold his own against the ridicule that was then poured out on Spiritualism and everything connected with it. He was liable to fits of great depression and to nervous crises difficult to understand, but he was withal of a simple, kindly, humorous, loving disposition that appealed to me... My friendship remained without change or diminution to the end."

There are few of the varied gifts which we call "mediumistic" and St. Paul "of the spirit" which Home did not possess - indeed, the characteristic of his psychic power was its unusual versatility. We speak usually of a Direct Voice medium, of a trance speaker, of a clairvoyant or of a physical medium, but Home was all four. So far as can be traced, he had little experience of the powers of other mediums, and was not immune from that psychic jealousy which is a common trait of these sensitives. Mrs. Jencken, formerly

Miss Kate Fox, was the only other medium with whom he was upon terms of friendship. He bitterly resented any form of deception, and carried this excellent trait rather too far by looking with eyes of suspicion upon all forms of manifestations which did not exactly correspond with his own. This opinion, expressed in an uncompromising manner in his last book, Lights and Shadows of Spiritualism, gave natural offence to other mediums who claimed to be as honest as himself. A wider acquaintance with phenomena would have made him more charitable. Thus he protested strongly against any séance being held in the dark, but this is certainly a counsel of perfection, for experiments upon the ectoplasm which is the physical basis of all materializations show that it is usually affected by light unless the light is tinted red. Home had no large experience of complete materializations such as were obtained in those days by Miss Florence Cook, or Madame d'Esperance, or in our own time, by Madame Bisson's medium, and therefore he could dispense with complete darkness in his own ministry. Thus, his opinion was unjust to others. Again, Home declared roundly that matter could not pass through matter, because his own phenomena did not take that form; and yet the evidence that matter can in certain cases be passed through matter seems to be overwhelming. Even birds of rare varieties have been brought into séance rooms under circumstances which seem to preclude fraud, and the experiments of passing wood through wood, as shown before Johann Zöllner and the other Leipzig professors, were quite final as set forth in the famous physicist's account in Transcendental Physics of his experiences with Henry Slade. Thus, it may count as a small flaw in Home's character that he decried and doubted the powers which he himself did not happen to possess.

Some also might count it as a failing that he carried his message rather to the leaders of society and of life than to the vast toiling masses. It is probable that Home had, in fact, the weakness as well as the graces of the artistic nature and that he was most at ease and happiest in an atmosphere of elegance and refinement, with a personal repulsion from all that was sordid and ill-favoured. If there were no other reason the precarious state of his health unfitted him for any sterner mission, and he was driven by repeated haemorrhages to seek the pleasant and refined life of Italy, Switzerland and the Riviera. But for the prosecution of his mission, as apart from personal self-sacrifice, there can be no doubt that his message carried to the laboratory of a Crookes or to the Court of a Napoleon was more useful than if it were laid before the crowd. The assent of science and of character was needed before the public could gain assurance that such things were true. If it was not fully gained the fault lies assuredly with the hidebound men of science and thinkers of the day, and by no means with Home, who played his part of actual demonstration to perfection, leaving it to other and less gifted men to analyse and to make public that which he had shown them. He did not profess to be a man of science, but he was the raw material of science, willing and anxious that others should learn from him all that he could convey to the world, so that science should itself testify to religion while religion should be buttressed upon science. When Home's message has been fully learned an unbelieving man will not stand convicted of impiety, but of ignorance.

There was something pathetic in Home's efforts to find some creed in which he could satisfy his own gregarious instinct - for he had no claims to be a strong-minded individualist - and at the same time find a niche into which he could fit his own precious packet of assured truth. His pilgrimage vindicates the assertion of some Spiritualists that a man may belong to any creed and carry with him the spiritual knowledge, but it also bears out those who reply that perfect harmony with that spiritual knowledge can only be found, as matters now stand, in a special Spiritualist community. Alas! that it should be so, for it is too big a thing to sink into a sect, however great that sect might become. Home began in his youth as a Wesleyan, but soon left them for the more liberal atmosphere of Congregationalism. In Italy the artistic atmosphere of the Roman Catholic Church, and possibly its record of so many phenomena akin to his own, caused him to become a convert with an intention of joining a monastic Order - an intention which his common sense caused him to abandon. The change of religion was at a period when his psychic powers had deserted him for a year, and his confessor assured him that as they were of evil origin they would certainly never be heard of again now that he was a son of the true Church. None the less, on the very day that the year expired they came back in renewed strength. From that time Home seems to have been only nominally a Catholic, if at all, and after his second marriage - both his marriages were to Russian ladies - he was strongly drawn towards the Greek Church, and it was under their ritual that he was at last laid to rest at St. Germain in 1886. "To another discerning of Spirits" (1 Cor. xii. 10) is the short inscription upon that grave, of which the world has not yet heard the last.

If proof were needed of the blamelessness of Home's life, it could not be better shown than by the fact that his numerous enemies, spying ever for some opening to attack, could get nothing in his whole career upon which to comment save the wholly innocent affair which is known as the Home-Lyon case. Any impartial judge reading the depositions in this case - they are to be found verbatim in the second series of

Incidents in My Life - would agree that it is not blame but commiseration which was owing to Home. One could desire no higher proof of the nobility of his character than his dealings with this unpleasant freakish woman, who first insisted upon settling a large sum of money upon him, and then, her whim having changed and her expectations of an immediate introduction into high society being disappointed, stuck at nothing in order to get it back again. Had she merely asked for it back there is little doubt that Home's delicate feelings would have led him to return it, even though he had been put to much trouble and expense over the matter, which had entailed a change of his name to Home-Lyon, to meet the woman's desire that he should be her adopted son. Her request, however, was so framed that he could not honourably agree to it, as it would have implied an admission that he had done wrong in accepting the gift. If one consults the original letters - which few of those who comment upon the case seem to have done - one finds that Home, S. C. Hall as his representative and Mr. Wilkinson as his solicitor, implored the woman to moderate the unreasonable benevolence which was to change so rapidly into even more unreasonable malevolence. She was absolutely determined that Home should have the money and be her heir. A less mercenary man never lived, and he begged her again and again to think of her relatives, to which she answered that the money was her own to do what she pleased with, and that no relatives were dependent upon it. From the time that he accepted the new situation he acted and wrote as a dutiful son, and it is not uncharitable to suppose that this entirely filial attitude may not have been that which this elderly lady had planned out in her scheming brain. At any rate, she soon tired of her fad and reclaimed her money upon the excuse - a monstrous one to anyone who will read the letters and consider the dates that spirit messages had caused her to take the action she had done.

The case was tried in the Court of Chancery, and the judge alluded to Mrs. Lyon's "innumerable misstatements on many important particulars - misstatements upon oath so perversely untrue that they have embarrassed the Court to a great degree and quite discredited the plaintiff's testimony." In spite of this caustic comment, and in spite also of elementary justice, the verdict was against Home on the general ground that British law put the burden of disproof upon the defendant in such a case, and complete disproof is impossible when assertion is met by counter-assertion. Lord Giffard might, no doubt, have risen superior to the mere letter of the law had it not been that he was deeply prejudiced against all claims to psychic power, which were from his point of view manifestly absurd and yet were persisted in by the defendant under his nose in his own Court of Chancery. Even Home's worst enemies were forced to admit that the fact that he had retained the money in England and had not lodged it where it would have been beyond recovery proved his honest intentions in this the most unfortunate episode of his life. Of all the men of honour who called him friend, it is not recorded that he lost one through the successful machinations of Mrs. Lyon. Her own motives were perfectly obvious. As all the documents were in order, her only possible way of getting the money back was to charge Home with having extorted it from her by misrepresentation, and she was cunning enough to know what chance a medium - even an amateur unpaid medium - would have in the ignorant and material atmosphere of a mid-Victorian court of law. Alas! that we can omit the "mid-Victorian" and the statement still holds good.

The powers of Home have been attested by so many famous observers, and were shown under such frank conditions, that no reasonable man can possibly doubt them. Crookes's evidence alone is conclusive[140]. There is also the remarkable book, reprinted at a recent date, in which Lord Dunraven gives the story of his youthful connexion with Home. But apart from these, among those in England who investigated in the first few years and whose public testimony or letters to Home show they were not only convinced of the genuineness of the phenomena. but also of their spiritual origin, may be mentioned the Duchess of Sutherland, Lady Shelley, Lady Gomm, Dr. Robert Chambers, Lady Otway, Miss Catherine Sinclair, Mrs. Milner Gibson, Mr. and Mrs. William Howitt, Mrs. De Burgh, Dr. Gully (of Malvern), Sir Charles Nicholson, Lady Dunsany, Sir Daniel Cooper, Mrs. Adelaide Senior, Mr. and Mrs. S. C. Hall, Mrs. Makdougall Gregory, Mr. Pickersgill, R.A., Mr. E. L. Blanchard, and Mr. Robert Bell.

Others who went so far as to admit that the theory of imposture was insufficient to account for the phenomena were: Mr. Ruskin, Mr. Thackeray (then editor of the Cornhill Magazine), Mr. John Bright, Lord Dufferin, Sir Edwin Arnold, Mr. Heaphy, Mr. Durham (sculptor), Mr. Nassau Senior, Lord Lyndhurst, Mr. J. Hutchinson (ex-Chairman of the Stock Exchange), and Dr. Lockhart Robertson.

Such were his witnesses and such his works. And yet, when his most useful and unselfish life had come to an end, it must be recorded to the eternal disgrace of our British Press that there was hardly a paper which did not allude to him as an impostor and a charlatan. The time is coming, however, when he will be

---

[140] Researches in the Phenomena of Spiritualism, and SPR Proceedings, VI., p. 98.

recognized for what he was, one of the pioneers in the slow and arduous advance of Humanity into that jungle of ignorance which has encompassed it so long.

Arthur Conan Doyle on His Cycle

Harry Houdini and His Cycles

HARRY HOUDINI - DOING NEEDLE THREADING - 192

Henry Slade
by Arthur Conan Doyle

Henry Slade, the celebrated slate-writing medium, had been before the public in America for fifteen years before he arrived in London on July 13, 1876. Colonel H. S. Olcott, a former president of the Theosophical Society, states that he and Madame Blavatsky were responsible for Slade's visit to England. It appears that the Grand Duke Constantine of Russia, desiring to make a scientific investigation of Spiritualism, a committee of professors of the Imperial University of St. Petersburg requested Colonel Olcott and Madame Blavatsky to select out of the best American mediums one whom they could recommend for tests.

They chose Slade, after submitting him to exacting tests for several weeks before a committee of sceptics, who in their report certified that "messages were written inside double slates, sometimes tied and sealed together, while they either lay upon the table in full view of all, or were laid upon the heads of members of the committee, or held flat against the under surface of the table-top, or held in a committeeman's hand without the medium touching it." It was en route to Russia that Slade came to England.

A representative of the London World, who had a sitting with Slade soon after his arrival, thus describes him: "A highly-wrought, nervous temperament, a dreamy, mystical face, regular features, eyes luminous with expression, a rather sad smile, and a certain melancholy grace of manner, were the impressions conveyed by the tall, lithe figure introduced to me as Dr. Slade. He is the sort of man you would pick out of a roomful as an enthusiast." The Seybert Commission Report says, "he is probably six feet in height, with a figure of unusual symmetry," and that "his face would attract notice anywhere for its uncommon beauty," and sums him up as "a noteworthy man in every respect."

Directly after his arrival in London Slade began to give sittings at his lodgings in 8 Upper Bedford Place, Russell Square, and his success was immediate and pronounced. Not only was writing obtained of an evidential nature, under test conditions, with the sitter's own slates, but the levitation of objects and materialized hands were observed in strong sunlight.

The editor of THE SPIRITUAL MAGAZINE, the soberest and most high-class of the Spiritualist periodicals of the time, wrote: "We have no hesitation in saying that Dr. Slade is the most remarkable medium of modern times."

Mr. J. Enmore Jones, a well-known psychic researcher of that day, who afterwards edited THE SPIRITUAL MAGAZINE, said that Slade was taking the place vacated by D. D. Home. His account of his first sitting indicates the business-like method of procedure: "In Mr. Home's case, he refused to take fees, and as a rule the sittings were in the evening in the quiet of domestic life; but in Dr. Slade's case it was any time during the day, in one of the rooms he occupies at a boarding-house. The fee of twenty shillings is charged, and he prefers that only one person be present in the large room he uses. No time is lost; as soon as the visitor sits down the incidents commence, are continued, and in, say, fifteen minutes are ended." Stainton Moses, who was afterwards the first president of the London Spiritualist Alliance, conveys the same idea with regard to Slade. He wrote: "In his presence phenomena occur with a regularity and precision, with an absence of regard for 'conditions,' and with a facility for observation which satisfy my desires entirely. It is impossible to conceive circumstances more favorable to minute investigation than those under which I witnessed the phenomena which occur in his presence with such startling rapidity. There was no hesitation, no tentative experiments.

All was short, sharp, and decisive. The invisible operators knew exactly what they were going to do, and did it with promptitude and precision."[141]

Slade's first séance in England was given on July 15, 1876, to Mr. Charles Blackburn, a prominent Spiritualist, and Mr. W. H. Harrison, editor of THE SPIRITUALIST. In strong sunlight the medium and the two sitters occupied three sides of an ordinary table about four feet square. A vacant chair was placed at the

---

[141] THE SPIRITUALIST, Vol. IX, p. 2.

fourth side. Slade put a tiny piece of pencil, about the size of a grain of wheat, upon a slate, and held the slate by one corner with one hand under the table flat against the leaf. Writing was heard on the slate, and on examination a short message was found to have been written. While this was taking place the four hands of the sitters and Slade's disengaged hands were clasped in the centre of the table. Mr. Blackburn's chair was moved four or five inches while he was sitting upon it, and no one but himself was touching it. The unoccupied chair at the fourth side of the table once jumped in the air, striking its seat against the under edge of the table. Twice a life-like hand passed in front of Mr. Blackburn while both Slade's hands were under observation. The medium held an accordion under the table, and while his other hand was in clear view on the table "Hone, Sweet Home" was played. Mr. Blackburn then held the accordion in the same way, when the instrument was drawn out strongly and one note sounded. While this occurred Slade's hands were on the table. Finally, the three present raised their hands a foot above the table, and it rose until it touched their hands. At another sitting on the same day a chair rose about four feet, when no one was touching it, and when Slade rested one hand on the top of Miss Blackburn's chair, she and the chair were raised about half a yard from the floor.

Mr. Stainton Moses thus describes an early sitting which he had with Slade:

A midday sun, hot enough to roast one, was pouring into the room; the table was uncovered; the medium sat with the whole of his body in full view; there was no human being present save myself and him. What conditions could be better? The raps were instantaneous and loud, as if made by the clenched fist of a powerful man. The slate-writing occurred under any suggested condition.

It came on a slate held by Dr. Slade and myself; on one held by myself alone in the corner of the table farthest from the medium; on a slate which I had myself brought with me, and which I held myself. The latter writing occupied some time in production, and the grating noise of the pencil in forming each word was distinctly audible. A chair opposite to me was raised some eighteen inches from the floor; my slate was taken out of my hand, and produced at the opposite side of the table, where neither Dr. Slade nor I could reach it; the accordion played all round and about me, while the doctor held it by the lower part, and finally, on a touch from his hand upon the back of my chair, I was levitated, chair and all, some inches.

Mr. Stainton Moses was himself a powerful medium, and this fact doubtless aided the conditions. He adds:

I have seen all these phenomena and many others several times before, but I never saw them occur rapidly and consecutively in broad daylight. The whole séance did not extend over more than half an hour, and no cessation of the phenomena occurred from first to last.[142]

All went well for six weeks, and London was full of curiosity as to the powers of Slade, when there came an awkward interruption.

Early in September, 1876, Professor Ray Lankester with Dr. Donkin had two sittings with Slade, and on the second occasion, seizing the slate, he found writing on it when none was supposed to have taken place. He was entirely without experience in psychic research, or he would have known that it is impossible to say at what moment writing occurs in such séances. Occasionally a whole sheet of writing seems to be precipitated in an instant, while at other times the author has clearly heard the pencil scratching along from line to line.

To Ray Lankester, however, it seemed a clear case of fraud, and he wrote a letter to THE TIMES[143] denouncing Slade, and also prosecuted him for obtaining money under false pretences. Replies to Lankester's letter and supporting Slade were forthcoming from Dr, Alfred Russel Wallace, Professor Barrett, and others. Dr. Wallace pointed out that Professor Lankester's account of what happened was so completely unlike what occurred during his own visit to the medium, as well as the recorded experience of Serjeant Cox, Dr. Carter Blake, and many others, that he could only look upon it as a striking example of Dr. Carpenter's theory of preconceived ideas, He says: "Professor Lankester went with the firm conviction that all he was going to see would be imposture, and he believes he saw imposture accordingly." Professor Lankester showed his bias when, referring to the paper read before the British Association on September 12 by Professor Barrett, in which he dealt with Spiritualistic phenomena, he said, in his letter to THE TIMES: "The discussions of the British Association have been degraded by the introduction of Spiritualism."

---

[142] THE SPIRITUALIST, Vol. IX, p. 2.
[143] September 16, 1876.

Professor Barrett wrote that Slade had a ready reply, based on his ignorance of when the writing did actually occur. He describes a very evidential sitting he had in which the slate rested on the table with his elbow resting on it. One of Slade's hands was held by him, and the fingers of the medium's other hand rested lightly on the surface of the slate. In this way writing occurred on the under surface of the slate. Professor Barrett further speaks of an eminent scientific friend who obtained writing on a clean slate when it was held entirely by him, both of the medium's hands being on the table. Such instances must surely seem absolutely conclusive to the unbiased reader, and it will be clear that if the positive is firmly established, occasional allegations of negative have no bearing upon the general conclusion.

Slade's trial came on at Bow Street Police Court on October t, 1876, before Mr. Flowers, the magistrate. Mr. George Lewis prosecuted and Mr. Munton appeared for the defence. Evidence in favour of the genuineness of Slade's mediumship was given by Dr. Alfred Russel Wallace, Serjeant Cox, Dr. George Wyld, and one other, only four witnesses being allowed. The magistrate described the testimony as "overwhelming" as to the evidence for the phenomena, but in giving judgment he excluded everything but the evidence of Lankester and his friend Dr. Donkin, saying that he must base his decision on "inferences to be drawn from the known course of nature." A statement made by Mr. Maskelyne, the well-known conjurer, that the table used by Slade was a trick-table was disproved by the evidence of the workman who made it. This table can now be seen at the offices of the London Spiritualist Alliance, and one marvels at the audacity of a witness who could imperil another man's liberty by so false a statement, which must have powerfully affected the course of the trial. Indeed, in the face of the evidence of Ray Lankester, Donkin, and Maskelyne, it is hard to see how Mr. Flowers could fail to convict, for he would say with truth and reason, "What is before the Court is not what has happened upon other occasions-however convincing these eminent witnesses may be-but what occurred upon this particular occasion, and here we have two witnesses on one side and only the prisoner on the other." The "trick-table" probably settled the matter.

Slade was sentenced, under the Vagrancy Act, to three months' imprisonment with hard labor. An appeal was lodged and he was released on bail. When the appeal came to be heard, the conviction was quashed on a technical point. It may be pointed out that though he escaped on a technical point, namely, that the words "by palmistry or otherwise" which appeared in the statute had been omitted, it must not be assumed that had the technical point failed he might not have escaped on the merits of his case. Slade, whose health had been seriously affected by the strain of the trial, left England for the Continent a day or two later.

From the Hague, after a rest of a few months, Slade wrote to Professor Lankester offering to return to London and to give him exhaustive private tests on condition that he could come without molestation. He received no answer to his suggestion, which surely is not that of a guilty man.

An illuminated testimonial to Slade from London Spiritualists in 1877 sets out:

In view of the deplorable termination of Henry Slade's visit to this country, we the undersigned desire to place on record our high opinion of his mediumship, and our reprobation of the treatment he has undergone.

We regard Henry Slade as one of the most valuable Test Mediums now living. The phenomena which occur in his presence are evolved with a rapidity and regularity rarely equalled.

He leaves us not only untarnished in reputation by the late proceedings in our Law Courts, but with a mass of testimony in his favour which could probably have been elicited in no other way.

This is signed by Mr. Alexander Calder (President of the British National Association of Spiritualists) and a number of representative Spiritualists. Unhappily, however, it is the Noes, not the Ayes, which have the ear of the Press, and even now, fifty years later, it would be hard to find a paper enlightened enough to do the man justice.

Spiritualists, however, showed great energy in supporting Slade. Before the trial a Defence Fund was raised, and Spiritualists in America drew up a memorial to the American Minister in London. Between the Bow Street conviction and the hearing of the appeal, a memorial was sent to the Home Secretary protesting against the action of the Government in conducting the prosecution on appeal. Copies of this were sent to all the members of the Legislature, to all the Middlesex magistrates, to various members of the Royal Society, and of other public bodies. Miss Kislingbury, the secretary to the National Association of Spiritualists, forwarded a copy to the Queen.

After giving successful séances at the Hague, Slade went to Berlin in November, 1877, where he created the keenest interest. He was said to know no German, yet messages in German appeared on the slates, and were written in the characters of the fifteenth century. The BERLINER FREMDENBLATT of November 10, 1877, wrote: "Since the arrival of Mr. Slade at the Kronprinz Hotel the greater portion of the educated world of Berlin has been suffering from an epidemic which we may term a Spiritualistic fever." Describing his experiences in Berlin, Slade said that he began by fully converting the landlord of the hotel, using the latter's slates and tables in his own house. The landlord invited the Chief of Police and many prominent citizens of Berlin to witness the manifestations, and they expressed themselves as satisfied. Slade writes: "Samuel Bellachini, Court Conjurer to the Emperor of Germany, had a week's experience with me free of charge. I gave him from two to three séances a day and one of them at his own house. After his full and complete investigation, he went to a public notary and made oath that the phenomena were genuine and not trickery."

Bellachini's declaration on oath, which has been published, bears out this statement. He says that after the minutest investigation he considers any explanation by conjuring to be "absolutely impossible." The conduct of conjurers seems to have been usually determined by a sort of trade union jealousy, as if the results of the medium were some sort of breach of a monopoly, but this enlightened German, together with Houdin, Kellar, and a few more, have shown a more open mind.

A visit to Denmark followed, and in December began the historic séances with Professor Zollner, at Leipzig. A full account of these will be found in Zollner's "Transcendental Physics," which has been translated by Mr. C. C. Massey. Zollner was Professor of Physics and Astronomy in the University of Leipzig, and associated with him in the experiments with Slade were other scientific men, including William Edward Weber, Professor of Physics; Professor Scheibner, a distinguished mathematician; Gustave Theodore Fechner, Professor of Physics and an eminent natural philosopher, who were all, says Professor Zollner, "perfectly convinced of the reality of the observed facts, altogether excluding imposture or "prestidigitation." The phenomena in question included, among other things, "the production of true knots in an endless string, the rending of Professor Zollner's bed-screen, the disappearance of a small table and its subsequent descent from the ceiling in FULL LIGHT, in a private house and under observed conditions.

Slade during all these occurrences."

Certain critics have tried to indicate what they consider insufficient precautions observed in these experiments. Dr. J. Maxwell, the acute French critic, makes an excellent reply to such objections. He points out[144] that because skilled and conscientious psychic investigators have omitted to indicate explicitly in their reports that every hypothesis of fraud has been studied and dismissed, in the belief that "their implicit affirmation of the reality of the fact appeared sufficient to them," and in order to prevent their reports from being too unwieldy, yet captious critics do not hesitate to condemn them and to suggest possibilities of fraud which are quite inadmissible under the observed conditions.

Zollner gave a dignified reply to the supposition that he was tricked in these cord-tying experiments: "If, nevertheless, the foundation of this fact, deduced by me on the ground of an enlarged conception of space, should be denied, only one other kind of explanation would remain, arising from a moral code of consideration that at present, it is true, is quite customary. This explanation would consist in the presumption that I myself and the honourable men and citizens of Leipzig, in whose presence several of these cords were sealed, were either common impostors, or were not in possession of our sound senses sufficient to perceive if Mr. Slade himself, before the cords were sealed, had tied them in knots. The discussion, however, of such a hypothesis would no longer belong to the dominion of science, but would fall under the category of social decency."[145]

As a sample of the reckless statements of opponents of Spiritualism, it may be mentioned that Mr. Joseph McCabe, who is second only to the American Houdini for wild inaccuracies, speaks of Zollner as "an elderly and purblind professor," whereas he died in 1882, in his forty-eighth year, and his experiments with Slade were carried out in 1877-78, when this distinguished scientist was in the vigour of his intellectual life.

So far have opponents pushed their enmity that it has even been stated that Zollner was deranged, and that his death which occurred some years later was accompanied with cerebral weakness. An inquiry from

---

[144] "Metapsychical Phenomena" (Translation 1905), p. 405.

[145] Massey's Zollner, pp. 20-21.

Dr. Funk set this matter at rest, though it is unfortunately easy to get libels of this sort into circulation and very difficult to get the contradictions. Here is the document:

"Spiritualism. A Popular History from 1847," p. 161.

"The Widow's Mite," p. 276.

Your letter addressed to the Rector of the University, October 20, 1903, received. The Rector of this University was installed here after the death of Zollner, and had no personal acquaintance with him; but information received from Zollner's colleagues states that during his entire studies at the University here, until his death, he was of sound mind; moreover, in the best of health. The cause of his death was a hemorrhage of the brain on the morning of April 25th, 1882, while he was at breakfast with his mother, and from which he died shortly after. It is true that Professor Zollner was an ardent believer in Spiritualism, and as such was in close relations with Slade.

(Dr.) KARL BUCHER, Professor of Statistics and National Economy at the University.

The tremendous power which occasionally manifests itself when the conditions are favorable was shown once in the presence of Zollner, Weber, and Scheibner, all three professors of the University. There was a strong wooden screen on one side of the room:

A violent crack was suddenly heard as in the discharging of a large battery of Leyden jars. On turning with some alarm in the direction of the sound, the before-mentioned screen fell apart in two pieces. The strong wooden screws, half an inch thick, were torn from above and below, without any visible contact of Slade with the screen. The parts broken were at least five feet removed from Slade, who had his back to the screen; but even if he had intended to tear it down by a cleverly devised sideward motion, it would have been necessary to fasten it on the opposite side.

As it was, the screen stood quite unattached, and the grain of the wood being parallel to the axis of the cylindrical wooden fastenings, the wrenching asunder could only be accomplished by a force acting longitudinally to the part in question. We were all astonished at this unexpected and violent manifestation of mechanical force, and asked Slade what it all meant; but he only shrugged his shoulders, saying that such phenomena occasionally, though somewhat rarely, occurred in his presence. As he spoke, he placed, while still standing, a piece of slate-pencil on the polished surface of the table, laid over it a slate, purchased and just cleaned by myself, and pressed the five spread fingers of his right hand on the upper surface of the slate, while his left hand rested on the centre of the table. Writing began on the inner surface of the slate, and when Slade turned it up, the following sentence was written in English: "It was not our intention to do harm. Forgive what has happened." We were the more surprised at the production of the writing under these circumstances, for we particularly observed that both Slade's hands remained quite motionless while the writing was going on.[146]

In his desperate attempt to explain this incident, Mr. McCabe says that no doubt the screen was broken before and fastened together afterwards with thread. There is truly no limit to the credulity of the incredulous.

After a very successful series of séances in St. Petersburg, Slade returned to London for a few days in 1878, and then proceeded to Australia. An interesting account of his work there is to be found in Mr. James Curtis's book, "Rustlings in the Golden City." Then he returned to America. In 1885 he appeared before the Seybert Commission in Philadelphia, and in 1887 again visited England under the name of "Dr. Wilson," though it was well known who he was. Presumably his alias was due to a fear that the old proceedings would be renewed.

At most of his séances, Slade exhibited clairvoyant powers, and materialized hands were a familiar occurrence. In Australia, where psychic conditions are good, he had materializations. Mr. Curtis says that the medium objected to sitting for this form of manifestation, because it left him weak for a time, and because he preferred to give séances in the light. He consented, however, to try with Mr. Curtis, who thus describes what took place at Ballarat, in Victoria:

Our first test of spirit appearance in the form took place at Lester's Hotel. I placed the table about four or five feet from the west wall of the room. Mr. Slade sat at the end of the table furthest from the wall, whilst I took my position on the north side. The gaslight was toned down, not so much but that any object in the room could be clearly seen. Our hands were placed over one another in a single pile. We sat very still

---

[146] "Transcendental Physics," p. 34, 35.

about ten minutes, when I observed something like a little misty cloud between myself and the wall. When my attention was first drawn towards this phenomenon, it was about the size and colour of a gentleman's high-crowned, whitish-grey felt hat. This cloudlike appearance rapidly grew and became transformed, when we saw before us a woman-a lady. The being thus fashioned, and all but perfected, rose from the floor on to the top of the table, where I could most distinctly observe the configuration. The arms and hands were elegantly shaped; the forehead, mouth, nose, cheeks, and beautiful brown hair showed harmoniously, each part in concord with the whole. Only the eyes were veiled because they could not be completely materialized. The feet were encased in white satin shoes. The dress glowed in light, and was the most beautiful I ever beheld, the color being bright, shiny silvery grey, or greyish shining white. The whole figure was graceful, and the drapery perfect. The materialized spirit glided and walked about, causing the table to shake, vibrate, jerk and tilt considerably. I could hear, too, the rustling of the dress as the celestial visitant transiently wended from one position or place to another.

The spirit form, within two feet of our unmoved hands, still piled up together in a heap, then dissolved, and gradually faded from our vision.

The conditions at this beautiful séance-with the medium's hands held throughout, and with enough light for visibility-seem satisfactory, provided we grant the honesty of the witness. As the preface contains the supporting testimony of a responsible Australian Government official, who also speaks of Mr. Curtis's initial extremely sceptical state of mind, we may well do so. At the same séance a quarter of an hour later the figure again appeared:

The apparition then floated in the air and alighted on the table, rapidly glided about, and thrice bent her beautiful figure with graceful bows, each bending deliberate and low, the head coming within six inches of my face. The dress rustled (as silk rustles) with every movement. The face was partially veiled as before. The visibility then became invisible, slowly disappearing like the former materialization.

Other similar séances are described.

In view of the many elaborate and stringent tests through which he passed successfully, the story of Slade's "exposure" in America in 1886 is not convincing, but we refer to it for historical reasons, and to show that such incidents are not excluded from our review of the subject. The BOSTON HERALD, February 2, 1886, heads its account, "The celebrated Dr. Slade comes to grief in Weston, West Virginia, writes upon slates which lie upon his knees under the table, and moves tables and chairs with his toes." Observers in an adjoining room, looking through the crevice under the door saw these feats of agility being performed by the medium, though those present in the room with him were unaware of them. There seems, however, to have been in this as in other cases, occurrences which bore the appearance of fraud, and Spiritualists were among those who denounced him. At a subsequent public performance for "Direct Spirit Writing" in the Justice Hall, Weston, Mr. E. S. Barrett, described as a "Spiritualist," came forward and explained how Slade's imposture had been detected. Slade, who was asked to speak, appeared dumbfounded, and could only say, according to the report, that if his accusers had been deceived he had been equally so, for if the deceit had been done by him, it had been without his consciousness.

Mr. J. Simmons, Slade's business manager, made a frank statement which seems to point to the operation of ectoplasmic limbs, as years later was proved to be the case with the famous Italian medium, Eusapia Palladino. He says: "I do not doubt that these gentlemen saw what they assert they did; but I am convinced at the same time that Slade is as innocent of what he is accused of as you (the editor) yourself would have been under similar circumstances. But I know that my explanation would have no weight in a court of justice. I myself saw a hand, which I could have sworn to be that of Slade, if it had been possible for his hand to be in that position. While one of his hands lay upon the table and the other held the slate under the corner of the table, a third hand appeared with a clothes-brush (which a moment previously had brushed against me from the knee upwards) in the middle of the opposite edge of the table, which was forty-two inches long." Slade and his manager were arrested and released on bail, but no further proceedings seem to have been taken against them. Truesdell, also, in his book, "Spiritualism, Bottom Facts," states that he saw Slade effecting the movement of objects with his foot, and he asks his readers to believe that the medium made to him a full confession of how all his manifestations were produced. If Slade ever really did this, it may probably be accounted for by a burst of ill-timed levity on his part in seeking to fool a certain type of investigator by giving him exactly what he was seeking for. To such instances we may apply the judgment of Professor Zollner on the Lankester incident: "The physical facts observed by us in so astonishing a variety in his presence negatived on every reasonable ground the supposition that he in one solitary case had taken refuge in wilful imposture." He adds, what was certainly the case in that particular instance, that Slade was the victim of his accuser's and his judge's limited knowledge.

At the same time there is ample evidence that Slade degenerated in general character towards the latter part of his life. Promiscuous sittings with a mercenary object, the subsequent exhaustions, and the alcoholic stimulus which affords a temporary relief, all acting upon a most sensitive organization, had a deleterious effect. This weakening of character, with a corresponding loss of health, may have led to a diminution of his psychic powers, and increased the temptation to resort to trickery. Making every allowance for the difficulty of distinguishing what is fraud and what is of crude psychic origin, an unpleasant impression is left upon the mind by the evidence given in the Seybert Commission and by the fact that Spiritualists upon the spot should have condemned his action. Human frailty, however, is one thing and psychic power is another. Those who seek evidence for the latter will find ample in those years when the man and his powers were both at their zenith.

Slade died in 1905 at a Michigan sanatorium to which he had been sent by the American Spiritualists, and the announcement was followed by the customary sort of comment in the London Press. THE STAR, which has an evil tradition in psychic matters, printed a sensational article headed "Spook Swindles," giving a garbled account of the Lankester prosecution at Bow Street. Referring to this, LIGHT says[147]:

Of course, this whole thing is a hash of ignorance, unfairness and prejudice. We do not care to discuss it or to controvert it. It would be useless to do so for the sake of the unfair, the ignorant, and the prejudiced, and it is not necessary for those who know. Suffice it to say that the STAR only supplies one more instance of the difficulty of getting all the facts before the public; but the prejudiced newspapers have themselves to blame for their ignorance or inaccuracy.

It is the story of the Davenport Brothers and Maskelyne over again.

If Slade's career is difficult to appraise, and if one is forced to admit that while there was an overpowering preponderance of psychic results, there was also a residuum which left the unpleasant impression that the medium might supplement truth with fraud, the same admission must be made in the case of the medium Monck, who played a considerable part for some years in the 'seventies. Of all mediums none is more difficult to appraise, for on the one hand many of his results are beyond all dispute, while in a few there seems to be an absolute certainty of dishonesty. In his case, as in Slade's, there were physical causes which would account for a degeneration of the moral and psychic powers.

Monck was a Nonconformist clergyman, a favourite pupil of the famous Spurgeon. According to his own account, he had been subject from childhood to psychic influences, which increased with his growth. In 1873 he announced his adhesion to Spiritualism and gave an address in the Cavendish Rooms. Shortly afterwards he began to give demonstrations, which appear to have been unpaid and were given in light. In 1875 he made a tour through England and Scotland, his performances exciting much attention and debate, and in 1876 he visited Ireland, where his powers were directed towards healing. Hence he was usually known as "Dr." Monck, a fact which naturally aroused some protest from the medical profession.

Dr. Alfred Russel Wallace, a most competent and honest observer, has given an account of a materialization séance with Monck which appears to be as critic-proof as such a thing could be. No subsequent suspicion or conviction can ever eliminate such an incontrovertible instance of psychic power. It is to be noted how far the effects were in agreement with the subsequent demonstrations of ectoplasmic outflow in the case of Eva and other modern mediums. Dr. Wallace's companions upon this occasion were Mr. Stainton Moses and Mr. Hensleigh Wedgwood. Dr. Wallace writes:

It was a bright summer afternoon, and everything happened in the full light of day. After a little conversation, Monck, who was dressed in the usual clerical black, appeared to go into a trance; then stood up a few feet in front of us, and after a little while pointed to his side, saying, "Look."

We saw there a faint white patch on his coat on the left side.

This grew brighter, then seemed to flicker and extend both upwards and downwards, till very gradually it formed a cloudy pillar extending from his shoulder to his feet and close to his body.

Dr. Wallace goes on to describe how the cloudy figure finally assumed the form of a thickly draped woman, who, after a brief space, appeared to be absorbed into the body of the medium.

He adds: "The whole process of the formation of a shrouded figure was seen in full daylight."

---

[147] 1886, p. 433.

Mr. Wedgwood assured him that he had lead even more remarkable manifestations of this kind with Monck, when the medium was in a deep trance, and in full view.

It is quite impossible after such evidence to doubt the powers of the medium at that time. Archdeacon Colley, who had seen similar exhibitions, offered a prize of a thousand pounds to Mr. J. N. Maskelyne, the famous conjurer, if he could duplicate the performance. This challenge was accepted by Mr. Maskelyne, but the evidence showed that the imitation bore no relation to the original. He attempted to gain a decision in the courts, but the verdict was against him.

It is interesting to compare the account given by Russel Wallace and the experience later of a well-known American, Judge Dailey. This gentleman wrote[148]:

Glancing at Dr. Monck's side we observed what looked like an opalescent mass of compact steam emerging from just below his heart on the left side. It increased in volume, rising up and extending downward, the upper portions taking the form of a child's head, the face being distinguished as that of a little child I had lost some twenty years previously. It only remained in this form for a moment, and then suddenly disappeared, seeming to be instantly absorbed into the Doctor's side. This remarkable phenomenon was repeated four or five times, in each instance the materialization being more distinct than the preceding one. This was witnessed by all in the room, with gas burning sufficiently bright for every object in the room to be plainly visible.

It was a phenomenon seldom to be seen, and has enabled all who saw it to vouch for, not only the remarkable power possessed by Dr. Monck as a materializing medium, but as to the wonderful manner in which a spirit draws out.

Surely it is vain after such testimony to deny that Monck had, indeed, great psychic powers.

Apart from materializations Dr. Monck was a remarkable slate-writing medium. Dr. Russel Wallace in a letter to the SPECTATOR [149] says that with Monck at a private house in Richmond he cleaned two slates, and after placing a fragment of pencil between them, tied them together tightly with a strong cord, lengthways and crosswise, in a manner that prevented any movement.

I then laid them flat on the table without losing sight of them for an instant. Dr. Monck placed the fingers of both hands on them, while I and a lady sitting opposite placed our hands on the corners of the slates. From this position our hands were never moved till I untied the slates to ascertain the result.

Monck asked Wallace to name a word to be written on the slate. He chose the word "God" and in answer to a request decided that it should be length ways on the slate. The sound of writing was heard, and when the medium's hands were withdrawn, Dr. Wallace opened the slates and found on the lower one the word he had asked for and written in the manner requested.

Dr. Wallace says:

The essential features of this experiment are that I myself cleaned and tied up the slates; that I kept my hands on them all the time; that they never went out of my sight for a moment; and that I named the word to be written, and the manner of writing it after they were thus secured and held by me.

Mr. Edward T. Bennett, assistant secretary to the Society for Psychical Research, adds to this account: "I was present on this occasion, and certify that Mr. Wallace's account of what happened is correct."

Another good test is described by Mr. W. P. Adshead, of Belper, a well-known investigator, who says of a séance held in Derby on September 18, 1876:

There were eight persons present, three ladies and five gentlemen.

---

[148] BANNER OF LIGHT, Dec. 15, 1881.
[149] October 7, 1877.

The Madness of Sherlock Holmes

Sherlock Holmes is probably the most famous detective in the world. The tales of his exploits have been seen in magazines, books, television screens, the movies and even in computer games. And yet, there is a mysterious side to this fictional character that has eluded and yet drawn us for decades. In a way reminiscent of Holmes' art of deduction, this film gets to grips with the creator of Sherlock Holmes, Sir Arthur Conan Doyle, and uncovers an even more bizarre and mysterious tale than anybody could have expected. From secret societies to the occult, from peer pressure to inner turmoil, this is a story of such depth that it will speak to one and all. Uncovering dark secrets of Conan Doyle, this film finally explains what experiences and influences helped to forge the character of not just Sherlock Holmes, but also Moriarty and Watson.

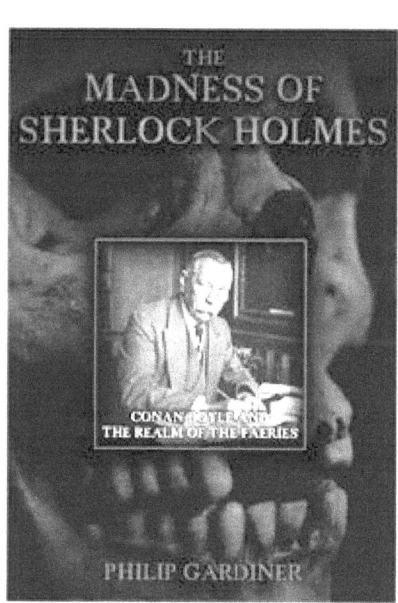

The Madness of Sherlock Holmes;
Conan Doyle and the Realm of the Faeries
75 minutes - $20 + $5 s/h

Global Communications, Box 753, New Brunswick, NJ 08903
Credit Card Orders 732 602-3407   MRUFO8@hotmail.com

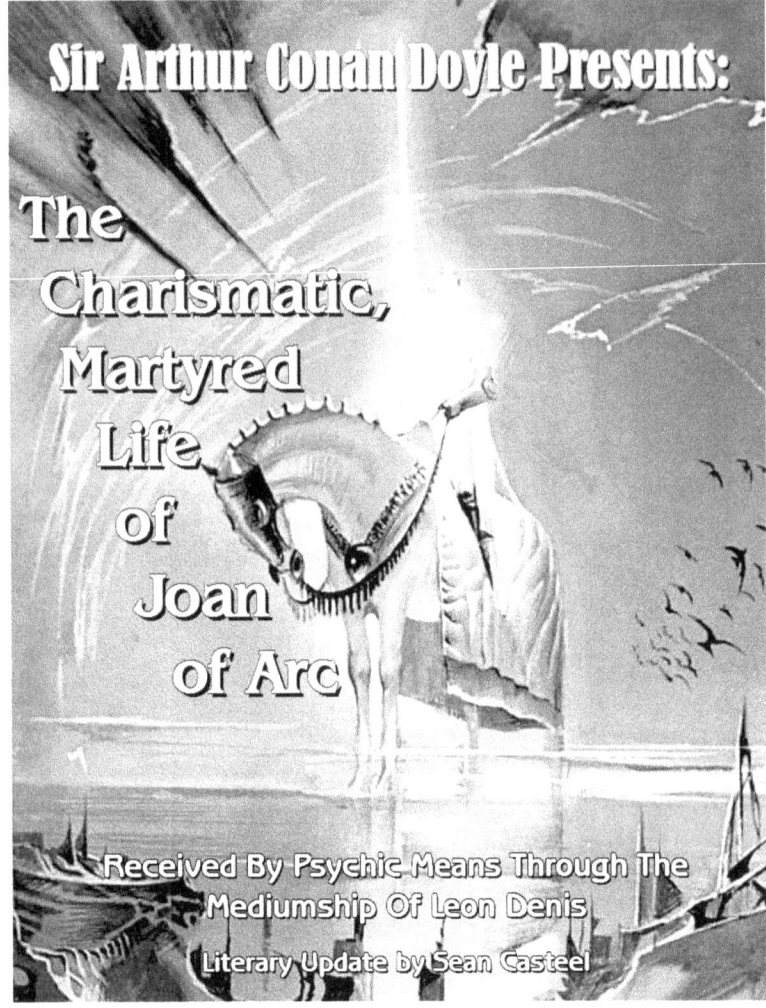

WARNING!
THIS IS NOT AN ORDINARY HISTORY BOOK ABOUT THE FRENCH MARTYR JOAN OF ARC

It is much more than that.

It may be a book that Joan of Arc helped to write herself.

For it was not written by the author by "ordinary means" -- instead, it came directly "from spirit."

And this is not a fanciful statement by some humdrum psychic -- in fact, this book has the backing of one of the greatest literary minds of all time: none other than the creator of Sherlock Holmes, Sir Arthur Conan Doyle, who translated what has become a rare classic in the early 1920s.

The voices in Joan's head ... The materialization of angels and saints: "I saw them with these very eyes, as well as I see you!" ... The witchcraft trial ... Being burned at the stake. These are all a matter of public record. But so much more is now brought to light by a French spiritist named Leon Denis, who not only traveled across France tracing Joan of Arc's footsteps, but, says Denis, "There is not one place that she has passed where I have not meditated, prayed and mourned ... I have (even) followed the melancholy road which led the great martyr to her doom"

Here then is the powerful voice of Joan of Arc crying out once more, as she did while being burned alive for her strong convictions in the day of our Lord, May 29, 1431, when a court of thirty seven judges decided unanimously that Joan was an unrepentant heretic.

Large Print!

$29.95 +$6.00 Shipping & Handling

Global Communications, Box 753, New Brunswick, NJ 08903
Credit Card Orders 732 602-3407   MRUFO8@hotmail.com

Shocking Psychic Solution; The Lizzie Borden Case

You know the chant...

"Lizzie Borden took an axe
And gave her mother forty whacks
When she saw what she had done
She gave her father forty one."

But, Lizzie was acquitted. So what really happened that hot August day in 1892? Was she unjustly accused? Can the riddle of the Lizzie Borden case ever be solved?

Using psychic means, Richard and Debbie Senate pierce the veil of time and discover the shocking truth. Lizzie didn't kill her stepmother or her father; you'll be surprised at who did.

$27.95 +$6.00 Shipping & Handling

THE MEDIUMSHIP OF SPIRIT
YOUR PATH TO HEALTH, WEALTH AND IMMORTALITY

William Alexander Oribello
With Aurora Thyme

ASCENDED MASTER WILLIAM ALEXANDER ORIBELLO GIVES YOU THE KEYS TO THE HIGHEST INITIATION INTO GOD'S KINGDOM

William Alexander Oribello was the founder of the Mystic Light Society and author of such classic metaphysical works as *Candle Burning With The Psalms*, *Sacred Magic* and *Godspells*. Inner Light Publications has been his only publisher and remains so today. Bill was called to the Divine Plane in 1996, leaving behind a number of unfinished manuscripts.

Now an Ascended Master, Oribello has returned to the Earth Plane to continue his great work, assisted by the mediumship of psychic Aurora Thyme. In this blessed work, Oribello reveals God's greatest desire for all of us to be happy and prosperous and to live our lives as He intended during the Golden Age of Mankind.

These great secrets are available to anyone willing to cast aside the negative aspects of the modern world and accept help from the Ascended Masters whose mission is to bring the Great Wisdom of God the Creator to Planet Earth and usher us back to the Golden Age of Mankind that has eluded us for so long.

$17.95 +$6.00 Shipping & Handling

Global Communications, Box 753, New Brunswick, NJ 08903
Credit Card Orders 732 602-3407   MRUFO8@hotmail.com

DO OUR FAVORITE PETS, SO NEAR AND DEAR TO US, SURVIVE DEATH? AND ARE COMMON HOUSE PETS MORE LIKELY TO SENSE THE PRESENCE OF A GHOST THAN THEIR HUMAN OWNERS?

DO WILD ANIMALS HAVE A SOUL? IF SO, DO SOME DECEASED ANIMALS HAUNT THE LIVING OUT OF A NEED FOR VENGEANCE?

IS THERE A 'DOGGIE' HEAVEN? AND WILL WE EVER 'MEET UP' WITH OUR MUCH BELOVED PETS ON THE OTHER SIDE?

WHAT ABOUT THE ANIMALS THAT HAVE THE GIFT OF SPEECH? ACCORDING TO THE BIBLE, A TALKING DONKEY CAUSED A WICKED MAN TO REPENT, WHILE IN 1930'S ENGLAND A TALKING MONGOOSE MOVED IN WITH A FARM FAMILY AND BECAME A TERRIFYING MEMBER OF THE HOUSEHOLD.

AND ARE HUMAN 'MAD SCIENTISTS' AND ALIEN ABDUCTORS WORKING SECRETLY TO CREATE HUMAN/ANIMAL HYBRIDS CALLED 'CHIMERA'? WHAT KIND OF MONSTROUS CREATIONS AWAIT US NOW THAT WE'VE LEARNED TO COMBINE DIFFERENT FORMS OF DNA?

COME EXPLORE THE SUPERNATURAL SIDE OF MAN'S BEST – AND WORST – FRIENDS AS RELATED IN THE SPOOKIEST ANIMAL STORIES EVER TOLD!

Here is proof of a psychic – occult – paranormal connection between humans and every manner of species. . . and the ghostly chills they often confront us with. For indeed there are as many animal phantoms as there are human specters, perhaps many more as the TRUE tales in this book will certainly prove in due course.

AND YES, MY DEAR FRIENDS. . .'CATS AND DOGS'
DO FALL FROM THE SKY!

$21.95 +$6.00 Shipping & Handling

Come along with paranormal journalist Tim Beckley as he explores a mysterious mountain that has a reputation for being the most supernatural locale in North America, if not the world.

Here are stories of Lemurians and survivors of other "lost civilizations" who roam the woods freely and occasionally wander into town to trade gold for supplies.

Little men who seldom come out except at night to collect edibles and then return to their secret cavern homes deep within the mountain.

Native Americans residing in the backwoods say they have not only heard the screams of Bigfoot, but have seen these hairy creatures close-up!

Mt. Shasta is said to contain the capital of the subterranean world known as Telos, occupied by the Ascended Masters of Wisdom. This city is rumored to be connected to the Hollow Earth through a worldwide network of secret tunnels.

Accounts of miraculous healings, including those whose eyesight has been regenerated after being struck by mysterious blue beams of light coming from inside the mountain.

$21.95 +$6.00 Shipping & Handling

Global Communications, Box 753, New Brunswick, NJ 08903
Credit Card Orders 732 602-3407   MRUFO8@hotmail.com

www.ingramcontent.com/pod-product-compliance
Lightning Source LLC
Chambersburg PA
CBHW081916170426
43200CB00014B/2743